P9-EJU-664

Merry Christmas 199.

Rick & Heil

A History of the Vikings

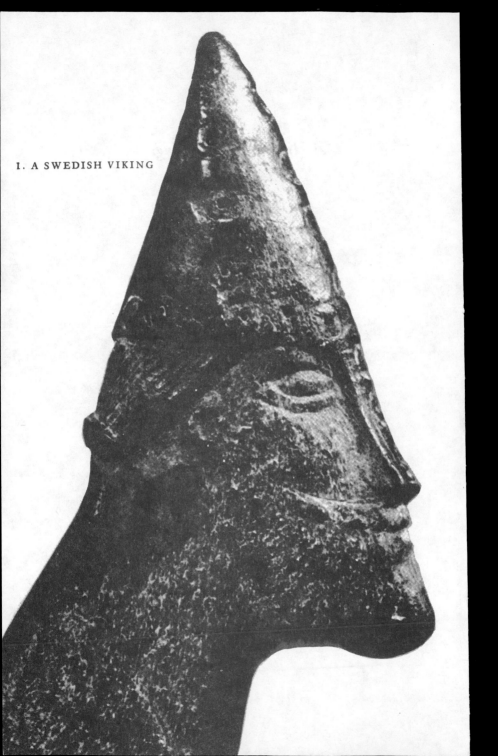

I. A SWEDISH VIKING

Gwyn Jones

A History of the
VIKINGS

REVISED EDITION

Oxford   New York

OXFORD UNIVERSITY PRESS

1984

Oxford University Press, Walton Street, Oxford OX2 6DP

London Glasgow New York Toronto
Delhi Bombay Calcutta Madras Karachi
Kuala Lumpur Singapore Hong Kong Tokyo
Nairobi Dar es Salaam Cape Town
Melbourne Auckland
and associated companies in
Beirut Berlin Ibadan Mexico City Nicosia

Oxford is a trade mark of Oxford University Press

© Oxford University Press 1968, 1973, 1984

First published 1968. First issued as an Oxford University Press paperback 1973.
Revised edition 1984.

All rights reserved. No part of this publication may be reproduced,
stored in a retrieval system, or transmitted, in any form or by any means,
electronic, mechanical, photocopying, recording, or otherwise, without
the prior permission of Oxford University Press

This book is sold subject to the condition that it shall not, by way
of trade or otherwise, be lent, re-sold, hired out or otherwise circulated
without the publisher's prior consent in any form of binding or cover
other than that in which it is published and without a similar condition
including this condition being imposed on the subsequent purchaser

British Library Cataloguing in Publication Data

Jones, Gwyn, 1907–
A history of the Vikings.—Rev. ed.
1. Vikings
I. Title
948'.02   DL65
ISBN 0-19-215882-1
ISBN 0-19-285139-X pbk

Library of Congress Cataloging in Publication Data

Jones, Gwyn, 1907–
A history of the Vikings. (Oxford paperbacks)
Originally published: 1968.
Bibliography: p.   Includes index.
1. Civilization, Scandinavian. 2. Vikings
I. Title.
DL31.J6 1984   948   83–13303
ISBN 0-19-215882-1
ISBN 0-19-285139-X (pbk.)

Contents

Illustrations

MAPS

Note Prefatory to the Revised Edition, 1984

A History of the Vikings was first published in 1968. The intervening sixteen years have seen impressive developments in matters Viking. On the one hand we have watched the refinement and expansion of archaeological research on land and underwater, the accumulation and plotting of illuminative factual detail, and the purposeful pursuit of numismatic, place-name and linguistic information. On the other we have witnessed a remarkable expansion of popular interest in the Vikings, fostered and maintained by visually exciting television programmes, the publication of lavishly illustrated books dealing with the more dramatic and assimilable chapters of the Viking story, and by a noble array of large-scale exhibitions presented by the British Museum in London, the Metropolitan Museum of New York, the National Museum of Man in Ottawa, the Museum of Science and Industry, Chicago, and on a smaller but telling scale the 'Vikings in England' exhibition at York. Irish-Norse Dublin and Anglo-Scandinavian York in the British Isles, the Danevirke and Vorbasse in Denmark; the confirmation of a Norse presence at L'Anse-aux-Meadows in the New World; more (and more varied) ships found in northern waters, leading to a fuller picture of Scandinavian maritime achievement; kings, kingdoms, and the nature and extent of royal power from Ragnar Lodbrok and the dark of legend to Harald Hardráði and the murk of history; art styles and stylistic influences; and increasingly the non-viking Viking, i.e. the Dane, Norwegian, Swede at home, the non-collective image replacing the stereotype, and the modes and manner of his non-violent everyday life—it has been a time of new knowledge and re-appraisal for us all.

My revisions of fact or belief (they will be found in the main on pp. 99–103, 116–17, 183, 189–90, 207, 218–19, 293–8, 302–8, 360–6, 424, 430) update my *History* in various particulars, but do not affect its original character as a general and comprehensive survey, both narrative and interpretative, of the Viking Age and Viking World. The need for, and desirability of, such a survey appear to me today even more compelling than when I first settled to my pleasurable task almost a quarter of a century ago.

G. J.

1984

Acknowledgements

I have received much help and kindness during the writing of this book, and wish I could find new words to express my gratitude. As with my *Norse Atlantic Saga*, I have received hospitality, gifts of published and unpublished material, a wealth of reference (sometimes to sources of information beyond my linguistic means), grants of time, money, and my friends' learning. I owe thanks to several institutions: the British Broadcasting Corporation for a commission which took me to Iceland and Greenland in 1964; the Dansk-Engelsk Selskab for asking me to Copenhagen in 1965; the Smithsonian Institution for inviting me to take part in its Symposium on the Vinland Map in Washington in the autumn of 1966; my College for a grant which allowed me to visit various Scandinavian museums and libraries in the summer of 1967. I have three major obligations to individuals. My friends Dr. Olaf Olsen of the National Museum of Denmark and Dr. Henry Loyn, Reader in History at the University College of South Wales and Monmouthshire, have read and commented closely on my manuscript; and Mr. Helmuth Schledermann has read through my Hedeby material and what I have to say about ninth- and tenth-century kings and kingship in Denmark and Norway. All three have saved me from error in fields where they are expert, and such faults or misjudgements as survive their amendment may be charged to me alone. Others who have shown me courtesies of different kinds include Antikvar Harald Andersen, Mr. D. G. Bridson, Mr. and Mrs. Sigurjón Einarsson, Dr. Kristján Eldjárn, my colleagues Professor Thomas Jones and Dr. R. G. Thomas, Professor Julia McGrew, Frøken Elisabeth Munksgaard, Mr. C. R. Musson (to whom I owe many of my maps), Mr. P. H. Sawyer, Professor H. M. Smyser, Professor Erik Tengstrand, Museumsinspektør C. L. Vebaek, Mrs. Eva Wilson, and Mr. Michael

Wolfe. My obligations in respect of illustrations are in general expressed where the plates, text figures, and maps are listed.

I am much indebted to the following for the use of copyright material: Columbia University Press for F. J. Tschan's translation of *The History of the Archbishops of Hamburg-Bremen*, 1959; the Medieval Academy of America for the Cross and Sherbowitz-Wetzor translation of *The Russian Primary Chronicle*, 1953; the late Professor G. N. Garmonsway for his translation of the Anglo-Saxon Chronicle; and the late Professor A. H. Smith for his place-name map.

Also, no one can write a general history of the Vikings without levying a viking-style tribute on other men's riches. I am conscious of my many exactions, and trust that every bibliographical reference will be held indicative of gratitude and esteem.

University College   GWYN JONES
Cardiff

For timely assistance during the revision of my *History* I stand, as ever, in debt to many. Of institutions I would mention the American-Scandinavian Foundation, the Archaeological Institute of America, the Archaeological Association of Canada, the York Archaeological Trust, the Chicago Museum of Science and Industry, Cornell University, the University of Iowa, and the British Council; and of friends and colleagues Hilmar Foss, Henry Loyn, Olaf Olsen, Else Roesdahl; Eleanor Guralnick, Robert McGhee, Patricia Sutherland, Birgitta Wallace; R. T. Farrell, Howard Laster, Kathleen Campbell, Richard Lloyd-Jones, Dick Ringler, and the late John H. Parry. To my wife Mair I owe my warmest thanks of all.

G. J.

Introduction

THE SUBJECT OF THIS BOOK IS THE VIKING REALMS, Denmark, Sweden, and Norway, their emergence and development, civilization and culture, and their many-sided achievement at home and abroad. It is an extensive field to survey. For even when we set aside the almost trackless millennia of my opening pages, there remain a thousand years of history to be charted in an area of Norse activity extending from the North Cape and White Sea to the Pillars of Hercules, from Newfoundland and Baffin Island to the Volga Bend and Byzantium. However, my concern is primarily with the 'Viking Age' proper, equated as this generally is with the three-hundred-year period *c.* 780–1070—the period, that is, of the so-called 'Viking Movement' overseas. The Viking Movement is that manifestation of the Viking Age which most powerfully, because most painfully, impressed itself upon non-Scandinavian chroniclers abroad. By their emphasis on the destructive effects of the Movement in western Europe, and their neglect of its contributions to trade, discovery, colonization, and the political and cultural institutions of the countries affected, these chroniclers produced for the contemporary world and posterity alike a picture at once incomplete, lurid, and distorted. They made little inquiry into the lands, peoples, beliefs, and civilizations from which (as they saw it) these priest-murderers and robbers of churches emerged— a lack of dispassionate comment made more serious by the shortage of contemporary records in Scandinavia itself, with its attendant problem of an abundance of late, unreliable written sources, mainly from the hands of twelfth- and thirteenth-century Icelandic antiquaries and historians. Consequently, to see the Viking Age in terms of the Viking Movement, and this last through the eyes of west European Christian annalists and chroniclers, is to see it, in every sense of the word, partially. It turns a many-faceted and durably important contribution to our European heritage into a sensational tale of raid, rapine, and conquest, and an interplay of complementary aspects of the European genius into a brutal saga. Not least, it gives the Age a sudden, inexplicable beginning and offers inadequate reasons for its end, whereas on examination it will be found to evolve out of the centuries preceding it and merge with the years which followed.

Who were the vikings (*víkingar*), whose name is used descriptively for this significant period of European history? They were men of the North, the inhabitants of Scandinavia, and it is important to see them in fair perspective. The *Norðmenn* or *Nordmanni*, despite southern witness and the image-making of their own authors and artists, were, one almost apologizes for saying, first and foremost men. Second, they were the men of Rogaland, Vestfold, Zealand, Skåne, Södermanland, or whatever other region or patria gave them life and nurture. As time went on and the northern kingdoms took vague, prophetic shape, no doubt a proportion of them felt themselves to be subjects of the king of the Danes, Swedes, or Norwegians. But though they had many ties, including those of language and religion, to remind them of a shared northernness, they had but little sense of a separate Danish, Swedish, or Norwegian nationality. For the rest, they were neither super-human nor sub-human; but precisely and generically human—in their greed, treachery, cruelty, and violence, as in their energy, generosity, loyalty, and familial kindness, and recognizably one and the same species as their neighbours, whether Franks and Germans, Petchenegs and English, Wends and Bulgars, Bretons and Irish, Eskimos and American Indians, Muslims and Greeks, whenever and wherever encountered. It was the pressures of history, geography, and economics, and their religion and seafaring arts, which made them distinctive in their day, not original sin or primal virtue. Being men, they lived under a compulsion to make life bearable and if possible good. In an agrarian world they needed land for their children and grass for their stock; in an era of opening trade-routes they craved silver and the chattels silver could provide; in a hierarchical, warlike, and still part-tribal society their leaders sought fame, power, wealth, and sustenance through action. Thus it was chiefly land-hunger which led them to the windy sheep-runs of the Faroes, the butter-laden grass of habitable Iceland, and the good and fragrant pasture of the west Greenland fjords. It was an ambition to distinguish themselves, win land and wealth to reward and enlarge their armed following, which impelled generation after generation of northern kings, jarls, and sea-captains to assault the territories of their southern and south-western neighbours. It was a desire for profit and material goods which encouraged the vikings to trade and carry in the Baltic and North Seas, the Black Sea and Caspian, across the Atlantic Ocean and along the great Russian rivers. They were particularly well placed to meet the inexhaustible European and Muslim demand for furs and slaves, but turned their hand to any saleable commodity: grain, fish, timber, hides, salt, wine, glass, glue, horses and cattle, white bears and falcons, walrus ivory and seal oil, honey, wax, malt, silks and woollens, amber and hazel nuts, soapstone dishes and basalt millstones, wrought weapons, ornaments, and silver. For this alone the viking peoples would be worthy of fame, for to this end they built ships and established market towns, developed trade routes and maintained spheres of influence, and fortified mercantile practice with piracy and conquest abroad.

To go viking was a trade or profession, a means to the good life, or at least to a living. Its three main elements, trade, piracy, and land-taking, often closely blended, had been northern activities long before the Viking Age, and would long outlast it. One moves back with no sense of dislocation from the commencement of the Viking Movement shortly before 800 to the purposeful mastery of sea-going techniques by the Scandinavian peoples and the eastward expansion of the Swedes into the Baltic lands soon after the year 700. Behind these lay the movements of the Angles, Jutes, Geats, and Eruli associated with the fourth, fifth, and sixth centuries, and still farther back the Folk Wanderings or Migrations of so many northern tribes or peoples. Historians have long debated whether we should see more than superficial resemblances between the late and early manifestations of northern unrest, and that there were substantial intermissions is evident, but though we shall be wise to reserve the word 'viking' for its agreed post-780 context, there are convincing reasons for seeing northern history, however diversified, as a unity, and the northern excursus as a continuing rather than a fortuitously repetitive or coincidental process.

Our three main sources of information about the viking and pre-viking north are archaeology, numismatics, and written records. Ideally they should complement and illuminate each other, so that hardly a corner of doubt or ignorance remains to us; in fact, all three are imperfect instruments to knowledge and understanding. For a start, there is no contrast here between the exactitude of science (archaeology and numismatics) and the subjectivity of the written word. Archaeologists, like other men, are not always free from nationalism, mysticism, or overconfidence, as is shown by the long debate over the extent and significance of Scandinavian material in Russian graves, the sad story of viking finds in America, the continuing argument over the origin and chronology of viking art styles, and the uncertainty as to what objects came out of what layer in so many nineteenth-century archaeological investigations. Even when the material evidence is agreed on it must be interpreted, and here again scholars of deserved reputation do not always see eye to eye. The dating of objects and sites is often difficult, and closer approximations than a century or half-century are hard to come by. Nature, which has been so prodigal of disasters, has even so been a little niggardly of such terminatory phenomena as a flow of lava, a drift of sand, or a river's change of course. Again, as we see at Hedeby, the archaeologists may have so huge a task in hand that they can do little more than issue interim reports, of great interest and importance, but disconcertingly open to revision in the light of next year's dig.

Yet, for all this, the contribution of archaeology to our knowledge of the viking world is immense. Investigators, grown more and more masters of their art, and drawing increasingly on scientific aids, have uncovered thousands of graves and many hundreds of dwellings; they have identified and sometimes explored Viking Age towns; and can inform us with confidence of ploughed fields, cattle byres, middens, drainage systems, farmsteads and smithies. They have found warriors with their weapons, boats and horses; merchants with scales and weights; great ladies furnished and provisioned out of this world for the next. They have found sleighs, carts, chests, spades and picks, horse-harness, dog-collars and leads; spinning weights and scraps of silk and woollen; garments, brooches, combs and other toiletry. We have a good idea of what people wore, and what tools they used from broad-axe to eating-knife, from spear to needle. We are sufficiently well informed about the viking ship to build a replica and cross the Atlantic in it. We know something of Norse religion and much of Norse funerary practice. We can study the viking at home, and accompany him abroad with his distinctive personal ornaments and ship-burials. We know his house patterns in Iceland and Greenland, can assess his grasp of constructional principles at the great strongholds of Trelleborg and Fyrkat, as well as at centres of trade like Birka and Hedeby. A carbon-14 dating of *c.* 1000 for some of the artefacts discovered at L'Anse-aux-Meadows in Newfoundland is crucial for the Norse discovery of North America; the examination and dating of buried treasure in Scandinavia is one key to the warlike or peaceful nature of particular decades back home. And not least, everything brought to light by the archaeologists is a check on the written records.

That is no less true of numismatics, the study of coins and coinage. Much northern history is characterized by chronological imprecision, and here, eventually, numismatics will solve many problems. Thus it is the record of the coins struck by various rulers in the Norse kingdom of York in the middle decades of the tenth century which does most to bring sense and order into the whirligig of change there; and by analogy, the close connection between coinage and royal power, or at least royal pretensions, holds out hope for a closer understanding of how royal power developed in the Scandinavian countries during the Viking Age. Coin-making was a late introduction into all three lands, beginning with copies of coins from the mint at Dorestad, the famous silver coinage of the emperor Charlemagne, with its obverse legend CARO-LUS and its reverse DOR-STAT, both highly stylized in Scandinavia over the years, and at times replaced by animal, bird, or human motifs (Plate 12). Where such copies were minted has been much argued: Hedeby and Birka appear the likeliest places, in that order. But the first royal coinages of northern kings owed much to England. Towards the end of his reign, possibly *c.* 888, the Danish king Guthrum of East Anglia had coins struck bearing his baptismal name Edelia or Edeltan (Æthelstan); between 890 and 895 East Anglia saw an extensive coinage associated with the name of king Edmund the Martyr, important evidence incidentally for the Conversion of the southern Danelaw; an unidentifiable Halfdan-Halfdene has left his name on three coins of the 890s; and during the same decade there was a lightweight coinage in the Five Boroughs which did not scruple to use the name of an English not a Danish king. It was a hundred years later, in the 990s, that the Irish vikings began to produce a local coinage, again in close imitation of English models.

The royal currencies of Scandinavia itself start late. In Denmark coins with a king's name begin with Svein Forkbeard, *c.* 985–1014; in Sweden with Olaf Skötkonung, *c.* 994–1022; and in Norway scantily and maybe transiently with Olaf Tryggvason, 995–1000, and St. Olaf, 1015–30. English influence is strong. Svein is the first Scandinavian king to appear in some kind of portraiture, by way of a bust on a coin inscribed partly in Latin, partly in rough-and-ready Old English, *Rex Addener*, 'Svein king of the Danes'. The reverse has an Old English legend naming 'Godwine (moneyer) of the Danes', but no mint. The first Norwegian coins were copies of Old English pennies, made by Old English moneyers for the 'king of Norway'; we must wait for the second half of the century for a clear indication of Norwegian mints at Nidarnes, Hamar, and Kaupang in the Trondelag. Harald Hardradi, as befitted a strong, ambitious king who had seen the civilization of the Byzantine, Muslim, and Mediterranean worlds, did much to develop a Norwegian currency, manage it in his own interest, and give it permanence. The Swedish coinage of Olaf Sköttkonung and his successor Onund Jacob was likewise strongly influenced from England, and much of it was produced by English moneyers at Sigtuna. After Onund Jacob's time (he reigned till 1050) this Swedish coinage failed to maintain itself, either because there was too much silver about for a coinage to have much meaning, or because of a pagan reaction against Christian innovations, of which coins with their religious symbols and legends might appear one of the more obvious. In Denmark, on the other hand, Svein's successor Knut managed his coinage well, and we have an impressive list of mints working for him: Ribe and Viborg in Jutland, Odense on Fyn, Slagelse, Roskilde, and Ringsted in Zealand, and Lund in Skåne. Coins were minted likewise at Hedeby, Århus, Ålborg, and Randers. After Knut's death we observe the same Byzantine influences on the designs of Danish coins as on Norwegian.

Like archaeology, numismatics is a check on the written word. The period of conquest and unrest in eastern and southern England is attested by no fewer than eighteen hoards from the decade *c.* 865–75, containing between them almost 2,500 English coins.

In the same way, the numismatist knows of a total of twenty hoards with more than 2,000 English pennies deposited round the shores of the Irish Sea during the decade 970–80, while from England east of the Pennines the tally is a solitary hoard of fewer than 400 pennies from

Tetney in Lincolnshire and two pennies of Eadgar from a rubbish-pit at York. Clearly little impact was felt in England from the resurgence of the power of the southern O'Neil which in 980 scotched the power of the Dublin Norse and of their allies from Man and the Isles, and in this way coin-hoards may be said to mirror the contrast between the disorder of the Hiberno-Norse world in the heyday of Maelsechlainn ('Malachy of the Collar of Gold') and of Anlaf Quaran ('Olaf of the Sandal') and the calm progress of the Anglo-Danish rapprochement which culminated in the reign of Eadgar the Peaceful.[1]

No less striking is the incidence of kufic coins throughout Scandinavia, with the heavy concentrations in eastern Sweden and Gotland indicative of the military and mercantile roles of those peoples in Russia and the Caliphate. The drying-up of the flow of kufic silver northwards helps explain the collapse of Birka *c.* 970, and the ensuing shortage of this precious and coveted metal throughout Scandinavia makes significant the heavy exactions of tribute and, later, soldiers' wages from eleventh-century England, and the acquisition of German silver by loot and trade after *c.* 950.

It is no severe criticism of the numismatist to recognize that like archaeology his science is less than perfect as a guide to early chronology and viking conquest, colonization, and trade. Like books, coins have their fates, and these are often obscure. To take an extreme example, the discovery of three Roman copper coins from the period 270–305 in the south-eastern corner of Iceland does not prove that the Romans visited that country. They are far more likely to have been carried there by a Norseman after 870. Dated coins supply for the most part one terminal date only: that before which they could not have arrived in a country, been used in trade or stolen as loot, or had their career suspended by being buried in a grave or hoard. Ideally it is their conjunction with other objects which allows a fair degree of chronological exactitude.[2]

---

[1] Michael Dolley, *Viking Coins of the Danelaw and of Dublin*, 1965, pp. 9–10.
[2] Readers of Sture Bolin, 'Mohammed, Charlemagne and Ruric', in *Scandinavian Economic History Review*, I, 1, Copenhagen, 1953, pp. 5–39; *Ur penningens historia*, Lund, 1962; and *Studier över Mynt och Myntfynd i Östra och Norra Europa under Vikingatiden* (unpublished in 1962, but excerpted by P. H. Sawyer); A. R. Lewis, *The Northern Seas*, Princeton, 1958; and P. H. Sawyer, *The Age of the Vikings*, 1962, will find a somewhat different viewpoint expressed in K. F. Morrison, 'Numismatics and Carolingian Trade: A Critique of the Evidence', in *Speculum*, 38, 3, Cambridge, Mass., 1963, pp. 403–32, and Brita Malmer, *Nordiska mynt före år 1000*, Acta Archaeologica Lundensia, Lund, 1966.

But probably the most important decision facing today's historian of the viking and pre-viking north is his use of written sources. While archaeology and numismatics, for all their imperfections, give him more and more, the written sources give him less and less. To be brief, our confidence in saga and chronicle, poem and inscription, has been deeply shaken. Well-trusted narratives, long-cherished beliefs, familiar personages, and celebrated events have been re-examined, re-assessed, and not infrequently discarded. In the dark backward and abysm of time before *c.* 750 we must expect to see all things darkly, their edges blurred, their content obscure, their shapes distorted. I have therefore entitled two of my early chapters 'The Legendary History of the Swedes and the Danes' and 'The Historical Traditions of Norway to 950', titles which mean exactly what they say. But northern written sources stay richly embroidered with legend, tradition, folktale, and invention to the end of our period, as the life story of Harald Hardradi from Stiklarstadir to Byzantium, from the Nissa to Stamford Bridge, amply demonstrates. This legendary material, both early and late, is part of Scandinavian historiography, highly important to the history of northern history, and for many still not fully differentiated from history; and it seems to me that in the interest of the English reader I should make a traverse through it, erecting as I go such monitory signposts as 'Here be Monsters', 'Myth-Makers at Work: Proceed with Caution', and 'Bravic War Department Property: Danger—Keep Out!' For it is *not* a historical landscape which here surrounds us, and should not be regarded as such.

There is difficulty enough in the sheer bulk of the material. Documents exist in many languages, but preponderantly in Old Norse (and there mainly in Old Icelandic), in Old English, Early Irish and Early Welsh, in Latin and Greek, Arabic and Persian, and in Russian. In kind they include annals, chronicles, sagas, travel-books, geographical treatises, laws, charters, treaties, entertainments, panegyrics, defamations, wills, tracts, ecclesiastical and royal missives, homilies, saints' lives, legends, folktales, myths, elegies, heroic lays, skaldic verses, and commemorative inscriptions. They even include works which within inverted commas may be described as 'histories', like Adam of Bremen's History of the Archbishops of Hamburg-Bremen (*Gesta Hammaburgensis Ecclesiæ Pontificum, c.* 1080), Ari Thorgilsson's Book of the Icelanders

(*Íslendingabók, c.* 1122), the *Historia de antiquitate regum Norwagiensium, c.* 1180, of Theodoricus Monachus, the synoptic histories of the Norwegian kings written by Icelanders, of which Snorri Sturluson's *Heimskringla, c.* 1225, is the best-known exemplar, and the Danish History (*Gesta Danorum, c.* 1185–1223) of Saxo Grammaticus. There are substantial compilations of a purposeful and responsible nature, like the *Anglo-Saxon Chronicle*, the *Annales Bertiniani*, and the *Annals of Ulster*, to which the epithet indispensable may be forthrightly applied, and lucky interpolations like the narratives concerning Ohthere and Wulfstan inserted in king Alfred's translation of Orosius's History of the World, or the account of Harald Hardradi's war service in Byzantium to be found in the anonymous 'Book of Advice', known in our day by reason of its late nineteenth-century publication with the *Cecaumeni Strategicon* of *c.* 1070–80. There are runic inscriptions to Swedes who died in Russia and the Muslim countries, and Muslim accounts of the Rus who descended the Volga and Dnieper in search of silks and silver. There are inscriptions to men who received Danegeld in the west, gave meat to eagles in the east, cleared roads or built causeways at home, did not flee at Uppsala while they held sword in hand, or died while the drengs besieged Hedeby; inscriptions to fathers, mothers, wives and husbands, and many a mourned-for son; inscriptions to comrades. A whole saga of viking endeavour stares back at us from a standing stone like that at Högby in Östergötland. 'Thorgerd raised this stone to her mother's brother Ozur. He died in the east in the land of the Greeks. Five sons had the good bondi Gulli. The brave soldier Asmund fell at Fyris; Ozur died in the east in the land of the Greeks; Halfdan was slain on Bornholm, Kari at (. . . ?); Bui too is dead.' In short, if we have the necessary languages and the will to read, we possess at a first uncritical glance the material for a dozen books about the vikings in the written sources alone, ranging as these do from far horizons and the honoured names of heroes and peoples to the quiet intimacies of family and home.

But the reliability and helpfulness of these sources varies a good deal. Only a few deserve a full confidence, most demand caution, and many a bleak distrust. It was all of half a century ago that the brothers Curt and Lauritz Weibull in Sweden and Halvdan Koht in Norway began their devastating examination of northern written sources. As a result vast quantities of unhistorical tradition have been swept from northern history books and can never be reinstated. This remains the most fundamental contribution to viking history made from any quarter during this century.[1] We place far less reliance than we did on the faithfulness of oral transmission, and are increasingly conscious of the limited or partisan aims of many chroniclers. Indeed, the historical validity of the sagas is today less well regarded than it was even a decade ago.[2] The most significant change is in respect of Snorri Sturluson's *Heimskringla*, which can no longer be held to give coherence to early Norwegian history; but all the Icelandic historians and sagamen are under suspicion and scrutiny. (The sagas relating to Greenland and Vinland are exceptional in that their general thesis is receiving confirmation from archaeology and, possibly, cartography.) Eastwards, the Muslim sources descriptive of the Rus clearly require a new evaluation. But our awareness of all this is gain not loss, in that it frees us from error and conducts to truth. For when the heaviest discount has been made on grounds of error, confusion, origin, transmission, invention, bias, propaganda, sources, influences, analogues, and dating; when entire works are jettisoned, like *Jómsvíkinga Saga*, or sunk in historical estimation, like *Landnámabók*; or subjected to the higher criticism, like the *Anglo-Saxon Chronicle*, *Heimskringla*, the *Primary* or *Nestorian Chronicle*, the Irish and Muslim sources, northern *lausavísur* and skaldic verse, and the Latin chronicles of the Empire—when all this is done, a not too disappointing residue of acceptable material remains. In the pages that follow I offer what must be scores of observations on the acceptability of the sources dealt with in particular contexts. Here I shall be content to emphasize, then re-emphasize, the rigour with which all written sources must be tested and refer the inquiring, or possibly the relieved, reader to the recent books of Theodore M. Anderson, Fr. P. Walsh, P. H. Sawyer, and Lucien Musset listed in my Bibliography; and to the decisive studies of Curt and Lauritz Weibull and Halvdan Koht already referred to.

A related problem is the enormous modern literature bearing not only on the written sources but on every aspect of the subject. This, too, is to be found in a wide variety of languages, and he must

---

[1] Their more important essays and collections are listed in the Bibliography, pp. 433, 434, 444.
[2] A representative bibliography of the long debate on the historicity of the sagas will be found in the main Bibliography, pp. 441-2.

be a veritable Tongue-Master who has them all at command. There is a long-standing theory that by the time an actress is equipped to play Juliet she is too old for the part. The viking historian may equally fear that before he acquires all the languages, reads all the books, and flushes all the coverts of all the periodicals, he will have reached the blameless haven of senility without a word rendered. Patently, to wait on definitive knowledge is to wait on eternity. But in view of the marked advances of the last forty years, the need for a fresh explication, and one would hope, synthesis, and the spectacular increase of interest in the vikings during recent decades (currently reinforced by Mr. Helge Ingstad's discovery of Norse remains in Newfoundland, the publicity attendant on the discovery and publication of the Vinland Map, and the celebration of the nine hundredth anniversary of the Norman Conquest, with its Norse preliminaries at Gate Fulford and Stamford Bridge), this seems a better time than most to offer the student and general reader a view of the subject's present state and lasting value.

A substantial part of my History is by intention narrative, a progress through time, and deals with the growth and continuing political history of the three viking kingdoms at home and their warlike, mercantile, and colonizing activities abroad. I believe this to be essential in what is only the second viking history to be written for the English reader. It follows that I give fair space to the main figures of the Age. These were not always, or at any time the only, makers of power, but they were, or appear representative of, those who acquired and employed it. We must be careful not to think of even the best-known northern kings as rulers of nations in a modern sense. The kingdoms established in Denmark at the beginning of the ninth century, in Sweden some fifty years later, and in Norway a little before the year 900, were obviously more extensive, powerful, and more indicative of national possibilities than the petty kingdoms and independent lordships which preceded them, but there was nothing truly 'national' about them. They were personal aggrandisements of territory and wealth, based on sea-power, unstable in nature, eccentric of duration. In other words, the 'marauders of the great international trade-routes', as Lönnroth calls them, wore much the same colours at home as abroad. As late as the reigns of Knut or his regent in Denmark, Olaf Skötkonung and Onund Jacob in Sweden, and Harald Hardradi in Norway, there were at best only the most rudimentary notions of nationality current in the north, and practically nothing (many scholars would say nothing whatever) in the way of national institutions, national administration, or a national policy. A kingdom was what belonged to a king, and it is in this confined sense only that we can speak of the kingdom of the Danes, the king of the Swedes, and the Norwegian realm.[1]

However, if not shapers of kingdoms and moulders of events (a case can be made out that they were), such men as Godfred and Harald Fairhair, Harald Bluetooth, Olaf Tryggvason and Olaf Haraldsson, Svein Forkbeard and king Knut, were significant catalysts in their day and place. The enduring realities which lay behind them, of geography, race, language, social order, livelihood, trade, town, countryside, and the vital harvests of land and water, along with religion, art, literature, and law I have brought under review in three chapters on 'The Scandinavian Community', though some of them recur more or less continuously throughout. To that other ultimate reality of the viking situation, ships and seafaring, I have devoted half a chapter, for these and their end-product, power along coasts and sea-lanes, are fundamental to an understanding of the nature of northern kingship, the political vicissitudes of the northern realms, and viking trade and piracy, colonization and war overseas. Parts of the narrative are necessarily signposted with a maybe, a we-presume, or an *aiunt*, and much of the detail is obscure—including detail as considerable as the identity of the Geats and the mixture of peoples in the Danelaw, the administrative measures of Harald Fairhair and the legal improvements of Hakon the Good, the dynastic, political, and economic background of the early tenth-century Swedish domination in southern Jutland, the situation in Denmark which earned disfavour for Harald Bluetooth and led to the accession of his son Svein, and those events in Norway which ensured the overthrow of jarl Hakon and the downfall of Olaf Tryggvason. But when every difficulty has been acknowledged, and every doubt confessed, we know that the period under discussion saw the first shaping, admittedly incomplete, still largely personal, and subject to harsh vicissitude, of the

---

[1] There are brief summaries of present Scandinavian opinion on these matters in Erik Lönnroth, 'Probleme der Wikingerzeit', in *Visby-symposiet för historiska vetenskaper*, 1965; the same author's 'Government in Medieval Scandinavia', in *Recueils de la Société Jean Bodin*, Brussels, 1966; and Else Roesdahl, *Viking Age Denmark*, 1982, p. 25 and *passim*.

three northern kingdoms at home, the creation and development of the island-republic of Iceland and the duchy of Normandy abroad, and the occupation of the lesser Atlantic isles. It saw a firm Norse lodgement in Greenland, and the discovery and exploration of part of the Atlantic coast of North America. Eastwards there was a military and commercial presence carried by way of the Baltic lands and Lake Ladoga to the Russian rivers, the maintenance on their banks of armed trading posts, of which Novgorod and Kiev had the most notable history, the contact with Islam and Byzantium, and the Rus share in bringing into being the great Slav kingdom whose name perpetuates their own. There was the significant Danish contribution to the making of the English people, and the infusion of Danish and Norwegian blood, thought, and practice into the whole of the British Isles and much of western Europe. There was the important viking contribution to European trade, and the equally important religious, artistic, mercantile, and institutional borrowings from Europe, which ensured the northward expansion of the bounds of Christian European civilization. Finally there was the clear demonstration that because of dissension at home, the superior resources of their neighbours, an inability to evolve an exportable political and social system, and above all a lack of man-power, no Scandinavian king in viking times would achieve a durable empire held together by the North Sea and Baltic, or even a purely Scandinavian hegemony.

These are the matters which we must now seek to cover in a more or less chronological order.

I. THE NORTHERN PEOPLES TO A.D. 700

1. From the Beginnings to the Age of Migrations

THE THREE SCANDINAVIAN COUNTRIES KNOWN FOR more than a thousand years as Sweden, Denmark, and Norway have had a long if not continuously recorded history, and every stage of it helped mould the lands, peoples, and kingdoms as we behold them in the Viking Age. Twelve thousand years ago, in the earliest post-glacial period in Scandinavia, men were moving over its habitable areas, food-gathering, hunting, fowling, and fishing, leaving their mark on a flint here, an antler there, in Denmark by Bromme north-west of Sorø in Zealand, in Sweden in Skåne and Halland, in Norway in Østfold on the eastern side of the Oslofjord and, as now appears certain, in the south-western coastal region, and along the west coast from Bergen to Trondheim. These last were the Fosna folk, who had probably entered Norway from the south. Northwards again, facing the Arctic Ocean, were to be found people of the Komsa culture, their place of origin unknown. It is meaningless to talk of nationality in those distant times, and idle to speak of race; but these hunters, fishermen, and food-gatherers from the south who knew, or over the centuries came to know, the bow and arrow, knife, scraper, harpoon, and spear, who developed the skin-boat, would possess the first known tamed animals, the big wolflike dogs of Maglemose and Sværdborg, and buried their dead in shallow graves in close proximity to the living—these were the parent 'Scandinavians', and their way of life, closely adapted to their surroundings, persisted for many thousands of years. Indeed, Norwegian scholars in particular have found survivals or parallels of this ancient hunting culture of Scandinavia not only among the Lapps of Finnmark but among the Norse population of Norway almost to our own day.

Yet of these half-glimpsed wanderers in the northern wilderness, with every allowance for the piety which would have men look to the rock from which they are hewn, it is their remoteness from the viking scene which most impresses. Nor need we trace even in broad outline those developments in climate, environment, social practice, and cultural influence which made human progress possible in Scandinavia, or count the untellable generations of hunters and fishers, workers in flint and clearers of forest, stock-minders, crop-raisers, builders of dolmen and dysse, the artificers, traders, and colonizers who fill ten thousand years of northern prehistory till *c.* 1500 B.C. By then, with the Bronze Age under way, there is evidence from physical anthropology that the people of the far north dwelling in the village settlements of the Varangerfjord were of the same 'nordic' racial type as the inhabitants of the Oslofjord in the south; while Denmark and the more southerly regions of the Scandinavian peninsula were entering upon a period of comparative wealth, social change, modes of belief, and artistic achievement informative in themselves and prophetic of developments to come. To pay for tin and copper, and also gold from the peoples farther south, Denmark had the high-priced amber of Jutland, and soon native smiths and artists were rivalling and at times excelling their southern masters in the working of bronze. We see the Bronze Age handsome and clear in its weapons and personal ornaments, in such religious offerings as the sun-image of Trundholm, where the sun's disc stands with a bronze horse within a six-wheeled bronze chariot, so that worshippers might see their god in effigy make a progress across the northern heavens, and in the long, slender, gracefully curved lurs or trumpets, masterpieces beyond which the casters' art could hardly hope to progress. We see it, too, in the contemporary rock-carvings to be found almost everywhere in Scandinavia south of a line Trondheim-Swedish Uppland. For the carved rock-faces of Bohuslän and the pictured slabs of the Kivik barrow show these splendid artefacts in use, along with their users: swords and axes, spears, bows and arrows; ships beaked at both ends, with rowers (never with sails); sun-images ship-borne, man-borne, drawn by horses; chariots and wagons; there are men fighting, dancing, and turning somersaults, sharing in religious ceremonies, and almost every man of them with an immense erected phallus. Sometimes they depict gods and priests, occasionally a female figure, and a profusion of horses, cows, dogs, snakes, deer, birds, and fish. For today's student these rock-carvings are the picture-galleries of their age. Finally we see the Age in its funerary ritual, the thousands of graceful tumuli covering and enlarging a burial chamber proper, the wealth of grave goods, including not only weapons and adornments but, uniquely spared by time and corruption, garments and fabrics, boxes and pails, cups, beakers, and stools. Knee-length kirtles, overcloaks of woollen, shoes of cloth or leather and caps round and shaggy, blouses and jackets and woven fringed skirts, all are to be found, and most moving of all, miraculously preserved by the tannin of the 'oak cists' of Denmark, the very flesh and fell of the wearers, the bodies, faces, features, of the men and women themselves.

The Bronze Age came to an end some five hundred years B.C., not suddenly, but by gradual transition to a period characterized by the use of iron. The lap-over of the late Bronze and early Iron Age provides us with an evocative change in burial practice. Boat-shaped graves outlined with stones, and often with taller stones at either extremity to represent prow and stern (*skibsætninger*, 'ship-settings', sing. *skibsætning*), and inhumation are found together in Gotland and on Bornholm. The dead were now thought of as having to make a voyage, or at least as having need of a boat. The *skibsæt-ninger* direct our thoughts back to the formalized rock-carvings of the early Bronze Age, with their religious or ritualistic significance; outwards to the contemporary religions of the mediterranean civilizations; and a millennium and a half forward to the boat-shaped viking graves of Lindholm Høje, the boat-shaped viking houses of Trelleborg, Aggersborg, and Fyrkat in Denmark, the viking ship-burials of Norway, the pictorial stones of the Swedish mainland and Gotland, and the convex walls of the first Christian church in Greenland, at the Norse settlement of Brattahlid in Eiriksfjord.

The opening centuries of the Iron Age were a depressed period for most of Scandinavia. The wealth and liveliness of the Bronze Age dulled and contracted; there was little gold and as yet no silver; grave offerings became fewer and poorer, field and bog offerings came almost to an end. And whereas bronze and bronze artefacts had found their way as far north as latitude 68°, early iron fails at latitude 60°, approximately that of present-day Oslo and Uppsala. And everywhere artistic standards were in decline. Why should this be so? What impoverished the northern countries and for a time interrupted their lines of communication south? First there is the compelling fact of European history which has labelled these centuries the 'Celtic' Iron Age. This was an epoch of Celtic power and expansion, when the Celtic peoples who occupied the Upper Rhine and Danube basins and much of eastern France, spilled over into Spain, Italy, Hungary, the Balkans, and even Asia Minor, and westward pressed on to the Atlantic seacoast and into the British Isles. The core of their society was a military, but not heedlessly militant, aristocracy with a need for chariots and harness, weapons and personal adornments, and therefore the pragmatically minded patrons of artists and craftsmen who alone could make these splendid accoutrements for them. Their empire was military and cultural, based on the warrior with his two-edged iron sword, in turn based on the peasant with his plough and sickle, but with no enduring political structure which could make it a permanent threat to the urbanized mediterranean world. But the unrest into which they threw so much of Europe worked unhappily upon the north. Trade routes and cultural channels between Scandinavia and the Etruscan and Greek civilizations were in large measure blocked, and for a while the northern countries fell into that backwardness and isolation to which their geographical position and southern ignorance from time to time exposed them. By this time, too, Jutland had lost its lead in the amber trade, and the amber of Prussia was of no benefit to Zealand and the isles.

More serious was the climatic change which took place in Europe just as the Iron Age began. During the Bronze Age conditions in Scandinavia had been favourable to economic and cultural progress. A comparatively warm dry climate had made life easier for man and his domestic animals, and also for the animals he hunted and ate. The area of cultivation and pasture was enlarged, and agricultural skills improved. Deterioration when it came was quick and sharp, and was severest in the northerly parts of the peninsula, where the margin of existence throughout recorded history has been narrower than in Denmark and the southern portions of Norway and Sweden. The main problem everywhere would be the winter feeding of stock; but cold and wet are maimers of most features of civilized life. If we accept the identification of the mysterious Thule mentioned by the Greek geographer Pytheas of Massalia with some part of the west coast of Norway, it was during these unpropitious yet challenging times, when northern man was adjusting to harder grain, heavier ploughs, more lethal weapons, and longer trousers, that Scandinavia first appears in European historical and geographical records. In 330–300 B.C. Pytheas made a remarkable voyage west and north as part of his survey of the coasts of Europe from Cadiz to the Don. But the work which recorded this, his *Of the Ocean*, has not survived, and all too much is uncertain. Six days' sail north of Britain, he tells us (or, more accurately, later geographers rich in ignorance, confusion, and prejudice tell us), he came to a land which appears to lie close under the Arctic Circle. It was inhabited by barbarians who lived by agriculture. They were poorly off for domestic animals, but had millet and herbs, roots and fruit. From grain and honey they made a fermented drink, and this grain they threshed indoors, because the rain and sunlessness made outdoor threshing impossible. This dank, uncordial region, wherever it lay, was not Pytheas's only acquaintance with the north. He speaks of the amber island of Abalus (Heligoland?), whose inhabitants sold the sea's gift to a people called the Teutones. He speaks, too, of the Ingvæones and almost certainly of the Goths or Gutones. The Teutones were possibly the inhabitants of the Danish district of Thy, bounded east and south by the Limfjord and north by the Jammerbugt, in north-western Jutland. To the east of them, between the Limfjord, Mariager Fjord, and the Kattegat, was Himmerland, the presumed home of the Cimbri, and these two names usher in a second phase of personal contact between the peoples of early Iron Age Scandinavia and the sophisticated cultures of the Mediterranean. For Teutones and Cimbri were in hostile and often victorious contact with Roman armies in Gaul, Spain, and northern Italy in the decades immediately preceding 100 B.C. The bloody and destructive ceremonies which followed the heavy Roman defeat at Orange *c.* 105 are thus described by Orosius in his *History of the World*:

The enemy [the Cimbri] captured both camps and acquired an enormous quantity of booty. In accordance with a strange and unusual vow, they set about destroying everything which they had taken. Clothing was cut to pieces and cast away, gold and silver was thrown into the river, the breastplates of the men were hacked to pieces, the trappings of the horses were broken up, the horses themselves drowned in whirlpools, and men with nooses round their necks were hanged from trees. Thus there was no booty for the victors and no mercy for the vanquished.

An earlier witness to the victory-rites of the Cimbri is supplied by the geographer Strabo, of the first century B.C. Their priestesses, ancient women robed in white clothing, decked their captives with garlands before leading them to a huge bronze cauldron. Here one of their number, sword in hand and mounted on a step or ladder, cut each man's throat after he had first been suspended over the cauldron's edge, so that his blood, which served both for sacrifice and augury, flowed down into it. This is very much the scene portrayed on one of the panels of the silver bowl of Gundestrup, found in the Danish home of the Cimbri, Himmerland in Jutland, and itself in all its loveliness (it is Celtic work of the second or first century B.C., brought up maybe from northern France or further south-east) possibly just such a grisly receptacle. There are other passages in classical writers to confirm the alarming impression made in parts of continental Europe by this first documented eruption of warlike men from Scandinavia. Others besides the Teutones and Cimbri were now on the move. As though to set a long-enduring pattern, trouble in the northern homelands was found to mean trouble for lands further south. Driven in part by stringent changes in their economy, the Langobards set off from Skåne on the journey that would by the late sixth century carry them by way of the lower Elbe and middle Danube into Italy. The Burgundians, deriving by a most shaky tradition from Bornholm (Borgundarholm), would look for a better future in north-eastern Germany, while the Rugii of Rogaland in south-western Norway (the identification is a long way from certain) sought a better present on the south Baltic coast. Most famous of all were the Goths, inhabitants of the modern Öster- and Västergötland in Sweden (though a case for the island of Gotland as their original habitat can still be argued), who also found new lands in north Germany. The power of the Celts was on the wane; the peoples called Germani by Poseidonios of Apamea (_c_. 130 B.C.–5 B.C.) were pressing southwards for land, wealth, conquest, trade, plunder or glory; and Scandinavia, the 'big island Scandza', was establishing a reputation, which Jordanes would later confirm, as the factory (_officina_) of peoples and matrix (_vagina_) of nations.

The next phase of the Iron Age in Scandinavia, the Roman, is roughly coeval with the first four centuries of the Christian era. Once again southern influences proved stimulating, and the northern nations recovered strongly from their material and cultural impoverishment. The Celtic peoples found themselves no enduring match for Roman arms and discipline, and as these new masters of the Mediterranean extended their boundaries northwards and out-wards, and the tribes of Germania continued their wandering south, Roman and German must soon confront each other, sometimes in peace, sometimes in war, on the Danube and the Rhine. The cultural contacts were particularly close in the kingdom of the Marcomanni in Bohemia, from whence two great trade-routes proceeded north-wards, one by way of the Elbe to Jutland, the other by way of the Vistula to the Baltic islands and Sweden. Flanking these was an eastern route coming up from the Black Sea, or perhaps more routes than one, including that through Russia, which would prove of the first importance after A.D. 200, when the Goths would be the chief transmitters of goods and culture northwards; also a western sea-route from Gaul by way of the mouth of the Rhine and the Frisian islands to Holstein and so to Scandinavia. Not surprisingly, Zealand and its neighbouring islands stood to benefit most, and it was here and in Fyn that the choicest vessels of silver and bronze, like the decorated wine-service from a chieftain's grave at Hoby on Lolland, and painted cylindrical glass beakers as handsome as those from Nordrup, Varpelev, and Himlingøje, found their resting-place; but lovely and costly treasures from Rome reached Norway and Sweden, too, and its trade-nomenclature of values and weights was to leave a lasting and in the case of the öre (*aureus*) a permanent mark on the Old Norse reckoning system. Once more, and as always significantly, there was a shift in burial customs, too. Cremation can be found persisting almost everywhere, but inhuma-tion on the Roman model is also widespread, men and women buried in splendour, with wine and meat and the bowls and dishes and beakers and flagons of a costly banquet about them. Silver and gold poured north, masses of coin into Gotland, Skåne, Bornholm, and the Danish isles; and everything they saw of swords and brooches, rings and filigrees, hairpins and pots, was a challenge to native workmen. Southwards in exchange went skins and furs, amber, sea-ivory, and slaves. And with the profits of trade were combined the profits of war.

Slowly but surely the northern lands revealed their secrets to the geographers and ethnologists of the south. At the very begin-ning of the Christian era the emperor Augustus had dispatched a fleet beyond the Rhine up the north German coast, then round Jutland as far as the Kattegat, and as a consequence the Cimbri, Charudes, Semnones, and other Germanic peoples in this land 'sent ambassadors to ask for friendship with me [Augustus] and the Roman people'. In Nero's reign, *c.* A.D. 60, another fleet entered the Baltic; and soon Pliny the Elder was writing somewhat haphazardly in his *Natural History* of the bay Codanus beyond Jutland, which is full of islands, the largest of which is *Scadinavia*, which we may reasonably identify as the southern part of the Scandinavian peninsula. By the end of the first century A.D. Tacitus has firm and credible news of Scandinavia's most notable inhabitants, the Suiones, distinguished not only for arms and men but for their powerful fleets ('though the style of their ships is unusual in that there is a prow at each end'), who have high regard for wealth and accept one of their number as supreme, so that there is no limit to his power and no question of the obedience paid him. These can be none but the Svea (Svíar or Svéar), the Swedes of Uppland in central Sweden, already stronger and closer knit than their neighbours. Next to them dwelt the Sitones, resembling the Suiones in every respect save that they were so far degenerate as to

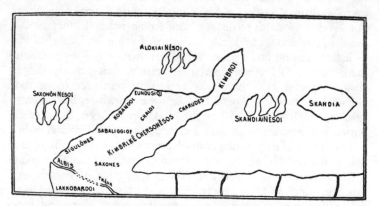

I. PTOLEMY'S CONCEPTION OF THE NORTH
South of the Elbe (Albis) dwell the Langobards, north of it the Saxons. In Jutland dwell the Cimbri (Himmerland?) and the Charudes (Hardsyssel?), but the other names do not lend themselves to identification. To the right (east) of Jutland are the Danish isles and Skåne.

take a woman as ruler. Most likely these were the Kainulaiset, the Kvenir or Kvænir of *Egils Saga*, the Cwenas of Ohthere (Ottar) and king Alfred, whose tribal name, whether Finnish or Lapp, lent itself to confusion with an Old Norse word for woman, *kván, kvæn*, gen. pl. *kvenna*, so that Kvenland, on the western shore of the Gulf of Bothnia, north of Uppland, became mistakenly a land of amazons, Adam of Bremen's *terra feminarum*. In another fifty years' time the tale has been carried further by the geographer Ptolemy. East of Jutland, he informs us, are four islands called Scandia. Three of them, presumably three of the Danish islands, are small, *Scandiai nesoi*, but the one lying furthest east, Scandia proper, opposite the mouth of the Vistula, is big. This must be the Scandinavian peninsula, and among the tribes inhabiting it are the Goutoi, in whom we seem to recognize the Gautar, and the Chaideinoi, whom we are tempted to identify with the Heidnir of Hedemark in Norway. Vast areas of the north are left unremarked, but several important regions are beginning to receive a clearer light. And we now glimpse beyond the Germanic peoples the primitive wondrous Finns and Lapps who enclosed them to the north.

Then, dismayingly, comes an almost unbroken silence of four hundred years before southern writers again attempt to enlarge our knowledge of the Scandinavian homelands. But in the sixth century the Roman Cassiodorus, minister and counsellor of Theodoric, king of the Ostrogoths in Italy (493–526), compiled a substantial historical work called *The Origin and Exploits of the Goths*, and the Gothic consciousness of a Scandinavian origin ensured from Cassiodorus a well-intentioned though at times puzzled northward glance. His book has not survived, but we have a summary of it in the *Getica* of Jordanes, written some thirty years later. Once again we read of the great island Scandza and its many and various peoples. Not all of them can be identified, but the advance in knowledge is considerable. Farthest north dwelt the Adogit, in a region where for two score days there was unbroken daylight in summer and in winter darkness unrelieved. Up there, too, were the Screrefennae, who live without benefit of grain, on the flesh of animals and birds' eggs. We hear of the Suehans or Swedes, with their fine horses and the prized dark furs they sent down to the markets of Rome, and of other tribes whose names are commemorated in Swedish provinces, the Hallin (Halland), Liothida (the medieval Lyuthgud, modern Luggude, near Hälsingborg), Bergio (maybe the Bjäre), and, more important, the Gautigoths (Väster-götland?), and the Swedes again, now called the Suetidi. There are the peoples of Raumarike and Ranrike, now Bohuslän, and specific-ally of Norway the Granni of Grenland, the Augandzi of Agder, the Harothi of Hordaland and the Rugi of Rogaland, 'over whom not many years since Roduulf was king who, despising his own kingdom, hastened to king Theodoric of the Goths and found what he sought'. These nations, says Jordanes, fought with the ferocity of wild animals, and were stronger than the Germans in both body and spirit. This view of the peoples of Sweden and Norway is more revealing than any glimpsed before, and consonant with the modern archaeological picture. And this is not the end of our debt to Jordanes. As Tacitus *c.* A.D. 100 had been the first to speak of the Swedes as an emergent kingdom, so it is Jordanes in the sixth century who first speaks of the Dani, the Danes, then settled in Denmark, from which they had driven the Eruli, its former occupants or recent usurpers.

The Swedes, Jordanes informs us, were famous for being taller than other northern peoples. Yet it was the Danes, of the same race as the Swedes, who claimed pre-eminence in this respect. The Norwegian tribes of Hordaland and Rogaland were likewise notably tall.

There remains Procopius, the Byzantine historian who accom-panied Belisarius on his campaigns against the Vandals and Ostro-goths and shortly after the year 550 commemorated the wars of Justinian in his *Histories of the Wars*. In tracing the fortunes of the Eruli after their shattering defeat by the Lombards *c.* 505, Procopius had occasion to mention the northern lands from which the Eruli had come and to which some of them were destined to return. He speaks of the land of the Danes and of the island Thule, which must be the Scandinavian peninsula. Here the Eruli found a new home close to the Gautoi, one of its most numerous peoples, presumably the Gautar dwelling somewhere south of the Swedes of Uppland. Much of Thule was barren and desolate, but the rest of it found room for thirteen nations, each with its king. Procopius is eloquent on the subject of the midnight sun, but his most striking informa-tion relates to the Scrithifinoi, Jordanes' Screrefennae, the Lapps whose way of life was like to that of beasts. They were a hunting people who drank no wine and raised no crops. They had no gar-ments of cloth and nothing that he recognized as shoes; their body's covering derived like its sustenance from the animals they hunted and slew, whose skins they fastened together with sinews. Even their children were nursed differently from the rest of mankind. They knew nothing of the milk of women nor ever touched their mother's breast, but were nourished on marrow from the bones of beasts. As soon as a woman had given birth she thrust the child into a skin which she afterwards hung from a tree. Then having put marrow in the child's mouth she went off with her husband a-hunting. The other inhabitants of Thule, Procopius judged, were not much different from the normality of men, though he found it worth recording that they had great numbers of gods and demons, to whom they offered human sacrifice in various cruel ways.

2. LAPPS HUNTING ON SKIS (OLAUS MAGNUS)
The presence of the woman is likely to be due to Olaus's reading in classical authors.

With Jordanes and Procopius we come clear by more than a century of the Roman Iron Age and move forward into that so-called Germanic Iron Age which leads to the Viking Age itself. Conveniently bridging these last two phases of the Iron Age, which occupy the first four and the second four centuries of the Christian era respectively, is the period of the Great Migrations, reminiscent of the outpouring of the Cimbri and Teutones just before the first century A.D. and the subsequent movements of the Langobards, Goths and Burgundians, though what took place now, under the impulse of the Hunnish invasion farther south in the second half of the fourth century and the diminution of Roman power first in her provinces, and eventually in Italy, was on a much bigger scale. The details of these migrations, with which medieval history may be said to begin, hardly concern us, neither the fictions of an imperial alliance which gave the Visigoths, Ostrogoths, and Burgundians their footholds on Roman territory, nor the more open assaults of the Langobards and Eruli, Alamanns and Franks. In fact, all these peoples were assailants, not sustainers. The Visigoths, Eruli, Ostrogoths, and Langobards forced their way into Italy; the Franks, Visigoths, Alamanns, Bavarians, and Burgundians partitioned and repartitioned Gaul; from Gaul the Visigoths swung south to conquer Spain, and the Vandals moved on by way of Andalusia to North Africa; in the mid-fifth century Angles and Saxons, some Jutes and Frisians, left their homes in and near the Danish part of Scandinavia to transform Roman Britain into Germanic England. To trace even the specifically Scandinavian share in these migrations would be a huge task, and is no part of this book; but a quick glance at three aspects of the subject will show that there was little new and nothing out of character for the Scandinavian peoples in the raids, campaigns, and colonial ventures which we shall find distinguishing the Viking Age proper, some three or four centuries ahead.

First, the Eruli, or as the classical authors tend to spell their name, Heruli. Their original home appears to have been somewhere in the Danish islands or southern Jutland, or maybe somewhere in both. It is not beyond belief that they had holdings in Skåne in Sweden. By reputation they were at all times a fighting tribe bent on exaction and piracy. In the third century A.D. their activities were receiving uncordial notice in the Black Sea area, whither a substantial body of them had removed themselves in the wake of the Goths. In 289 they are mentioned as having invaded Gaul along with the Chabiones, of whom little else is known. In the fourth century part of their race was subjugated by Ermanaric, famed king of the Ostrogoths, and not long afterwards they were defeated by the oncoming Huns. In the middle of the fifth century we hear of them plundering the coast of Spain, but whether these were wandering Eruli or Eruli raiding out of some northern home we do not know. For another hundred years wherever there was fighting and plunder there would be Erulian mercenaries, with their blue eyes and azured cheek-guards. Their defeats by Ermanaric *c.* 350, Theodoric *c.* 490, and the eunuch Narses in 556, set them among the most illustrious losers in early Germanic history. Procopius is notably severe on those that had fared south. Faithless, greedy, violent, shameless, beastly, and fanatical, he calls them, the vilest and most abandoned of men. Among other trenchant bad habits they cured the ills of old age by stabbing their ancients to death. Jordanes, as we shall see (p. 45 below), says that the Eruli were driven out of Denmark by the Danes, and if we accept that the disputed *egsode eorle* (MS. *eorl*) of Beowulf 6 means that Scyld Scefing, the eponymous ancestor of the Danish Scylding (Skjoldung) dynasty, 'terrified the Eruli' ('erul' is possibly the same word as *eorl*, *jarl*, a warrior of noble birth), we have testimony that their reputation for martial violence was well established in and around their own northern territories as well as abroad, for it would be Scyld's distinction not that he had terrified some puny collection of peace-lovers but a people of whom the whole north stood in fear. When this terrorization and expulsion of the Eruli took place we cannot say, perhaps toward the close of the fifth century. Where the dispossessed Eruli went we do not know, perhaps to join their compatriots in the general region of Hungary. But just as strong (or weak) a case, with growing archaeological and anthropological support, can be made out for a Danish expulsion of the Eruli around the year 200 or a little later, which would help account for their movements down through Europe in the third century. In either case, and whether the lapse of time was brief or long, eventually they would head back north, after their defeat by the Lombards *c.* 505, make their way through Slavic tribes and the lands of the Danes, and find a new home near the Gautar in southern Sweden. Perhaps, however, their most memorable contribution to northern history was not this unblest turbulence and commotion but their connection with the runic alphabet and runic inscription. Throughout Scandinavia there are inscriptions containing the word *erilaR* (*eirilaR*), which appears to mean 'Erulian', suggesting that the Eruli had such a reputation as rune-masters that their name became a descriptive title for such.

At roughly the time when the Eruli, according to Jordanes,

returned to live alongside the Gautoi or Gautar, this latter people, or a people whose name for some unknown reason was confounded with theirs,[1] was making its own much-chronicled contribution to the long list of Scandinavian sallies south. Their king at the time is best known by the Old English form of his name, Hygelac. The Old English epic poem *Beowulf* records how he was king of the *Gēatas*, how he planned hard fighting against the Franks (*Hūgas*) and brought his ships of war to Frisia, where he met his death in battle. 'That was not the least of close encounters in which Hygelac was slain, when the Geats' king, loving lord of peoples, Hrethel's son, died of the sword-drink in Friesland, hewn down by the blade in the rush of battle.' It was the Hetware of the lower Rhine who vanquished him, brought it about by their superior strength that the corsleted warrior must bow to the ground before them. This disastrous foray of Hygelac's which according to *Beowulf* (ll. 1202–14, 2354–68, 2910–21) cost him the lives of all save one of his followers, took place *c.* 521, and is vouched for by two Frankish sources, the *Historia Francorum* of Bishop Gregory of Tours (d. 594) and the anonymous eighth-century *Liber Historiæ Francorum*, and also by an English work of the eighth century about monsters and strange beasts, *Liber Monstrorum* (*De Monstris et de Belluis Liber*). From these we learn how a king named Ch(l)ochilaicus-Huiglaucus-Hyglac(us) made a piratical naval raid upon the land of the Attuarii, a Frisian people living within the Merovingian empire between the lower Rhine and the Zuyder Zee. Here he plundered a village and carried the booty out to his ships. The king himself remained ashore, where he was caught and slain by an army led by Theudobert, son of the Frankish king Theudoric. Next his fleet was routed and the booty restored to its owners. The skeleton (*ossa*) of king Huiglaucus, who ruled the Geats (*qui imperavit Getis*), a man so huge that from the age of 12 no horse could carry him, was preserved on an island at the mouth of the Rhine, and for a long time displayed there to the curious as a marvel of the human creation. That the two Frankish chronicles refer to Ch(l)ochilaicus as a king of the Danes not the Geats need not surprise us. Unless Gregory of Tours and his two successors had a more precise knowledge of

---

[1] The much-debated identity of the Geats of *Beowulf* will be touched on later (see pp. 34–44). For the moment we are concerned with the event itself, and whether the expedition of *c.* 521 was mounted by the Gauts of southern Sweden or the Jutes of Jutland is of secondary significance.

events and peoples in early sixth-century Denmark and Sweden than we have, any confusion of Danes and Geats, especially as to habitat, is understandable enough. The Danes they knew of, and the use of their name for various peoples 'up there' is well attested over many centuries.

The *aduentus Saxonum*, the entry of the Anglo-Saxon peoples into Britain, and their centuries-long successful struggle to establish Germanic kingdoms there, is among the most famous ventures of the Age of Migrations, but like other historical events of the time it is obscure in much of its detail: the identity and place of origin of the peoples taking part, the needs or desires that moved them to entry and conquest, the lines of invasion, the quality and duration of native resistance, the role of Hengest the Dane, the historicity of the British Arthur. Fortunately, in a brief survey of Viking ante-cedents these are points which do not bear too sharply at us. For even if we remain uncertain of the 'Jutish' connection with Jutland, the precise limits of Bede's *Angulus*, and of the country 'now called the land of the Old Saxons',[1] we know that the majority of the migrating peoples (who first and foremost were seeking land to live on) came from the general area of the lesser Danish islands; from southern Jutland (i.e. Slesvig), which according to Bede was left denuded of its inhabitants—a circumstance, if we can trust to it, highly significant for the westward progress of the Danes from the islands to Jutland; from the neck of the Cimbric peninsula (i.e. Holstein); and from the neighbouring territories of the upper Elbe, Weser and Ems rivers as far west then south as the Zuyder Zee and the mouths of the Rhine. Our earliest authority for the post-Conquest inhabitants of Britain is Procopius, who is thought to have

---

[1] The references are to Bede's famous statement in the *Historia Ecclesiastica*, I, 15: '(The newcomers) came from three most powerful nations of the Germans, the Saxons (*Saxones*), Angles (*Angli*), and Jutes (*Iutae*). From the Jutes are descended the people of Kent (*Cantuarii*) and the *Uictuarii*, that is, the people which holds the Isle of Wight, and that which to this day is called *Iutarum natio* in the province of the West Saxons, situated opposite the Isle of Wight. From the Saxons, that is, from the country which is now called the land of the Old Saxons, came the East Saxons, South Saxons, and West Saxons. From the Angles, that is, from the country which is called *Angulus*, and is said to have remained uninhabited from that day to this, between the provinces of the Jutes and Saxons, are sprung the East Angles, Middle Angles, Mercians, the entire Northumbrian stock—the people, that is, who live north of the river Humber—and the other peoples of the Angles.'

talked with some Englishmen (*Angiloi*) sent shortly after the middle of the sixth century to the emperor Justinian in Constantinople as part of an embassy from king Theudobert of the Franks. They were a curious miscellany, these inhabitants, for among them Procopius numbered the souls of the dead ferried to Britain across the Channel from Gaul. More tangible were the Angles, Frisians (*Frissones*), and Britons, each ruled by their own king and each so fluently fertile that every year they sent large numbers of men, women, and children overseas to the land of the Franks. That many Britons emigrated in the first half of the sixth century to Armorica (Brittany) is an attested circumstance; that waves of the Germanic invaders of Britain flowed back to the Continent when temporarily checked and baffled seems to be confirmed by the independent Fulda tradition of the *Translatio Sancti Alexandri*, and for an earlier period by Gildas. Significantly enough, according to the monk of Fulda, the sixth-century migrants returned to the mouth of the Elbe, from whence some of them had sprung.

That the Angles were a Scandinavian people is vouched for by Bede and king Alfred, and their continental home was probably in Slesvig and those islands near by mentioned by the Norwegian Ottar to king Alfred and by him regarded as the home of the English (*Engle*) before they came to this country. The Old English poem *Widsith* placed Angel and its king Offa north of the river Eider (Fifeldor). The Saxons, however we interpret their name, whether as the title of one people or, as is more likely, the group title of the related peoples from Holstein to the Ems (or still more widely as a general description of all peoples given to piratical activity in these and the contiguous parts of Europe), were as certainly not a Scandinavian people, but their geographical position helped shape the history of south-west Scandinavia for at least seven hundred years. They were a restless, stirring folk, these Men of the Sax, skilled clearers of swamp and forest and practised in war, and in the three centuries following *c.* A.D. 150 had elbowed their way into a considerable territory. In particular it is their arrival in the terpen area of Frisia in the period 400–50 which invites our attention. 'God made the sea, but the Frisians made the coast', says the old proverb. The terpen were man-made mounds built over many centuries against the sea's invasion of the Frisian coast between the Weser and the Zuyder Zee, small at first, but later big enough to support sizeable agricultural communities. This Saxon influx of the early fifth century into Frisia explains why Procopius speaks of the *Frissones* in Britain, while for other early authorities they were lost sight of under the name of *Saxones*. Later all separate titles of tribal origin, nationhood, and language would fall together under *Angli*, *Angelcynn*, and *Englisc*, and these in their turn under *English*, though by an interesting survival the Welsh and Gaelic speakers of the Island of Britain have preserved to our own day their ancient usage, *Saesneg* and *Sassenach*, words not entirely without savour of Teutonic piracy and barbarism.

2. The Legendary History of the Swedes and the Danes

FROM THESE WANDERINGS ABROAD BY ROAD AND flood we return to Scandinavia and the emergent kingdoms of the Swedes and Danes. Initially the progress of Norway towards nationhood was slower, and with the possible exception of the conquests of Halfdan Whiteleg we shall see scant approach to anything more than regional kingdoms in that long, narrow, sea-and-mountain-boundaried, northward-running eel-stripe of a country till the Viking Age has dawned and Halfdan the Black, father of Harald Fairhair, is fighting his way to the overlordship of the south and west. Nor have we much in the way of firm historical fact for the developing supremacy of the Swedes of Uppland and the Danes—mainly signs and pointers in poetry and legend, the story of the graves and other archaeological finds, and the unarguable circumstance that it was these two peoples, and no others, who after many shifts and balances of power imposed their rule on the areas which still bear their names.

The two cardinal facts of homeland Swedish history during the first millennium of our era are, first, that about the year 100 they were, on the testimony of Tacitus, more powerful and better organized in their Uppland province than any of the tribes that surrounded them, and second, that at a date which still remains bewilderingly uncertain (it might be as early as post-550 or as late as c. 1000) they would so impair the strength of their southern neighbours in Väster- and Östergötland that thereafter, apart from some forced interchanges of territory with Denmark, they would prove masters in their own part of Scandinavia. The most significant written source of information for the benighted sixth and early seventh centuries in Sweden is the Old English heroic elegy

Beowulf, in its several passages relating to Swedish-Geat affairs. These have been the subject of whole libraries of disquisition, most of it seeking to answer the question, Significant of what?

Wherever we end we must begin with the classical synthesis of our greatest English *Beowulf* scholar, R. W. Chambers, outlined and sustained by him in his *Introduction* to this greatest of Old English poems.[1] It proceeds from an identification of the Geats (OE. *Gēatas*) of the poem with the Gauts (OI. *Gautar*, OSw. *Gøtar*) resident, as we have just said, in the provinces south of the Swedes. Unfortunately we have still less knowledge of the Gauts at this time than of the Swedes, and outside *Beowulf* and *Widsith* no knowledge at all of the Geats. But it would be overgloomy to conclude that we therefore survey the problem out of two blind eyes. It helps that the tone of the *Beowulf* passages is always serious and thoughtful, sometimes brooding and melancholy. In this respect there is no difference between the poem's account of the wars between the Swedes and Geats and its account, retailed above, of Hygelac's expedition to Frisia. Both are offered to an intelligent and informed audience in good faith as a record of deeds wrought and destiny endured. It is not history in our modern sense, we shall look in vain for political and economic causation: deeds are done, and their consequences borne, by great men, kings and leaders: the motives to action are pride, greed, revenge, though these are usually presented in conventional disguises, the defence or enriching of a people, loyalty to a king or kinsman, the inexorable demands of feud, the workings of Wyrd. But *Beowulf* in its Geat-Swedish passages is, we believe, more than a tale of who killed whom, and why.

Soon after the sixth century opened the Swedes of Uppland were ruled by an aged but formidable monarch, the anglicized form of whose name was Ongentheow. In Old Norse this should be represented by a form like Angantyr (Angantýr, Anganþér), but this is not found in the two essential enumerations of the kings of Sweden,

---

[1] R. W. Chambers, *Beowulf, an Introduction to the Study of the Poem, etc.*, 1921, 1932, and with a Supplement by C. L. Wrenn, 1959. The Supplement includes a chapter on the significance of the Sutton Hoo finds for *Beowulf*, but does not otherwise concern itself with dissentient Scandinavian opinion about Swedish-Geat relations. See, too, Ritchie Girvan, *Beowulf and the Seventh Century*, 1935, especially the chapter 'Folk-Tale and History'; and Birger Nerman, *Det svenska rikets uppkomst*, Stockholm, edition of 1941.

the verse *Ynglinga Tal* composed at an early date by the ninth-century
poet Thjodolf of Hvin, and the prose *Ynglinga Saga* of *c.* 1225, in both
of which his place in the list is occupied by king Egill. Nor have we
outside documentary confirmation of any save one of the contemporary kings of the Geats. The earliest mentioned of these was
Hrethel, whose three sons were Herebeald, Hæthcyn, and Hygelac.
By an unlucky accident Hæthcyn killed his elder brother Herebeald
with an arrow from his bow, and such was Hrethel's grief that he
died, leaving the kingdom to Hæthcyn. The Swedes and Geats
were natural enemies, and Hæthcyn, in answer to the onslaughts and
ambushes of Ongentheow's sons, led a raid into Swedish territory
and carried off Ongentheow's aged wife. But the Swede, 'old and
terrible', gave pursuit, killed Hæthcyn, and rescued the lady,
though stripped of her ornaments of gold. The Geat survivors
escaped to an unidentified Ravenswood, where he surrounded and
throughout the night taunted them with a prospect of the gallows
in the morning. But before first light they heard the warhorns of

3. HUMAN MASK FROM VALSGÄRDE

Hygelac as he came hastening along their bloody track with the
chivalry of the Geats. It was the Swede's turn to seek a fastness, but
in vain; Hygelac's warriors overran his entrenchments and brought
him to bay: he died under the protecting shield. Then the Geats
withdrew to their own country, and Hygelac was their ruler till
he was killed south among the Hetware. His successor was Heard-

red, his son. There was no long peace between the peoples. Ongentheow had been succeeded by his son Ohthere (the poem does not tell us this, but it is a fair assumption), but on Ohthere's death the throne was usurped by his younger brother Onela, and Ohthere's sons Eanmund and Eadgils fled for help to the traditional enemies of the Swedish royal house, the Geats. Onela, 'best of those sea-kings who gave out treasure in Sweden', went after them, killed his nephew Eanmund, and with him Heardred king of the Geats, then once more sought his own country, 'and let Beowulf hold the throne, rule the Geats'. But the chain of family, dynastic, and national feud was not yet run out. The Geats supported Ohthere's surviving son with an army either 'across the wide sea' or 'across the wide lake' (*ofer sæ side*), and after a campaign described as cold and grievous Onela was slain and Eadgils became king of the Swedes. And still nothing was compounded, for it is implicit in the ending of *Beowulf* that disaster will wait upon the Geat people, that their maidens shall tread a path of exile, and the raven and wolf contend over their warrior-dead.

West Norse sources, more particularly *Ynglinga Tal*, *Ynglinga Saga*,[1] and Arngrímur Jónsson's late sixteenth-century Latin abstract

---

[1] 'Thjodolf the Learned of Hvin was a poet of king Harald Fairhair [of Norway]. He made a poem about king Rognvald the Glorious which is called *Ynglinga Tal*, the List or Count of the Ynglings. Rognvald was the son of Olaf Geirstada-Alf, brother of Halfdan the Black [Harald Fairhair's father]. In this poem are named thirty of his forebears, with a word about the death and burial-place of each . . . [My] Lives of the Ynglings are written in the first place from Thjodolf's poem and augmented from the accounts of learned men.' (Snorri Sturluson, *Heimskringla*, *Prologus*.) Twenty-seven of Thjodolf's stanzas, wholly or in part, have been preserved in *Ynglinga Saga*, a prose account of the Ynglings with which Snorri opened his *Heimskringla* or compendium of the Lives of the kings of Norway. They were called Ynglings because they traced their line from Frey, God of the World and Sovereign of the Swedes, who established the holy place at Uppsala and made his chief residence there. Another name of Frey was Yngvi, 'and the name of Yngvi was kept for a long while thereafter in his line as a royal name, and the men of his line were thereafter called Ynglings'. Historically speaking, no reliance is to be placed on the first seventeen of these. Even in terms of fiction, nothing in their lives became them like the leaving of it. King Fjolnir rose in the night to make water, fell into a vat of mead and drowned instead; Sveigdir ran after a dwarf when drunk and vanished into a boulder; Vanlandi was trampled to death by a nightmare; Domaldi was sacrificed for good seasons; Dag was struck on the head with a pitchfork when seeking revenge for his sparrow; and so on down to the fifth century.

or version of the lost *Skjöldunga Saga* (presumably of *c.* 1180-1200), in general confirm though in places they vary this Old English account of Geat-Swedish relations. For a start there is no Beowulf in the Norse sources, yet paradoxically he is the person we can best spare from the roll-call of the Geat kings. His fifty-year reign must be accounted a fiction: he is the occasion of the historical passages, but no true part of them. And there are further difficulties posed by the West Norse sources. Instead of a war between Swedes and Gautar *Ynglinga Saga* makes the antagonists Swedes and Danes, even Jutes. Ottar (Ohthere) the Swede took a fleet to Denmark and devastated Vendil in Jutland, but was overwhelmed in a naval battle in the Limfjord. The victorious Danes carried his body ashore and exposed it on a mound for beasts and birds to ravage. They took a tree-crow (or a crow of wood) and sent it to Sweden with the taunt that Ottar their king was of no more account than that. However, it has been argued that this part of *Ynglinga Saga* is a chapter of error. Ottar was nicknamed not from Vendil in Jutland but from Vendil (modern Vendel) in Uppland in Sweden, where the chief burial mound has traditionally been known as Ottars Hög, King Ottar's Howe, or the mound of Ottar Vendel-crow. It is Ottar's father Egill who is called *vendilkráka*, Vendel-crow, by such comparatively reputable authorities as the twelfth-century Icelandic historian Ari Thorgilsson and the *Historia Norwegiæ*, which appears to derive from an original of about 1170. Inevitably there has been speculation whether Egill the father of Ottar and Ongentheow (i.e. Angantýr) father of Ohthere are one and the same man, and the possibility is surprisingly strong.[1] But first let us note that *Ynglinga Saga* has also managed to distort the Eadgils-Onela story. In *Ynglinga Saga* Athils is Ottar's son and immediately succeeds him. That Ali (Onela) was his uncle and a Swede had been forgotten. Ali was still described as a king, but over Uppland in Norway, erroneously, not Uppland in Sweden. However, the issue of their contest was the same:

---

[1] The philological progression, it has been suggested, is a form of Angantyr > *Angila (an affectionate diminutive) > *AgilaR > Egill. This is less convincing than the genealogical coincidence taken in conjunction with *Beowulf*'s account of Ongentheow's death at the hand of Eofor ('Boar') and *Ynglinga Tal*'s reference to Egill's blood reddening the boar's snout, *farra trióno*. Though Snorri Sturluson in his *Ynglinga Saga* certainly read *farra* as 'bull'.

King Athils had great quarrels with the king called Ali the Upp-lander: he was from Norway. They had a battle on the ice of [Lake] Väner, where king Ali fell and Athils had the victory. There is a long account of this battle in *Skjöldunga Saga* [*Ynglinga Saga*, 27].

Skjöldunga Saga, however, is as strong in error as *Ynglinga Saga* concerning the nationality of Ali, whom it describes as *Opplandorum* [*rex*] *in Norvegia*. The Athils of *Ynglinga Saga* was a true Swede in his love of fine horses, but the poets and sagamen have not dealt kindly with him: it is a grotesque and baffled mischief-maker who squinnies at us from their pages. Even with horses his touch was not held to be infallible: according to the *Kálfsvísa* he fell off one, a grey, at Lake Väner, 'when they rode to the ice,' and according to Snorri fell off another at a sacrifice and knocked his brains out on a stone. This happened at Uppsala, and he was buried in a mound there.[1]

Ynglinga Saga records of three Swedish kings of this period that they were howed at Uppsala: Aun, Egill, and Athils; and it is hardly a coincidence that there stand at Gamla Uppsala, Old Uppsala, three mighty grave mounds on a line north-east to south-west, known as Odinn's Howe, Thor's Howe, and Frey's Howe. In the two of these which have been excavated there were found the charred remains of a man of rank and wealth, without question Swedish kings, and almost without question two of those named. The burial mound of Ottar twenty miles to the north at Vendel completes a roll of kings covering most of the sixth century. These superb monuments at Old Uppsala, each thrown up over the place of a king's burning, are impressive witness to the martial dynasty which was busy extending the power of the Swedes over their neighbours in mainland Götaland and offshore Gotland; while a succession of Vendel and Valsgärde graves from the sixth to the ninth centuries show great lords laid to rest without cremation in boats of 30 feet and upwards, with horse and harness, dog and leash (and in one case a hunting falcon), fine weapons, bronze plates for belts and horse-trappings, cooking-pots and food. In other graves of the same period and region there are glass beakers, ornamentation in semi-precious stones and enamel, ring-swords whose pommel-ring is of gold, and magnificent helmets on the Roman cavalry

---

[1] Saxo Grammaticus would have us believe that he died of strong drink, while celebrating 'with immoderate joviality' the death of his enemy Hrolf (Hrothulf).

4. PICTURED STONE FROM ALSTAD, NORWAY
It appears to portray the Sigurd legend. 'Below a large ornamental bird, possibly of symbolic import, is a man on a horse—with a
hawk in his hand and followed by his dogs. The man is possibly
Sigurd setting out on his fateful journey. Beneath this scene is a
horse without a rider: Grani coming home after the death of his
lord. Lastly comes a man riding with a mighty raised weapon:
which could be the murderer, Hogni.' The reverse side with its
tendrils is a good example of the Ringerike style. The pictures
have also been plausibly interpreted as portraying the arrival of
the dead in the Otherworld.

pattern. This is the world of *Beowulf*: graves and poem are parallel revelations of an age.[1]

Taken in conjunction with those passages of *Beowulf* which tell of the Geat attack on Frisia *c.* 521 (pp. 30–31 above), this is a coherent and attractive synthesis of Old English poetry, Norse and Continental documentary sources, and archaeological evidence. But not everyone believes in it. A great many Danish and Swedish scholars do not accept the Geat-Gaut equation, and the most critical school of Swedish historians, led by the Weibulls and speaking from Skåne, dismisses all notion of a collapse of the Gautish kingdom towards the year 600.[2] Their viewpoint may be crudely

---

[1] The same is true of *Beowulf* and the *c.* mid-seventh century ship-burial of a royal personage at Sutton Hoo in East Anglia. The full implications of the discoveries at Sutton Hoo are as yet not understood, but the correspondence between the treasures found there and the way of life they represent (the big ship-cenotaph or mound, the weapons, shield, and banded (**walu*) helmet, silver spoons and dish, the man-with-monster(s) motif, the goldsmith's and jeweller's work, the coins, the harp and royal standard) and those passages in *Beowulf* which tell of similar things is extraordinarily close. Some of the grave goods had travelled far to their long resting-place: the silver dish bears the hallmark of the emperor Anastasius of Byzantium (*ob.* 518); the two-score gold coins from the royal purse are Merovingian tremisses; the helmet and shield closely resemble Swedish work of the early sixth century. Professor Birger Nerman speculated whether the warrior-king for whom the Sutton Hoo ship-burial was planned was a Swede ('Sutton Hoo; en svensk Kunga- eller hövdinggrav', in *Fornvännen*, 1948), which seems unlikely; Professor Sune Lindqvist believes that *Beowulf* and the Sutton Hoo burial may both be seen against a background of the Swedish origin of the East Anglian royal house of the Wuffingas or Wulfingas ('Sutton Hoo and Beowulf', in *Antiquity*. 1948). The English reader will be best helped by Charles Green, *Sutton Hoo*, 1963; R. L. S. Bruce-Mitford, *The Sutton Hoo Ship Burial*, I, 1975, II, 1978; *The Sutton Hoo Ship-Burial. Reflections after Thirty Years*, 1979; and R. T. Farrell, '*Beowulf* and the Northern Heroic Age' in his *The Vikings*, 1982, pp. 180–216. In our present context the parallels between Sutton Hoo and Vendel are hardly less striking than those between either place and *Beowulf*.

[2] In addition to the books listed in the footnote on p. 35 above the indispensable references are C. Weibull, 'Om det svenska och det danska rikets uppkomst', *Historisk tidsskrift för Skåneland*, VII, 1921; E. Wadstein, *Norden och Västeuropa i gammal tid*, Stockholm, 1925; Kemp Malone, 'The identity of the Geats', *Acta Philologica Scandinavica*, IV, 1929; E. Wadstein, 'The Beowulf poem as an English National Epos', ibid., VIII, 1933; O. Moberg, 'Svenska rikets uppkomst', *Fornvännen*, 1944. There is a succinct statement in Lucien Musset, *Les Peuples Scandinaves au Moyen Age*, Paris, 1951, pp. 23–6, and a

expressed thus: when the statements of a poet who for the most part deals in legendary and folktale material conflict with what otherwise may be assumed as to the historical or geopolitical situation in sixth-century Sweden, those statements should not be allowed an authority they do not deserve. So first, who were the Geats? Philologically their name corresponds precisely with that of the Gauts, but can by a series of postulations be made to approximate to that of the Jutes, as this is preserved in Old English and West Norse sources (*Iuti, Iutæ, Eote, Yte,* and *Jótar, Jútar*). This pro-Jute philological argument on the whole commends itself to non-philologists. There is the further possibility that the Old English poet, no wiser in his generation than we in ours, confused the two peoples, Jutes and Gauts, whose names he found not too dissimilar, and about whose location, it is suggested, he was not well informed—but this is supposition. If the West Norse sources have their errors relating to Denmark, Jutland, Vendil, Sweden, and Gautland, why, we are asked, should the Old English sources be held above suspicion or invariably receive a favourable explication? None of this is notably helpful to the Jutish case, but good arguments remain. If the Geats were the Jutes, their descent upon Frisia seems a likelier occurrence, especially when we consider the kind of ships at their disposal early in the sixth century, than that the Gauts of Sweden should be raiding there. There had been a long period of trade and other contact between the mouths of the Rhine and the Jutland peninsula, and a clash between their peoples is unsurprising. The Frankish recorders of it speak of the raiders as Danes, *Dani*, not Gauts, and the *Liber Monstrorum* describes Huiglaucus as king of the *Getæ* not the *Gauti*, though it is difficult to believe that *Getæ* could mean Jutes. For what it is worth we have a reference in Venantius Fortunatus, bishop of Poitiers (530–609), to the defeat of a Danish fleet in Frisia *c.* 565; and Viking Age evidence for close trading and political relations between Denmark (including Jutland) and Frisia is so strong that it encourages us to believe that this was the continuation of relationships already existing. It has even been argued that the ancient trading town of Hollingstedt in Slesvig preserves in the medieval form of its name (Huglæstath, 1285) reminiscence of a Huiglaucus-Hugleik-Hygelac who may or may not have been he

---

looser one in V. Starcke, *Denmark in World History*, Philadelphia, 1962, pp. 99–107. See too J. A. Leake, *The Geats of Beowulf*, Wisconsin, 1967.

qui imperavit Getis—though this at best is inconclusive. At this point one might not unfairly conclude that while the philological evidence is strong for the Gauts, the historical and economic facts are, in respect of Hygelac's expedition to Frisia, strong for the Jutes.

But the passages concerning the Geat-Swedish wars remain, and here it is difficult to believe that by the Geats the English poet meant any people other than the Gauts. The view that they were Gauts resident in northern Jutland would reconcile the opposed arguments, but there is next to no evidence for it. On the whole we must settle either for a prolonged Jutish-Swedish war during the sixth century, which is certainly not impossible, or a Gautish-Swedish war, which is highly probable. The 'facts' can be made to fit either hypothesis, but go more naturally with the second, in that it would appear wellnigh impossible for our sea-conscious poet to avoid mention of ships and naval encounters in his account of three generations of seaborne expeditions between Jutland and Sweden. Gautish origins are to be sought in Västergötland, but they were a strong people and spread steadily into Östergötland, Dalsland, Närke, Värmland, and part of Småland. They were inevitably rivals of the Swedes, and warfare between the two peoples could not be avoided. The Chambers thesis, if not surely right, is more likely to be so than any of its rivals. But what we need not deduce from *Beowulf* is that the Gauts were so decisively overthrown in the later sixth century that the Swedes then assumed control of their territories. In Curt Weibull's view they kept their independence till near the year 1000, and it may well have been Olaf Skötkonung who first enjoyed the title *rex Sveorum Gothorumque*. West Norse sources carry numerous references to the Gauts and Gautland down to that time, including the well-known but not necessarily reliable ones in Snorri's *Heimskringla* to jarl Rognvald's realm in Gautland and Olaf Tryggvason's hope of enlisting him as an ally against the confederacy including Olaf Skötkonung.[1] Others lay stress on the circumstance that whereas early 'authorities' speak of many tribes in

[1] But nothing may be taken as certain. We know little more concerning the early (sixth-century) kings of Gautland than that their claim to rule was fundamental: the Gautish throne stayed empty till a posterior of twice our mortal size was advanced to fill it. We are hardly wiser in respect of the later jarls. Curt Weibull thinks that Rognvald was a Swedish chieftain ('Sverige och dess nordiska grannmakter', 1921 pp. 118 ff.); he has been placed in Gardariki (Russia); and he has been seen as a subject of the king of the Danes.

Sweden, visitors in the ninth century like Anskar speak only of the Swedes, thus suggesting that the struggle for power was by then concluded.[1] In any case it is more reasonable to suppose that the Gauts became a junior partner in the Swedish realm than that they were ground out of existence. We hear of their laws and lawspeaker, their Thing and their jarls, to the end of the viking period. That the Swedes became more powerful than the Gauts is certain, but we are unsure of the decisive stages and dates of the process.

If now we turn to the realm of Denmark our first, if spurning, steps must still be taken on Swedish soil, whether we begin with Jordanes' puzzling statement that the Danes, men of the same stock as the Swedes, at an unstated time (post A.D. 200 or *c.* 500), took or recovered possession of the Erulian lands in Denmark, or whether we cautiously grope our way into the mirage-strewn hinterland of legend, to find the eponymous Dan son of Ypper, king of Uppsala in Sweden, 'from whom [i.e. Dan], so saith antiquity, the pedigrees of our kings have flowed in glorious series, like channels from some parent spring'. It was Dan who left Sweden to take possession of Zealand and its sister isles of Falster, Lolland and Møn. Together these formed the realm of Vithesleth, the Wide Plain. Later Jutland, Fyn and Skåne accepted the authority of Dan, and the kingdom was named Danmörk after him. According to Saxo, Dan had a brother by the name of Angul, who immortalized his name by attaching it to the people known afterwards as Angles, and in the unprophesied course of history as English. This is wild and whirling stuff, not to be pressed to a meaning, much less a conclusion (there is no consistency even in the legend: according to the *Chronicle of the Kings of Lejre* the eponymous sons of Ypper were Nori, Östen, and Dan), yet it may belatedly point to the strength, wealth, and strategic importance of Zealand, the isles, and Skåne on the one hand, and Jutland (possibly with Fyn) on the other, divided as they are by the Great Belt, as contributory to the creation of a kingdom of Denmark. This does not mean that 'Greater Denmark' quickly achieved definitive boundaries and held them without variation, or that it was

[1] The most recent Swedish summary of this phase of native history, M. Stenberger, *Sweden*, 1963, pp. 152–7, concludes that the union of Götaland with the Svea kingdom in central Sweden probably took place before the beginning of the ninth century. The Sparlösa stone of *c.* 800 may be evidence in favour of this (see p. 79).

not frequently a prey to civil war and fragmentation; but some increasing consciousness there must have been of a Danish identity and separateness from the Swedes and Norwegians. This was felt soonest and strongest by leading individuals and families: it was to these, not to the concept of nationhood, that ordinary folk felt allegiance and gave service. Also, with every allowance made for the sometime expulsion of the Eruli,[1] and the emigration of the Angles and (some) Jutes, we do not know to what extent the Dani filled the emptied seats of other peoples, or whether their name came to cover a confederacy of tribes resident in Zealand, the lesser islands, and Jutland, originally with names of their own. What we do know is that the people or collection of peoples bearing the name Dani were dominant in geographical Denmark and Skåne soon after the beginning of the sixth century.

The most celebrated of the legendary kings of Denmark were the Skjoldungs (*Skjöldungar*), the Scyldings of *Beowulf*, Men of the Shield, descended from Skjold, who according to *Ynglinga Saga* was the son of Odinn, according to Saxo the grandson of Dan, and according to *Beowulf* either the son of Sheaf, Scyld Scefing, or distinguished as Scyld 'with the Sheaf'. According to *Beowulf*, too, he came to the Danish shore a helpless child, no one knew from where or across what waters, but with a heap of treasures about

---

[1] The passage in Jordanes relating to the Dani and Eruli is as follows: Sunt et his exteriores Ostrogothæ, Raumarici, Aeragnarici [Raumariciae, ragnaricii], Finni mitissimi, Scandzæ cultoribus omnibus mitiores [minores]; nec non et pares eorum Vinoviloth; Suetidi, cogniti in hac gente reliquis corpore eminentiores: *Quamvis et Dani, ex ipsorum stirpe progressi, Herulos propriis sedibus expulerunt*, qui inter omnes Scandiæ nationes nomen sibi ob nimis proceritate affectant præcipium (ed. Mommsen, MGH, V, 58). Much argument has been concentrated on Jordanes' text, and particularly on the meaning here of *stirps* and *proprius*: whether Jordanes understood the Danes to be of Swedish descent, or along with the Swedes of Scandinavian descent; and whether Jordanes is informing us that the Danes expelled the Eruli from their [i.e. Erulian] dwelling-places, or from their own [Danish] dwelling-places, which the Eruli had seized or maybe encroached on, as, for example, they might have done soon after the year 505 on their return by way of the land of the Danes to the south of Sweden. On the one hand is the continuing legendary tradition that the Danes came from Sweden; on the other the high likelihood that the Danes were indigenous in Denmark, above all in Zealand; in between are the ambiguities (or what in our ignorance we judge to be the ambiguities) of Jordanes. On the whole the documentary evidence is uncertain in support of the Swedish hypothesis, and the archaeological evidence can be offered both for and against it.

him; for when in the fullness of time he died, having succoured the Danes, terrified their enemies, and established their royal line, his subjects placed him on a ship, their glorious lord by the mast, and having heaped him with no lesser dowry of weapons and treasures than he had brought with him, and set a golden standard high over his head, they let the sea take him, gave him to the ocean. Nor could any man from that day to this, whether hero under heaven or counsellor in hall, tell who received that load.

For the names of the kings who followed him there are more authorities than authority: Saxo Grammaticus, shortly after 1200; Sven Aggeson, c. 1185; the *Chronicle of the Kings of Lejre*, some time after 1160 (later incorporated in the fourteenth-century *Annals of Lund*); the *Chronicle of Roskilde*, c. 1146; *Langfeðgatal*, of the eleventh century; and *Beowulf*, composed probably between 700 and 750; to which may be added *Hrólfs Saga Kraka* and the Latin abstract already referred to of *Skjöldunga Saga*. Some of these sources, Sven Aggeson in particular, are spare; some, like Saxo, are voluminous. All demand circumspection, and most excite disbelief. It is with Halfdan, the 'high Healfdene' of *Beowulf*, that we reach some slight, some possible assurance of history, presumably at the beginning of the second half of the fifth century. His son Hrothgar was an aged guardian of his people when we read of him in *Beowulf*, an unspecified while before the death of Hygelac the Geat, c. 520, but presumably in the first two decades of the sixth century. He lived in a great hall called Heorot, or Hart, lofty and wide-gabled, at Lejre in Zealand. Gamle Lejre today is to be found some five miles west-south-west of the cathedral city of Roskilde, a quiet little village.on a quiet little stream (the Kornerup Å; the Lejre Å has dried up) which flows three miles or so to the southern extremity of Roskilde Fjord. Today's student of *Beowulf* and its Norse analogues is likely to visit it with emotion: like many other places in Denmark, a place of burial since the Stone Age, so that its ancient approaches are watched over by many a treed and grassy mound; the site of the biggest *skibsætning* in the country; by Thietmar of Merseburg's witness a sanguinary shrine of the heathen; royal seat of the Skjoldungs; and in saga tradition the never-to-be-forgotten scene of the nurture and destruction of Hrolf Kraki and his champions. He is likely to leave it deeply impressed—and baffled. Lejre was clearly inhabited some time in the tenth century by a chieftain rich enough to be given a fine burial, but of Hrolf's sixth-century court no trace has been found. It is sad to think of those high lords without a roof to their heads,[1] but in respect of Lejre that is the case, and likely to remain so. Nor has anything been found of the sacrificial site described in Thietmar's early eleventh-century Chronicle, where every ninth year, in the month of January, ninety-nine men and the same number of horses, dogs, and cocks, were sacrificed to the gods. But this last is not surprising.

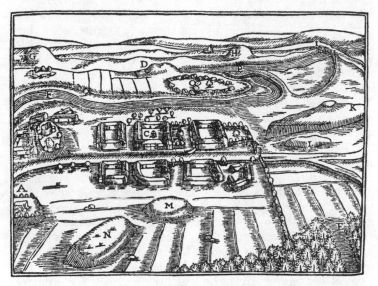

5. LEJRE FROM THE WEST (OLAUS WORMIUS)
A. Sepulchrum Haraldi Hyldetandi; C. Locus ubi Regia olim erat;
O. The main skibsætning.

Here let us again remind ourselves that while it would be timorous not to draw from such an abundance of legendary and pseudo-historical material the conclusion that Halfdan-Healfdene, Hroar-Ro-Hrothgar, Helgi-Halga, and Hrolf-Hrothulf were kings who existed and ruled in Denmark, we know hardly an unchallengeable fact about them. We do not even know whether Halfdan's name, meaning presumably 'Half-Dane', implies that the Skjoldungs were

[1] '—*en smule hjemløs*' is Harald Andersen's phrase, the leader of the excavations there. See *Fra Nationalmuseets Arbeidsmark*, 1960, and *Skalk*, 1958, 2 and 4.

a dynasty at first part-alien to the inhabitants of Denmark. He would be a man supremely bold or learned who claimed to know the exact relationship, habitat, or even identity, of Danes, Jutes, Eruli, Heathobeards, and Angles. And so with Hrolf: we must sift a bushel of legend to win a grain of history, and even then have no minute particulars. In English writings Hrolf is mentioned for the most part with foreboding. He was a hero, certainly, and prominent in the defence of Heorot against the attack of Ingeld and his Heatho-beards. 'For a long, long time', says *Widsith*, 'that nephew and uncle, Hrothulf and Hrothgar, kept the peace together, after they had driven away the viking race, made Ingeld's vanguard stoop, cut down at Heorot the Heathobardan host.' But Hrothulf has a murkier claim to fame: he usurped the Danish throne, and to this end set aside and probably killed his cousins, Hrothgar's sons. Icelandic and Danish sources ignore or obscure this grievous deed, so foreign to Hrolf's later character and reputation, but cannot dispose of it altogether. Stripped of its grosser accretions of legend and folktale (and the Icelandic *Hrólfs Saga Kraka* is a corridored museum of such), Hrolf's role in Denmark's early traditions may be summarized thus. Halfdan, king of Denmark, had two sons, Hroar and Helgi. Halfdan was basely killed by his brother Frodi, the monarch of a separate kingdom, and his sons took a bloody ven-geance. Helgi, the more assertive of the two, then became king of Denmark. In his dealings with women he was as ill-fated as he was heavy-handed, which is saying a lot, and his favourite vice bred instruments to plague him. His son, the glorious Hrolf, was the issue of his unwittingly incestuous marriage with his daughter Yrsa. Later Yrsa, her unhappy lot now known, left Helgi and married Athils king of the Swedes—none other than that hard-drinking, horse-loving Athils-Eadgils who slew Ali on the ice of Lake Väner, and was buried in the kings' mounds at Old Uppsala. It was to Uppsala that king Helgi made a journey across the sea, to fetch Yrsa home again. He went ashore with a hundred men, and Athils welcomed him to court with open arms. But on his way back to his ships Athils had him ambushed, took him 'between anvil and hammer', and the Danes perished to the last man. So Hrolf in-herited, and built up a mighty army and mightier kingdom. He established his chief seat at the place called Lejre (Hleiðargarðr). 'That is in Denmark, a big, powerful stronghold; and in every aspect of munificence there was more pomp and splendour there than in any place whatsoever—more indeed than any had ever heard tell of.' To Lejre came champions from all the northern lands, among them the bear-begotten Bothvar Bjarki, who married into Hrolf's family and with the freedom proper to a kinsman suggested it was time to restore the Danish image in Sweden. What followed was Hrolf's Uppsala Ride, in which he carried off a large helping of treasure from Athils's court, but was forced to abandon it, in a picturesque delaying tactic, on the plain of Fyrisvellir, before Uppsala. A hint in *Beowulf* allows us to think that Hrolf's attack on Athils was an intervention on behalf of Ali's widow, a kinswoman of his. If so, it failed, for Athils kept his throne, though Hrolf, with the connivance of the story-tellers, snatched the glory. This Swedish expedition was the turning-point of his life, in legend because an offended Odinn now deserted him, in fact, one suspects, because his swelling ambition led his enemies to combine against him. Their leader was his first cousin Hjorvard, according to *Skjöldunga Saga* king of the island of Öland off the south-eastern coast of Sweden, who led an army of Swedes and Gauts to Lejre, and in a night attack slew him and his entire bodyguard, none of whom chose to survive his lord. Hjorvard likewise fell, and Lejre perished by 'the hostile surges of malignant fire'.

Legendary history such as this is a heady brew, and still headier is to follow with Harald Wartooth, Sigurd Hring, and their bloody congress at Bravellir. Briefly, then, let us remind ourselves that heroes' deeds and dynastic struggles, confusedly if excitingly recorded, are never the whole of the story. Something real and un-legendary was going on in Denmark and Sweden during these same blurred and unlit times. The general area of 'Denmark' was taking shape, to include Zealand (its heart and centre), Falster, Lolland and Møn, and then other islands, and the territories immediately across the Øresund, i.e. Skåne and Halland, but, not in all probability, Bornholm. Later there would be a movement of Danes west into Jutland north of the Eider, which eventually would play as important a part in Danish affairs as Zealand. The Great and Little Belts, together with the Øresund, bound these lands together; the effective barriers to movement, and therefore to expansion, were the swamp and forestland at the neck of the Jutland peninsula and the im-penetrable forests of Småland in Sweden. Early in the Christian era Skåne (ON. Skáney), bounded by water and wilderness, was to all intents and purposes itself an island, a circumstance which alone makes its early attachment to the Danish interest intelligible. That there was considerable political and military vicissitude within this area between the third and the eighth centuries is a safe assumption, and archaeology suggests that the third, seventh, and eighth centuries were particularly important for the future kingdom of the Danes. But detail is almost completely lacking.

Even so, two assured deductions may be made. While poets and story-tellers looked to heroes and kings, always spectacular, often unreal, and at best tangential to truth, life as men live it went steadily on. Its basis was agrarian, agricultural, and in that sense one century differed little from another. The setting might vary somewhat in Denmark, and vastly throughout the three Scandinavian countries, with their plain and mountain, heathland, forest and clearing, coast and interior, rock, sand, and clay; but the means were recognizable everywhere, and the end was the same, to produce food: corn and grass for man and beast, and beast for man alone. In addition there was the endless garner of nature's second bounty, fish, game, animals; a selection of men travelled and traded, native goods went out and foreign goods came in, some for daily use, some for magnificence and pride; yet others plied their crafts, smiths, woodcarvers, boatbuilders, potters, the makers of cables and harness, the healers of bodies and builders of howes. All this is obvious enough, and mentioned only that it may not be forgotten. Without a worker there can be no hero, without an economy no kingdom.

Second, the kingdom of Denmark (and those of Sweden and Norway too) grew from units both modest and ancient, homestead, hamlet, village, and from the developing institutions of a defined community, a recognized district, known in Denmark as a herred (ON. *hérað*). Our factual knowledge of the herred hardly precedes the Viking Age, but clearly the social unit then defined was a long-standing one. The word seems originally to have indicated a body of mounted men, with a warlike connotation, but came to mean an area within which men rode to the same Thing (*þing*), the public gathering for law and consultation on matters affecting that area. The topography of Denmark, with the sole exception of western Jutland, and the Danish parts of what is now southern Sweden, lent itself to the grouping together of homesteads to form villages, and some of these last were found to be well placed to provide an area composed of more than one herred with facilities for law, religion, marketing, and the discussion of other matters affecting the well-being of free men and owners of land and chattels. The importance of such a centre and of its leading family would grow together. As in Norway and Sweden, the unrest of the times either removed a local chieftain altogether or fostered his strength and prestige. The community's wealth in land and people had to be defended against outside aggression, and when occasion offered outside wealth had to be acquired. In both Zealand and Jutland we can from time to time assume the existence of a number of 'kingdoms', each with its 'king', and in Jutland we know that some of them survived, fitfully, till at least the time of Gorm in the tenth century. Probably the key to a fuller knowledge of this pattern of small kingdoms lies in the regional Thing linked with a market-place. A backward glance from the year 1000 confirms what in any case seems the safe deduction that such key-places included Hedeby, Ribe, Århus, Viborg, Aggersborg, and Lindholm Høje in Jutland, Roskilde and Ringsted in Zealand, Odense on Fyn, and no doubt Lund in Skåne—though we know that some of these acquired different characteristics as the result of political change, or even in course of time removed to a different site.

Also, the early petty kingdoms, however entitled, were subject to vicissitude. By conquest, inheritance, coalescence, or act of god, their boundaries and fortunes changed. Probably many individual and dynastic episodes which attain epic, or at least heroic, dimension in the legendary sources were local and contained. Occasionally a ruling house had a run of successes which made it overlord of substantial parts of Denmark. Hrolf Kraki and Harald Wartooth, if we cannot accept that they were flesh and blood and conquering kings, may serve as legendary exemplars. Expansion and triumph depended less on shield-biting berserks and the deceptive favour of this god or that valkyrie than on wealth gained from agriculture and trade, then used to sustain the process of war. In the legendary history of Denmark no ruling house established a durable supremacy. This conforms not only to the requirement of heroic literature that triumph is the prelude to disaster. It conforms also to the broad facts of the Danish situation.

That said, we return to the heroes and kings, and confess that the ramifications of Danish history for a hundred and fifty years after the death of Hrolf (*c.* 550?) defeated all medieval inquirers and continue to defeat us today. We can assume an immediate and painful disintegration followed by sharp struggles for power within the country, but the personalities, territories, and procedures involved are unknown.[1] Even with Ivar Vidfadmi (Far-reacher, Wide-grasper) in the seventh century we dazzle with fantasies. He was, we hear, king of Skåne when Ingjald, called the Wicked, of the Yngling line, was king of the Swedes at Uppsala. Ingjald had widened his kingdom by slaying twelve kings, all of them treacherously. Confronted with the wrath of Ivar he withdrew into his hall with his daughter and people, and when the company was dead drunk he had fire laid to it, so that they all perished. According to *Ynglinga Saga*, this pyromanic imbecility cost the Ynglings their realm of Uppsala, and future kings of Sweden and Denmark came of the line of Ivar, though what Ivar could be except another Yngling is hard to say. We hear that he now conquered Sweden and came to possess all Denmark. Also he won for himself a large part of Germany, the entire Austrriki (presumably the lands east of the Baltic, including a little of Russia), and the fifth part of England—a traditional description of Northumbria. Much of this is plainly nonsense. The authors of *Skjöldunga Saga* and *Heimskringla* have bestowed these conqueror's laurels on the legendary Ivar in precisely the same way as Geoffrey of Monmouth ascribed to our British Arthur (and Malgo) the conquest of Ireland, Iceland, Gothland, the Faroes, Norway and Denmark: it sounded well and who could disprove him? Saxo, surprisingly, does not mention Ivar.

But of Ivar's grandson, Harald Hilditonn or Wartooth, he has much to tell. With Harald, still more than with Ivar, we must prise a few facts and conclusions from the concreted legend in which we find them embedded. If he existed at all, he was an ambitious and

---

[1] The Danish kings of the *Chronicle of the Kings of Lejre* and the *Annals of Lund* yield nothing in picturesqueness to the Swedish kings of *Ynglinga Saga*. Five in particular are not to be passed over in silence: the little dog Rakkæ whom the Swedes imposed on the Danes as their king for a while, till he grew overexcited and jumped from table to hall floor, where hounds of lower degree but taller stature tore him to Hel (the same well-attested folktale is told later of the Tronds); his successor king Snio who was eaten alive by lice at a Thing in Jutland; and, most famous of all, Amblothae the Jutlander (Saxo's Amleth, Amlethus), Horwendil's son, Feng's nephew, husband of a princess of Britain, paramour of a Scottish queen, Rorik Ringslinger's tributary, Wigleik's victim, Shakespeare's inspiration, Hamlet prince of Denmark. Rakkæ and Snio preceded Hrolf; Hamlet came somewhat later. Later again came blind Wermund and his son Offa, who, says *Widsith*, 'drew the boundary against the Myrgings [a people related to the Saxons] at Fifledor [the Eider]'.

warlike king who overcame his rivals in Denmark, including the islands, Jutland and Skåne, and then extended his power over the ancient kingdom of the Gautar and maybe over Uppland itself. He lived to a great old age, the ruler of a loose-strung empire or confederacy rather than a compacted kingdom, in which sub-kings recognized his authority, and when occasion favoured would be prepared to challenge it. The challenge that finally undid him came from his nephew Hring, also styled Sigurd Hring. Early sources are almost unanimous in describing Hring as Harald's nephew; but thereafter a tangle of witness makes him a sub-king in Denmark, in Sweden, in East Gautland, or in Sweden and East Gautland together. The first of these appears the least likely. If Hring existed at all, he existed east of the Øresund.

The rivalry of Harald and Hring led to the battle of Bravellir, a clash as famous in northern story as Hrolf's last stand at Lejre, and equally embellished with fictions. Harald, we hear, came to earn the dislike of his subjects for old age and cruelty, and they planned to get rid of him by some ignoble stratagem. He preferred to die in battle and sent a challenge to king Hring. Each monarch collected a great host, with champions drawn from every northern nation, including the as yet undiscovered Iceland, with Germans and Slavs, Kurlanders and Livonians, ironclad amazons and the one eyed War-God himself, in the guise of Harald's charioteer. The waters between Zealand and Skåne were so packed with Harald's fleet that a man could cross dryfoot; while the unfurled sails of the Swedes obscured all view over the ocean. The armies came formally to the place of slaughter, probably near Bråviken, north of modern Norrköping, on the north-eastern boundary of East Gautland. Here they were drawn up in battle order and harangued by Harald and Hring. Then the trumpets sounded and the fell incenséd points of mighty opposites bore furiously together. 'The sky seemed to fall suddenly on the earth, fields and woods to sink into the ground; all things were confounded, and old Chaos come again; heaven and earth mingling in one tempestuous turmoil, and the world rushing to universal ruin.'[1] The carnage ended only when Harald was dead, tumbled from his chariot and clubbed to death by Odinn, who thus gathered him to his peers in Valhalla. Hring treated his uncle's corpse with honour; according to Icelandic sources he was conveyed

[1] So Saxo, Book VIII. All my quotations from Saxo are taken from Oliver Elton's translation, 1894. (New trans. by Peter Fisher, ed. Davidson, 1979)

6. BRAVELLIR

in his chariot into a cairn filled with the donated treasures of the victors; according to Saxo he was burned on a sumptuous pyre and his ashes transferred to Lejre.[1]

'So ended the Bravic war.' And so ends a chapter. Dead reckoning places Bravellir in the early eighth century, but guesses hardly more hazardous have placed it as far back as the seventh and even the sixth. All we can be sure of is that 'it was a famous victory', and that with the death of Harald Wartooth another Danish-Swedish confederacy had fallen to pieces. In Norway all this while there were stirrings, gropings towards the amalgamation of various petty kingdoms, evidence of European connections, elaborate burials, splendid works of art in favoured centres of habitation, and perhaps the first indications that from Vestfold on the western shore of the Oslofjord would come the chief moulders of the future kingdom of Norway, and from Halogaland by way of the Trondelag, three hundred miles north of Vestfold, their most important rivals. But it is still too early to detect significant political movement north of the Skagerrak, and Norway's story may be postponed to its place in our chapter on the ninth- and tenth-century history of the viking realms.

[1] The *Sepulchrum Haraldi Hyldetandi* of Ole Worm's famous 'prospect' of Lejre, 1643, the Hyldetandshøje whose mangled remains are visible today, is not a burial mound of the seventh or eighth century but a *langdysse* of the Stone Age.

II. THE VIKING KINGDOMS TO THE CLOSE OF THE TENTH CENTURY

1. The Scandinavian Community,
I: Diversity and Unity

So FAR IN OUR ACCOUNT OF THE SCANDINAVIAN PEOPLES we have assumed that despite a threefold division into Danes, Swedes, and Norwegians, and the internal division of each of these into tribes and regions, with a more or less constant pattern of neighbourly aggression, dynastic struggle, extra-territorial conquest, and folk migration—despite these things we have assumed that Scandinavia is an entity and have talked of it as such. Before proceeding with the political history of the peoples we had better ask ourselves why.

First there is the geographical position of the three countries in the north of Europe. They are grouped together, it is true; but the grouping is less neighbourly than that of the countries of the British Isles or the city states of Italy. The old Cimbric peninsula, modern Jutland, is an extension of the north German plain, and a long run of wars from the beginning of the ninth century to the middle of the twentieth has failed to draw what nature left undrawn, a definitive frontier. The flat and fertile countryside of the Danish isles from Fyn to Zealand, of Bornholm, and Skåne in Sweden, has more in common with lands south of the Fehmarn Belt and the Baltic than with Norway and Swedish Norrland. On the peninsula itself, the upturned keel of mountains running south from Finnmark almost to Stavanger and Värmland made vast areas of eastern and western Scandinavia almost inaccessible to each other throughout the Middle Ages.[1] Eastwards there is no natural division

---

[1] The two best lines of land communication between Norway and Sweden were the Trondheim gap and the area south of Lake Mjøsa. There are two well-known accounts of the hardships to be encountered from both natives and

between Sweden and Finland: the chief virtue of the Muonio and Torne rivers as a frontier is that they happen to flow into the head of the Gulf of Bothnia. It is arguable that in terms of mass the Scandinavian peninsula without Denmark but with the Kola peninsula and the territory west of a line drawn from the head of Kandalaks Bay to the head of the Gulf of Finland would be more coherent and form a more logical entity than the three-nationed Scandinavia we know. But logic counts for little in the affairs of men, and it is unlikely that a grouping of Baltic nations rather than Scandinavian would have presented the medieval world or posterity with a tidier or more genial spectacle. And if there is little obviously compulsive to unity in the geographical situation of the viking nations, neither is the nature of their countries notably similar. The following account of how it looked to a near contemporary is taken from Saxo's Preface to his Danish History, written shortly after the year 1200.

The extremes, then, of this country [Denmark] are partly bounded by a frontier of another land, and partly enclosed by the waters of the adjacent sea. The interior is washed and encompassed by the Ocean; and this, through the circuitous winds of the interstices, now straitens into the narrows of a firth, now advances into ampler bays, forming a number of islands. Hence Denmark is cut in pieces by the intervening waves of ocean, and has but few portions of firm and continuous territory; these being divided by the mass of waters that break them up, in ways varying with the different angle of the bend of the sea. Of all these Jutland, being the largest and first settled, holds the chief place in the Danish kingdom. It both lies foremost and stretches furthest, reaching to the frontiers of Teutonland, from contact with which it is severed by the bed of the river Eyder. Northwards it swells somewhat in breadth, and runs out to the shore of the Noric Channel [Skagerrak]. In this part is to be found the

---

terrain on the southern route from Norway by way of Eid forest to Sweden. The first is in *Egils Saga*, 70–6, the second is the *Austrfararvísur*, or Eastern Journey Verses, of the poet Sighvat Thordarson, preserved in *Óláfs Saga Helga*, 71 and 79. Sighvat was zestfully appreciative of his experiences, which included blisters, sores, weariness, hunger, inhospitality, and heathendom. Egill, whose sense of humour was more formidable, made a troll-like journey through the great snows, and suffered cold, hunger, ambush, and perfidy. Both accounts are literary set-pieces, beautifully done, and to be taken with a grain of salt.

MAP I. VIKING SCANDINAVIA

fjord called Lim, which is so full of fish that it seems to yield the natives as much food as the whole soil . . .

Eastwards, after Jutland, comes the Isle of Funen [Fyn], cut off from the mainland by a very narrow sound of sea. This faces Jutland on the west, and on the east Zealand, which is famed for its remarkable richness in the necessaries of life. This latter island, being by far the most delightful of all the provinces of our country, is held to occupy the heart of Denmark, being divided by equal distances from the extreme frontier; on its eastern side the sea breaks through and cuts off the western side of Skaane; and this sea commonly yields each year an abundant haul to the nets of the fishers. Indeed, the whole sound is apt to be so thronged with fish that any craft which strikes on them is with difficulty got off by hard rowing, and the prize is captured no longer by tackle, but by simple use of the hands . . .

But since this country, by its closeness of language as much as of position, includes Sweden and Norway, I will record their divisions and their climates also as I have those of Denmark. These territories, lying under the northern pole, and facing Boötes and the Great Bear, reach with their utmost outlying parts the latitude of the freezing zone; and beyond these the extraordinary sharpness of the cold suffers not human habitation. Of these two, Norway has been allotted by the choice of nature a forbidding rocky site. Craggy and barren, it is beset all around by cliffs, and the huge desolate boulders give it the aspect of a rugged and a gloomy land; in its furthest part the day-star is not hidden even by night; so that the sun, scorning the vicissitudes of day and night, ministers in unbroken presence an equal share of his radiance to either season . . .

And now to unfold somewhat more thoroughly our delineation of Norway. It should be known that on the east it is coterminous with Sweden and Gothland, and is bounded on both sides by the waters of the neighbouring ocean. Also on the north it faces a region whose position and name are unknown, and which lacks all civilization, but teems with peoples of monstrous strangeness; and a vast interspace of flowing sea severs it from the portion of Norway opposite. This sea is found hazardous for navigation, and suffers few that venture thereon to return in peace.

Moreover, the upper bend of the ocean [i.e. the Baltic and the Gulf of Bothnia], which cuts through Denmark and flows past it, washes the southern side of Gothland with a gulf of some width; while its lower channel [i.e. the Arctic Ocean], passing the northern sides of Gothland and Norway, turns eastwards, widening much in breadth, and is bounded by a curve of firm land. This limit of the sea the elders of our race called Gandvik [i.e. The White Sea]. Thus between Gandvik and the Southern Sea there lies a short span of mainland, facing the seas that wash on either shore; and but that nature had set this as a boundary where the billows almost meet, the tides of the two seas would have flowed into one, and cut off Sweden and Norway into an island. The regions on the east of these lands are inhabited by the Skrit-Finns [Lapps]. This people is used to an extraordinary kind of carriage [ski? sledge? the Lappish *akja*?] and in its passion for the chase strives to climb untrodden mountains, and attains the coveted ground at the cost of a slippery circuit. For no crag juts out so high, but they can reach its crest by fetching a cunning compass. For when they first leave the deep valleys, they glide twisting and circling among the bases of the rocks, thus making the route very roundabout by dint of continually swerving aside, until, passing along the winding curves of the tracks, they conquer the appointed summit. This same people is wont to use the skins of certain beasts for merchandise with its neighbours.

Now Sweden faces Denmark and Norway on the west, but on the south and on much of its eastern side it is skirted by the ocean. Past this eastward is to be found a vast accumulation of motley barbarism.[1]

Three comments seem called for. In terms of human geography the Scandinavian axis lies north-south (physically it is nearer north-east by south-west). The more fertile and level areas are all in the south, most abundantly in Denmark and the Swedish provinces south of Uppsala, in Bornholm, Öland, and Gotland, but also on both sides of the Oslofjord and from there round the sea's edge to Stavanger, and by way of the great fjords northwards to the Trondelag. The northern half of the peninsula is generally mountainous, often inhospitable, and cold. Distances are formidable. It is salutary to be reminded in Malmö that one is nearer as the crow flies to Turkey than to the North Cape, and in Oslo that Rome is more accessible than Kirkenes. The coastline of Norway, not counting fjords and bays, is more than 1,600 miles long. Denmark begins at *c.* 55°N., and Norway ends at *c.* 71°N. Such great distances,

[1] *Gesta Danorum*: Preface (the translation is by Oliver Elton, but I have emended some of the proper names). Geographical information of an allied kind has been preserved by, *inter alia*, Adam of Bremen in the eleventh century and Snorri Sturluson in the thirteenth. Einhard, writing in the 820s (*Vita Karoli Magni*, cap. 12), speaks of the Danes and Swedes, 'whom we call *Nordmanni*', occupying the northern shores of the Baltic and all the islands, while Slavs and others occupied the southern—most prominent among them the Wilzi.

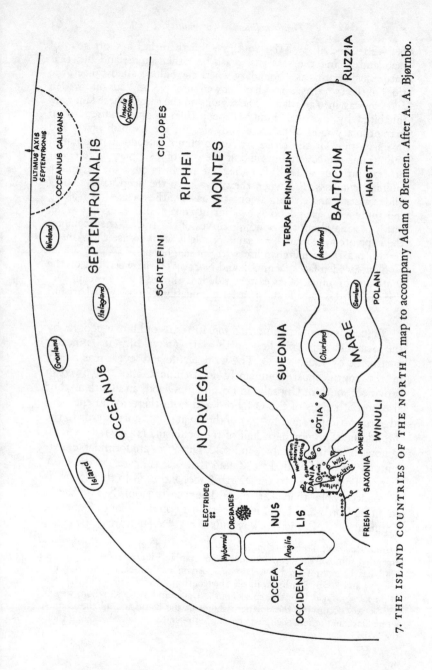

7. THE ISLAND COUNTRIES OF THE NORTH A map to accompany Adam of Bremen. After A. A. Bjørnbo.

together with a marked variation of appearance, nature, climate, wild life, and vegetation, would seem designed to prevent a sense of belonging rather than promote it. Even today's traveller, cosseted and encapsuled, feels himself move out of one world into another if he starts his journey at the ancient Hedeby near the old south Danish border,[1] goes by road or rail to Hirtshals in north Jutland, from there takes ship across the Skagerrak to Kristiansand, sails west then north to Stavanger, Bergen, Trondheim, past the Arctic Circle to Malangen and Tromsö, so onwards to the huge brown block of the North Cape, and from there by Ohthere's route eastwards to Vadsö and the White Sea. The sensation of change is hardly less marked if he entrains at Malmö in Sweden for Stockholm and Uppsala, thence to Östersund and by the inland railway to the iron mountain of Kiruna, just south of latitude 68°N.[2] Beyond lie Lappland and Finnmark, less forbidding than might be expected, but even so too formidable to be occupied by Norwegians or Swedes during the viking period. North of the line Oslo-Stockholm we are in a belt of latitude which contains Greenland south of Disco, Baffin Island, and the Bering Strait. Most of the peninsula lies farther north than Kamchatka. What differentiates Scandinavia from these cruel lands is that the western coast of Norway is laved by the Gulf Stream; the sea never freezes, and communication need never cease. The Baltic, too, is not normally to be compared for winter rigour with the ice-bound waters of Greenland, Arctic Canada, and Siberia. And Nature has been kind in a second way. The coastline of Norway (*mutatis mutandis*, this is true of Baltic-laved Sweden and Bohuslän, too) is protected by a strong fence of islands, some 150,000 in number, which secure shipping at almost every point from the heaviest Atlantic weather. It is as though Nature, having made communication by water compulsory, relented and made it possible. And finally she made these waters teem with fish. The harvest of the land varied from the corn and stock-bearing farms of the franklins of the south to

---

[1] Nowadays, of course, in the German province of Schleswig.

[2] This is little more than a twentieth-century paraphrase of Adam of Bremen in the eleventh. 'When one sails past the Danish islands a new world opens up in Sweden and Norway, two vast northern countries still very little known to our world. The well-informed king of Denmark [Svein Estridsson] has told me that it takes a month or more to travel through Norway, and that one can hardly journey through Sweden in two.' (Trans. Tschan.)

the reindeer herds and fur-bearers of the northern plateaux on which the Lapps paid tribute, but the harvest of the waters was constant.

The retardive effect of high latitude, long winters, severing distance, and a barriered landscape upon the development of the northern kingdoms was considerable. The exertion of kingly authority was easiest in Denmark, where Jutland and the isles, Zealand and Skåne, even Vestfold in the north, could from time to time be held on a more or less loose rein by a Danish king with command of the sea. The southern and western sea-fringe of Norway offered parallel but more limited opportunities to the sea-going progeny of Yngvi; and in Sweden the Baltic islands and coastal provinces proved assimilable by the king who controlled Uppland and the waterways of Lake Mälar. But this left much unaccounted for. In early times Denmark was at best a loose and straining confederation; considerable tracts of inland Norway by reason of their inaccessibility were more or less permanently divorced from the policies and economies of the Trondelag, Rogaland, and the Vik; and large regions of Sweden, notably Västergötland, Östergötland, and Uppland, were held apart by dense forests. The trend to separatism was marked to the end of the Viking Age. Farmer communities, remote and inward-looking, and resistant to change, persisted throughout Harald Hardradi's time

8. HERRING HARVEST OFF SKÅNE (OLAUS MAGNUS)

in Norway and Onund Jacob's in Sweden; and the old viking aristocracy, blest with estates, privileges, and ships, was slow to break up. No king in the north could survive except by force. It sounds less than flattering to describe Godfred the Dane, Olaf Tryggvason, Svein Forkbeard, and Eirik the Victorious as mere top-dogs in their separate domains, but it falls short of a libel. Their almost-peers were a hard-jawed pack. Such was the nature of the northern realms.

The viking peoples who lived between the neck of Jutland and the Lofotens, Sogn and Uppsala, were not all alike, and emphatically not of one 'pure' nordic race. But two main types of Scandinavian have always been recognizable: the one tall of stature, fair or ruddy complexioned, light-haired, blue-eyed, long of face and skull; the other shorter, dark-complexioned, brown- or dark-haired, brown-eyed, broad-faced and round of skull. The earliest evidence comes in uncertain and arguable form from the megalith graves; during Roman times Danish skeletons show a preponderance of long-skulled types; the earliest documentary evidence, apart from comment by classical authors on the tall stature of the Swedes, Danes, Gauts, and Burgundians, is Icelandic. The poem *Rígsþula*, probably of the first half of the tenth century, and showing signs of Celtic influence, describes in folktale fashion the origin of three main classes of viking society, the serfs, free peasants, and warrior-chieftains, and in so doing offers telling if exaggerated pictures of the types. Rig's son by Edda (Great-Grandmother) was black-haired and ugly, the skin of his hands wrinkled and rough, with lumpy knuckles and thick fingers, his back gnarled, his heels long— the image of that enduring toiler on the land who through most of history has carried the world on his back. Rig's son by Amma (Grandmother) was ruddy-faced, with sparkling eyes. But it is his son by Mothir (Mother) who fulfils the nordic dream. Of Mothir we read:

> Her brows were bright, her breast was shining,
> Whiter her neck than new-fallen snow.

And of her son:

> Blond was his hair, and bright his cheeks,
> Grim as a snake's were his glowing eyes.[1]

[1] The translations are by Henry Adams Bellows, *The Poetic Edda*, New York, 1923. For *Rígsþula* see, too, pp. 145–7 below.

Fortunately these picturesque notions never became the systematized and malignant myth that race has become in our own day. At the time when *Rígsþula* was being written there is no evidence of prejudice or dissension between the two types. Harald Fairhair was the first king of all Norway; his father was Halfdan the Black (*svarti*), and two of his sons were likewise called Halfdan, one nicknamed the White (*hvíti*), the other, reminiscently, the Black. According to *Egils Saga*, of the two famous sons of Kveldulf, Thorolf was tall and handsome like his mother's people, but Grim took after his father and was black and ugly. Grim's sons, Thorolf and Egill, born out in Iceland, repeated the pattern: Thorolf was the image of his uncle, tall, handsome, and sunny-natured; Egill was black, even uglier than his father, tortuous and incalculable. He became the greatest poet of his age, and many a hard-hewn line of verse testifies to his pride in his craggy head, broad nose, heavy jaw and swart visage. In the next generation Egill's eldest son would be styled Thorstein the White. These colour nicknames were purely descriptive, like the Short, the Tall, the Fat, the Slender, the Bald or the Hairy-breeked, and contain nothing of obloquy. Much has been written about the differences of temperament between these blond and dark types. The dolichocephalic, we are instructed, is an innovator and adventurer, not easily discouraged and steady under pressure. His view of life, rational and hopeful, sees things much as they are. He can command others and drive himself. He can also relax. The brachycephalic is conservative, distrustful not only of change but of himself, quick to enthusiasm, prompt to despair, emotional in politics, personal relationships, and religion. And on him, like moonlight on water, or phosphorescence on a rotten log (the image goes with one's own cephalic index), will be found the gleam of poetry and music. The classification is too glib, but if we allow generously for exceptions not unhelpful. The percentage of tall, long-skulled, blue-eyed people is today highest in Sweden and lowest in Denmark, which probably reflects their degree of intercourse with other European peoples over a long period of time. Certainly a community which combines the practical with the visionary, intellectual curiosity with emotional fervour, the power to innovate with the will to endure, and which can embrace the future without forsaking the past, need not complain of its inheritance. The Scandinavian peoples were fortunate in their ancestral stock; they received helpful, undistorting contributions from abroad; and the hard demands made by different regions proved as beneficial as they were unending. The long, flat, wind-swept wastes of Jutland, the axe-resisting, isolative forests of central Sweden, the sundered Bothnian archipelago, the mountain wildernesses of the Keel, the hostile frozen tundra of the north, and perhaps most of all the fjords, islands, and skerried waterways of the west Norwegian coast—when we add to these distance, cold, and the intimidating darkness of winter, when we add, too, the dreams of power and delusions of grandeur which built and rebuilt and shattered and reshattered the northern realms from long before the Viking Age till long after it, we see that Scandinavia could never be the nursery of weaklings. In 1047, so the Icelander Saemund the Learned tells us, in a year of wondrous cold wolves ran the ice between Norway and Denmark. Six centuries later it was men not wolves who crossed the frozen Belts to ravage Copenhagen. But the Scandinavian peoples were a well-tempered instrument of survival: they survived the ice, they survived the wolves, and, not least, survived each other and themselves.

So far it may appear that the concept of Scandinavian 'one-ness' is not too strongly based. But land and people are not the whole story. In many decisive respects the Swedes, Danes, and Norwegians were closely bound together. They shared the same language, religion, law, social organization, art, and general culture. And they shared the same heroic tradition, the same legendary and part-historical past. That their language was common may be proved in the first place from a comparative study of the languages of modern Scandinavia. As Wessén says, at the beginning of his history of the Swedish language:

Even to this day there is a great and obvious resemblance between the languages of the Northern countries: this applies to the dialects as well as to the literary standards evolved in the course of centuries. If we trace these languages backwards in time by exploring the written record, as well as forms of living colloquial speech, this resemblance grows increasingly apparent. Gradually the differences diminish up to a point where they disappear altogether. We have then come to the *Primitive Nordic language*, the parent tongue of the present Nordic vernaculars, common to the Scandinavian countries down to the beginnings of the Viking Age.[1]

[1] Elias Wessén, *Svensk Språkhistoria*, Stockholm, 1943–5.

**9. EARLY GERMANIC IRON AGE GOLD BRACTEATE
WITH AN INSCRIBED FUTHARK**
Swedish, used as a personal ornament. The central design shows
a man (head only) on a horned horse, and a large bird. Around
this is inscribed a runic alphabet, the older futhark, starting mid-
left and ending at the hasp, with a further group of runic letters
in the upper left quarter.

Likewise such information as can be assembled from early sources about the oldest form of the Old Norse language suggests that it was used by all the Norse Scandinavians. The earliest runic inscriptions, such as that on the Stabu spearhead (Norway), the Mos spearhead (Gotland), the scabbard, belt-buckle, comb and plane from Vimose (Fyn), the shield-boss and chape from Thorsbjærg (Slesvig), all of the period A.D. 200–300, are evidence of this, as are the memorial-stone (*bautasteinn*) inscriptions which began in the fourth century at Einang in Valdres (Norway) and flourished early in Sweden as well. These laconic written evidences of Old Norse are exciting, baffling, and precious. The Stabu spearhead bears one pointed word, *raunija(R)*, 'the tester'; the fibula from the noble lady's grave at Himlingøje in Zealand preserves a name (presumably the lady's), *WiduhudaR*; on the Einang stone may be read, *DagaR þaR runo faihido*, '[I], Dag, fashioned these runes'; on the Möjebro stone in Uppland, Sweden, above a warrior on a horse and accompanied by his two dogs is the inscription, *FrawaradaR ana hahai slaginaR*, 'FrawaradaR slain on his horse' or 'FrawaradaR [scil. lies here]. Ani the one-eyed is slain'; the Thorsbjærg chape commemorates a man and a sword, *Owlþuþewa R ni wajemariR*, 'Ullþer: may Márr [the sword] spare no one'; and the magnificent golden drinking horn of Gallehus in south Jutland, now lost, recorded the name of its maker: *ek hlewagastiR holtijaR* (or *holtingaR*) *horna tawido*, 'I, HlewagastiR (Hlegest) of Holt (Holstein? son of Holt?), fashioned the horn.' Hundreds of years later runic inscriptions of the eighth, ninth, and tenth centuries are eloquent in the same fashion. The men who lettered the stones at Eggjum in Norway (*c.* 700? *c.* 800?), Glavendrup on Fyn in Denmark (*c.* 900–25), and Rök in Östergötland in Sweden (*c.* 900), were working within one convention and one language, and the circumstance that their inscriptions are of different date and represent various degrees of development of the primitive Old Norse tongue emphasizes their overall similarity.[1]

Throughout the viking period the nordic peoples continued to speak a mutually intelligible language. The familiar division between West Norse, the tongue spoken in Norway (more specifically western Norway), Iceland, and the other Norwegian colonies overseas, and East Norse, the tongue spoken by the Danes and

---

[1] For a note on runes see pp. 419–20 below.

Swedes, was becoming defined about the year 1000. Subsequently dialectal and even language distinctions would sharpen, and linguistically the nations would go their own way. *Dönsk tunga, norræn tunga, norrænt mál*, would become a fiction and a sentiment. But this 'Danish tongue' or, more rarely, 'Norse tongue' had proved

10. PICTURED STONES AND RUNESTONES IN SKÅNE (OLAUS WORMIUS)
Of these stones portrayed by Ole Worm in the 1640s only 1, 2, and 4 are now to be found (at Lund). Nos. 1 and 2 are memorial stones to brothers; no. 4 appears to be a representation of the giantess Hyrrokin riding on her wolf with a serpent for reins.

a noble instrument, not only for intercourse and intelligibility among home-staying and outward-bound Scandinavians of all regions and origins, but for every mode of human expression. It catered for the affections and emotions, for history and literature, the formulae of law and religion, and the everyday needs of men and women busied with land, sea, war, trade, animals, home, and all aspects of life and death in the four seasons of the year. Again, and highly important, the language frontier was clearly defined. The 'Danish tongue' began at the Eider and ended where the Norsemen ended. It was a world apart from most of the languages surrounding it, whether Lappish, Finnish, or Slavonic; and clearly differentiated from Germanic languages neighbouring it to the south. By historical design or geographical accident it became the language of Iceland, Greenland, and the Atlantic isles, and in the mouths of traders, warriors, rulers, would spread into countries east of the Baltic, and down the Russian rivers to the Black Sea and Constantinople; it would be known in the British Isles, densely, and echoed faintly in verses written east over Jordan and west in Labrador-Newfoundland. Much of this was transient, though by a nice irony it was Iceland which saw the most splendid flowering of the Norse tongue in literature and preserved the bulk of Scandinavian tradition on vellum. In Scandinavia itself the glory of the 'Danish tongue' was that it served as a shield-wall to the cultural unity of Sweden, Denmark, and Norway, and encouraged them to think of themselves as members of one family, however unruly.

It was the same with the Old Norse religion, its modes of worship, and apparatus of myth. Since we shall discuss these matters in some detail later (pp. 315–33 below), one comment will for the moment be sufficient. This religion was a powerful unifying force in the minds of the northern nations for two reasons: it was their only religion, and before the Viking Age opens it was theirs alone. Many of the Germanic peoples had embraced Christianity early. Some of them had even embraced its heresies. Visigoths, Ostrogoths, Burgundians, Lombards, Alamanni, all abandoned the faith of their fathers; and in 496 Clovis king of Tournai called on the Lord and the Lord called on Clovis, with imperial consequences for the Franks. The European boundaries of Catholicism steadily widened. The peoples the vikings would encounter in and around the Mediterranean were Christians, with the exception of the Arabs, who like the Christians were monotheists. The Germanic and Celtic peoples they encountered in the British Isles were Christians; and with the forceful conversion of the Saxons by Charlemagne after the campaigns of 772–85, Christianity reached the Eider. But the three northern nations were slow to change. Harald Bluetooth of Denmark underwent conversion *c.* 965, and before he was driven from the throne by his son Svein *c.* 986 he claimed to have 'made the Danes Christians', which is after a fashion true. At the death of Olaf

Tryggvason in the year 1000 Christianity was the titular, and after the death of Saint Olaf in 1035 the actual, religion of most of Norway. The Swedish royal house was the last to accept Christian baptism, and though Olaf Skötkonung did so accept it with his court in 1008, it was a hundred years later that the renowned centre of heathen worship at Uppsala was razed to the ground. But for a long while before these definitive changes took place Scandinavia had been isolated in her heathendom, and, by those whose business it was to hate, hated for it. For many northerners, that they were not Christians was a stronger bond than that they were worshippers of Odinn, Thor, or Frey. If the Old Norse tongue was the shield-wall, the Old Norse religion was the byrnie of the peoples.

Again, there is a remarkable homogeneity about the arts and culture of the three nations. As with religion, the more relevant matters will be treated in a later place (pp. 333–45 below), and here it is enough to mention the identity, resemblance, or parallelism characteristic of personal ornaments and weapons of war, ships and furnishings, the techniques of poetry and the substance of saga (the Icelandic family histories, *Íslendingasögur*, excepted), the methods of woodcarving, metalwork, and incision on stone, the similarities of costume and architecture, and shared standards of quality and design. This is not to brand Scandinavian culture and art with tame uniformity; nothing could be farther from the truth. Artists differed in skill and vision; whole regions were open to special influences, both native and foreign; there was not just a Scandin-avian style, but styles. But viking culture and viking art are legitimate terms, in poetry from Bragi to the end of the skaldic tradition, in the plastic arts from Oseberg to Urnes. And if we allow the word culture to include habits, practices, the entire complex of social belief and organization, here, too, the resemblances heavily outnumber the differences. Even the art of war was a common art, and different in various features from that of other peoples; and their sea-lore was unique to them for at least three hundred years.

In addition, the pattern of possession and dominion in many parts of Scandinavia was an intricate one. Leaving aside all legend-ary and half-historical kings, many Danish monarchs, among them Harald Bluetooth, his son Svein Forkbeard, and the great Knut, ruled over extensive areas of southern Norway and southern Sweden. Skåne in particular and the eastern shore of the Oslofjord were part of Denmark throughout the Viking Age. There was a Swedish reigning house at Hedeby in south Jutland during the first third of the tenth century, and for what it is worth Adam of Bremen reports renewed Swedish influence in Svein Forkbeard's Danish kingdom before the century ended. Towards the middle of the eleventh century Denmark would be ruled over by king Magnus the Good of Norway. The leading families of Scandinavia were much intermarried for sound business reasons, and their estates were far-spread. Great ones do not ride alone: there was a leaven of Danes in Norway and Sweden, Norwegians in Sweden and Denmark, Swedes in Denmark and Norway, ruling, serving, fighting, buying and selling, toiling and moiling, mating and marrying, seeking or losing the world's good—in short, comporting themselves after the immemorial habit of mankind and the particular customs of time, place, and circumstance. Neither host nor guest appears to have found anything unnatural about this, and the ties of consanguinity were endlessly reinforced by the contacts and common interests of individuals.[1] Most of this human commerce took place in the coastal regions with their marts and manors, their centres of wealth and power. Large areas in the Scandinavian interior would, of course, remain isolated, conservative, and wanting nothing so much as to be left alone to the end of the Viking period.

The rest of Europe had little doubt that the Scandinavian peoples had more in common than they had apart. Occasionally they distinguished them with some sort of accuracy by their regional or national title, like the Norwegians from Hordaland who killed the king's reeve at Dorchester *c.* 789, or the men from Vestfold (West-faldingi) who attacked Aquitaine in the 840s; but the accuracy is more apparent than real. Thus the *Anglo-Saxon Chronicle*, after speaking of the three ships of the Norwegians of Hordaland, goes on to say that these were the first ships of the Danes to come to England. Sometimes southern chroniclers gave their tormentors a common title, Norsemen or 'vikings, *Nordmanni, wicingas*

---

[1] One recalls Hroar Tungu-Godi of Skogahverfi in Iceland. His father was Uni the Dane, son of Gardar the Swede (for whom see p. 273 below). Uni served king Harald Fairhair of Norway. Hroar's mother was Thorunn, daughter of Leidolf Kappi, a Norwegian settler in Iceland. Thus Hroar belonged to all four Scandinavian lands and had kinsfolk everywhere (*Land-námabók*, St. 284).

(*Norðmenn, víkingar*),[1] or as with the Arabs of Spain, *majus* (*al-majus,* incestuous fire-worshippers, warlocks, heathen), with the Germans *ascomanni,* ashmen or shipmen, and with the authors of Byzantium, Rhos (ῥῶς, Slavonic *Rus'* and Muslim *Rūs*), or βάραγγοί. But they made no scruple of describing all by the name of one: *Nordmanni* and *Dani* are convertible terms, as anyone will quickly realize who reads the arguments of Norwegian and Danish scholars as to who among their forefathers established the duchy of Normandy. Even northern chroniclers showed the same tendency. Adam of Bremen could hardly be more specific. 'The Danes and the Swedes, whom we call Norsemen, Northmen [*Nordmanni*] . . . The Danes and the Swedes and the other peoples beyond Denmark are all called Norsemen by the historians of the Franks [*ab historicis Francorum omnes Nordmanni vocantur*]' (IV, xii).[2] According to the two Icelandic authorities, *Íslendingabók,* the Book of the Icelanders, and *Landnámabók,* the Book of the Settlements, it was *Norðmenn* who colonized the island, which almost certainly means Norwegians, for the Danes who came there by way of south-west Norway and the admittedly few Swedes were lumped under the name of the majority. English records are overwhelmingly concerned with the *Dene,* the Danes, and let them include Norwegians and Swedes, save when the *Chronicle* drew a distinction between them in its entry for 924 (see p. 236 below). The Norsemen in Kiev in 1018, despite their unquestioned Swedish origin, were described by Thietmar of Merseburg as being for the most part Danes. The Irish annalists were a lesson to all with their division of Norse invaders into White Foreigners, Norwegians (*Finn-gaill*), and Black Foreigners, Danes

---

[1] There is still less than full agreement as to the original meaning of the two Norse nouns *víking* and *víkingr.* In the written sources they certainly mean, *víking,* piracy or a pirate raid, and *víkingr,* a pirate or raider. The first element of the words, *vík-,* has been explained in various ways. A viking was one who lay up or lurked in or came from a bay, fjord, or creek (*vík*); he was a man of the camp (O.E. *wīc, wīcing*), i.e. a soldier or fighter; or a man of the town (*wīc,* Latin *vīcus*), i.e. a seafaring man or trader. Reference to the ON. verb *víkja* made him a fast mover, or one who turned, receded into the distance, made a detour or a tour away from home. The association with piracy makes it something of a misnomer to call an entire period of Scandinavian history and civilization the Viking Age, but it has proved too convenient to be abandoned.

[2] The reference is primarily to Einhard, who in his *Vita Karoli Magni,* cap 12, referred in almost the same words to the Danes and Swedes, 'whom we call *Nordmanni*'. See p. 63, n. 1.

(*Dubh-gaill*), but it was a lesson no one heeded; nor do we know why they distinguished them by colour.[1] Cartographical knowledge of the North was still imprecise; the Norsemen came from 'up there'; and the best-known name was good enough for them all. The Irish monk grateful in his cold cell for the gale which kept the vikings off the sea; the merchant of Dorestad or Quentowic surveying the blackened ruins of his once flourishing town; the Frankish fighting man who saw five score and eleven of his fellows dangling like rooks from an island-gallows in the Seine; the outraged wife of a thousand homesteads from Sutherland to Sicily; the mourners for menfolk and daughters snatched away to slavery; and the chroniclers of these and similar ills, seething with grief and fury—these could not be expected to inquire too nicely into which island or promontory, what fjord or mountainside, had sloughed these monsters southwards. 'From the fury of the Norsemen, O Lord, deliver us!' was a litany without need of vellum. It was graven on the hearts of men wherever and for as long as that fury fell.

[1] The Welsh chroniclers, for example, made no such clear distinction. The Danes coming in by way of England and the Norwegians by way of Ireland were pretty well all black: Black Gentiles (*y Kenedloed Duon*), Black Norsemen (*y Normanyeit Duon*), Black Host, Pagans, Devils, and the like. The *History of Gruffydd ap Cynan* mentions both Danes and Norwegians, and the unknown author of *Breuddwyt Rhonabwy* makes brilliant if fantastic play with the 'pure white troop' of Llychlyn (Lochlan) and the 'pure black troop' of Denmark, but even so the generalization carries truth. See B. G. Charles, *Old Norse Relations with Wales*, Cardiff, 1934, pp. ix–x.

2. The Historical Traditions of Norway to 950

Our first section on the northern peoples concluded with the legendary victory of Sigurd Hring at Bravellir, the improbable obsequies of the Dane Harald Wartooth, and a prospect of confusion and obscurity in the immediate fortunes of Sweden, Denmark, and Norway. In the case of Sweden our knowledge of what was happening at home, as distinct from the exploits of Swedes abroad, stays meagre till the beginning of the tenth century. There is the evidence supplied by archaeology that from the sixth century onwards Swedish power and influence grew stronger in the eastern and central provinces, and that there was close connection at times between Sweden and the more accessible regions of Norway. There is evidence, too, of Norwegian cultural influences spreading east by way of Sweden to Finland. The Swedes throve continuously if not without vicissitude. The mart on Helgö in Lake Mälar seems to have been operating from at least the fifth century, with much profit to the king of the Svea, and in Birka, close by, they possessed by the year 800 the most famous of all Scandinavian marts trading with the eastern Baltic and the Volga region. It was at Birka that the missionary Anskar was received by king Bjorn in 829. Bjorn, we are asked to believe (though few things are less believable), had sent messengers to Louis the Pious, inviting him to dispatch a Christian mission to the Swedes, which he did, though its success, foreseeably, was limited. About 850 Anskar returned to Birka, whose king was now that Olaf who reconquered Kurland and made the Chori pay him tribute. He may not have been the only king in Sweden at this time.

As for the political nature and geographical extent of his kingdom, the precise relationship between the ancient Uppland realm and mainland Götaland on the one hand and the island Gotland on the other, we are gravely underinformed. An inscription on the Sparlösa stone of *c.* 800 has been interpreted to mean that a king Alrik, son of king Eirik of Uppsala, ruled over Västergötland at that time, which would suggest an Uppland dominance, and Wulfstan's testimony in the 890s (it is quoted on page 110 below) would seem to confirm this. Presumably it was in Olaf Skötkonung's time, *c.* 1000, that the non-Danish regions of central and southern Sweden were drawn closely together in one Swedish kingdom; but well before this the power of Uppland, its wealth, and progress in trade and war, had given it a clear lead over its rivals. Swedes, Gauts, and Gotlanders were active in the Gulf of Bothnia and the eastern Baltic; they had pressed beyond the area of Lake Ladoga to the Russian rivers Dnieper and Volga, and by the year 839 emissaries of the 'Rus' had reached the Black Sea and Constantinople. Swedes were not unknown in the British Isles, and report would have a Swede circumnavigate Iceland in the 860s; shortly before the year 900 the Swedes 'seized royal power in Denmark by force of arms', and held sway in southern Jutland for not less than a third of the century; but this helps us little in respect of the Swedes at home. Even the creative imagination of Snorri Sturluson does not reach beyond mention of a king Eirik at Uppsala not long after 850, and yet another Bjorn, who is said to have ruled for fifty years.

In respect of Norway, thanks to archaeological research, the study of ancient farms and their holdings, our knowledge of trade-routes, the different economic characteristics of various parts of the country, and a few winnowable grains of information in the written sources, both verse and prose, we are a little better placed to watch the centuries-long coalescence of a considerable number of small communities into overlordships, republics, and petty king-ships, and the resolution of various of those last into an extensive though incomplete and loose-girt kingdom north of the Skagerrak during the long and forceful career of Harald Fairhair, *c.* 870–945. The far-reaching fragmentation of pre-viking and early viking Norway (and the tendency to fragmentation persisted into the eleventh century) was to be expected from the country's historical and geographical heritage. There were three major divisions, and far more minor ones. Most important of all for the political destinies of Norway in the Viking Age was the so-called Østland or Eastern region, consisting of the settlements, aggregations, republics,

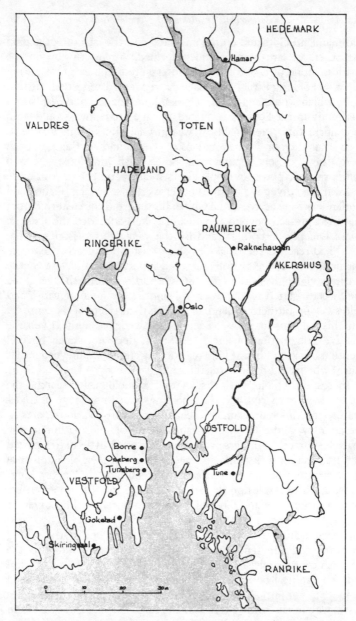

MAP 2.   NORWAY: VESTFOLD AND THE OSLOFJORD
PROVINCES

kingdoms, either lying alongside the Oslofjord or culturally, economically, and in the long run politically, bound up with it, i.e. Vestfold, Raumarike, Hedemark, Østfold. Much of the best farming land in Norway was to be found here, crop and animal husbandry could be profitably pursued, and in viking times a succession of market towns, Kaupang-Skiringssal, Tunsberg, Oslo, throve on the region's attraction for merchants native and foreign. Wealth accumulated, especially in Vestfold, so that the farmer had his axe and plough, the estate-owner his tenants and slaves, the royal progeny of Frey its martial following, and the artist-craftsman his patron. It followed that of all the petty kingdoms of Norway Vestfold was likeliest to produce a Norwegian royal house, the most notable monuments of Norwegian viking art, and prove in other ways the heartland of the slowly and intermittently developing Norwegian realm. At the same time it was in close touch with Denmark and Sweden, and through them with the quickening influences of central European civilization.

II. VIKING SHIPS IN TUNSBERGSFJORD

The second main region of Norway lay well to the north. This was the Trondelag, with its natural centre on the southern shore of the Trondheimsfjord (Hladir, Nidaros, Trondheim). Here, and east of the fjord and past Snåsavatn, lies an extensive tract of good farming land, and the whole area north of Trollheimen and west of the Keel, while testing, is not inimical to man. On the higher ground and in favoured spots even on quite high mountains there were stretches of excellent grass, and the local inhabitants (not only in the Trondelag, but everywhere in Norway) had early learned to make use of such. Throughout the summer their flocks and herds grazed these pastures, were driven up in the spring, and back down in the autumn. In places the pasture was common to all, but increasingly the husbandman came to have his own upland grazing, his seter (*seter*, Swedish *säter*). Sometimes the seter was of a permanent nature, but whether permanent or seasonal it was a factor of high significance for the economic, social, and political development of district, region, and nation. Equally important, perhaps, the Trondelag had maintained trade with the Frisians over many centuries. Trade and agriculture together led to the emergence of a class of well-to-do landowning farmers whose interests were best served by social stability and the rule of law. It was a decisive moment for this great northern region of Norway when the men of the coast and the men of the inland farms and seter took steps to secure these benefits.

The third distinctive region of Norway was the coastal region of the west between the Jaeder and the southern Trondelag, whose districts bore the famous viking-time names of Rogaland, Horda-land, Sogn, Firthafylki, Sunnmoer, and Raumsdal. The area is generally mountainous, its coasts rocky and penetrated by narrow and often precipitous fjords. Good farming land is scarce in proportion to the size of the area, and the possibilities of expansion eastwards and northwards limited. It would be quick to feel the pinch of an increasing population, and quick to do something about it. Holmsen rightly speaks of the Vestland's 'spartansk kultur' in Merovingian times;[1] there was a significant change of weapons there *c.* 600 from the old two-edged sword to the short one-edged frankish scramasax, and from the old-style comparatively light types of spear to the heavy, broadbladed lance. These were weapons unfavoured by the rest of Scandinavia, and show that the Vestland had interests and contacts which were not those of their neighbours to the north and east. Generalizations are never the whole truth, but while the Oslofjord appeared cast for the task of national unification, and the Trondelag for advances in law and administra-

[1] *Norges Historie*, Oslo-Bergen, 1961, pp. 85–6.

tion, the Vestland appears the destined breeding-ground of viking individualism from the Age of Migrations to the mid-eleventh century. Robbing your richer neighbours was a simple way of redressing the injustices of nature. If we can trust to heroic story and lay, the men of Rogaland, Hordaland, and Sogn were foraying among the Danes and eastwards in the Baltic during the seventh and eighth centuries; their scramasaxes have been found on Bornholm and in Finland; they were well placed to prey on the Frisian traffic in hides and furs and sea-ivory with the Trondelag, Halogaland, and Finnmark. They were skilled shipbuilders and sailors and naturally productive of a warlike aristocracy.

When the Age of Migrations drew to a close towards the end of the fifth century there was a substantial number of independent units south of Halogaland, each based on self-interest, a need for religion and law, and the power of a ruler, whatever his style and title. The numerous hill-forts built throughout the inhabited areas of Norway and Sweden during the period 400–600 testify to a need for military defence which must have led to the growth of a local leader's power. The profits of trade and a plenitude of iron which could be made into tools, agricultural implements, and weapons, brought wealth into strong, greedy, and purposeful hands. Everywhere there would be found individuals or families distinguished for riches, landed possessions, skill in war or piracy or general acquisitiveness, who by consent, election, or force, claimed support and obedience from their neighbours, and in return offered authority, protection, public ceremony, and law. Thus there were eventually many kings and still more jarls, or earls, in Norway. Sometimes they joined together to make and obey a code of custom and law helpful to a wider community. At its humblest level a number of families living in the same neighbourhood formed a settlement or *bygð*, and to regulate conduct within the *bygð* there was inevitably need of some kind of consultative assembly. This was the Thing (*þing*), one of the most typical of Scandinavian institutions, which maintained customary law, safeguarded the rights of free men, controlled the blood-feud by apportioning penalties and compensations, and knit its *bygð* more closely together. In the same way there was frequently a grouping of *bygðir* for law and defence, and these larger units (sing. *hérað*, *fjórðungr*, *fylki*, and the like) were in turn the constituents of the 'kingdoms', many of their names ending in the significant territorial suffixes *-rike*, *-land*, or *-mark*, from which during the Viking Age the rulers of Vestfold would shape a more identifiable though still far from complete Norway.

This would be a long, hard process, for there was small prospect that the chieftains, jarls, kings who cluttered Norway would lightly curtail their authority in the interest of a cause they knew nothing about, and would disapprove of strongly when they did. So, many of these fought for trade, plunder and land, glory and revenge, or because their fathers had fought before them; a kingdom here grew bigger, a kingdom there disappeared. These are the men whose masks and reflections are mirrored in the pages of Snorri's *Ynglinga Saga*, engage our attention by some amiable or ferocious eccentricity, then grimace and disappear. Their world is that of tradition and folktale rather than history, and everything related of them in the written sources of the twelfth and thirteenth centuries must be regarded with scepticism or downright disbelief. Olaf the Wood-cutter, who cleared the forest north of Lake Väner with axe and fire and called it Värmland, before his subjects sacrificed him to Odinn for good seasons; Halfdan Whiteleg, who is said to have established a mighty kingdom including Raumarike, Hadaland, much of Hedemark and Vestfold, and Värmland in Sweden, before he died of old age and was buried in a mound at Skiringssal in Vest-fold; Eystein Fart, who became king of all Vestfold before, a warlock helping, he was knocked overboard by a ship's boom and howed at Borre; Halfdan the Generous with Money but Stingy with Food, likewise howed at Borre—all these inhabit that morning world of half-remembered dreams which precedes the light of historical day. Gudrod the Hunting King looms closer to the frontiers of history, in that he was the father of Halfdan the Black and grandfather of Harald Fairhair, but can hardly be said to have crossed them. According to his story, he was a high-handed man who after the death of his first wife asked for Asa daughter of the king of Agdir. She was refused him, so he made a sudden descent on Agdir, killed Asa's father and brother, and carried her off with much booty. They had a son whom they called Halfdan. When Halfdan was one year old king Gudrod perished of a spear-thrust one dark evening, gross and full of beer. The slayer was a servant lad of queen Asa's, and the queen never denied responsibility for the deed, which if it took place at all took place *c.* 840. Neither of Gudrod's sons, Olaf Geirstada-Alf by his first marriage, and Halfdan the Black by his second, made any move against her, and it has been conjectured (though conjecture is all that it is) that it was this resolute and imperious lady who was buried so splendidly in the Oseberg ship-mound, with sleigh and wagon, her slave woman, four dogs, fifteen horses, combs, pins, eating-knife, apple- or water-bucket, spindle, scissors, loom, spades and dung-fork, and all things else meet and requisite for a ninth-century northern queen in the afterworld. Olaf, who was twenty years older than his half-brother Halfdan, succeeded his father to the kingdom, but is reputed to have suffered such setbacks that finally only Vestfold was left to him. He had a son, king Rognvald, who acquired the nickname *heiðumhár*, *-hæri*, the Glorious or High-honoured, concerning whom the skald Thjodolf composed *Ynglinga Tal*, but oddly enough he is the one Yngling king about whom Thjodolf tells us nothing, neither how he won his honorific title nor the manner of his death and interment. The usually resourceful Snorri and his sources are equally silent, and we are left to infer that the future of Norway lay with one man only, Asa's son Halfdan, nicknamed the Black.

With him, too, we remain knocking at the door of verifiable fact. Like many a folktale hero, he had been raised by his mother for safety's sake in her father's realm in Agdir. He became ruler there at the age of 18, and later received the eastern half of Vestfold from his half-brother Olaf. If we believe in him at all we must believe in his ambition, too, for he immediately embarked on a long series of campaigns against his fellow kings in Vingulmark, Raumarike, Hedemark, Gudbrandsdal, Toten, and Hadaland. His second marriage was to Ragnhild, daughter of Sigurd Hart, a king in Ringerike, but its manner and telling in late sources are heavy with the accoutrement of fictional saga. She had, says *Heimskringla*, been abducted by her father's slayer, the berserk Haki, who planned to marry her; but before he died in an ambush the lordly Sigurd killed twelve men, wounded Haki in three important places, and cut off one of his arms. He lay abed the winter through, healing his wounds and savouring his bridal-to-be, but one fine morning Half-dan the Black, who was informed of all these happenings, summoned his retainer Harek Gand and told him to get after Haki—'and bring me Ragnhild, Sigurd Hart's daughter'. Harek set off, surrounded Haki's hall, rescued Ragnhild and her brother Guthorm with all the valuables they found there, then fired the building. Haki was still alive and gave chase. The rescued pair had been lifted into a magnificent tented wagon, and raced away across an ice-covered lake. When Haki reached the lakeside, shorn of glory, bride, arm, and all hope of revenge, he turned down the hilt of his sword, fell on its point and died. Halfdan saw the tented wagon from afar, spread a great banquet and invited the neighbours, and that same day, in the highest tradition of the Sagas of Old Time, wedded and bedded the rescued princess. Whence sprang Harald, to the glory of Norway.

According to Halfdan's saga in *Heimskringla*, Ragnhild was a niece of queen Thyri of Denmark, Gorm the Old's wife, but sense and chronology speak against it. Halfdan is the first royal person to get a saga to himself in *Heimskringla* and likewise in *Fagrskinna*. The saga is short, and if our regard is for history unadorned, could well be shorter; for its second half Snorri relies almost exclusively on legend, folktale, and dreams. But we can accept that Halfdan was a warlike, acquisitive, intelligent, and powerful ruler over the Vestfold territories. That he was more powerful than some of his half-glimpsed predecessors is incapable of proof, but Snorri, our main source of information, was looking ahead to Harald Fairhair, and the father profited by the son. He was 40 years old, we are advised, when he died accidently by drowning.

Harald, his son, was 10. His, too, was a life's span heavily embroidered with folktale and legend, but he is so dominating a figure in Norwegian history that we must seek to find how much of truth, and where that fails of likelihood, lies under *Heimskringla*'s draperies. We start conventionally enough. It had been revealed to his mother in a dream[1] that her progeny would flourish like a great tree with blood-red roots, green trunk, and snow-white branches which would cover the whole of Norway and lands farther afield. Yet the opening years of Harald's reign must have been heavy with danger. His first task, or rather that of his mother's brother Guthorm, who acted as regent for a while, was to repel various of his father's old enemies who saw in a boy's accession their opportunity

[1] Dreamed by the begetters of other conquering heroes, from Cyrus the Persian down to Sigurd Jerusalem-farer. King Halfdan, normally no dreamer, likewise had a dream, in a pigsty. It seemed to him that he had the longest hair of any man on earth, and that it hung down in ringlets, some to the ground, some to his thigh, some to his waist, some merely to his neck, while the shortest curls came sprouting out as nothing more than little horns of hair. The strands were of all colours, but one excelled the rest in beauty, brightness, and length. Thorleif the Wise, who had recommended the pigsty, identified this particular lock as St. Olaf.

to throw off dependence and recover their former territories. Battles were fought, kings slain, realms subjugated, till eventually Harald was master of a much enlarged Vestfold, possibly including Ringerike, Hedemark, Gudbrandsdal, Hadaland, Toten, Raumarike, and northern Vingulmark.

Whatever his motive so far, a great and continuing ambition must have bred in him now. Norway, after all, was one country, its long coastline traversed over many centuries by the laden ships of the Frisians and Halogalanders. Southwards, in close and often embarrassing relationship with the Vik, was Denmark, and more especially Jutland, with its lesson in kingdom-making for a man as ready to look beyond his nose as Harald. West over sea Norwegians, including members of Harald's own family like Olaf or Amlaibh, had won or were winning kingdoms in the British Isles. At home there was the example set by his father Halfdan, and farther north that of the Trondheim jarls. In their original home by the Malangenfjord (modern Tromsö), in latitude 69°N, these last had entered the race for power with fewer advantages than the rulers of Vestfold. But they had read the times correctly: Europe needed furs, hides, cables, sea-ivory and down, and these they possessed, or could obtain, in abundance. What was required was that they should be safe on the long haul from Bjarmaland and Halogaland to Skiringssal, Hedeby, and marts beyond. The best way of ensuring this was to control the sea-route; so with the backing of their northern neighbours this active and far-sighted family extended its influence southwards and in the ninth century reached the mouth of the Trondheimsfjord. Here they found communities whose interests were similar to their own, and without too much disturbance became dominant over them. It followed that they would next explore the possibilities of taking over the entire Trondelag, and base their further plans for safeguarding the trade-route south on two main bases of power, the land animals and sea-mammals of the remote north and the self-sufficient farming and trading community of the Tronds. How successful Hakon Grjotgardsson would have been in his inevitable move against the sea-kings of the Vestland we cannot say. The two greatest men in Norway came to terms; Hakon strengthened his grip on the Trondelag and settled in as jarl of Hladir. In return he recognized Harald's overlordship, an unirksome and not overmeaningful gesture, and Harald found himself free to marry Hakon's daughter, enlarge his father-in-law's already large patrimony, and wage war on the viking kingdoms in the west. On a longer view Harald had bolstered up the strongest challengers to the Yngling line, set a barrier across his descendants' way to the unification of Norway, and ensured a more or less independent status for the Tronds, who would long remain the most rebellious and uncooperative section of the Norwegian realm.

12. SEAL HUNTERS (OLAUS MAGNUS)

Harald's campaign against the Vestland was a long, arduous, and interrupted affair. He had a more or less unified Vik and a more or less pacified Trondelag behind him, but he was now confronted by a warlike aristocracy and a breed of sea-going pirates who had long been raiding west over sea and taking toll of their Norwegian neighbours, too. It would be a minority of them who were not prepared to fight for stakes of all or nothing. There was much bitter fighting as Harald attacked and removed his many obstacles on the west coast on the way to the final reckoning at Hafrsfjord. The sea-battle fought there was among the most decisive in medieval Scandinavian history. A confederacy of disaffected kings and jarls throughout the south-west drew a host together and encountered Harald's fleet where it lay ready for battle in a little fjord west of Stavanger. Not for the first time Harald had moved faster than his foes. The fight was long, hard, and costly on both sides, but Harald emerged the unquestioned victor. *Heimskringla*, *Egils Saga*, (probably from the same hand), and the poem *Haraldskvæði*, the Lay of Harald, sometimes called *Hrafnsmál*, the Raven's Sayings, supply many details of the fray, how Thorir Haklang was killed and his ship cleared, how Kjotvi the Rich fled to an island stronghold, and the men of his host slung their shields on their backs and fled helter-skelter through the Jaeder. There have been many attempts to determine the year of the battle. Traditionally the three principal dates of Harald's life were long held to be *c.* 850 for his birth, *c.* 872 for Hafrsfjord, and *c.* 932 for his death. These were the dates to be drawn from Ari's *Íslendingabók*, which Snorri Sturluson accepted in the early thirteenth century, and Guðbrandur Vígfússon sought to confirm in the mid-nineteenth. They are now judged to be too early. Koht suggests 865–70 for Harald's birth, 900 for Hafrsfjord, and 945 for the accession of Hakon Athelstan's fosterling to the throne left empty by Harald's death and the misfortunes of his chosen heir, Eirik Bloodaxe. A consensus of recent opinion would place Hafrsfjord earlier than 900, but not before 885; that is, during the second half of the reign of king Alfred in England.[1]

[1] Vígfússon's first big contribution to saga chronology was his *Um Tímatal í Íslendinga Sögum*, Copenhagen, 1855, and while various of the assumptions on which it was based are now abandoned or severely questioned, this was a fundamental work of scholarship. Almost thirty years later he challenged his own almost universally accepted conclusions in *Corpus Poeticum Boreale*, II, 487–500, but such was the authority of the earlier work that his emendations went largely unheeded. The new landmark was Halvdan Koht's 'Um eit nytt grunnlag for tidrekninga i den elste historia vår', *Innhogg og Utsyn*, Oslo, 1921. The dates relating to Harald, Eirik, and Hakon are essential to the chronology of *Egils Saga*, which has been elaborately studied by Per Wieselgren, *Författarskapet til Eigla*, Stockholm, 1927, and Sigurður Nordal, *Egils Saga Skalla-Grímssonar* (Íslenzk Fornrit), Reykjavík, 1933. They agree on *c.* 885 for Hafrsfjord and 947 for the expulsion of Eirik Bloodaxe in favour of Hakon. There are excellent brief statements for the English reader in T. D. Kendrick, *A History of the Vikings*, 1930, pp. 108–9 and 111 (with its footnotes 1 and 2); G. Turville-Petre, *Víga-Glúms Saga*, 1940 (2nd ed. 1960), pp. xliii ff., and *The Heroic Age of Scandinavia*, 1951, pp. 115–17. This last also offers an explanation of the discrepancy of a decade or more between the actual and the early Icelandic dating: Icelandic tradition held that the country was settled by men in flight from the tyranny of Harald Fairhair; the first and most famous settler was Ingolf Arnarson, *c.* 870; Ingolf had fled from oppression in Norway; the battle of Hafrsfjord caused men to flee from Norway; therefore it must have been fought about 870. There is an elaborate summary of the chronological argument by Bjarni Aðalbjarnason in his *Heimskringla*, I, Formáli, pp. lxxi–lxxxi.

But though after Hafrsfjord so many of his worst enemies were dead or in flight, the time was not yet ripe for Harald to trim his hair and take his royal ease. For at least fifty years before Hafrsfjord there had been considerable viking activity in western Europe, and the Norwegians had established colonies in the British Isles, but northern tradition is insistent that it was in the years after Hafrsfjord that considerable numbers of Norwegians fled from the tyranny of king Harald to Shetland, Orkney, and the Hebrides, and from there practised viking in reverse. Instead of spending their winters in Norway and their summers raiding in the British and Atlantic islands, they now lived out west and did their raiding back in Norway. For a while Harald tried to control this by a naval patrol of the islands and skerries of Vestland, but against fast-moving foes who had no intention of being brought to battle these measures proved ineffective. True to his nature and his lifelong strategy he now used his command of the sea-lanes to tackle the trouble at its source, sailed with his fleet to the Atlantic islands, and put all he caught to the sword in Shetland, Orkney, and the Hebrides. He is reported to have harried on the mainland of Scotland, and to have sailed south to Man; but Norse accounts of this western expedition are hard to reconcile, and the Celtic hard to credit.[1] Having extirpated his enemies, Harald laid claim to both Shetland and Orkney, then bestowed them on the family of jarl Rognvald of Moer. The first earl of Orkney was Rognvald's brother Sigurd, notorious for his assaults on Scotland, the second Rognvald's base-born son Einar, ruthless, capable, one-eyed, an archetypal turf-cutter and middling poet, who is said (incorrectly, as we think) to have acquired the same kind of rights over odal land in Orkney as Harald in Norway.

To early historians Harald Fairhair was now 'king of Norway', but the title is a misleading one. Up north it made no odds who was king over various of the regions down south, and Harald's tokens of authority would produce little deference in the eastern hinterland. But certainly he was a king *in* Norway such as the land had not known before, and his personal authority in the coastal regions of the west was unrivalled. The very length of his loosely defined 'reign', which on the most niggardly count lasted more than half a century, added to his stature and subsequent reputation. About his

[1] The account of Harald Fairhair in the thirteenth-century Welsh *Hanes Gruffydd ap Cynan* (ed. A. Jones, Manchester, 1910), including what is said of his family and his two expeditions to Ireland, invites a profound distrust.

methods of rule and government we hear comparatively little, and most of that requires a cautious interpretation. Thus we are told by Snorri that wherever in the course of his conquests Harald gained power he appropriated the hereditary estates, and all farmers had to pay him dues. In every shire (*fylki*) he appointed a *jarl* whose duty it was to administer law and justice and collect the king's fines and dues, one-third of which he kept for his own expenses. Every jarl had four or more *hersar* under him, and while each jarl provided sixty men for the royal army, every hersir provided twenty. Further, king Harald increased all taxes so swingeingly that his jarls were richer than the petty kings of old, and for this reason many great ones threw in with him.

But we cannot believe that Harald evolved a system of government and revenue as tidy as this. Snorri is arguing back from his knowledge of the jarls and fylkir of Norway in the early thirteenth century, and offers a misleading picture of the less systematized situation *c.* 900. Certainly king Harald needed wealth and would not be overscrupulous how he raised it. That he took a profit from everyone and everything he could may be counted sure, but it is hard to believe that the hostile words of later Icelandic tradition mean what they say: 'All husbandmen should become his tenants, and those too who worked in the forests, and saltmen, and all takers of prey by sea and by land—all these were now made subject to him' (*Egils Saga*, 4). There could be mulctings without this kind of tenure. Similarly: 'King Harald seized possession in every district of all odal rights [i.e. hereditary rights to land], and the whole land, settled and unsettled, and equally the sea and the waters.'[1] That he would dispossess and confiscate, impose redemptive fines on foes left in possession of their estates, and top and tail the resources of potential enemies, was to be expected, and his unrivalled conquests allowed him to do this on an unparalleled scale; but it is unbelievable that the great landowners of the ninth century would compromise much less abandon their *oðal*. Harald was strong-willed and energetic, with a need and desire for riches; but he had sense and judgement, too. Once the initial and deliberately punitive exactions were over he would not be short of means. The lucrative fur trade of the north and all imports from Iceland paid him a toll; his private holdings were large, and the sequestrated estates of the Vestland vikings on which he lived in later life presented him not

[1] For a comment on this aspect of late Icelandic tradition, see p. 279 below, n. 1.

only with land and tenants but with the material profits of generations spent in piracy at home and overseas.

He would in any case be tempted to remove from Vestfold in the
Oslofjord to the famed viking territories of the south-west, because
it was they that most needed to feel his hard and steadying hand.
He lived in style there, with his headquarters at Avaldsnes on
Karmøy, but making royal progresses by land or water to other
main farmsteads of his. His court moved with him, whose skalds
and warriors and material splendour would quickly become part of
his legend. The government of other regions he entrusted to friends,
kinsmen, or local chieftains who for a variety of reasons recognized
his personal overlordship. Between some of these and Harald the
ties were slender and would not outlast his life. The most notable of
contemporary jarls were Hakon Grjotgardsson, who retained control
of the Trondelag, and his reconciled foe Rognvald of Moer, three of
whose sons made their mark on Norse history, Thorir succeeding to
the jarldom of Moer, Einar to the jarldom of the Orkneys, and
according to Icelandic tradition the in-every-sense-great Hrolf
(Göngu-Hrólfr) becoming the first duke of Normandy. In most of
these more or less dependent states life went on much as usual.
Farmers farmed and traders traded, smiths forged tools and weapons,
women spun and wove. Norwegians for the most part continued to
live under the rule of local custom and Thing-law, and the Things
continued in usefulness and advanced in importance. By now, we
think, there were possibly three lagthings or supra-Things in
Norway. The small states about Lake Mjøsa in the eastern Norwegian Uppland recognized the laws of the Eidsivathing as binding
upon them all. The many shires of the Trondelag congregated for
law every June at the Eyrathing near the mouth of the river Nid;
and most famous of all, if only because it provided a model for the
law of Iceland in 930, was the Gulathing, held just south of the
mouth of the Sognfjord, and serving the three great shires of Sogn,
Hordaland, and the Fjords. At least two of these had been established before Harald Fairhair's time, and possibly all three, but the
Gulathing owed much to his determination to control and pacify the
Vestland. 'With law shall the kingdom be built up, and with lawlessness wasted away.' And, 'If we break the law we break the peace.'
Harald was appreciative of the stability brought into everyday
affairs by the supra-Things, and confirmed their standing and
authority. The right of the assembled congregation to approve a

ruler by public acclamation would be an asset of the Ynglings till the end of the viking period.

There was another sphere of negotiated agreement between king and freeman, provision for which was built into the later codes of law, and whose regulations would grow steadily more elaborate till Harald's successor Hakon the Good formulated them for the Gulathing Law and the Frostathing Law. This was coastal defence. It had always been the right of a local chieftain to call on his people to resist attack from without. When states were small this was not too difficult. At news or sight of a marauder the summons went forth, men took up their weapons and rations, and hastened to the place of assembly. But Harald's situation was less easy. He must arrange for a wide-ranging not a local muster; ideally he should prepare his defence measures in advance; and he needed a fleet more or less instantly at command. His personal retainers were not enough. For political as well as military reasons, for the stronger assertion of his personal and royal authority, the king wanted all he could get in terms of manpower, arms, and length of service. But the peace-loving farmer sought to give as little as he could of these commodities. It could be agreed that for defence purposes the land, or such part of it as a king like Harald Fairhair controlled, fell into regions and districts, and that it would be fair for each district to furnish a ship and a crew. But how big a ship? How large a crew? How choose the men? Who gives the orders?[1] In short, the world-over groan of the conscripted man: Why me? Details for Harald's time are scanty or non-existent, but in the later Gulathing Law we read that three families of free farmers must put up one man between them, and that he must be supplied with rations of meal and meat for two months. When he stood down from service he was given provisions for a fortnight, presumably to get him back home hale and hearty. It is reasonable to suppose that the sea-going, viking-ridden, and turbulent Vestland took more kindly to ship-service than the more settled agrarian divisions elsewhere.

During his long life (he lived into his eighties) Harald fathered many sons, some of them to Norway's bane. Some sources say there were twenty of them, the *Historia Norwegiæ* names sixteen, Eyvind Skaldaspillir (Despoiler of Skalds or Plagiarist) in his panegyric on Hakon the Good calls him one of nine, and this is likely to be right.

[1] These and other questions are part of Holmsen's lively and precise discussion in *Norges Historie*, pp. 146–8.

They were by several mothers. The two who bore most immediately upon Norway's story were Eirik, nicknamed Bloodaxe, and the child of Harald's old age, Hakon, called the Good, who was fostered in England with king Athelstan. By the time Harald was forty we hear that many of his sons were self-seeking and turbulent, than which nothing could be more natural. To enforce one's rights to land and title was part of the business of being a king's son. Eirik's mother was Ragnhild, daughter of a king Eirik in Jutland; we can believe that he was the son on whom Harald set his highest hopes, if only because of the Danish connection, which was strengthened when Eirik married Gunnhild, daughter of Gorm the Old, king of Denmark. Some such attempt to safeguard the ancestral lands in the Vik was common prudence. What we need not believe is that when Harald was 80 and prepared to slough his royal cares, he led Eirik to his high-seat in the Vestland and gave him power over his entire kingdom. We may be confident that Harald would not make such an anachronistic gesture, and that if he did it would prove meaningless. The rest of Harald's sons would look for their rightful inheritance in this petty kingdom and that—and if they did not, there would be other claimants in plenty. Then Harald died, and was buried in a mound on Karmøy or by Haugasund in Rogaland, where he had long chosen to live, the greatest king that Norway had ever known. The personal nature of his rule was immediately apparent, the former petty kingdoms spurned the authority of the Ynglings, and leading men everywhere looked to their separate advantage. Harald left behind him no system of government to preserve his achievement, and from the closing of his howe the race was to the swift and the battle to the strong. As always, this meant the man with sea-power.

Eirik, with most at stake, and the soubriquet of a man of action, seems to have moved briskly. But 'For a short while only hand is fain of blow'. In England the 15 year-old Hakon heard of his father's death, and presumably with his fosterers' support sailed for Norway.[1] He arrived in Trondheim, no doubt by prior agreement with jarl Sigurd of Hladir. We have only late and biased written sources to go on: in them the enterprise appears a model of political manoeuvre, backed by force, but so exact in its timing that force was not

[1] *Heimskringla* is unreliable as to chronology here. Like *Egils Saga* (in all probability from the same hand), it sees Athelstan as reigning till the late 940s, whereas he died in 939.

used. With no battle joined, Eirik, for reasons we do not know, recognized the weakness of his position and sailed west over sea with any that cared to follow him. With all his faults (and they have been greatly exaggerated by Icelandic tradition) he was his father's son, strong-willed, valiant, resourceful. By 948 he was a king in York in England. Within the year his subjects drove him out to placate the English king Eadred. In 952 he was back again, but was once more driven forth in 954, and soon afterwards he died with

13. NINTH-CENTURY NORSEMAN
A carving in wood from the Oseberg wagon.

five other Norse kings in the skirmish at Stainmore in the kingdom of Northumbria. He left behind him his wife and a wolf-pack of sons who would resume with skill and daring that power-game in Norway which their father had somewhat inexplicably abandoned. The winners' prize was becoming bigger. It would be a serious exaggeration to say that there was by this time any concept of a united nation, or even kingdom, in Norway. But Harald's achievement could not be lost sight of, and to the end of the Viking Age the glittering prize in Norway would not be a kingdom of Vestfold, the Upplands, the Vik, a shire or shires in the fjord-indented west, or a jarldom of the Trondelag, but the overlordship of all those regions whose control ensured agrarian wealth, the profits of trade, and a dominant sea-power. It was a prize, sometimes only half glimpsed, and never achieved, for which Harald Greycloak and his banesman Gold-Harald the Dane, jarl Hakon, Olaf Tryggvason, and St. Olaf would one after the other yield up their lives. For Harald had made Norway more than the North Way (*Norðrvegr, Nóregr*), the route to the north as seen from the south. Yet wars and counter-wars, native jealousies and foreign aggression would all too frequently set Norwegians at each other's throats; hardly a province but would again have its petty king, and the jarls of Hladir would wax as never before; the Danes in particular would not cease to have local or dynastic ambitions north of the Skagerrak. It is to the Danes after Bravellir that we now return.

3. Denmark to the Death of Gorm the Old

WHATEVER PLACE WE ACCORD THE 'BRAVIC WAR' in history as opposed to legend our knowledge of Danish affairs in the eighth century stays meagre. We are near the century's end when in the pages of Frankish chroniclers we meet with Danish kings whose names and policies invite confidence and permit us to draw reasonable if wary conclusions about the Danish realm. The death of Carloman in 771 made his brother Charles, or Charlemagne, sole king of the Franks, and it was the territorial ambitions of this resplendent monarch in respect of his northern neighbours which brought Sigfred king of the Danes and thereafter Godfred into the light of recorded history. In 772 Charlemagne launched against the Saxons the first of a series of campaigns which would be pressed hard for more than thirty years before they ended in complete victory. Saxonia was bounded by the rivers Elbe and Saale to the east and by the Rhine to the west. Northwards its frontier ran flush with that of the Danes along the river Eider; but southwards it was less defined, and relations with the Franks had been consistently bad since the days of Charles Martel. It could be expected that an empire-builder like Charlemagne would, in modern phrase, seek to settle the Saxon question once and for all. It was an ugly war. In general the Saxons had no one ruler who could speak on their behalf, and they were heathens who believed in Thunaer or Woden. It became more and more difficult to distinguish tribal resistance from rebellion or treachery, with the inevitable reprisals; and the forcible conversion of the Saxons to Christianity was as brutal and shameless as such operations seem fated to be. The war which began with the destruction of the Irminsul, the World Pillar or Column of the Universe, upholding all things, sacred to the Saxon nation, proceeded inexorably to the pronouncement at Quierzy that extermination waited on every Saxon who did not embrace the faith of the Franks.

The massacre at Verden on the Aller in 782, the transportation of every third Saxon from his native soil which was begun in 794-5, and the uprooting of whole settlements of the Nordalbingians in 804, showed that in matters civilizing and evangelical Charlemagne was a man of his word.

These events could not pass unnoticed among the Saxons' northern neighbours. In 777 the Saxon chieftain Widukind had fled for shelter to king Sigfred in Nordmannia (i.e. Denmark). It was a moment for diplomatic overtures, and Charlemagne invited Paul the Deacon to make them in person. But Paul demurred. He had no wish, he said, to contemplate that ferocious northern visage. Besides, king Sigfred was a bumpkin who knew no Latin. Diaconal urbanity would be wasted on him. So Paul was excused. Which is a pity, for the description of a contemporary Scandinavian court by a mildly malicious and well-trained southern historian would be both helpful and entertaining.

Sigfred died about 800 and then or a little later was succeeded by the famous Godfred, an energetic and audacious man, keenly alive to the southern threat to his kingdom's welfare. Charlemagne's dedicated conquest of the heathen Germanic Saxons and his politically expedient alliance with the heathen Slavonic Abodrits, whom he encouraged to move into East Holstein, disposed the Danish monarch to utter a warning. In the year 804 he demonstrated with a fleet and army at Sliesthorp, on the frontier between his kingdom and Saxony. South of the Elbe stood Charlemagne. Maybe their available forces were too evenly matched, for there was no battle. Proposals for a personal meeting between the kings came to nothing for fear of treachery, but there was a resort to negotiation, which if it achieved nothing else at least kept the peace. Four years later Godfred acted more decisively, invaded the land of the Abodrits, and so ravaged it that they sued for peace and agreed to pay him tribute. Their chieftain Drosuk (Drasco) he carried back with him into captivity, and their commercial centre, the town of Reric, he destroyed. His campaigns, we are told, were not concluded until he had brought other Slavonic communities of the western section of the south Baltic coast under tribute, including the Wilzi.

His action against Reric is significant. By an extension of their power over Frisia and their alliance with the Abodrits the Franks were at a point to control all trade between the Baltic and the west

European coasts. But this trade was of the highest importance to Denmark, which had enjoyed prosperity for more than two thousand years by virtue of her position on two main European trade routes, that leading east by west across the base of the Jutland peninsula, and that leading northwards from western and southern Europe up the peninsula itself. The first of these, from Hollingstedt to the Schlei, linked Frisia and the west with Birka, Wollin, Truso, the eastern Baltic and Russia; the second, the so-called Army Road, led on to Norway and the Kattegat. They intersected by the emporium of Hedeby, and it was to Hedeby that Godfred now sacrificed the Abodrits' chief mart, Reric, of whose precise location we are still uncertain, though it was probably either at Alt Gaarz in the Bay of Wismar or in the vicinity of modern Lübeck. The last thing Godfred wanted to do was to injure the movement or volume of wealth and goods: he just wanted them to be by way of his own territories. At Hedeby geography was already on his side, and he determinedly fortified its natural advantages. The *Annales Regni Francorum* record how in 808 after the destruction of Reric he sailed with his entire force to that same harbour of Sliesthorp from which he had glowered threateningly at Charlemagne in 804. Here he gave orders that to protect the northern bank of the Eider the frontier between Danes and Saxons should be fortified with a rampart reaching from the western ocean to that selfsame eastern fjord which conducts to the Mare Balticum. It should have but one gate for the ingress and egress of horsemen and wagons. This clearly refers to the Danevirke, a defensive system of earthworks covering the base of the Jutland peninsula; and while Godfred is not to be credited with its inception, its further development, along with the enlargement of the already established trading-town of Hedeby, just south of Sliesthorp, much enhances Godfred's claim to be considered a far-sighted as well as a forceful king of Denmark in the Viking Age. By this double stroke of policy and action, goods and ships could avoid the long and inhospitable west coast of Jutland and the waters of the Skagerrak in favour of an eight-mile portage and quick access to the Belts and the Baltic—and all on Danish territory.[1]

[1] The Danevirke as it now exists or is traceable does not extend from the Baltic to the North Sea, nor does it protect the entire northern bank of the river Eider. Even so it is a considerable work, in that a series of ramparts built over a long period of time (*c.* 737– *c.* 1160) served to defend against invasion the vulnerable part of the frontier of Jutland, i.e. the narrow neck

Godfred and Charlemagne were now in open confrontation, the stirring king of a small northern realm and the emperor of a dominion extending from the Eider to Ebro and Tiber, and from the Atlantic to Elbe and Raab. On the whole, Charlemagne's reaction was less vigorous than Godfred might have expected, for he had much to attend to, what with wars in Spain and Italy, negotiations with Nicephorus in Constantinople and Harun-el-Rashid in Baghdad, support for the exiled Eardwulf of Northumbria, problems of succession at home, and the thousand and one cares of a vast imperial administration. But the Abodrits had been his allies, he had to do something, so he sent an expedition northwards under the command of his son Charles to chastise the Danes and the Wilzi, but the prudent Charles sought easier game on the south Baltic coast, and left these hard-hitting enemies in peace. Godfred now suggested a Danish-Frankish conference at Beidenfleth on the river Stör in Holstein, whose main result was that Drosuk was permitted to return to his own people, a concession nullified a short while later when Godfred had him executed. But there was still no set trial of

---

between Hollingstedt on the river Treene in the west and the head of the Sliefjord in the east. Four main ramparts may be distinguished (see pp. 104–5). The first (the Hovedvold or Main Rampart) begins near Gottorp, runs for almost three miles south-west to Kurburg, and from Kurburg roughly six miles west to Hollingstedt (the Krum- or Krummevold, the Crooked or Curved Rampart). The second starts near Thyraburg and the dried-up Danevirke Sø, and runs almost two miles east to the ramparts of Hedeby town (the Forbindelsesvold, or Connecting Rampart). The third starts at the head of Selker Noor, Selk Cove, a mile or more south of Hedeby, and follows a straight line for three and three-quarter miles west, to end about a mile short of Kurburg (the Kovirke). Part of the ramparts was demolished during the Second World War when the Germans needed airfields and defences against an anticipated but in the event undelivered British attack. The fourth rampart, the Østervold, or Eastern Rampart, about two miles long, of which few traces remain, protected the base of the Schwansen peninsula, and may therefore be said to reach the Baltic at Windeby Noor. Supplementing these four ramparts were a number of minor walls, outworks, strong-points, and some substantial moats and dikes. The main walls varied in height and width: the Kovirke was perhaps 6 feet high, the middle section of the Hovedvold about 18 feet—and 95 feet wide. This same middle section was strengthened on perhaps as many as ten occasions, most notably by a stone parapet 9 feet by 9 feet, and by king Valdemar the Great's buttressed brick wall, 6 feet thick and some 20 feet high, built in the 1160s. Undoubtedly the completed Danevirke was a formidable obstacle to invasion from the south and closed the gap between the natural defence line of the

strength between the two monarchs, and it is clear that Charlemagne had no thought of conquering the Danes. When Godfred made his next demonstration it was by sea. In 810 with a strong fleet he scoured the Frisian coast, won minor victories over small local forces and returned home with a tribute of one hundred pounds of silver. According to Einhard, his swollen head now demanded a bigger crown. He talked of conquering all Germany: Frisia and Saxony were but provinces of Denmark, and the Abodrits his scat-men; soon he would be coming to Aix-la-Chapelle itself, to beard the emperor in his court and water his horses at the palace well. Charlemagne had earlier styled his adversary a crazy king, and this may appear the proof of it. The emperor promptly gave orders for a fleet to be built, and meantime saw that his coastal defences were in trim. In 811 he reviewed his naval forces in the Scheldt and off Boulogne, but the emergency was already over. Godfred had been murdered by one of his retainers in 810, and his nephew Hemming, who succeeded him, agreed to terms of peace which confirmed Denmark's southern frontier on the Eider. His reign lasted just one

---

Sliefjord and the swamps and water meadows of the rivers Rheide and Treene. It is more difficult to assess its deterrent value in its early stages, i.e. in the reigns of Ongendus (possibly) and Godfred. But though our doubts are encouraged by our ignorance, we can conclude that by the time of Godfred's death in 810 the Danevirke was a meaningful undertaking, and that the meaning was not wasted on his southern neighbours.

About Godfred's contribution to the Danevirke there is still a difference of opinion. The author of the *Annales Regni Francorum* had certainly not seen the Danevirke for himself, and we cannot conclude from his generalized statement which part of it was constructed first. The Dane Vilh. la Cour in his *Danevirkestudier* (Copenhagen, 1951) argued that the Kovirke could not have been built by Godfred, but belongs to the period which saw the construction of the forts at Trelleborg, Fyrkat, and Aggersborg. This would leave Godfred with what we may call the first version of the Hovedvold or Main Rampart. Jankuhn in his mighty *Haithabu, ein Handelsplatz der Wikingerzeit* (Neumünster, 4 ed., 1963) argues that since the town of Hedeby quite certainly existed in Godfred's day, and since Godfred wished to protect it and bar the Army Road, Godfred built the Kovirke. But the debate continues, and is summarized in Roesdahl, *Viking Age Denmark*, pp. 141-6. Three successive stages or complexes have been argued for: 1, the Nordvold, the first version of the Hovedvold, and maybe the Ostvold; 2, the Kovirke; 3, Hedeby's semicircular protecting wall (c. 950 or later), and its Forvold, the Forbindesvold and Krumvold. Architectural and constructional features of some of the tenth-century ramparts are now thought to point to Harald Bluetooth and the German threat rather than to his son Svein Forkbeard. With

year; his two would-be successors died in battle, and their two successors were driven out by the sons of Godfred returning home from Sweden. Charlemagne died in January 814, and in 815 his son Louis the Pious undertook a campaign into Jutland. The Danevirke was no bar, but Godfred's sons withdrew to the island of Fyn and found shelter behind their formidable fleet. The invading army was glad to depart back south, whereupon the Danes under a leader named Glum attacked in their turn, failed to take Itzehoe, an administrative centre of the Franks north of the Elbe, and were as glad to depart back north. This was the situation shortly before 820.

An important and difficult problem now presents itself, perhaps more for discussion than answer. How real was Danish royal power at this time? What was Godfred's status? Was he, as we have assumed, ruler over a kingdom which can, not unfairly, be called Denmark, or was he one among many small and circumscribed kings, albeit the strongest and best known of them. Curt Weibull was of the opinion that Denmark was not a united kingdom in any acceptable sense of the term till the time of Harald Bluetooth, i.e. post-950; and in this he has been followed by many scholars, including Erik Arup and H. Jankuhn. Indeed, it was Arup's belief that there was no true royal power in Denmark to the very end of the viking period, not even under Svein Forkbeard and his son Knut.[1] By implication this is a matter of importance for the other Scandinavian realms, too, and for many of their rulers. But, to stay with Godfred, there are strong reasons for thinking him a king in more than name of a more than regional kingdom. His actions and

---

the stabilization of the southern frontier in the thirteenth century the Danevirke lost much of its practical significance, though it was to hear the noise of battle once again during the Prussian assault of 1864. Most ramparts from the Viking Age were of earth strengthened with timber. The more elaborate works belong to later periods.

[1] C. Weibull, 'Om det svenska och det danska rikets uppkomst', in *Hist. tidsk. f. Skåneland*, 1921; *Källkritik och historia*, Stockholm, 1964; E. Arup, *Danmarks Historie*, I, Copenhagen, 1925; H. Jankuhn, *Haithabu*, Neumünster, 1963. The subject is well ventilated, with extensive bibliographical reference, by Helmuth Schledermann, 'Slesvig-Hedebys tilblivelse, I, Stednavne og fund', in *Sønderjyske Årbøger*, I, 1966, pp. 1–65; 'II, Historiske meddelelser om kongemagten og byen', ibid., I, 1967, pp. 1–73; to which I am much indebted. The historical sources are conveniently assembled in O. Scheel and P. Paulsen, *Quellen zur Frage Schleswig-Haithabu im Rahmen der fränkischen, sächsischen und nordischen Beziehungen*, Kiel, 1930.

policies, so far as we can trace or reconstruct them, appear to be those of a man possessed of real power. He made war east against the Slavs, and west into the region of the Elbe and Frisia, and in each case was concerned with more than a quick profit. Of the two great north-south trade routes, the eastern one, running from the Baltic by way of Oder or Vistula to the Danube, North Italy and the Balkans, had experienced disturbance ever since the sixth century; this increased the importance of the western, by way of the Rhine or Scheldt to the North Sea, and so along the coast northwards. From the mouth of the Scheldt up to and including the neck of Jutland was a pro-fitable, strategically important, and therefore sensitive area, and unmistakably Godfred was aware of this, and strong enough to act on his convictions. His move against Reric, his patronage of Hedeby, his furthering of the Danevirke, his provision of asylum for the Saxons, his prolonged and successful opposition to Charlemagne, and his trust in sea-power to check Charlemagne's superiority on land, are not the thoughts and actions of a minor king.

His resort to non-military measures and negotiation as between one state and another (the same is true, if to a lesser degree, of his predecessor Sigfred, and abundantly so of his successor Hemming) is not less revealing of his royal status. It may be too much to say that he maintained diplomatic relations with the emperor, but there is no doubt that the two monarchs established diplomatic contact, with its apparatus of overture, embassy, negotiation, bluff, and démarche. In today's language, Godfred had vital interests in Frisia, Saxony, and Wendland. There were trade-routes to be safe-guarded, and tribute to be collected from the Slavs. Frankish ambitions threatened both, and clearly the Danish kings had a foreign policy in respect of Holstein, the Abodrits and Slavs generally, and the Franks. There was considerable negotiation with the Franks in 782, 784, 804, and 809, because Charlemagne, too, had problems south of the Danish border. He wanted Slavonic protégés or allies not too prone to give the Danes trouble and so provoke them to action; on the other hand, he did not want them overfriendly with the Danes. The culmination of Godfred's skilful policy of talk and blows came after his death, in the peace treaty between Hemming and Charlemagne in 811. This written trans-action was the first of its kind to which any Scandinavian political unit is known to have been a party. Finally we may note that in Godfred's time German and Frankish sources speak of Denmark as a

kingdom, though at times it might have more than one holder of
power and be subject to civil war. If Godfred held sway over Jutland and Skåne, and maintained an interest in the Norwegian Vik,
as southern sources record, for these reasons, too, we may with propriety style him king of Denmark—but with equal propriety note
what must have been in various places the personal nature of his
rule.

But after his and Hemming's death we know surprisingly little
about events and persons within Denmark. Surprisingly, because
Danish activities outside Denmark were becoming well documented
in the annals and chronicles of many lands south and west of her,

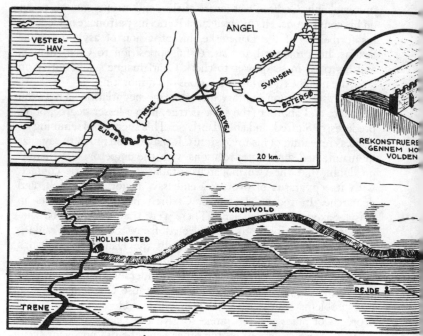

14. THE DANEVIRKE (A PICTORIAL RECONSTRUCTION)
The main picture shows the various ramparts, with two cuts
illustrative of the construction of the Hovedvold (Main Rampart)
and the Kovirke. It is now thought unlikely that there was a
passage at the place called Kalegat (Kahlegatt); it was rather
where the Hærvej or Army Road meets the rampart. The inset
shows the position of the Danevirke in relation to the base of the

England, Ireland, France, and Germany in particular. But the compiling of medieval European historical records was a by-product of Christianity, and Denmark would remain heathen for at least another century. Certainly there were internal wars in Denmark as the sons of Godfred fought descendants of an earlier king Harald for supremacy there, and as certainly Louis the Pious tried to take advantage of this. Two names emerge, Horik son of Godfred and Harald Klak son of Harald, each with the title of king. To engage the emperor's more favourable attention Harald not only fought against Horik, but became a Christian. Briefly he was some kind of co-king with Horik, but was driven out for good in 827. The Franks had already

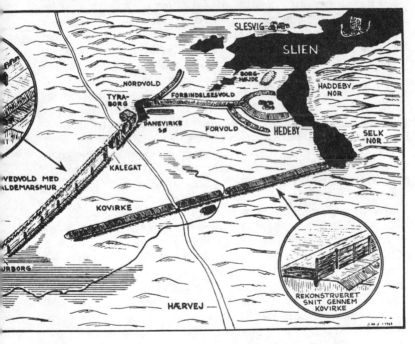

Jutland peninsula between the North Sea (Vesterhav) and the Baltic (Østersø).
(Krumvold, Crooked or Curved Rampart; Nordvold, North Rampart; Forbindelsesvold, Connecting Rampart; Forvold, Outer Rampart; Borghøjde, Hill Fort. The names are the Danish ones throughout.)

considered the possibility of using disaffected Danes to guard the coast of Frisia against attack from the north, and in 826 Harald Klak had received a substantial territory there in fee from the emperor. It was here, either in Nordalbingia or Rustringen, that Harald lived out his life, and various kinsmen of his, including his brother Rorik, held high office in Frisia down through the ninth century. At home Horik maintained his power as a viking king till his death in battle in 853-4.

His reign was notable for something more than civil wars, territorial ambitions, and viking raids south, searing though these last were. Most of his recorded actions show him to have been a strong and martial monarch, determined and unscrupulous; and that he was no stranger to the pragmatic view appears in his dealings with the Christian missionary Anskar. The first recorded Christian mission to the Danes had taken place early in the eighth century, when the Northumbrian Willibrord visited king Ongendus (Angantyr), described by Alcuin as 'fiercer than a wild beast and harder than any stone'. In the event the king's tolerance and restraint under provocation contrasted favourably with the high-minded boorishness of his visitor. For a century thereafter contacts between Denmark and Christianity were less direct. Merchants and raiders south were bound to learn something of the religion practised there and report it along with other curiosities back home; merchants from abroad brought their Christian observances to various northern marts; it seems unlikely that the Norsemen at any time forced their Christian slaves to pick a god from the Norse pantheon; and Norse ornament and decorative patterns were markedly influenced by the work of Christian artists in England and France. By c. 804 Charlemagne brought the frontier of Christianity up to the Eider itself, but it was his son Louis the Pious who encouraged the second mission to the Danes when in 823 he sped the papal legate, Ebo archbishop of Rheims, in search of souls there. Ebo made a few converts, and maybe it was due to him that in 826 Harald Klak and four hundred of his followers were, in the picturesque phrase of the *Vita Hludovici*, 'drenched in the wave of holy baptism' at Ingelheim, near Mainz. When Harald returned to Denmark with the emperor's backing it was part of the deal that a Christian missionary should go with him. This was Anskar, the monk of Corbey, then a young man of 25, whose sweetness and light were probably much lightened and sweetened by his biographer Rimbert, but whose zeal and courage

are undoubted. As for his patron, Harald's baptism assuredly owed
more to mortal ambition than to hopes of eternal heal. Anskar was in
Denmark for a short time only. With his brother monk Autbert he
established a small school for the instruction of a dozen or more
youths, probably at Hedeby, and probably already Christians, but
few Danes loved Harald, the emperor's man, and when he was driven
out the monks perforce left with him. Anskar's next mission was to
Sweden in 829. With a new helper, Witmar, he made the perilous
journey; at sea they were attacked by vikings, lost their holy books
and very nearly their lives, and eventually arrived in Birka on Lake
Mälar on foot. Birka, like Hedeby, was an important mart, and
among its mixed population and numerous visitors they were certain
to find some Christians. If only from a desire not to offend the
Empire king Bjorn made him not unwelcome. His best gain for
Christianity was Herigar (Hergeir), who was prefect of the town:
he built and maintained a church on his own land, and after Anskar
returned to Germany, bearing letters from king Bjorn to Louis,
continued, we are told, to labour for the faith in Sweden.

In 831 Anskar was consecrated archbishop of the new arch-
diocese at Hamburg, and when he went to Rome pope Gregory IV
named him, jointly with Ebo of Rheims, papal legate to all the
northern peoples, Swedes, Danes, Slavs, and such others, named or
nameless, as dwelt in those regions. There is an Icelandic saying that
no boy becomes a bishop without beating. In the ninth century no
man of the northern mission became an archbishop without beating
others. Anskar was clearly a shrewd and unflinching servant of the
Church. But both in Denmark and in Sweden there were reverses to
be endured. Gautbert's mission to Birka was moderately successful
for a while, but suddenly the heathens prevailed, his companion
Nithard was killed, and he himself expelled. In Denmark king Horik
turned hostile for other than religious reasons. When Anskar's
friend and patron the emperor Louis died in 840 the Empire became
a stage for bloody faction among his three sons. The northern
defences were left to their own devices while Lothar, Charles the
Bald, and Louis the German fought with brotherly ferocity among
themselves. Nothing could be more pleasing to the Danes. They at
once intensified their attacks south, and among other depredations
carried out the sack of Hamburg in 845 with a fleet reputedly of six
hundred ships. Anskar escaped with his life and some of the sacred
relics, but church, school, and library were destroyed with the rest

of the city.[1] Louis the German's administrative remedy for the
resultant ecclesiastical disorder was to combine the two sees of
Hamburg and Bremen, and it was as archbishop of Bremen that
Anskar undertook his next mission to Denmark in 849. It was undoubtedly an awareness of political pressures and the hope of
reciprocal benefits which made Horik in 850 give Anskar permission to build a church at Hedeby. In the same year Anskar re-
sumed the mission to the Swedes, first sending the hermit Ardgar
to make contact with Herigar in Birka, then after the death of
Herigar and the return of Ardgar, travelling there himself. There
was opposition to be faced, but yet another Swedish king, this time
Olaf, proved generous and forbearing. When Anskar returned to
Bremen he left the missionary Erimbert behind him.

Meantime Horik's long and vigorous reign in Denmark was
approaching its violent end. Various members of his family rose
against him and may even have wrested away part of his kingdom;
after an assortment of murderous encounters their numbers thinned,
and tradition has it that it was the one and only survivor, Horik
the Younger, who came to the throne in 853-4. He was at once
under pressure to do away with the church in Hedeby, and for a
time it was closed, but presumably political or economic considerations saved it from destruction, and a visit from Anskar did the rest.
In 854 the church was reopened, furnished with a bell—and a bell it
was permitted to ring, which hitherto had been as a scandal to the
heathen. Over in Ribe a site was earmarked for a second church,
and in time that, too, was built and opened. The three churches at
Birka, Hedeby, and Ribe, modest though they must have been, were
landmarks on the road which brought Christianity to Scandinavia.[1]

[1] A greatly increased knowledge of ninth- and tenth-century Hamburg was
an unforeseen consequence of the destruction wrought there in the Second
World War. It appears that the fortress proper, the Hammaburg, and everything inside its big loosely quadrangular wall, including Anskar's church,
was indeed destroyed by fire; but the merchants' quarters situated outside
the fortress along the Reichenstrassenfleet, survived the assault. It was
clearly a rich and prosperous town. See R. Schindler, *Ausgrabungen in Alt-
Hamburg*, Verlag Gesellschaft der Freunde des vaterländischen Schul- und
Erziehungswesens, Hamburg, 1957.

[1] It is noticeable that these early missions to the north concentrated their
effort upon market-places open to foreign trade, where there would at any
time be a small number of Christians temporarily resident. Their spiritual
needs were a natural concern of the Church and would take precedence over

From the accession of Horik the Younger till well into the tenth century we stay much in the dark as to political conditions in Denmark. In the 850s a viking leader named Rorik, probably a brother of Harald Klak, who had received Walcheren in fee from Lothar, made a lodgement in South Jutland, the part lying between the Eider and the sea. By 873 Denmark had at least two kings of name and repute, the brothers Sigfred and Halfdan, and according to Adam of Bremen there were yet other kings among the Danes at this time who practised piracy by sea upon their southern neighbours. It looks as though some kings could manage without a kingdom, though none could manage without a fleet and an armed following, call it what we will. The two Danish kings who perished on the Dyle in 891 were named Sigfred and Godfred, but nothing is known of their realm or status back home. Anskar's successor (and biographer) Rimbert continued his missionary work in Denmark for a time—we hear of his ransoming Christian slaves in the market at Hedeby—but after his death in 888 the connection between Bremen and the north was broken, and we lack even the exiguous and tendentious information about native events to be gleaned from the recorded activities of earlier workers for the faith. Thus we do not know to what extent Denmark was now one dominion, whether any monarch between the elder Horik, *c.* 850, and Gorm the Old, *c.* 936, ruled it as an undivided realm, or where the boundaries between the smaller kingdoms into which Denmark was periodically divided were drawn. And we would give much to know the pattern of relationship between North and South Jutland on the one hand and between Jutland and the islands, especially those east of the Great Belt, on the other. The witness of the Norwegian Ottar (OE. Ohthere) in his report on west Scandinavian geography and trade-routes to king Alfred, and incorporated by the king in his translation of Orosius's *History of the World* in the 890s, is less decisive than at first appears. He outlines his voyage from Skiringssal (Sciringesheal, i.e. Kaupang) on the western shore of the Oslofjord to Hedeby thus:

From Skiringssal he said that he sailed in five days to the port which is called Hedeby (*et Hæþum*), which stands between the Wends, the

---

the conversion of the disbeliever, especially the disbeliever in the large benighted hinterlands. The turn of many of these last would not come for another hundred and fifty years (Olaf Olsen, *Hørg, Hov og Kirke*, p. 116).

Saxons, and Angeln, and belongs to the Danes. While he sailed thither from Skiringssal, he had Denmark (*Denemearc*, i.e. the Danish lands in Sweden) to port and the open sea to starboard for three days; and then for two days before he reached Hedeby he had Jutland (*Gotland*) and South Jutland (*Sillende*) and many islands to starboard. And those two days he had to port the islands which belong to Denmark.

A second traveller who spoke of Hedeby to king Alfred was the Englishman (or Norwegian?) Wulfstan, who made a voyage from there to Truso at the mouth of the Vistula.

Wulfstan said that he left Hedeby and reached Truso in seven days and nights, and that the ship was under sail the whole way. To starboard lay Wendland; and to port he had Langeland and Lolland, Falster and Skåne, and all these lands belong to Denmark.[1] Then to port we had Bornholm, where the people have a king of their own. Then after Bornholm we had to port those lands which are called, first, Blekinge, and Möre, Öland and Gotland, and these lands belong to the Swedes. And we had Wendland to starboard the whole way to the mouth of the Vistula.

The more relevant remarks in the accompanying description of Europe are these:

West of the Old Saxons is the mouth of the river Elbe, and Frisia; and north-west from there is the land which is called Angeln (*Ongle*), and south Jutland (*Sillende*), and part of Denmark (*Dene*) . . . West of the South-Danes is that arm of the ocean which surrounds the land of Britain; and north of them is the arm of the sea which is called the Baltic (*Ōstsǣ*); and to the east and to the north of them are the North-Danes, both in the mainlands and in the islands; and east of them are the Afdrede, and south of them is the mouth of the river Elbe and part of the Old Saxons. To the north of them the North-Danes have that same arm of the sea which is called the Ostsæ, and east of them is the people of the Osti, and the Afdrede to the south.

In these passages the term Denmark clearly signifies a geographical unit including Jutland and the islands together with the Danish territories in what is now Sweden, i.e. Skåne, but excluding

---

[1] The phrases translated 'belong(s) to' are *hyrð in on Dene*; *þe in Denemearce hyrað*; *hyrað to Denemearcan* (of Langeland, etc.); and (to come) *hyrað to Sweon*. Whether the first two should be differentiated from the straightforward *hyrað to*, and if so how ('belong with', 'are associated with', 'go together with', or even 'are the same people as'), I cannot say.

2. PRE-VIKING DRAGON HEAD. The terminal of the wooden stem-post of a Migration Age ship.

3. WARRIORS ATTACKING A HOUSE

4. SAGA SCENE

5. NORSE TOOLS. Including hammers, tongs, shears, moulds, ladle, wedges, chisel, and anvil. The hammer-shafts and anvil-base are modern.

6. NORSE WEAPONS. Swords, axe-heads, spears, shield boss, and helmet.

7. BAPTISM OF KING
HARALD BLUETOOTH OF
DENMARK BY BISHOP
POPPO

8. TRADE FOLLOWS THE
HAMMER—AND THE CROSS.
A smith's mould for making
both religious emblems,
together with some hammer-
amulets.

9. JELLING. The smaller stone to the left is that raised by Gorm to his wife Thyri. The larger stone to the right is that raised by Harald Bluetooth to his parents Gorm and Thyri and to 'that Harald who won for himself all Denmark and Norway, and made the Danes Christian'.

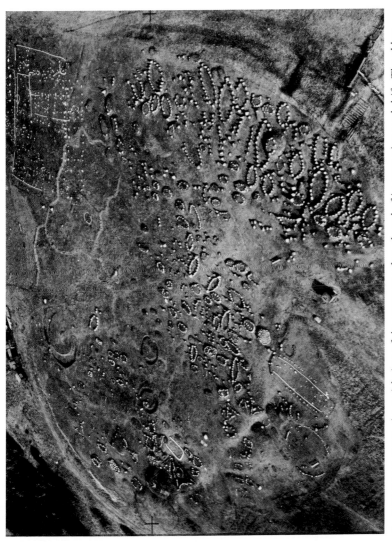

10. LINDHOLM HØJE. An aerial view of the cemetery when cleared of its protecting sand-drift. The oldest section, of the seventh and eighth centuries, is to the left. On the sloping ground centre and right are viking graves, of which the *skibsætninger* are the most striking. Upper right is the outline of a large rectangular farm of the eleventh century.

11. GAMLA UPPSALA. Aerial view of the three great burial mounds and, in line to the right, the smaller 'Tingshög' or Thing-mound.

12. THE OLDEST DANISH COINS FROM THE VIKING AGE. Farthest left is a copy of Charlemagne's coinage minted at (Dor)stat. The others are more independent adaptations.

participation in the flow of wealth and goods between Byzantium, the Arab world, and Russia on the one hand, and western Europe as well as Scandinavia on the other. It would be a curiously modern concept if some of the foremost Swedish vikings and merchants thought how then their main trade-routes would lie in the great ring of waterways surrounding Europe as the Midgard Snake of their mythology lay in the ocean encompassing the Middle World of Men, and like him might hope to lie there till the northern crack of doom.[1] Either way, as a domination of the trade through South Jutland, or an extension of Swedish influence as carriers on what we may call 'world-routes', it was an attractive prospect to strong, venturesome, profit-seeking chieftains.

The extent of Olaf's kingdom is not known, but it certainly included the all-important region of Hedeby, and probably a number of areas linked by and controlling the important sea-routes of southern Denmark. Two memorial stones with runic inscriptions found in the Hedeby area help confirm Svein Estridsson's tenuous recollections. The first of these, from between Selker Noor and Haddeby Noor (and by some considered to show significant traces of Swedish runic practice), says: 'Asfrid made this memorial after Sigtrygg, her son and Gnupa's.' The second, discovered in one of the bastions of Gottorp Slot, north of Hedeby, says: 'Asfrid, Odinkar's daughter, made this memorial after king Sigtrygg, her son and Gnupa's. Gorm carved the runes.' Gnupa is a satisfactory Norse form of Chnob, and Sigtrygg will serve for Sigerich. So we have supporting evidence for at least three kings of 'Swedish' origin, Olaf, Gnupa, and Sigtrygg. Gnupa's wife Asfrid, judging by her father's name, was a Danish lady—than which nothing could be more natural. Finally, there is the testimony of Widukind's late tenth-century *Res gestæ Saxonicæ* and other German chronicles, that to punish the 'Danes' for harrying in Frisia Henry the Fowler invaded their territory in 934, chastised them soundly and forced

[1] See the passage from the *Russian Primary Chronicle* quoted on p. 163 below. It was the genius of Pirenne which in modern times drew attention to the profound effects of the assertion of Arab power in North Africa, Sicily, and Spain upon the old and, by implication, new trade-routes between the Levant and northern and western Europe. (See his *Economic and Social History of Medieval Europe*, 1937, and *Mohammed and Charlemagne*, 1939). For the view that he overstated a good case, see R. Latouche, *The Birth of Western Economy*, (1961, chapter IV, 'The so-called Grand Commerce of the Merovingian Period', and pp. 165–7.)

Bornholm and Blekinge. It was probably a political unit, too, in the sense that its inhabitants thought of themselves as Danes subject to some variety of Danish rule. Ottar, it is true, leaves the political situation of Jutland tantalizingly open to speculation, and it seems safe to assume that at times of general dissension and disunity, which were not infrequent, it had, like Bornholm and no doubt other areas, rulers of its own over some fair-sized portion of the peninsula. But North-Danes or South-Danes or Danes whatsoever, the Danes were a people, and had a country. What they must still await, and for a very long time, was a last licking into shape as a kingdom.

This was demonstrated at almost exactly the time of king Alfred's witness. In the 890s Danish armies abroad had suffered many defeats and heavy losses. After the carnage on the Dyle in 891, there was a king in Denmark named Helgi (Heiligo), to whom Adam of Bremen, following his authority king Svein Estridsson, devotes precisely one sentence, informing us that he was well beloved for his justice and piety. But he must have reigned over a shaken, almost a broken, kingdom, for, adds Adam, 'To him succeeded Olaf who came from Sweden and seized royal power in Denmark by force of arms.' Olaf had many sons, two of whom, Chnob and Gurd, possessed the realm after their father's death. Finally, says the same source, a king named Sigerich ruled over Olaf's kingdom; but after a short while Hardegon Sveinsson, who came from Nortmannia, took it from him. The sequence of events seems to have been as baffling to king Svein Estridsson as it is to us; for whether some of these many kings, more correctly styled *tyranni*, ruled in due succession or at one and the same time, he confessed he did not know.

This Swedish interlude in Denmark is curious but explicable. At its simplest it would appear to be a well-executed coup designed to lay hands on a region, South Jutland and Hedeby, famous for the influence and profit it brought its rulers. We know that at this time, *c.* 900, the Swedish kings disposed of much power and wealth, and were well able to take advantage of Danish weakness. As Wulfstan informs us, the big islands Gotland and Öland belonged to the Swedes, as did the mainland province of Blekinge. Swedish military and merchant venturers were exploiting the East Baltic lands, controlled profitable trading-routes along the Russian rivers, and had established the kingdom or khaganate of Kiev. Maybe then, by extending their influence, or conquests, as far as South Jutland and its mart at Hedeby, the great men of the Swedes could ensure their

them to pay him tribute, and made their king Chnuba submit to baptism.

Just how, when, and why the Swedish kingdom in southern Jutland ended are among the all too many things we do not know. But end it did. When archbishop Unni renewed the long-inter-rupted mission of Hamburg and Bremen to the Danes in 935 he encountered, according to Adam, not a submissive king Gnupa but an obdurate heathen, king Gorm, whose appearance on the scene, whatever Unni thought of it, must be warmly welcomed by students today, for he can hardly be other than Gorm the Old, husband of Thyri, and father of the renowned Harald Blátonn, or Bluetooth, and of Gunnhild Mother of Kings, the wife and widow of Eirik Bloodaxe of Norway. Even so Adam is an inaccurate witness in that he puts Gorm on the throne too early, and a cantankerous or biased one in that he describes him as a malignant persecutor of Christians. Again, it is hard to reconcile Adam's story of a Hardegon Sveinsson from Nortmannia (Normandy? Norway?) overcoming Sigerich-Sigtrygg, and so ending the Swedish line in Hedeby, with the tradition recorded in the Greater *Óláfs Saga Tryggvasonar* of how Gorm Hardaknutsson invaded Jutland, slew its king Gnupa, then another king Silfraskalli, and finally destroyed or routed all the kings as far as the river Slie in the south. Still, somewhere in these fecund waters swims the minnow of truth, and we may not unreasonably conclude that during the years 935–50 Olaf's kin was supplanted by a father and son, Hardegon-Hardaknut Sveinsson and Gorm, North Jutland Danes with holdings in Norway, who made Jelling in Jutland their royal seat, and established that mighty line of kings, Harald Bluetooth, Svein Forkbeard, Knut the Great, Hardaknut and Svein Estridsson, whose span of dominion carries us beyond the Viking Age.

As for Gorm himself, his realm and rule, once we set aside the dreams and folktales of *Jómsvíkinga Saga*, the bias of Adam, and the misconceptions of Saxo and Sven Aggeson, who thought him old and slothful, we are left with very little: he was a king, he was a pagan, he had offspring, and he raised a memorial stone to his wife Thyri, who predeceased him.[1] The Greater *Óláfs Saga Tryggvasonar* informs us that not only did he clear Jutland of a rash of kinglings

[1] The reader is referred to the excellent articles of Asgaut Steinnes, 'Gorm og Hardegon' in *Afhandlinger tilegnede . . . Axel Linvald*, Copenhagen, 1956, pp. 327–42; and Bent Ousager, 'Gorm Konge', in *Skalk*, 1957, nr. 2, pp. 19–30.

but won himself a realm in Wendland, too. The 'Hardecnudth Wrm' of Adam of Bremen ('a savage worm, I say'), perhaps Gorm, son of Hardaknut, was a heathen persecutor of Christian men, who so angered Henry the Fowler that he invaded Denmark and made his unheroic adversary sue for peace, whereupon Henry 'drew his kingdom's boundary at Slesvig, which is now called Hedeby, established a march [i.e. a borderland], and ordered that a colony of Saxons should become resident there'. In the light of Henry's invasion of the same area in 934, when he humbled the heathen Gnupa, and his own death soon afterwards in 936, there must be a substantial confusion of events and persons here; but German pressure was strong upon Denmark at this time, and, to continue with Gorm, it is unlikely that he was strong enough to resist it entirely.

Among the best-known and most-discussed runic inscriptions of Denmark is that cut on the smaller of the two memorial stones which stand by the church of Jelling in central Jutland. It reads thus: 'King Gorm made this memorial to his wife Thyri, amender [*or* glory *or* adornment] of Denmark.' The historical Thyri (or Thyra) stands far back in the murk which surrounds her husband; she may have been the daughter of a jarl of Jutland, she may have been descended from an English royal house; but later tradition made much of her beauty, chastity, wisdom, and saintliness, and in the most literal sense her great works on behalf of Denmark, in that she was credited, erroneously, with the construction of the Danevirke. It has been argued that the phrase 'amender (or however else we translate it) of Denmark' (*tanmarkaR but*, or in conventional Old Norse, *Danmarkar bót*) applies not to Thyri but to Gorm himself, his welding of minor kingdoms into one, or almost one Denmark, and his re-establishment of the old southern frontier; but this is unlikely. In either case this is the first use in native sources of the term *Danmark*.[1]

But this is not all we learn from the antiquities at Jelling about Gorm. Still to be seen are the two large mounds or barrows associated with Gorm and his son Harald Bluetooth, which stand north and south of the twelfth-century romanesque church; also

[1] It had been used in the English form *Denemearc* in king Alfred's preface to his translation of Orosius in the 890s. *Denimarca* occurs in the Chronicle of Regino of Prüm, which was concluded in 908 (ed. Kurze, SSRG, Hanover, 1890).

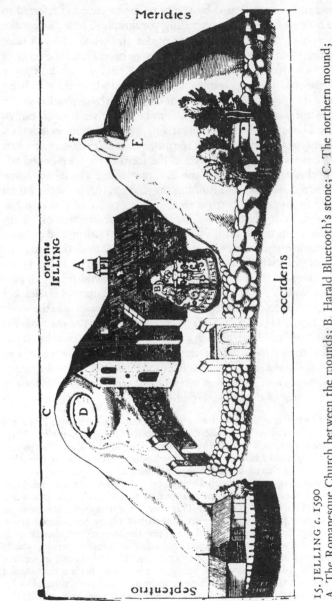

15. JELLING c. 1590
A. The Romanesque Church between the mounds; B. Harald Bluetooth's stone; C. The northern mound; E. The southern mound. D. (described as a well) and F. (a stone of considerable size) are objects less surely identifiable.

the two runic stones raised by the same monarchs, and referred to in the first sentence of our preceding paragraph. These alone make an impressive complex, but they are not the whole story. Under the square choir of the present church have been found the remains of three wooden buildings, one an oak-built stave church at some time destroyed by fire, another a demolished structure which by virtue of its age and position in front of the north barrow has in the past not unreasonably been assumed to be a heathen temple, but is, in fact, likelier to be a post-heathen, i.e. Christian foundation. Finally, excavation has revealed the outlines of an enclosure, marked out by large standing stones set in the form of an open-ended triangle enclosing one quarter of the quadrant of a circle, its axis some two hundred metres long, running north by south from the burial chamber in the north barrow to the sharp point of the triangle. There were evidently two main stages in the construction of Viking Age Jelling. The first was the work of the heathen Gorm, and includes the triangular enclosure, the northern mound, and the inscribed memorial stone which he raised after queen Thyri. This mound contained a large burial chamber lined with wood, intended for two persons, but when opened in modern times it was empty of bodies and almost everything else of significance. The second stage was the work of the Christian Harald, who so to speak took over the site from his father. It looks as though he built a first wooden church on what, if not the site of an utterly vanished heathen shrine, may well have been a place of ancient religious significance, and raised his southern mound, some seventy metres long and eleven metres high, where it must obliterate a substantial area of the triangular enclosure.[1]

[1] The precise nature of the enclosure eludes us. It has been argued by Ejnar Dyggve in a number of publications (a convenient summary in 'Three Sanctuaries of Jelling Type', *Scripta Minora: Studier utg. av Kung. Humanistiska Vetenskapssamfundet i Lund*, 1959–60: 1) that it was a particular kind of heathen sanctuary. He believed he had discovered similar V-shaped enclosures at Tibirke and Tingsted, each with a church near the open northern end. More recent excavations by Olaf Olsen run counter to Dyggve's conclusions and dispose of Tibirke and Tingsted. This leaves the triangular *stensætning* at Jelling without parallel, unless we see it as part of a huge boat-shaped grave, or *skibsætning*. In any case, there is not 'the slightest doubt that it is an illusion to suppose that a V-shaped enclosure, with apex pointing south, represents a particular type of pagan cult site. This leaves the impressive enclosure by the north barrow at Jelling, but whether this is a boat-shaped burial or not, it is above all a monument to the dead and not a ritual place for the living.' (Olaf Olsen, *Hørg, Hov og Kirke*, Copenhagen, 1966, p. 288.)

Presumably he would remove his parents' bodies from the double burial chamber in the northern mound to his new church. For his Christian mother he would find this a compulsive duty; while as for his father, there is good analogy for moving a well-loved pagan into holy ground. The southern mound was not built as a grave but as a memorial or cenotaph, to whom we do not know.[1] On its summit there may possibly have been a watch-tower. One thing still remained to do: to match, or rather outmatch, Gorm's runic stone. So near the church, and between the mounds, he had raised a magnificent stone carved and inscribed on three sides; one of them with a figure of Christ, the oldest such representation in Denmark; the second portraying a great beast locked in struggle with a snake; and the third carrying the bulk of an inscription which reads in its entirety: 'King Harald had this memorial made for Gorm his father and Thyri his mother: that Harald who won for himself all Denmark and Norway, and made the Danes Christian.'

It is the background of these expansive claims to glory which we must next consider.

For a summary of recent developments in respect of Jelling see Roesdahl, *Viking Age Denmark*, pp. 171–6. 'The grandest Viking Age grave and monuments in Denmark—one can almost say in the whole of Scandinavia—are at Jelling. According to inscriptions on the two rune stones, they are associated with King Gorm and Queen Thyre, and their son Harald Bluetooth. In addition to the rune stones, the elements of the monument known today are a burial-mound (the North Mound), a mound without a grave (the South Mound), remains of a large stone setting and a large wooden church built in association with a chamber-grave. The church was succeeded by two wooden churches and lastly by the present church built of calcareous tufa about the year 1100. A fragment of another rune stone was found in the churchyard and wall a couple of years ago, but does not necessarily belong to the rest of the complex. The interpretation of all these features is still under discussion, and the newly found grave and the first wooden church are as yet unpublished. But the complex can be explained in brief as a grave for King Gorm and possibly also Queen Thyre, as a memorial to King Gorm, Queen Thyre and King Harald, and finally as a proclamation of Denmark's official conversion to Christianity' (p. 171).

[1] There is nothing strange in this. The mightiest of all northern howes, Raknehaugen in the well-knit Raumarike, twenty-two miles north-east of Oslo, over a hundred metres in diameter and some eighteen metres high, is an empty cenotaph. Farmanshaugen by Jarlsberg near the Tunsbergsfjord, and Sutton Hoo in East Anglia likewise appear to be cenotaphs, not burial mounds.

4. Denmark and Norway from the Accession of Harold Bluetooth to the Death of Olaf Tryggvason (c. 950-1000)

THE EXTENT OF DANISH INFLUENCE IN NORWAY, considerable though it was, is hard to define in any detail right down to the middle of the tenth century, when it grows clearer, or at any rate more demonstrative, in part through Harald Bluetooth's strongly incised claim to have won Norway as well as all Denmark for himself, in part through certain sparse winnowings from the copious but late and untrustworthy West Norse and more specifically Icelandic written sources. For the Danish part of Harald's claim, we judge that his father Gorm was dead by 950 at the latest, and that Harald may have enjoyed a good deal of authority during his father's later years. With an eye to the Empire and political reality, he seems to have weighed the advantages to himself and to Denmark of the Christianity to which Gorm was unresponsive, and authorized Christians to worship publicly in Jutland. His prestige was high from the moment of his accession. Other kings, like Godfred and Horik the Elder during the ninth century, may have enjoyed sole dominion over the Danish realm, but to some extent their claim must be based on fair assumption and the absence of a named rival. In Harald Bluetooth's case there is no room for doubt. He ruled alone, and an attack upon Jutland, the islands or Skåne, by anybody and from any direction, was an attack upon Harald and dealt with by him as such.

But his power was not without check, and his boundaries were less than inviolate. In 954 or a little later Hakon the Good of Norway ravaged the coasts of Jutland, Zealand, and the Danish lands in Sweden; and to the end of his reign Harald was subject to diplomatic, ecclesiastical, and military pressures from the German emperors ruling south of him. But Norwegian and German were foes from outside, not of his own people; and when much later, in the years of his decline, power was wrenched from his hand, the inheritor was once again a sole king, his son Svein Forkbeard, the conqueror of England.

When Hakon the Good, son of Harald Fairhair and foster-son of Athelstan king of England, by sea-power, good timing, and the support of jarl Sigurd of Hladir seized power in south-west Norway in the 940s and drove out his brother Eirik Bloodaxe, the Yngling interest there was strongly reaffirmed. His change of religion might be expected to ensure his denigration by later and Christian historians; but, in fact, Hakon's reputation is that of a purposeful but humane king, attached to the principles of law, and desirous of peace and order. He had a strong sense of what was practicable, and could trim his ambitions to match his prospects. Thus he confirmed Sigurd in his overlordship of the Trondelag, and allowed two of his own nephews, Tryggvi Olafsson and Gudrod Bjarnarson, to rule as sub-kings over part of eastern Norway. His power was based on the royal lands of the south-west and an amicable arrangement with jarl Sigurd of the Trondelag. His grasp of political reality was shown not least in respect of religion. Hakon was a Christian, come from Christian England, and desirous of introducing Christianity into his kingdom. But once he found the new religion obnoxious to the great majority of his subjects he promptly embraced the old.

No king acquires, and still less retains, the title of 'Good' without merit, and on the evidence of the *Bersöglivísur* or Plainspeaking Verses of Sighvat Thordarson (*c.* 1038) Hakon acquired it early. His fame with posterity rests traditionally on his prowess as a law-giver and the land's defender. *Ágrip, Fagrskinna,* and *Heimskringla* credit him with devising the Gulathing Law for the fylkir of Rogaland, Hordaland, Sogn, and the Firths, and with the help of jarl Sigurd of Hladir establishing the Frostathing Law for the fylkir of the Trondelag together with those of Nordmoer, Naumudal, and, later, Raumsdal, too. The Plainspeaking Verses praise him for both law and justice. These are large claims, and not all verifiable, but it is likely that he fostered and made use of the old supra-Things, making them consultative and representative bodies with which the monarchy could treat in their several regions, and so seek both legal and popular acceptance for measures of national as well as local purport. The closer integration of the fylkir to form large

16. FARMANSHAUGEN BY TUNSBERGSFJORD

regional units, and the building up of the lagthing as a consultative
assembly, recognized the realities of Norwegian geography,
fostered good law, strengthened the notion of the king as a more
than regional figure, and at the same time denied him autocratic
power. The lagthing and the monarchy between them would now
ensure that the heyday of the small states was over: each institution
was essential to the other. Further, Hakon is reputed to have
improved the laws of these Things, giving them a wider application
and fitting them better to the needs of the times, though significant
detail is lacking.

It is hardly more in evidence when we seek to define his
improvements in the realm's defences. His father Harald Fairhair
had earlier made arrangements for a call-out of ships and fighting
men from the shires (see p. 93 above), and it is probable that these
were modelled on Danish practice in those parts of Norway, Vestfold and the districts east of the Oslofjord, where Danish power was
long paramount. Nor can king Alfred's measures of national defence
in England have escaped the notice of the Scandinavians against
whom they were so skilfully directed. Harald Fairhair had also
faced the problem of guarding his coasts against disaffected or displaced vikings raiding Norway from overseas. We are told in the
written sources that Hakon developed Harald's measures further.

Danger was to be looked for from the south, from Denmark; to meet it he reorganized his coastal defences, in part by a system of beacons, in part by dividing the coastal districts and 'as far inland as the salmon swims farthest upstream' into *skipreiður*, ship levies, comparable to the Danish *skipæn* and the Swedish *skipslag*, and organized shire by shire. What we are not clear about is how systematized this was, and to what extent it had a legal and political sanction. The right to levy men, ships, provisions, and money for war must be sought by any northern king whose ambitions extended beyond his patrimony, but it was a right won very slowly in Scandinavia, and we have to wait till the beginning of the eleventh century (some would say much later), and the military and naval dispositions of Svein and Knut, so significantly related to England, before it grew effective. We must either interpret the term 'leidang' (*leiðangr*, Danish *leding*), naval levy, in a very general way in late written sources dealing with the Viking Age or, preferably, consider it an anachronism foisted in by analogy with much later times. The same may be true of the 'hird' (*hirð*), the private army maintained by a king or other great man.

But Danish ambitions in Norway were not to be foiled by laws, beacons, or levies. In the nature of things Harald Bluetooth had territorial claims there, and by 955 was under compulsion to implement them. When Eirik Bloodaxe met his death in battle at Stainmore in Northumberland in 954, his widow Gunnhild fled with her sons to find succour at her brother Harald's court in Jutland. The recovery of a kingdom in Norway for these same sons was a justifiable project for a mother and a prudent for an uncle. About Gunnhild, unfortunately, we know next to nothing, her image is so consistently distorted by the written sources, which show her clear-headed, hard-hearted, retentive of personal loves and hates, and as wife and widow wedded to policies of disaster; while her sons were turbulent, self-seeking, treacherous, and brave. The harsher of these adjectives arise out of the picture of Eirik, Gunnhild, and their sons supplied by twelfth- and thirteenth-century Icelandic historians, more especially by Snorri Sturluson in his *Heimskringla* and *Egils Saga*, and are most profitably regarded as the penalty paid by those who are not of the poets' party.[1] The eldest

[1] The origin and growth of the hostile Icelandic tradition relating to Gunnhild, Eirik Bloodaxe, and their sons cannot be fully determined, but it reached full flower with Snorri Sturluson in the two works named. Instead

of Eirik's sons, Harald Greycloak or Greypelt (*gráfeldr*), was clearly a man of character and authority. In any case, Harald Bluetooth's support for his nephews was easily secured: it would suit him to see the strong, sagacious, and at times militant Hakon dispossessed by any rival whatsoever. And the mere act of restoring the sons of Eirik would assert his overlordship of them and their territories alike.

The opening rounds of the Danish-Norwegian conflict went to Hakon. He repelled Danish attacks on the Vik, set up strong vice-roys, and carried the war to Denmark itself, with raids on Jutland and Zealand and an exaction of tribute from Skåne. Three times thereafter the sons of Eirik made assaults on Norway.[1] The third time they came was to the island of Stord, off the mouth of the Hardangerfjord, and here at Fitjar Hakon's luck ran out. He suffered a mortal wound and lost his kingdom to those who were at once his bitterest foes and closest kinsmen. His court poet,

---

of a Danish princess nurtured in courts, he made her the daughter of Ozur Toti of Halogaland, and had Eirik find her up in Finnmark, where she was the beautiful neophyte of two Lapp magicians. She helped him murder them and became his queen. Thereafter her ambitions for him, and in turn for their sons, made her the evil genius of them all, and of Norway, too. Like most beautiful sorceresses, she was beautifully amorous, especially (according to Icelandic sources) of handsome young Icelanders, and her favours as she grew older were liable to cost them their happiness, hopes, heads, or some other significant trifle. How this can be reconciled with her loyalty to her husband no saga attempts to explain. Yet for all his slanders Snorri was clearly fascinated by what his imagination made of her. Wicked she might be, but it is a regal lady who lives in his pages. In *Egils Saga*, we assume, he had need of strong, unscrupulous, and at times spell-weaving rulers in Norway and at York, to explain the defeats and expulsions of his own heroic ancestors, and from a few hints in history and tradition he created them. One wonders who among his relations or acquaintance supplied him with a model for the Kings' Mother? In fact, there is no evidence that Eirik, Gunnhild, and their royal brood were greedier, crueller, more devious or ambitious than their fellow contenders for rank and riches in Norway.

[1] Early historians see this train of events in different ways. The *Historia* of Theodoricus tells of a five-year war but only one battle; the *Historia Norwegiae* and *Fagrskinna* speak of two battles; *Ágrip* and *Heimskringla* of three; Saxo of one. But all agree on the outcome of the struggle, the death of Hakon, and the accession of Harald Greycloak. See A. Campbell, 'Saxo Grammaticus and Scandinavian Historical Tradition', *Saga-Book*, XIII, 1 (1946), pp. 5–7, and Bjarni Aðalbjarnarson (ed.), *Heimskringla*, Reykjavík, 1946, I, lxxxv–vii.

Eyvind the Plagiarist (*Skáldaspillir*), sounded more than official notes of grief, praise, and foreboding in his *Hákonarmál*, whose last verses are these:

> Unbound
> Against the world of men
> The Fenris-wolf shall fare,
> Before a king so good and true
> Shall fill his empty place.

> Cattle die,
> Kinsmen die,
> Land and realm lie waste;
> Since Hakon's sped to the heathen gods
> Many a man's in thrall.

The king's body was borne to Saeheim in North Hordaland, where he was laid to rest in a howe, in full armour and his richest array. With splendid rites his people sped him on his way to Odinn, and the once-Christian king, now praised as the defender of temples, and welcome to the Æsir, joined his eight heathen brothers, the sons of Harald Fairhair, in Valhalla.

This was *c.* 960–5. The five sons of Eirik returned to Norway, together with their mother Gunnhild, now fairly to be entitled *konungamóðir*, Mother of Kings. Hakon's nephew Tryggvi Olafsson still held his eastern territories and Gudrod Bjarnarson ruled over Vestfold. North, in Trondheim province, jarl Sigurd held sway.

17. A HERO ENTERS VALHALLA
Motif from a Gotland pictured stone.

Harald Greycloak was paramount in the central and south-western provinces only, and with four royal brothers to be provided for it might well have looked as though Norway must revert to what it had been before the unifying campaigns of Harald Fairhair. In fact, this did not happen. Greycloak was bent on conquest not bargainings, on growth not dismemberment, and in this he received the support of his brothers and, we are invited to believe, the encouragement and advice of his mother. But he would not succeed in emulating his grandfather's feats in Norway, and in reputation has paid the full price of failure: like Eirik, his father, he was short on luck or judgement, and after a good start the joint power of Harald Bluetooth and the Hladir jarls took him in a vice, at a time when he had grown too strong for their good and not strong enough for his own. His gifts and accomplishments were many; he is thought to have been the first king of Norway to lead an expedition to the fur-bearing areas north of northern Halogaland and onwards to the waters of the White Sea, a region and enterprise hitherto usurped by or delegated to the chieftains of the north; and after a few years' campaigning he appeared to have destroyed his chief enemies in western and southern Norway. Why then did he fail?

We can only speculate. He and his brothers had won their kingdoms with the help of the Danes, and for some Norwegians the shadow of Harald Bluetooth maybe hung over and disfigured them. Then, like Hakon the Good, Greycloak was a Christian, and like him unable to make much impression on his heathen subjects; but whereas Hakon bowed to the inevitable Greycloak persisted in well-doing, and with his brothers broke up the sacrifices and despoiled the sacred places, thus angering both gods and men. Men could do little except grumble and hope for a change, but the Æsir defended themselves with bad harvests, bad fishing, bad weather. The snow lay through midsummer and cows stayed in stall as north among the Lapps—which may be a poetic way of saying that the all-important farmer class felt itself pinched and alienated. There were still some attached to the memory of the good Hakon, and far more devoted to the cause of the jarls of Hladir up in the traditionally separatist Trondelag—to Sigurd till the Eirikssons slew him, and thereafter to his son jarl Hakon. Nor was the sudden destruction of the regional kings Tryggvi and Gudrod down in the Vik as clever as the brothers thought it. The Danish king was sensitive to every happening in that Danish sphere of influence, and after its sequestration his love for Greycloak grew cooler. Soon we find him on terms of friendship or alliance with none other than jarl Hakon of Hladir, which led in its turn to the death of Greycloak, who was caught (the written sources say betrayed) off Hals at the narrow eastern entrance of the Limfjord in north-east Jutland, overborne by superior force, and killed.

The more profitable areas of Norway were now divided between Hladir's jarl and the king of Denmark. Hakon was to hold the seven western provinces of Norway from Rogaland to Nordmoer as the king's liege, and be sole master of the Trondelag, while king Harald took the eastern provinces, the Vik and Uppland. This we assume, together with Hakon's pledge of allegiance, was the basis of his claim to have made Norway his. There was tribute to be paid—we have a kenning for Norway as 'Harald's hawk-isle', a picturesque acknowledgement of his overlordship there—but in the matter of revenues Hakon was to fare handsomely. Gunnhild and her two surviving sons fled to the Orkneys; for a while they plagued the Norwegian coasts (it was some twenty-five years later, in the days of Olaf Tryggvason, that Gudrod the last of them was killed while raiding there), but they got no footing. Hakon never took the title of king; he was jarl Hakon for the rest of his life, and for most of it the effective ruler of western Norway. It is uncertain how long he continued to pay tribute to king Harald, and the fact that Hakon was a heathen devoted to the old gods was as a hair on the tongue of the Dane. He restored the sacred places the sons of Eirik had plundered, and maintained the sacrifices. The Æsir were not ungrateful; they sent him fine weather and good crops, and in the first winter of his rule the herrings came in shoals everywhere along the coasts.

For a while he gave king Harald military service. From the beginning of his reign, as we have noticed, the king was subject to German pressure. Like Henry the Fowler before him, Otto I was an active champion of Christianity, and when in 948 pope Agapetus addressed a bull to Adaldag archbishop of Hamburg confirming that he was head of the Church in Denmark, with a right to appoint bishops there, we have it on the authority of Adam of Bremen that Otto was much to the fore in defining the first three Danish dioceses of Hedeby, Ribe, and Århus, all in Jutland. Their bishops, Hored, Liafdag, and Reginbrand, attended the ecclesiastical conference held at Ingelheim that same year. Judging by their names, they were not all three Danes. In 965 Otto exempted the three churches from imperial taxes on their lands, in a missive which like so many church documents of the time may be a forgery, may be a recognition of the fact that the taxes had anyhow proved impossible to collect, or may be a tactical assertion that Otto regarded these lands (and by implication Jutland, if not the whole of Denmark) as being under his suzerainty. To find a reason for this last we must look back to the year 960 or so, when Harald formally received the Christian faith. The circumstances in which he did so are confused by bad history and good legend, but the conversion itself is not in doubt. According to a confused Adam (II, 111), it was part of the price paid for an unsuccessful war against the emperor; according to Widukind's Chronicle (III, 65) it arose out of a debate at Harald's court as to the nature and worship of gods. The Danes agreed that Christ was a god, but a god less powerful and manifest than the Æsir, whereas the missionary Poppo maintained that there was but one God, the Father, his son Jesus Christ, and the Holy Ghost, and that the Æsir were a pack of demons. Harald challenged him to prove his faith by ordeal, to which the bishop, confident of his non-combustibility, assented. The next day he underwent ordeal by white-hot iron glove, and when the king saw that his hand was undamaged, not surprisingly he conceded that Christ was the one true God, and he alone should be worshipped in Denmark. Yet on the whole it was a wasteful miracle, for by this time there must have been many Christians in Denmark, especially in the marts and havens, partly through the influx of traders and travellers, partly as a result of the missions from Hamburg-Bremen, partly by virtue of the Christianized Danes of the Danelaw with their substantial influence on the Danish homeland.

However, the Danish king had ambitions and spheres of interest which made a degree of conflict between Denmark and the Empire unavoidable. It is fairly certain that bishop Poppo came to Denmark at the instigation of Otto, and more than likely that when Harald accepted the Christian faith this was interpreted in Germany as an acknowledgement of Otto's authority, if not his overlordship. About the year 960 Harald was busied with Norway, was by no means without plans to extend his domains in Sweden, and was active in Wendland. It was important for him to secure his southern frontier with the Empire; and to embrace Christianity and avoid contention with the emperor was the simplest and most efficacious way of doing so, since it deprived Otto of his two best excuses for aggression. For at least a decade Harald showed himself adept at forwarding his own schemes without too overtly upsetting those of Otto. The Slavonic Wends, holding sway along the south Baltic coast from Denmark to the Vistula, offered him prospects both peaceful and profitable. They were hunters, farmers, and pastoralists, on terms of mutual detestation with their German neighbours, who more or less thought of them as animals to be hunted and slaves to be sold. Harald appears to have married at least twice, and the last of his wives, wed probably after 965, was a Wendish princess. A runic stone found in the west wall of Sønder Vissing church, in mid-eastern Jutland, bears the inscription, 'Tovi [or Tova], Mistivoj's daughter, wife of Harald the Good, Gorm's son, had this memorial made for her mother'. A further twofold tradition associates Harald with Wendland: it was to Wendland that he fled for shelter from his son Svein near the end of his life, and it was in Wendland that he is credited with establishing the viking fortress of Jomsborg, the home of the legendary Jomsvikings. This if it stood anywhere stood at the mouth of the Oder, probably on its eastern outlet, the Dievenov, on the site of the little town now known as Wollin, the Jumne of Adam of Bremen. *Pace* Adam, it was not 'the largest town in Europe', and no trace has been found there of its artificial harbour for 360 warships, or of a citadel, unless the near-by hill of Silberberg is accepted as the site of such; but there were Norsemen there around the year 1000, and the archaeological finds reveal a mixed population of vikings and Slavs. It is difficult, indeed impossible, to accept saga notions of Jomsborg as a warrior community of men between the ages of 18 and 50, their services for sale to the highest bidder, bound by iron laws to keep peace among themselves and avenge each other's death, with a fortress of their own holding inside which no woman was ever allowed; but that Harald Bluetooth by persuasion or force imposed a market-place with its Danish garrison on the Wends in the interests of trade and an expansionist policy is credible enough. Misconceptions and pseudo-heroic (which means romantic) embroidery of a later age would do the rest.[1]

[1] The best account of the town is that of the excavators, O. Kunkel and K. A. Wilde, *Jumne*, '*Vineta*', *Jomsburg*, *Julin: Wollin*, Stettin, 1941. There is a brief summary for the English reader in N. F. Blake, *The Saga of the Joms-vikings*, 1962, pp. xii–xv. There is no doubting the fictional nature of *Jóms-*

A tenuous tradition preserves remembrance of a Danish exploit in Sweden during Harald's reign. Styrbjorn Starki, nephew of the Swedish king Eirik Sigrsæll (the Victorious), and husband of Thyri, Harald's daughter, led an expedition in which vikings from Jomsborg-Wollin or Danes generally were involved, against his uncle and sought to deprive him of his kingdom. He advanced as far as Uppsala, where he was routed with heavy losses. He seems to have been badly let down by his Danish auxiliaries. Several runic stones from Skåne, the Danish part of Sweden, commemorate men who did not flee at Uppsala, but fought so long as they held weapon in hand, and may (or on the other hand may not)[1] refer to this disaster. Disaster to the Danes, that is, for it was from this encounter that king Eirik of Sweden earned his nickname, 'the Victorious'.

Harald's relations with the emperor Otto I, though less than whole-heartedly obedient, had all this while stayed peaceful. When the emperor returned from Italy to Germany in 972-3, Harald was one of a number of monarchs who did him homage at Quedlinburg. A few months later Otto was dead, and Harald wasted no time in testing the mettle of his successor Otto II by some raids on Holstein. This was a mistake. Otto drew together a big army, including Saxons, Franks, Frisians, even Wends, and advanced upon Hedeby and the ramparts of the Danevirke. Harald invoked his rights with jarl Hakon, who came swiftly south with his Norwegians and manned a portion of the walls. Norse poetry and saga record their unbreakable defence, but the contemporary German chroniclers seem not to have heard of it. What they record is that the emperor broke through the Danevirke, pursued his enemies far into Jutland, imposed his own terms of peace, and built a fortress to secure the 'mark' or march established almost fifty years earlier by Henry the Fowler. In addition we may conclude that it was under German pressure that king Harald now took steps to evangelize Norway. But the unnatural honeymoon between Denmark and Norway was already over, the heathen Hakon was back in the heathen Trondelag,

---

víkinga Saga, but Lauritz Weibull's denial that Jomsborg and the Jomsvikings ever existed (*Kritiska undersökningar*, pp. 178-95, *Historisk-kritisk metod*, pp. 79-88; see the reprints in *Nordisk Historia*, I, 349-58, 432-55) has not universally commended itself. But it has induced a proper caution and prudence. There are some good comments in Bjarni Aðalbjarnarson, *Heimskringla*, I, cxi-ii and 272 ff.

[1] L. Weibull, *Nordisk Historia*, I, pp. 293-300, 411-16, 436.

and in the west and north of Norway Christianity made no headway. Though no doubt there were converts in king Harald's lands in the south and east.

Almost a decade passed and Harald Bluetooth was growing blunt of fang. One more triumph lay ahead of him before he would be driven to his corner like some broken-toothed old dog. In the 980s the emperor Otto was involved on behalf of Christendom against the Saracens in Italy, and in 982 was severely defeated at Cap Colonne in Calabria. The opportunity was too good to miss. Maybe it was a Christian scruple which inhibited Harald from conducting the campaign in person, maybe his authority was now on the wane, but in 983 the Danes under Svein Forkbeard, his son, captured and destroyed Otto's fortress in Slesvig and drove the Germans south. Concurrently his father-in-law, king Mistivoj of Wendland, invaded Brandenburg, and then or later Holstein, and sent Hamburg up in flames. The Germans had no counter for Dane or Wend, and now, if not before, Harald had won all Denmark for himself. Within a year or two he had lost it, and sought refuge from his son, Svein, in Wendland. The likeliest explanation of this astonishing reversal is that he had by now alienated a significant proportion of the landowning aristocracy by his policies in respect of religion, land, and monarchical power. Church and monarchy were the immediate beneficiaries of their mutual alliance, and there must have been many men disfavourable to and adversely affected by Harald's insistence on Christianizing Denmark. Not all of these could find themselves a new life overseas. They must bide their time at home, till Harald's declining powers and the increasing stature of the warlike Svein offered them their opportunity of change. It is likely, too, that various great lords found their ancient rights in land threatened and in some cases diminished. As in Norway, a king must eat, and the bigger the king the bigger his appetite. Harald may also have been called upon to pay, undeservedly, for the long-continued German pressure upon Denmark, whose worst effects he seems, in fact, to have evaded by tact, gesture, and occasional concession. Patience under duress is rarely appreciated by the politically immature. It did not help that the Church in Denmark had been foisted on her from Germany and continued to look to Germany and serve German interests. Finally Harald had lost face in his dealings with Norway and jarl Hakon. Even so, his flight to Wendland surprises. According to Adam of Bremen and the

Encomium Emmae, he was wounded in battle against his son Svein, fled to the Slavs (Adam: *ad civitatem Sclavorum quae Iumne dicitur*), and died within a few days. His body was carried home to Denmark and buried in his church of Roskilde. The fictitious *Jómsvíkinga Saga* gives him a less credible and the erratic Saxo a more gruesome end.

Some time in the latter part of his reign Harald, a late tradition would have us believe, had made a last and famous effort to dash down his former confederate and present enemy jarl Hakon.[1] A naval expedition left the south presumably for Hladir, and the result was the battle of Hjorungavag. The attacking force consisted of Danes with some Wends, but late tradition as overwhelmingly as inaccurately attributed the exploit to Jomsborg vikings from Wendland. A fleet said to be of sixty ships reached or was assembled at the Limfjord, and from there sailed north to Horundarfjord in Norway, just south of the modern Ålesund. There, at Hjorungavag, they blundered into the prepared position of a far more powerful fleet commanded by Hakon, with the help of his son, the valiant Eirik. Whatever the fictions that soon engirt it, and they were many, the sea-fight that followed was a crushing defeat for the Danes, and jarl Hakon seems not to have been under serious threat from that quarter again.

[1] Just when is uncertain. Snorri, who devoted to this event one of the most elaborate set-pieces of his *Heimskringla*, ascribes it to the winter of 994–5, in the reign of king Svein, but this is probably too late. Saxo, not that he is over-reliable, places it in the reign of king Harald, and the historian P. A. Munch, *Det norske folks Historie*, Christiania, 1852–63, I : 2, 103–6, found reasons why we should accept this. But it is not possible to find a date less generalized than 974–83. As for the campaign itself, the flamboyant narrative of *Jómsvíkinga Saga* must be set aside, *Heimskringla* treated with distrust, and most reliance placed upon the skaldic verses incorporated in Snorri's narrative. Lauritz Weibull, *Nordisk Historia*, I, 349–58, 432–3, 450–5, allows neither the (to his mind fictional) Jomsborg and Jomsvikings, nor Harald Bluetooth, any share in the encounter, and it is true that the skaldic verses mention none of them, nor any other Danish king. In Weibull's opinion, expressed in uncompromising terms, Harald's connection with Hjorungavag was first put about by Saxo and P. A. Munch. It does, however, require a highly debatable textual emendation of *Vinða sinni*, 'band of Wends' (verse 141) to eliminate that people. Nor is *Eydönum*, 'Danes of the isles', acceptable for *eyðöndum*, 'destroyers, vikings' (verse 139). Hjorungavag was a fight between jarl Hakon and the Danes, who received some help from the Wends. Bjarni Aðalbjarnarson, *Heimskringla*, I, cix–xii, 278–86, offers his usual clear and unheated summary.

But it was not in Hakon's stars to die old and honoured, at peace with the gods and men. Yet the reasons for the decline in his popularity and authority offered by written sources are plainly inadequate. According to Snorri, a great change took place in him; like some cautionary figure in old legend, an Ermanaric or Heremod, he grew arrogant and careless of good name; the Trond farmers found him harsh and greedy, and the great men felt themselves under threat; he began to break the laws he should have maintained, and his appetite for women, by monkish reckoning always excessive, was now grown inordinate. Everywhere there was discontent at his various oppressions. Even the Tronds, loyal but never subservient, were muttering in each other's ear. Men's minds were turning from the jarl to the race of Harald Fairhair, from an ugly present to a golden past. 'And now things took an ill turn for the jarl, in that a great leader arrived in the land just as the farmers fell out with him.'

This was the most spectacular viking of the age, Harald's great-grandson, Olaf Tryggvason. He was the son of that Tryggvi Olafsson, king over part of the Oslofjord in Hakon the Good's day, who had been tricked and killed by the sons of Eirik shortly before Olaf was born. His mother Astrid, like some fair, distressed heroine of folktale, escaped the massacre and fled to a small island in a lake where she gave birth to her son, traditionally in the year 968–9.[1] None desired her death more ardently than that wicked ogress of folktale, Gunnhild Mother of Kings, but with her infant son, her foster-father Thorolf Lousebeard, and a couple of her women, she found various hiding-places in eastern Norway and Sweden till the boy was three years old. Her brother Sigurd was a man of rank at the court of Valdimar 'king of Holmgard', i.e. that Valdimar (Vladimir) who achieved power at Novgorod in 972 and in 980 became Grand Duke (Great Prince) of Kiev and of all Russia. The hard-pressed band of fugitives set off to find him, but as they sailed east across the Baltic were captured by pirates from Esthonia, and sold into slavery. Astrid's (and Olaf's) foster-father they killed because he looked too old for work. Six years later Sigurd, in Esthonia on his royal master's business, saw this handsome young foreigner in a market-place, inquired who he was, ransomed him, and took him back to Holm-

[1] *Agrip* tells us that Olaf was 3 years old when his father was killed. That he was named Olaf after his grandfather suggests that his father was still alive at the time of his birth.

gard, Novgorod. Here he had the good fortune one day to recognize the man who had killed his foster-father, and promptly sank his hand-axe into the slaver's brain, a deed which secured him the brief displeasure of a populace inclined to fair trade and the lasting regard of a queen inclined to fair men. Soon she and Sigurd brought him into the king's good books; he throve in all manly accomplishments, and was prominent in the king's battles. When he was 18 he began his viking career with a cruise in the Baltic. First he attacked the island of Bornholm and was then storm-driven to Wendland, where he engaged the favourable attention of another noble lady, Geira daughter of king Boleslav (Miesco?), who married him. Three years later she died of a sickness, and Olaf went back to viking. So far, clearly, Olaf's story owes almost everything to the patterns of legend and his biographers' notions of the kind of youth they would wish so gallant and colourful a man to have had, but that he grew to manhood in Russia, was early a Baltic viking, and visited Wendland, is all likely to be right. More certainly, he was fighting in the British Isles in the early 990s, possibly at Maldon in 991, assuredly as an ally or follower of the Danish king Svein Forkbeard in 994. According to Snorri his raids were as widespread as Northumbria, Scotland, the Hebrides, Man, Ireland, Wales, and Cumberland, with France (Valland) thrown in for good measure. We lack the details, but in his early twenties Olaf was already a leader of rank and reputation, and his men shared in some huge Danegelds. Shortly before 995 he adopted the Christian religion. A hard-worked legend informs us that he was converted by a wise hermit in the Scillies; the *Anglo-Saxon Chronicle*, more credibly, reports that he received baptism shortly after the unsuccessful attack on London in 994 and the subsequent Danegeld of 16,000 pounds of silver. 'Then the king sent bishop Ælfeah and ealdorman Æthelweard to fetch king Anlaf [Olaf], and hostages were sent meanwhile to the ships. They conducted king Anlaf with great ceremony to the king at Andover, and the king stood sponsor for him at confirmation, and gave him royal gifts; whereupon Anlaf gave him his word, and kept it to boot, that he would never come to England as an enemy again.'

This was the moment which the triumphant viking chose for his return to Norway. He was rich, successful, and popular, fortified with a twofold sense of mission: to recover the kingdom of his forebears and convert it to Christianity. Also he had intelligence of Hakon's weakening position at home, and that catastrophic decline in his prestige among the Tronds which with all his named faults, and his bad press from Christian sagamen, we still find it hard to account for. Yet the explanation may be a simple one, and in accord with the central facts of Norwegian tenth-century history. The long rivalry between the northern jarls and the Ynglings, and the constantly assertive power of the Vestland and the Vik, are likelier reasons for Hakon's overthrow than lechery and lawlessness. We are almost completely in the dark regarding the political permutations of his later years, but one thing seems clear—he received no help from anywhere against Olaf's bid for power. With a strong fleet, which gave him the power to strike when and where he liked, and a following of war-hardened vikings, as well as a complement of English or English-trained priests, Olaf is said to have sailed for home by way of the Orkneys. He came to land at Moster, on one of the southern entrances to the Hardangerfjord, and from there moved north with speed. Either Hakon was by now in dishonoured flight, or (more likely) he was taken completely by surprise. Opposition was slight and quickly brushed aside, and the local landowners and farmers came to meet Olaf and offer him allegiance. Late sources record that Hakon and his thrall Kark had sought refuge in Gaulardal with his mistress Thora of Rimul, and there is an enduring tradition that during a night of horror the thrall cut his master's throat. Soon, at the Thing in Trondheim, Olaf was proclaimed king, as his great-grandfather Harald Fairhair had been. Later, the Uppland districts and the shires down in the Oslofjord, so long under the overlordship of the king of Denmark, are said to have recognized his sovereignty.

But there was to be no golden age. For all the panegyrics of his thirteenth-century admirers, the reign of Olaf Tryggvason was short and filled with stresses. We are freely informed as to his handsome person, gallant spirit, physical strength, and bodily feats; his labours for Norway and achievements for the Faith are generously expounded; and the events of his life, from his folktale birth to his legendary death, have been brilliantly recorded. It is the greater shock, then, to consider how little we really know about him. For good and bad, he was the stuff legends are made of—and legends can be heedless of truth.[1]

Even in the matter of his Christianity there is a head-on clash

[1] For an extended treatment of this theme see my 'The Legendary History of Olaf Tryggvason', the W. P. Ker lecture for 1967–8, University of Glasgow.

between Adam of Bremen writing *c.* 1080 and the Icelandic historians who wrote a hundred and fifty years later. Adam, more than normally atrabilious when writing about Olaf, says, 'Some relate that Olaf had been a Christian, some that he had forsaken Christianity; all, however, affirm that he was skilled in divination, was an observer of the lots, and had placed all his hope in the prognostication of birds. Wherefore, also, did he receive a byname, so that he was called Craccaben (Crowbone). In fact, as they say, he was also given to the practice of the magic art and supported as his household companions all the magicians with whom that land was overrun, and, deceived by their error, perished' (II, xl (38)). Norwegian and Icelandic sources say the exact opposite, and are likely to be right. We need not assume that Olaf had much awareness of the doctrinal aspects of the Christian faith, and on the most favourable witness he appears little touched by its spiritual values. But like Hakon the Good and the sons of Eirik Bloodaxe in Norway, and Harald Bluetooth and Svein Forkbeard in Denmark, he was alive to the advantages of being part of the Christian community of Europe; and like other travelled vikings he had observed at first hand the dignity, wealth, and ceremonial of the Church in other countries. Here was a splendour, an enrichment and fellowship, from which the northern barbarian stood excluded. To stand by Thor and Odinn in these late days was to be a dog howling in the wilderness. To bring the Norwegians to Christ would be followed by realizable benefits to Norway and Norway's king, and in particular it put a weapon in his hand against the less accessible and more unruly parts of the kingdom.

He could expect to meet with most success down in the Vik, where Harald Bluetooth had already done spadework for the faith. In the western provinces, the ancient lairs of vikings from Rogaland to the Firthafylki, men were aware of Christianity from their raids on Christian countries and the proselytizing of Harald Greycloak; but in the Trondelag heathendom was stubborn, even rampant, and farther to the north in Halogaland it was as yet undisturbed. It is probable that Icelandic historians, having accepted the doubtful tradition that their own country's conversion was brought about by Olaf Tryggvason, transferred to him some of the zeal and achievement of the other Olaf, Haraldsson, king and saint. Thus they report that the south and south-west both felt his heavy hand, and that in Trondheim he broke up the altars and knocked down the idols. At much the same time he established a small market-town near the mouth of the river Nid, for he did not fancy Hladir, with its odour of jarls and stench of graven images. Over the years this would grow into the royal town of Nidaros, and at length be renamed Trondheim. Also he strove mightily with the heathen of Halogaland. And as though this was not enough, we read of him drawing traders, voyagers, visiting poets, willy-nilly into the ranks of Christ's army, then packing them off home to spread the glad tidings. In the course of time he was given credit for Christianizing Norway (which is an exaggeration), the Shetlands and Faroes (about which little is known), Iceland (which is overgenerous), and Greenland (which is wrong). He stands before posterity as one who in his day and place was Christ's best hatchet-man, and the Icelandic retailers of his life approved the role.

By the year 1000 his position could hardly be worse. He was first and foremost a sea-king, and it was the coastal provinces of the west and south-west which engaged his attention. The inland regions saw little of him, and the leading men there, many of them self-styled kings, still peddled their local ambitions. But the intimidated west had no love for him either, and a veneer of Christianity did nothing to bind ruler and ruled in common purpose. The situation was worst in the Trondelag. To make the Tronds Christian and obedient he had to live among them, and the longer he did so the less they liked it. In five short years this splendidly dowered leader of men, whose reign in its beginning seemed the answer to Norway's needs, lacked real support throughout his kingdom. In valour a lion, in wit and resource he was now as a squirrel on the ground.

Meantime his enemies had been busy. These were his former comrade-in-arms, Svein Forkbeard of Denmark, covetous not only of his lost provinces in the Oslofjord but of all Norway; Olaf Skötkonung, the first Swedish king named as overlord of the Gauts, and greedy to develop realm and trade in a westward direction; and the dispossessed son of jarl Hakon, the clever and valiant jarl Eirik. The development of this menacing confederacy forced Olaf of Norway to act when his power of manoeuvre had become small. He had to find allies.

About king Svein of Denmark we would be willing to know more than we do. He was, we are told, foremost in destroying Olaf Tryggvason, but that is a context in which we may well be confronting one Iceland-fostered legend with another; and he conquered

England and was accepted as 'full king' there. But at home he appears something of a northern Laocoon entwined by unfriendly *exempla*. Thietmar of Merseburg describes him as *rex tyrannus*; Adam of Bremen, unctuously but with venom, presents him as the central figure in an Old Testament tale of sin, punishment, penitence, redemption; the *Chronicle of Roskilde* supplies him with a forked beard and quotes from Adam; Sven Aggeson polemicizes against the *Chronicle*, but is heedless as to sources; *Jómsvíkinga Saga* is as baseless and furious as ever; and Saxo attempts the grand consummation of all these, with Svein illustrating the ancient theme of *mutatio morum aut fortunae*. The *Gesta Cnutonis* (*c.* 1040), while admirably filled with admiration, is unadmirably short on fact.[1] We hear of his being kidnapped by Jomsborg vikings, driven from his kingdom by Eirik (Hericus) the Victorious of Sweden, skulking in exile in England and Scotland, and marrying the non-existent Sigrid the Haughty,[2] and can believe none of it. What we can believe is that he was a man of outstanding quality, and that unlike Olaf Tryggvason he was tolerant and sensible. He fostered Christianity, to which he was personally not much drawn, in a pragmatic and effective way; achieved the conquest of England by the classic procedure of making fewer and less important mistakes than his enemy; and finally, again unlike Olaf Tryggvason, left a son greater than himself to continue his policies.

The ruling families of Scandinavia had many close relationships. Olaf Skötkonung of Sweden was Svein's stepson; Olaf Tryggvason of Norway was his brother-in-law. Svein's sister Thyri had first been married to Styrbjorn Starki, the unsuccessful invader of Sweden, and after his death was bestowed on Boleslav (Burizleif) the Pole, king of Wendland, whom she detested, first because he was a heathen and second because he was old. In her distress she fled to Norway and married Olaf Tryggvason, who was neither. Two other

[1] All the above is in Inge Skovgaard-Petersen, 'Sven Tveskæg i den ældste danske historiografi', in *Middelalderstudie tilegnede Aksel E. Christensen*, Copenhagen, 1966, pp. 1–38.
[2] It was this same non-existent lady whose face the consort-seeking Olaf Tryggvason had once slapped, on the curious afterthought, 'And why should I want to marry you, you heathen bitch?' It is noticeable that Snorri Sturluson, who in life had an understandable liking for women who were pliant, in *Heimskringla* portrayed many who were masterful: Gunnhild Mother of Kings, Thyri the wife of Olaf Tryggvason, Astrid his mother, Sigrid the wife of Kalf Arnarson, and Sigrid the Haughty among them.

marriages deserve mention, the first that of Olaf Tryggvason's sister to Rognvald earl of Västergötland, a natural enemy of the king of Sweden, who was thus pushed further in king Svein's direction; and second the marriage of Svein's daughter Gyda to his ally jarl Eirik, the exiled son of jarl Hakon of Norway. The pieces were now on the board, the players confronting each other, and it was the king of Norway's move.

We are surer of its direction than its purpose. In *Óláfs Saga Tryggvasonar* we read that in the summer of the year 1000 Olaf set sail from Nidaros down the west coast of Norway, collecting strength on the way, so that he left Norway with a fleet of sixty warships, including the *Crane*, the *Short Serpent*, and the *Long Serpent*, this last the most powerful ship in northern waters. With an attendant train of auxiliaries this brilliant armada crossed the Kattegat, then entered the Øresund, passed the island of Hven, and with the low green shores of Zealand and Skåne temptingly in view held south for the opening Baltic, and came by way of Rügen to the mouth of the Oder. According to Snorri, his business was with Boleslav the Pole, the father of his first wife Geira and brief husband of his present wife Thyri. It was at Thyri's instigation he had come there at all, to recover the property she had left with Boleslav when she fled his unwelcome embraces. It was a friendly meeting, and Boleslav paid over the property in full. But it is likely that Olaf and Thyri had more in mind than this. Olaf needed an ally more than Thyri a dowry. Thietmar of Merseburg speaks of enmity between Boleslav and Svein, while the Baltic vikings were always potential allies for a man who could pay. By Snorri's account the Danes of Jomsborg-Wollin would betray the returning Olaf and a mere handful of his ships into an ambush laid by the kings of Denmark and Sweden and jarl Eirik by the island of Svold off Rügen. But Adam of Bremen, writing within seventy-five years of the battle, sees it differently. According to him Olaf Tryggvason (whose memory he detested for his adherence to the half-hatched clergy of England rather than to the pure elect of Hamburg-Bremen) learned at home that the kings of Denmark and Sweden were in league against him; his ever-ready anger was whetted by his wife Thyri, so that he assembled a fleet wherewith to chastise the Danes, and sailed south into the Øresund, where the sound is so narrow 'that Zealand is in sight from Skåne'. In this favourite resort of pirates the Norwegians were heavily defeated, and king Olaf, unable to get away, plunged into the sea 'and met the death his life deserved'. The battle took place not far from the modern Hälsingborg. However, the skaldic verse which celebrates the event helps convince us that the sea-fight occurred when Olaf was returning home to Norway from somewhere in the south (presumably Wendland). An attractive reconstruction, still leaving much unexplained, is that Olaf tried to counter the Danish-Swedish-jarl Eirik confederacy by an alliance with a natural enemy of the Danes, Boleslav the Pole, ruler of Wendland; that the Norwegian ship-levy, or perhaps his disaffected ships' captains, did not obey his summons to muster; and that he sailed for his rendezvous with Boleslav with a mere eleven ships. What followed conformed to the hard rule of viking politics: a sea-king without sea-power was doomed. Boleslav's fleet numbered sixty ships, and the viking jarl Sigvaldi may have been its commander. Either it was this joint fleet of seventy-one ships which was defeated by the confederates, or Sigvaldi treacherously or in prudence avoided battle, pulled out his ships (he was reputed to have done much the same thing at Hjorungavag), and left Olaf to his fate. But the treachery of Sigvaldi may well be an embroidery on the story. In any case the result was the same: after a heroic resistance against odds Olaf lost his life and kingdom. Where the fight took place is uncertain; there are good arguments for 'by an island' in the Øresund, either Hven or in the old Armager complex off (the later) Copenhagen, and for an unidentified island of Svold off Rügen. Earlier tradition favours the Øresund, later tradition Rügen.[1]

For Snorri Sturluson, never servile to fact, the glory of the day, in victory and defeat, lay with Norway.[2] Danes and Swedes are but

---

[1] Lauritz Weibull's searching study of these problems in his *Kritiska undersökningar* and *Historisk-kritisk metod* is conveniently assembled in *Nordisk Historia*, pp. 313-30 and 440-8.

[2] The details of the battle, as they are recounted in Snorri's brilliantly compulsive narrative, are entirely or in large measure fictitious. For whereas Adam of Bremen was concerned to denigrate Olaf, Snorri's aim was to glorify him, to which end he employed what suited him in Scandinavian tradition, the lore of other lands, and his own powers of literary composition. Thus, the long-sustained crescendo of interest and suspense as the two kings and jarl Eirik stand on the island and watch ship after ship come into sight, and the kings think each one the *Long Serpent* till jarl Eirik identifies it differently, was taken immediately from Odd Snorrason and ultimately from the late ninth-century *De Gestis Karoli Magni* of the Monk of St. Gall, who tells how Desiderius king of the Langobards stood with Otkar on a high tower in

18. AFTER SVOLD

the instruments of her fame. Adam, we recall, bestowed all the laurels upon the Danes. Still, the upshot was the same. The hard-pressed king, in his scarlet cloak, leapt overboard and was never seen again. He was a wondrous swimmer, and in time there would be tales that he had drawn off his mail-shirt under water and been rescued by a Wendish ship and carried safe to land. Many men were held to have encountered him in numerous countries, the Holy Land among them, but 'Be that as it may,' concluded Snorri, in a sentence which has so far eluded the correction of the severest critics of his veracity, 'king Olaf never again returned to his kingdom in Norway'.

Pavia watching the approach of Charlemagne's army, thought each new-comer the emperor, and was rhetorically corrected by Otkar. Likewise, Olaf resorts to epic and saga formula to establish the identity of his adversaries, the cowardly Danes in the centre, the bowl-licking heathen Swedes on their right, and the valiant Norwegians under jarl Eirik in the big ships to port. Even the last unforgettable stroke of dialogue between the desperate Olaf and his archer Einar Thambarskelfir ('What broke there so loudly?': 'Norway, from your hand, king!') belongs not to history, but with similar saga laconicisms and famous last words to heroic convention. And, alas, Einar's late-acquired nickname has nothing to do with *þömb*, a bowstring; it refers to his pendulous and quaggy belly.

Not even this was the whole truth. For he *would* return. Future generations would see in him an incarnation of the Norwegian ideal. But this was policy, and yet to come. The immediate consequences of Svold were a renewal of the Danish overlordship in Norway and Svein's direct acquisition of the Vik; the award to Olaf Skötkonung of Sweden of territory in the south-east and in the eastern provinces of Trondheim, part of which he delegated to jarl Eirik's brother Svein; and the bestowal upon jarl Eirik of all the western coastal districts. It looked like the familiar pattern of territorial disintegration, and the reassertion of regional interests, and would persist till 1015, when a new Olaf would arrive in Norway from England, and by virtue of his fifteen-year reign, his death, and sanctification, refurbish the notion of a separate Norwegian kingdom.

III. THE VIKING
MOVEMENT OVERSEAS

1. The Scandinavian Community, II: Aspects of Society

IN AN EARLIER CHAPTER UNDER THIS SAME TITLE WE examined the notion that for all their differences of circumstance and habitat, their wars, dissensions and rivalries, the Danes, Swedes, and Norwegians were a meaningful community of peoples. With the political and dynastic history of the Scandinavian homelands c. 750–1000 recounted, and the military, economic, and colonial history of the vikings overseas to be told, this seems the place to consider certain aspects of Scandinavian life and society which help correct what otherwise can be too violent or romantic a view of the viking north.

Viking society conformed to the Indo-European pattern. It was a class society, carefully organized as such, and the number of classes was three. There were the unfree, the free, and their rulers. A tenth-century poem,[1] *Rígsþula*, the Song of Rig, provides us with a stylized and memorable account of the origin of these three divinely ordained classes. In the poem's prose introduction Rig (*Rígr*, Irish *rí*, king, gen. *ríg*) is identified with the god Heimdall, the father of all mankind. One day (and for the story that follows the poet invokes ancient tradition) this traveller-god came to a poorish habitation where dwelt an ancient couple Ai and Edda, Great-Grandfather and Great-Grandmother. He entered and introduced himself as Rig. They fed him on coarse, husky bread, and for three nights he lay down in bed between them. Then he departed. Nine months later Edda bore a son whose description we have already noted (see p. 67 above): black-skinned and ugly, with lumpy knuckles and thick fingers, his back gnarled and his heels long. They called him Thrall (*þræll*), and in time he mated with the bandy-

---

[1] This dating is not universally agreed.

legged, sunburnt Slavey (*þír*) and begat on her litters of children, among them the boys Noisy, Byreboy, Roughneck, Horsefly, and the girls Lazybones, Beanpole, Fatty, and their like. Between them Thrall, Slavey, and their brood do the dirty work, carry loads, lug firewood, dung fields, feed pigs, cut peat, and from them are descended the race and varieties of thralls.

Meantime Rig had gone his ways and reached a second, more commodious home, where dwelt another couple, Afi and Amma, Grandfather and Grandmother. The man was making a loom, the woman spinning and weaving. Rig gave them good advice, and for three nights lay down in bed between them. Then he departed. Nine months later Amma bore a son, ruddy, fresh-faced, and with sparkling eyes. They called him Freeman or Peasant (*Karl*) and in time he married Daughter-in-law (*Snör*), and by her had many children, among them the boys Strongbeard, Husbandman, Holder, and Smith, and the girls Prettyface, Maiden, Capable, and their like. Karl's work was to tame oxen, build houses, barns and wagons, make and handle the plough; his wife managed the household, carried keys, and held the purse-strings; it was she who provided meals and clothes for her family. From them are descended the race and varieties of free men.

Once more Rig had gone his ways, this time to reach a splendid hall where dwelt a third couple, Father and Mother (*Faðir* and *Móðir*). The master was twisting a bowstring, bending his bow, fashioning arrows; the mistress, gaily attired, blonde and lovely, gave thought to her arms, smoothed her kirtle, pleated her sleeves. Rig gave them good advice, and soon Mother spread the table with a cloth of bright linen, white wheaten bread, pork and game, a wine-jug and drinking bowls of silver. They drank and talked together till the day ended. Three nights he lay down in bed between them. Then he departed. Nine months later Mother bore a son, fair-haired, bright of cheek, his eye piercing as a snake's. They called him Earl or Warrior (*Jarl*), and he grew up to use bow and arrow, shield and spear, to hunt with horse and ride with hound, practise swordsmanship and swimming. In course of time Rig returned to greet this special son of his, gave him his own name, taught him the magic art of runes, urged him to take possession of his hereditary estates. So Jarl went out into the world and stirred up war: he rode furiously, slew foes, reddened pastures, brought woe to earth. He came to own eighteen dwellings, and in true lord's fashion dealt out treasure to his friends and followers. He married a lady as well-born as himself, Lively (*Erna*), daughter of Lord (*Hersir*), fair and wise, slim-fingered, and by her had twelve sons, skilled and valiant, and no doubt daughters, too. Most notable of the sons was Kon the Young (*Konr Ungr, konungr*, King);[1] they grew up to tame horses, wield weapons, but in addition Kon the Young, Royal Scion, so mastered runes that with their aid he could save life, blunt sword, quell fire, soothe sea, and excel Rig himself in the mysteries. He had the strength and energy of eight men, knew the language of birds, hunted and slew them in the copses, till one day a crow said to him: 'Young Kon, why should you silence birds? Better for you to bestride steed, draw sword, fell a host. Danr and Danpr have finer halls and better lands than you. You should go viking, let them feel your blade, deal wounds. . . .' On which bloodthirsty advice both crow and poem (*Ormsbók*, AM 242 fol) fall silent for evermore.

The social order thus picturesquely presented by a well-born and socially secure poet is the one we observe, with minor local variation, in all the viking countries throughout the Viking Age. In the petty kingdoms of Norway before Halfdan the Black's day; in the confusion of realms in Denmark till the time of Godfred, and maybe of Gorm; and in Sweden by way of the Vendel monarchs down to Ivar Wide-Grasper and Bjorn, Olaf, Eirik, and Bjorn again, who held considerable but undefined sway in the ninth century, there was a ruling caste, a community of free men, and a substratum of thralls or slaves. Such was the situation in the more unified kingdoms of Harald Fairhair, Hakon the Good and Olaf Tryggvason in Norway, Harald Bluetooth and Svein Forkbeard in Denmark, and Eirik Sigrsæll and Olaf Sköttkonung in Sweden; and there would be no essential change in the days of Harald Hardradi (Norway), Svein Estridsson (Denmark), Onund Jacob and his brother Emund (Sweden), with whose reigns the Viking Age concluded. In Iceland and Greenland there was one significant difference: they were free there of the authority of 'kings and criminals' from abroad; but in every other essential they, too, had a ruling caste, free farmers, and slaves.

At the bottom of the social order crouched the thrall. Because

---

[1] The etymology is popular, not scientific. *Konungr* is properly a patronymic, of common Germanic ancestry, with the meaning 'scion of a (noble) kin', or 'scion of a man of (noble) birth'.

the laws of the Scandinavian peoples were unrecorded till after the
end of the Viking Age we know less about the slave's life and status
than we could wish, but a long succession of English laws and a
considerable number of references to thralls in Icelandic literature
provide us with information which if cautiously interpreted will
serve for homeland Scandinavia, too. The thrall might be an undis-
charged debtor or a man otherwise condemned to death; he might
be the son (or a woman slave the daughter) of slaves, as much his
master's property as the calf from his master's cow or the colt from
his mare; but the great recruiting grounds for slaves were war,
piracy, and trade. They came in great numbers from the British
Isles, either caught in the dragnet of the viking raids and invasions
or as straightforward objects of commerce; they came from all
other countries where viking power reached; and above all they
came from slave-hunts among the Slavonic peoples whose countries
bordered on the Baltic. The very name Slav (*Sclavus*) became confused with the medieval Latin *sclavus*, a slave. Droves of human cattle
came to the pens of Magdeburg, ready for their transfer west; there
was a big clearing-house later at Regensburg on the Danube; and
Hedeby in southern Jutland was well sited for its share of this
northern traffic in men. Southwards the burghers of Lyons grew fat
on slaves. The demand from Spain and the remoter Muslim world
was insatiable: men and girls for labour and lust, eunuchs for sad
service. By 850 the Swedes had opened up the Volga and Dnieper
as slave-routes to the eastern market. And just as the slave-trade was
essential to viking commerce, the slave himself was the foundation-
stone of viking life at home. The Frostathing Law thought three
thralls the proper complement for a Norwegian farm of twelve cows
and two horses; a lord's estate might well require thirty or more.
In the eyes of the law-makers a thrall counted as a superior kind of
cow or horse. He commanded no wergeld, but in England if you
killed him you had normally to pay his owner the worth of eight
cows; in Iceland you paid eight ounces of silver (one and a half
marks), and if this was paid within three days his master took no
further action. He could be bought and sold like any other chattel.
Hoskuld Dala-Kolsson of Laxardal in Iceland is said to have paid
three marks of silver, thrice the price of a common concubine, for
the Irish girl he purchased from a trader in a Russian hat in the
Brenneyjar (*Laxdæla Saga*, 12). She was one of twelve on sale in the
slaver's booth. In theory, and sometimes in practice, the thrall

could be put down like a horse or a dog once his usefulness was past. The male, and still more frequently the female, thrall could be sacrificed or executed to follow a dead owner, as we know from the most famous of all Norwegian graves, that at Oseberg, where a slave woman was buried with her mistress, from Birka in Sweden and Ballateare on Man,[1] from the 'beheaded slave's grave' at Lejre in Zealand, and as we read in Ibn Fadlan's account of a Rus burial ceremony on the Volga (see pp. 425–30 below). Rights he had none. Since he had no property he was exempt from fines; instead he was beaten, maimed, or killed. The mutineer or runaway could expect no quarter: the owning class would as soon tolerate a wolf on the foldwall as a slave on the run, and his end was a wolf's end, quick and bloody. For the slave born and bred life was hard. For a freeborn warrior taken in the wars, or a well-nurtured girl ravished from her burned home, it could be hell itself, and Icelandic sources record many a doom-laden attempt to wrest an impossible release from unbearable circumstance.

And yet the northern thrall was better off than his fellow in mediterranean and eastern lands. Where a master was bad or a thrall irreconcilable little could be hoped for; but there is evidence to suggest that most masters were reasonable and most thralls prepared to make the best of their lot. The ill-treatment of thralls was at least as bad a mark as the neglect of stock, and in so far as he was a member of a household the thrall could expect to benefit from the kindlier impulses of humanity. As the Viking Age wore on, and under the influence of Christianity, an increasing disquietude was felt about the ownership and sale of men. It operated most strongly on behalf of those of one's own nationality, and then those of one's own religion, but was a leaven in the whole situation. Sometimes we see economic pressures working on his behalf, as in the Icelandic *hreppar*. The slave, in fact, was not left devoid of means, possessions, and free time during which he could do work for himself. He had his peculium, and in favourable circumstances might hope to purchase, earn, or be rewarded with his freedom. Also, he was allowed to marry, though his children would be slaves.

[1] H. Shetelig, 'Traces of the custom of Suttee in Norway during the Viking Age', in *Saga-Book*, VI, 1910, pp. 180–208; H. Arbman, *Birka, Sveriges äldsta handelsstad*, Stockholm, 1939, pp. 77 and 87; G. Bersu and D. M. Wilson, *Three Viking Graves in the Isle of Man*, Society for Medieval Archaeology, Monograph Series, I, 1966, pp. 51 and 90–1.

Throughout our period the *freedman* (*leysingi, libertus*) was not a *freeman*. He was only half free, still dependent for a number of generations upon that former owner who was now his protector, and against whom he was not permitted to institute legal proceedings. There was much commonsense in this. The freedman had his human value, but this would protect him only as long as he had someone to champion it, and inevitably a great many freedmen had no free kinsman to do so. So he needed a patron or lawful master, and custom and law allowed for this. In a social sense the freedman had not quite arrived.

The overriding thing was to be free. The free peasant, peasant-proprietor, smallholder, farmer, call him what we will, was the realm's backbone. This class of free men was extensive; it ranged from impoverished and humble peasants at one extreme to men of wealth and authority (especially local authority) at the other; but what they had in common were legal and political rights, a wergeld, and land. As to this last there was much variation. Ideally a man had a farm, even a cot, of his own; in practice young men must often live with their parents, or farm land at the hand of a big proprietor. Even so their status was clear, and these were the men who tilled land and raised stock, bore witness and produced verdicts, said aye or no on matters of public concern at the Thing (including matters as important as the election or approval of a king or a change of religion), attended religious and lay ceremonies, worked in wood and metal, made and wore weapons, manned ships, served in levies, were conscious of their dues and worth, and so impressed these upon others that as a free peasantry they stood in a class of their own for Europe. Were so superior, for example, to their English counterpart that king Alfred's treaty with the Norse king Guthrum (Guthorm), *c.* 886, set the wergeld of a rent-paying English peasant and that of a Danish freedman at the same figure of two hundred shillings. The free Danish peasant of whatsoever kind was equated with the English peasant farming his own land, and his wergeld set with that of Danish and English noblemen at the high figure of eight half-marks of pure gold.[1]

Above the free men was the ruling caste, the aristocracy, most of it king-allied or god-descended. Here belonged the families with wealth, land, and rank. At different times during the Viking Age,

[1] The significance of, and reasons for, these equations have been much argued, but the higher standard accorded to the free Danish peasant is undoubted.

and in different parts of Scandinavia, we observe some of these families partly or fully independent of other authority, so that they enjoyed the rank of king or jarl over a defined territory. But we should not conclude that because the aristocracy existed by virtue of rank and descent and the recognition of degree it felt any automatic respect for a supreme monarch. Ideally a king to whom all the nation owed allegiance would head the hierarchy. But during most of the Viking Age Scandinavia presents us with a picture of too few supreme monarchs. In the case of Sweden we are ill-informed, but till at least the early tenth century we read that Danish Jutland bore its crop of kinglings, while in Norway the situation was worse. True, by the time Harald Fairhair felt the pressures of old age a great many petty kings had been tumbled out of their kingdoms, but he re-created almost as many in the persons of his sons. As late as the reign of Olaf the Stout, renamed the Saint, there were plenty calling themselves kings in none too remote stretches of the country, and it was not to be expected that a king in Heidmark or Raumarike, knowing himself to be lordly and of the seed of Frey, would readily give allegiance to a brother Yngling who planned to destroy his high-seat and his altars. Pride, piety, and self-interest bore weightily against it. The power of a Norwegian king had always been circumscribed, and not only by the exertions of those of his fellow countrymen with a claim to the same title. He depended heavily on the loyalty of the leaders of provinces, the farmer republics, and the jarls, the greatest of whom ruled the Trondelag, and at times, like jarl Hakon and jarl Eirik, held authority over most of the provinces of Norway which were not controlled by Danes or Swedes. He depended, too, on the approval of his free subjects. His very election depended upon their favourable voice at those public assemblies where he first presented himself to them. He had to carry them with him on all important decisions. We have already noted Hakon the Good's deferment to his subjects' preference for the old religion (see page 119 above), and reversals as spectacular are reported from Sweden. Snorri Sturluson is guilty of an anachronism when he portrays the victory of the Swedish farmers and Thorgny the Lawspeaker over king Olaf Eiriksson at the Uppsala Thing, *c.* 1020, but there is no doubting the limitation of royal power by the suffrage of the supra-regional Things. The king of the Swedes must make a progress (the so-called *Eiriksgata*) through his dominions and present himself for popular acclaim at all the Things. 'The Swedes,'

says the ancient West Gautish law, 'have the right to elect and likewise reject a king. . . The Thing of all the Götar must receive him
formally. When he comes to the Thing he must swear to be faithful
to all the Götar, and he shall not break the true laws of our land.'[1]
During the eleventh century the northern kingdoms grew stronger
and more integrated, which meant that the power of the aristocracy
vis-à-vis the king was diminished. In Norway particularly the status
of the old-style turbulent and self-seeking viking aristocracy
declined, and in large measure its place was usurped by landowners
emergent from and representing the élite of the bondi class. It is
therefore possible that the smaller farmer, too, was strengthened in
relation to the aristocracy. Certainly they helped change the
character of the Scandinavian kingdoms after 1035, and helped
bring the Viking Age to a close.

In what, then, did the king's prestige consist in these northern
lands, apart from his divine ancestry, his connection with shrine,
sacrifice, and sanctuary, and those personal qualities which command respect and obedience? Most of all it consisted in sea-power
and the ability to employ this for conquest and profit. Command of
the sea-lanes ensured exaction and tribute, and these in their turn
bought loyalty and service, without which a northern king immediately stood helpless, as the reigns and disasters of the Norwegian kings from Eirik Bloodaxe to St. Olaf confirm. Such startling
vicissitudes as the Swedish presence at Hedeby c. 900–35, the ups
and downs of Svein Forkbeard's early career, the overthrow of Olaf
Tryggvason, and the success of Magnus the Good in respect of
Denmark are all evidence of the striking power attendant on control
of the seas. A king's prestige consisted, too, in his wealth and
territory, for he could hardly be other than one of the greatest
landowners in a kingdom, and much of the profit of a successful war
went into his personal chest. With no capital city or town he moved
from one estate to another, he and his following more or less eating
their way through the countryside, sometimes receiving hospitality
from subjects great and small, but for the most part providing his
own sustenance in his own farms. With him travelled his *hirð* or
bodyguard, composed of hirdmen or retainers who had knelt and
set their right hands to his sword-hilt, so pledging him loyalty, if
need be to the death. In war these were the core of his army, in
peace the executants of his authority, and without them he was

[1] *Corpus Juris Sueogotorum Antiqui*, ed. C. J. Schlyter, Stockholm, 1834, I, 36.

nothing. Most would be men of his own country, drawn from the length and breadth of the land by report of a king's valour, good faith, and generosity; but some would be professional fighters plying their trade where the rewards looked best, Danes loyal to an English king, Norwegians and Swedes in Knut's Thingmannalíð. The hirdmen were the king's elect—or it might be better to say their lord's elect, for any great man with wealth, power, and fame could maintain a retinue, though here as elsewhere a king would seek pre-eminence. From them most was demanded, to them most was given. Swords, helmets and battle-harness flowed from the king, arm-rings and torques; he clothed their bodies with tunics of silk and cloaks of squirrelskin and sable, and their bellies he filled with choice foods and mead from the horn. For those who earned them there were axes inlaid with silver, and for those who wanted them women. And friendship with their own kind, and music and merriment in hall, with minstrels, jugglers, collared dogs, and skalds whose wrists were gold-haltered. And when the need arose, friendly embassies and punitive forays, the exaction of scat and recovery of dues, service at home and overseas, war and wounds, hard deeds and sometimes death. 'Sweet is mead—Bitter when paid for!' These were the two sides of the medal, service and reward, and kings throve best when both were unstinted.[1]

The royal revenues derived in large measure from the royal estates. It is uncertain what, if any, dues connected with religion and its practices might come the king's way, as is reported of Uppsala in respect of the king of the Swedes; but in any case his outgoing expenses would not be light either. He received a share of the confiscated property of outlaws and felons, and while the kingdoms were in the making the conquest of a neighbour or rival implied sequestration. He could make limited demands on his subjects for national works and instruments of defence; when his kingdom was at war he took command of its fighting forces. The

[1] These generalizations may seem to do less than justice to Hans Kuhn's researches on the *hirð* in 'Die Grenzen der germanischen Gefolgschaft', *Zeitschrift der Savigny-Stiftung für Rechtsgeschichte, Germanische Abteilung,* LXXIII, 1956, pp. 1–83. Kuhn's thesis is that there was a decisive break of some three and a half centuries between the abandoned *comitatus* of early Germanic times and the revived *hirð* of the late Viking Age. The new-style *hirð* should in that case be considered a product of Anglo-Danish civilization, welcomed and adopted at home in Scandinavia. I owe the reference to L. Musset, *Les Invasions: le second assaut*, pp. 251–2.

royal prerogative connected with the patronage of merchants and the safe conduct of goods, the very circumstance that trade could not take place except under a helm of power, was a considerable source of wealth to him. Of national taxes in the modern sense the viking world knew nothing, but clearly a king benefits by the prosperity of his subjects, whether this comes from good use of the soil, a developing trade, or the seizure of wealth abroad. Kings and kings' sons could take part in all these activities; Svein Forkbeard of Denmark and Olaf Tryggvason of Norway collected huge danegelds in England, and Olaf Eiriksson of Sweden earned the title Skött-konung, Scat-king, for his extra-territorial exactions; *Íslendingabók* (of the 1120s) records that the kings of Norway from Harald Fair-hair to St. Olaf levied a tax on emigrants from that land to Iceland; while the interest of the first of these monarchs in the trade out of Finnmark, and his stake in its profits, though rather freely presented by Snorri Sturluson in his *Egils Saga* (1220–5), is confirmed by his subjugation of the famed viking provinces of the south-west, whose inhabitants had long taken toll of the Frisian handlers of the northern trade in furs, hides, ivory, and down. Of Harald's son Bjorn we hear that he had merchant ships voyaging to other lands, acquiring thereby costly wares and such other goods as he needed. His brothers called him the Trafficker (*farmaðr*) or Chapman (*kaupmaðr*) (*Haralds Saga Hárfagra*, 35), and though the witness is late there is no reason for not believing it to be true in kind. Of the solicitude shown by Danish monarchs for the maintenance of trade we have already had occasion to speak in the case of Godfred and the Danevirke, Harald Bluetooth and the Wends, and king Svein, and we shall soon be observing the benevolent and profitable patronage bestowed on Helgö and Birka by the kings of central Sweden. Further, the right of a king to strike coins and control currency, though exerted comparatively late in Scandinavia, was a fruitful source of power. Part of the process whereby many kings became few, and the northern kingdoms achieved greater unity, we have already outlined in our Book Two, and the subject will be pursued in Book Four. In the later reaches of the Viking Period the power of a Christian king would be powerfully sustained by the Christian Church, with its learned clerks, diplomatic skills, and administrative experience. 'Men of prayer, men of war, men of work,' said our English Alfred. 'Without these [a king] cannot perform any of the tasks entrusted to him.' But with them, and a 'well-peopled land', he was a king indeed! In any case, the sense of dynasty was strong in the three northern countries, so much so that on the occasions when power in Norway was transferred to the lords of Hladir they never took the royal title, but were content, by will or perforce, to perpetuate their ancestral dignity of jarl.

The free man in possession of land and stock, the bondi (ON. *bóndi*, earlier *búandi*, from *búa*, to live, dwell, bide, have a household) ranging from smallholder to franklin, was, we have said, the backbone of a Scandinavia which, like the rest of Europe, was overwhelmingly pastoral and agrarian. Few such lived far or long from soil, seasons, crops, and beasts. Where arable land and pasture were extensive there would be many farms, and often small villages, as in much of Denmark, and southern and central Sweden; elsewhere the population would be thin and scattered, as almost everywhere in Norway and Iceland, northwards in Sweden, and in many of the Baltic islands. The bondi might be many things besides, such as sailor, trader, viking overseas, and in the northern areas hunter and fisher, but almost certainly he would still be a farmer, even if his absences or acres were extensive enough to require the labour of other men, free or thrall. There was a rough and ready (and persistent) classification of the Norse colonists of the Atlantic islands as farmers with a fishing-boat or fishermen with a farm, both categories being ploughers of land and sea; and it serves none too badly for dwellers on the prodigious littoral of the Scandinavian peninsulas and islands. The feeling for land of one's own was intense; in Icelandic tradition one of Harald Fairhair's chief enormities was his (reputed) infringement of the hereditary right to land of the *óðalsmaðr* or owner of an allodium.[1] Such love for one's

---

[1] The most famous written expression of this feeling is to be found in the Icelandic *Njáls Saga*, of the late thirteenth century, and owes much to art and nature. It tells how the saga-hero Gunnar of Lithend was riding off to exile when he was thrown by his horse and so alighted that he stood with his face looking back to his home. 'Lovely is the hillside,' he said, 'so that it has never looked lovelier to me, the cornfields white, and the new-mown hay. I shall ride back home and not leave it.' And so he did, knowing that death was the price of his return.

In the main the cornfields at Lithend would be of barley, which yielded both flour and malt and was of the first importance as a means to food and drink. Barley was the typical Scandinavian *korn*, though rye, oats, and (in the southern regions only) a little wheat were grown. Bread was made, and

patrimony was natural in those whose fathers felled trees, drained marshes, cleared fields of stones, tamed heath and mountain pastures, broke iron furrows, and when the frost-giants fought against them brought their little worlds through winters so cruel that in the spring the enfeebled animals had to be carried in arms from the barns on to the life-giving feeding-grounds. It was the same need and craving which carried Norwegians to the Atlantic islands and to America; while in England in the ninth century the Danes not only conquered land but are held by some to have purchased it with the price of conquest. A varying number of farms and cots with their ground, plus a varying amount of common land and grazing, constituted the minimal local unity, with varying title, but bound together by common interest, eleemosynary function, dues and services, law and religion. Aggregations of such units constituted a province, however entitled. And it was the aggregation of provinces which could lead to a boundaried king-

---

prized, but a great deal of *korn* was consumed in the shape of *grautr*, porridge or gruel.

Other foods grown in the Scandinavian lands, including the Atlantic colonies, were beans and peas, turnips and cabbage. ('Does he intend to be sole ruler over all the lands of the North?' asked the indignant St. Olaf concerning king Knut; 'Does he mean to eat up all the cabbage of England himself?') Garlic and angelica were culled and in places cultivated. Where nuts grew nuts were eaten; where berries were found berries were gathered, to be enjoyed fresh, strained for their juices, or employed in the manufacture of a winy drink. The Icelanders made moderate use of edible seaweed.

A most impressive piece of viking ploughland has been found at Lindholm Høje, where it had been preserved under a sudden sand-drift. Not only a 'washboard' of wide furrows is visible, but even the wheel-tracks of the viking farmer's last carting (Oscar Marseen, *Lindholm Høje, Beskrivelse af udgravninger og fund*, Ålborg Historiske Museum, n.d. (1962?)). There is a set of plough-marks on the floor of the grave at Gronk Moar, Isle of Man (See Plate XIII, G. Bersu and D. M. Wilson, *Three Viking Graves in the Isle of Man*, Society for Med. Arch., 1966).

For completeness' sake we mention meat and fish, much of this last dried, as staples of northern diet, and milk and its products, butter, cheese, and ambrosial skýr. And see Roesdahl, pp. 55–6 and 122–5.

Grass was of immense importance as the basis of animal husbandry. Among Icelanders of one's own generation one still encounters a passionate love of green growth, at times approaching a mystique. This, rather than a dubious philological argument, lends support to the notion that *Vínland* (Wineland, North America) began life as *Vinland* (Grassland), though the saga-writers and the land-naming practice of Eirik the Red's family speak against it.

dom. Thus the bondi, with a stake in the land and a voice in the law, the right of approval or dissent at a public assembly, was the key figure at all these levels, farm, parish, province, kingdom.

But throughout the viking period in Scandinavia we are aware of a second peaceful, or almost peaceful, activity hardly less important than husbandry. This was trade. Since the beginning of the second millennium B.C. Scandinavia had experienced the successive phases of the European culture existing south of it, and this could not have happened without trade and traders. There had to be goods up north which the south wanted, and wares down south which the north needed. Thus copper and tin came up the river routes from central and south-eastern Europe, notably by way of the Elbe to the sea, and thence along the west coast of Slesvig to Jutland, where he will be an unlucky searcher today who cannot garner some small blunted fragments to remind him of the brown and yellow amber-hoards of the past. It was amber, lovely, magical, prophylactic, which ensured that Jutland would be the starting-point of Bronze Age culture in the northern lands, and from Jutland the treasure was transferred by sea and land to Britain, France and the Iberian Peninsula, to Italy, the Mediterranean, Mycene itself. And as the centuries slid into the past, and Stone yielded to Bronze, and Bronze to Iron, always the north needed gold and silver, ceramics and filigrees, glassware, fine fabrics, jewels and wine; and the south was greedy for the winter harvest of bearskins and sables, squirrel and marten, for walrus ivory and reindeer hides, wax and ship's cables, and always slaves, and a little amber. Dealings in these or similar commodities would continue to the end of the Viking Age. Admittedly it is at times difficult to know whether certain goods and coin from abroad accumulated in the north as a result of warfare, piracy, or honest trade. Irish bronzes and the western European so-called 'Buddha bucket' of Oseberg; Scandinavian and Slavonic pottery at Wollin; Arabic, German, and Anglo-Saxon coins on Gotland; kufic silver, Arabic and Rhenish glassware, Frisian cloth, and Frankish weapons at Birka; Swedish iron ore and slag at Hedeby; these are not to be explained without some reference to trade. Or that entire rollcall of valuables we have listed before and will need to list again: slaves, weapons, furs, malt, wine, fruit, sea-ivory, cables, ornaments, silks, woollens, fish and fish products, timber, nuts, reindeer antlers, salt, millstones, livestock, combs, pots, fats, coins, hacksilver, even European hoods and gowns in Greenland.

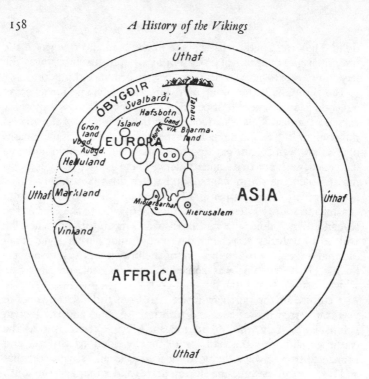

19. THE WORLD CIRCLE OF THE NORSEMEN
After A. A. Bjørnbo.

Also, the frequent occurrence of weights and scales, with bars of silver, in Scandinavian graves is substantive evidence of the mercantile calling. The total weight of trade is not calculable, but must have been considerable, and we have frequent mentions of trade goods and trading voyages in the written sources, too.

The best known of these to the English reader is Ottar (Ohthere) the Halogalander's account of his economy and travels, inserted by king Alfred of Wessex in his translation of Orosius, probably in the early 890s.

Ohthere said to his lord, king Alfred, that he lived farthest north oi all Norwegians.[1] He lived, he said, in the north of the country alongside the Norwegian Sea. He said, though, that the land extended a

[1] There is general agreement that he lived somewhere in the Malangenfjord-Senja-Kvaløy area, *c.* 69°N.

very long way north from there; but all of it is uninhabited, except that in a few places here and there Lapps make their camps, hunting in winter, and in summer fishing by the sea.

He said that on one occasion he wished to find out how far the land extended due north, and whether any one lived north of the uninhabited land. He proceeded then due north along the land (*or* coast). He kept the uninhabited land to starboard the whole way, and the open sea to port for three days. By then he was as far north as the whale-hunters go furthest. He then kept going still due north as far as he could sail in a second three days, whereupon the land veered due east, or the sea into the land, he knew not which[1]—save that he did know that he waited there for a wind from the west and a little from the north, and then sailed east along the land as far as he could sail in four days. At that point he had to wait for a wind from due north, because the land veered due south there, or the sea into the land, he knew not which. From there he sailed due south along the land as far as he could sail in five days. There a big river went up into the land. They turned up into the river, because they dared not sail on past the river for fear of hostilities, because the land on the other side of the river was all cultivated (*or* inhabited). Before this he had not met with any cultivated land since he left his own home; but he had had uninhabited land to starboard the whole way, save for fishers and fowlers and hunters (and these were all Lapps), and at all times to port the open sea. . . .

Chiefly he went there, apart from exploring the land, for the walruses, for they have very fine ivory in their tusks (they brought some of these tusks to the king), and their hide is very good for ship's cables. This whale is much smaller than other whales: it is not longer than seven ells long. But in his [Ottar's] own country is the best whale-hunting; they are eight and forty ells long, those, and the biggest fifty ells long. He said that in company with five other crews he killed sixty of these in two days. He was a very wealthy man in those possessions in which their wealth consists, that is, in wild animals. He had still when he visited the king six hundred tame unsold beasts. These beasts they call reindeer; six of them were decoy reindeer. These are very costly among the Lapps (*Finnum*), for with them they capture the wild reindeer. He was among the foremost men in the land; even so, he had not more than twenty head of cattle and twenty sheep and twenty pigs, and the little that he ploughed he ploughed with horses. But their wealth consists for the most part in the tribute which the Lapps pay them. The tribute consists in

[1] Ottar had reached the North Cape. He would thereafter proceed as far as the White Sea and Kandalaks Bay.

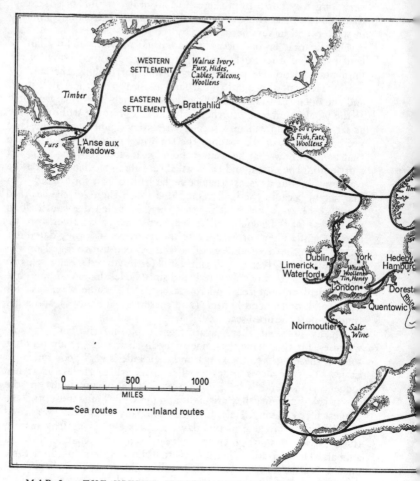

MAP 3. THE VIKING WORLD AND TRADE ROUTES

Walrus Ivory,
Furs.

Furs

Walrus Ivory,
Fish, Hides

Furs

Slaves

Staraja Ladoga

Volga

Novgorod

Bulgar

Tashkent

*Slaves, Furs,
Wax, Honey.*

Samarkand

Silver

Bokhara

Grobin

Amber

Gnezdovo

Chorezm

Wiskiauten

Truso

Itil

Wollin

Kiev

Slaves

Gurgan

Berezany

*ines, Pottery,
ass, Cloth, Weapons,
ewellery*

Danube

*Silk,
Silver,
Spices*

Byzantium

*Silk, Fruit,
Spices, Wine,
Jewellery*

Baghdad

Jerusalem

Alexandria

animals' skins and birds' feathers [i.e. down], in whalebone and the ships' cables which are made of whale's [i.e. walrus] hide or of seal's. Each pays according to his rank. The highest in rank must pay fifteen martens' skins, and five of reindeer, and one bearskin, and ten measures of feathers, a kirtle of bearskin or otterskin, and two ship's cables; each must be sixty ells long, the one to be made of whale's hide, the other of seal's. . . .

The land of the Norwegians, he said, was very long and very narrow. All of it that can be grazed or ploughed lies alongside the sea, and that moreover is in some parts very rocky. And wild mountains (*moras*) lie to the east, above and parallel to the cultivated land. On these mountains dwell Lapps.

Obviously Ottar did not require this abundance of ivory, furs, hides, and down for his own consumption. Some of it, maybe, he rendered up as scat to the king of Norway (at this time king Harald Fairhair), but the disposal of part of it was the reason for his month-long journey by the immemorial trade-route down the protected west coast of Norway, and so to Kaupang (Sciringesheal) on the western shore of the Oslofjord, thereafter to Danish Hedeby, and on occasion still farther to Alfred's court in England.

This was trade from the north. The reaching out after wealth from the west is indicated by these sailing directions preserved in the Sturla Thordarson and Hauk Erlendsson [H] versions of the Icelandic *Landnámabók* (Book of the Settlements).

Learned men state that from Stad in Norway it is seven days' sail west to Horn in the east of Iceland; and from Snæfellsnes, where the distance is shortest, it is four days' sea west to Greenland. And it is said if one sails from Bergen due west to Hvarf in Greenland that one's course will lie some seventy or more miles south of Iceland [H. From Hernar in Norway one must sail a direct course west to Hvarf in Greenland, in which case one sails north of Shetland so that one sights land in clear weather only, then south of the Faroes so that the sea looks half-way up the mountainsides, then south of Iceland so that one gets sight of birds and whales from there.] From Reykjanes in the south of Iceland there is five days' sea to Jolduhlaup in Ireland [H. *adds* in the south; and from Langanes in the north of Iceland] it is four days' sea north to Svalbard in the Polar Gulf. [H. *adds* And it is a day's sail to the unlived-in parts of Greenland from Kolbeinsey (*i.e.* Mevenklint) in the north.]

The great serpent-ring of Rus and Swedish trade is outlined thus by the author of the *Russian Primary Chronicle*:

A trade route connected the Varangians with the Greeks. Starting from the Greeks, this route proceeds along the Dnieper, above which a portage leads to the Lovat. By following the Lovat, the great Lake Ilmen is reached. The river Volkhov flows out of this lake and enters the great Lake Nevo [Lake Ladoga]. The mouth of this lake (*i.e.* the Neva River) opens into the Varangian Sea [the Baltic]. Over this sea goes the route to Rome, and on from Rome overseas to Tsargard [Constantinople]. The Pontus, into which flows the river Dnieper, may be reached from that point. The Dnieper itself rises in the upland forest, and flows southward. The Dvina has its source in this same forest, but flows northward and empties into the Varangian Sea. The Volga rises in this same forest but flows to the east, and discharges through seventy mouths into the Caspian Sea. It is possible by this route to the eastward to reach the Bulgars and the Caspians, and thus attain the region of Shem. Along the Dvina runs the route to the Varangians, whence one may reach Rome, and go from there to the race of Ham.[1]

The documentary evidence could be deployed at considerable length. Anskar travels to Birka in the company of merchants who forfeit most of their goods to pirates, while the saint himself loses almost forty books. The Norwegians supply timber to Iceland, Icelanders supply Eirik the Red in Greenland with meal and corn, and Greenlanders supply coloured cloth to the broad-cheeked inhabitants of America. From America come unblemished pelts and timber to Greenland and Iceland, and from those countries woollens, seal-oil, sea-ivory, fats, falcons and (save for floe-riders, from Greenland only) white bears, back to the marts of Scandinavia, whence they were dispersed southwards through Europe. Across the Irish Sea Norse merchants maintained a brisk trade in Welsh slaves, horses, honey, malt and wheat, and Irish or Irish-imported wine, furs, hides, whale-oil, butter, and coarse woollen cloth.[2] A treaty of 991 between Olaf Tryggvason and king Ethelred aims to secure the safety of foreign merchant ships, together with their crews and cargoes, in English estuaries, and a full respect for English ships encountered abroad by vikings. That Danes and Norwegians were frequent traders into London (the Danes with a 'more-favoured nation' clause) may be deduced from a twelfth-century city custumal which appears to refer to conditions during

[1] English translation S. H. Cross and O. P. Sherbowitz-Wetzor, *The Russian Primary Chronicle*, Cambridge, Mass., 1953, p. 53.
[2] A. H. Williams, *An Introduction to the History of Wales*, Cardiff, 1941, I, 157.

the reigns of Knut and Edward the Confessor.[1] Meanwhile the Church strove to bring humanity and sometimes theology into the slave-trade. We read of the Rus from Kiev buying silk in Byzantium and horses and slaves in Regensburg. 'Pereiaslav on the Dnieper,' said Svyatoslav their lord, 'where all riches are concentrated: gold, silks, wine and various fruits from Greece, silver and horses from Hungary and Bohemia, and from Russia furs, wax, honey, and slaves.' We read of the Arab merchant of Cordoba, Al-Tartushi, visiting Hedeby in the mid-tenth century, from whence the (English?) merchant Wulfstan had sailed to Truso some fifty years earlier. Al-Musadi and Muqqadasi report on the wares of the Rus at Bulgar on the Volga bend, just below the confluence of that river and the Kama: sables, squirrel, ermine, black and white foxes, marten, beaver, arrows and swords, wax and birchbark, fish-teeth and fish-lime, amber, honey, goatskins and horsehides, hawks, acorns, hazel nuts, cattle and Slavonic slaves. Some of these the Rus had brought a prodigious distance out of the cold and spectred north, by a three-months journey from a dark and sunless land facing the northern ocean. Ibn Fadlan describes the merchants themselves, as he saw them on the Volga in 922:

I have seen the Rus as they came on their merchant journeys and encamped by the Atil (Itil, Volga). I have never seen more perfect physical specimens, tall as date palms, blond and ruddy; they wear neither *qurtaqs* (tunics) nor caftans, but the men wear a garment which covers one side of the body and leaves a hand free. Each man has an axe, a sword, and a knife, and keeps each by him at all times. The swords are broad and grooved, of Frankish sort. . . . Each woman wears on either breast a box of iron, silver, copper, or gold; the value of the box indicates the wealth of the husband. Each box has a ring from which depends a knife. The women wear neck-rings of gold and silver. . . . Their most prized ornaments are green glass beads. . . . They string them as necklaces for their women.[2]

---

[1] Stenton, *Anglo-Saxon England*, p. 533.
[2] Amin Razi's version of Ibn Fadlan's *Risala*, of 1593 but maybe based on a good early MS., has the following interesting details: 'In place of gold the Rus use sable skins. . . . The Rus are a great host, all of them red-haired; they are big men with white bodies.' I have by kind permission used the version of H. M. Smyser, 'Ibn Fadlan's Account of the Rus with Some Commentary and Some Allusions to Beowulf', in *Medieval and Linguistic Studies in Honour of Francis Peabody Magoun*, New York, 1965, pp. 92–119. Other recent renderings will be found in Brøndsted, *The Vikings*, 1965; A. Zeki

. . . When they have come from their land and anchored on, or tied up at the shore of, the Volga, which is a great river, they build big houses of wood on the shore, each holding ten to twenty persons more or less. Each man has a couch on which he sits. With them are pretty slave girls destined for sale to merchants. A man will have sexual intercourse with his slave girl while his companion looks on. Sometimes whole groups will come together in this fashion, each in the presence of the others. A merchant who arrives to buy a slave girl from them may have to wait and look on while a Rus completes the act of intercourse with a slave girl.

. . . When the ships come to this mooring place, everybody goes ashore with bread, meat, onions, milk and *nabid* [an intoxicating drink, perhaps beer] and betakes himself to a long upright piece of wood that has a face like a man's and is surrounded by little figures [idols], behind which are long stakes in the ground. The Rus prostrates himself before the big carving and says, 'O my Lord, I have come from a far land and have with me such and such a number of girls and such and such a number of sables,' and he proceeds to enumerate all his other wares. Then he says, 'I have brought you these gifts,' and lays down what he has brought with him, and continues, 'I wish that you would send me a merchant with many dinars and *dirhems*, who will buy from me whatever I wish and will not dispute anything I say.'

Contemplating this picture (which might be considerably enlarged) of Danes, Norwegians, Swedes, Gotlanders, and Ålanders driving trade with peoples as varied and distant as the Lapps of Finnmark and the Baltic Fenns, the Greeks and Arabs of the East and Spain, Slavs and Germans, Franks and Frisians, Irish and English, and the Atlantic island-dwellers from Faroes to Labrador, we must not forget that there was much trade both between and within the Scandinavian countries themselves. Trade often allied to manufacture, in soapstone pots and iron goods, for example. The twelve rough-finished axe-heads found near Grenaa in eastern Jutland, threaded on a stave of spruce, were a Norwegian or possibly

Validi Togan, *Ibn Fadlan's Reisebericht*, Abhandlungen für die Kunde des Morgenlandes, xxiv, 3, Leipzig, 1939; M. Canard, 'La relation du voyage d'Ibn Fadlan chez les Bulgares de la Volga', in *Annales de l'Institut d'Études Orientales*, Algiers, 1958, xvi, pp. 41–6. I have not seen A. P. Kovalevsky's translation into Russian of 1939 and 1956. A new and direct translation from Arabic into English is needed, if only to reassure those who like myself know no Arabic.

a Swedish export to Denmark. We have already remarked on Swedish iron-ore and slag at Hedeby. But our pressing task now is to look briefly at the growth of the Scandinavian merchant towns.

The Viking Age was a period remarkable for the rise, development, and sometimes decline, of towns and market-places. The Norseman abroad, whether as invader, settler, or merchant, needed havens and bases. Sometimes he took into his use towns already in existence, sometimes he established them for his convenience, from Limerick on the Shannon to Kiev on the Dnieper. Many of these we have had, or shall have, occasion to mention in other contexts, and the same is true of certain of the Scandinavian home marts also. Most of the towns they established at home were shaped by two considerations: accessibility for the merchants who needed to use them, and protection from the pirates who wanted to prey on them. For the ampler the volume of trade the stronger the temptation to privateering.[1] Over long periods the south-west coast of Norway, the Øresund passage, and the Baltic were infested with pirates. Adam of Bremen is endlessly indignant on this theme. There is much gold in Zealand, says he, accumulated by pirates who ravage the coasts of southern Norway; between Zealand and Funen (Fyn) lies a pirate den, a place of terror for all who pass by; Fehmarn and Rügen are the haunts of robbers who spare none that pass that way; it is the distinction of the Sembi, or Pruzzi, that they succour mariners attacked by pirates;[2] even the natives of Greenland, greenish from the sea-water whence the country derives its name, trouble seafarers by their piratical attacks. Scores of references in the Icelandic sagas, and almost as many in Snorri's *Heimskringla*, relate to pirate haunts, ships' crews out viking in Skagerrak, Kattegat, and Baltic, raids on coastal and sometimes inland towns, and the

---

[1] And the ampler the volume of wealth secured from viking raids abroad the stronger the compulsion to trade at home. It is the merchant's immemorial privilege to redistribute the superfluous coin of wealthy clients. (See P. Grierson, 'Commerce in the Dark Ages', in *Trans. Royal Hist. Society*, 5th Series, IX, 1959, pp. 123–40.)

[2] This occasions a useful note on the fur trade. 'They (the Sembi) have an abundance of strange furs, the odour of which has innoculated our world with the deadly poison of pride. But these furs they regard, indeed, as dung, to our shame, I believe, for right or wrong we hanker after a martenskin robe as much as for supreme happiness. Therefore, they offer their very precious marten furs for the woollen garments called *faldones*' (IV, 18). Trans. F. J. Tschan.

taking of merchant ships in Scandinavian waters. That cool repository of Norse worldly wisdom, the *Hávamál*, advises the farmer not to move far from his weapons when out in the fields; the crew of a merchantman needed no such warning, for every sail was read as hostile till it proved friendly. Even as the merchant ship or ferry carried arms, so the towns between which they plied were protected by being sited away from the sea, inside narrow fjords like Hedeby and Lindholm Høje, on inland lakes like Birka and spray-free Sigtuna, on rivers leading from such lakes like Aldeigjuborg, Old Ladoga, or within bays where islands, shoals, and complicated channels made the approach slow and observable, as at Wiskiauten, Kaupang and, presumably, Truso. In addition many of the towns were given strong man-made defences, like the northern fort and look-out station and the semicircular rampart at Hedeby, the rock-fortress and town wall of Birka, and the earthwork stronghold of Grobin. Even so, the emergence of towns, and especially of towns with mints, was clearly consequential upon the growth of royal power and an increased social stability. Their number was substantial. 'Along the North Sea and the Baltic coasts, like blind eyes, lie the vanished towns of the Vikings, the sites of Northern Europe's oldest trading centres, following the winding route from the mouth of the Rhine along the coast of Jutland right up to Lake Mälar in the north. If you think of the traders of those times— wherever they came from or wherever they were bound—a picture of trading towns, once swarming with life, but now dead, springs to mind: the Frisian town of Dorestad; Hedeby in the south of Denmark; farther north, still in Denmark, Lindholm Høje, on the Limfjord; the Latvian Grobin; the Norse-Slav Wollin; the Estonian Truso; the Swedish Birka; and, in southern Norway, Skiringssal [Kaupang].'[1] And these were by no means all. By the end of the Viking Age Norway had seen the birth of Trondheim-Nidaros, Bergen, and Oslo; Sweden knew Skara, Lund, and Sigtuna; Denmark had well-established centres of population at Ribe, Viborg, Århus and Ålborg, Odense and Roskilde, some of them centres of mercantile and religious life, some royal creations. On the other hand, Old Uppsala and Helgö were much or entirely fallen away, and Lindholm Høje was about to disappear under its mantle of blown sand, so leaving the way open to the development of Ålborg at the same eastern end of the Limfjord.

[1] Brøndsted, *The Vikings*, pp. 149–50.

Many of the old market towns have been excavated and studied, Birka by the Swedes Hjalmar Stolpe and Holger Arbman, Hedeby by the German Professor Jankuhn, and Kaupang by the Norwegian Charlotte Blindheim. As a result we know a good and increasing deal about their structure and history, their daily life, and their role in the manufacture and distribution of goods. Kaupang, it appears, was a summer market only (the name means 'market-place'). The permanent settlement was strung out and without man-made defence-works. Many merchants died there and were buried in boats, together with their instruments for weighing gold and silver. The connection with England and Ireland was strong; ornaments and weapons from those countries have been found there, as well as Rhenish pottery and western glassware, and half a dozen assorted coins come from Mercia, the kingdom of Louis the Pious, the Arab world, and, possibly, Birka. Mrs. Blindheim thinks that large quantities of down were exported from Kaupang. There is evidence of metalworking, weaving, and manufacture in soapstone. The mart stood adjacent to the wealthy region of Vestfold, and presumably supplied many of its needs and luxuries. It would also appear to be a good point of assembly for merchants sailing south to Hedeby or proceeding by way of the Øresund to the Baltic. We know that merchant ships were glad to sail in company as a safeguard against piracy in those waters.

Security from enemies and accessibility to friends were considerations much in the minds of those who founded the trading town of Birka on the island of Björkö in Lake Mälar. The incoming merchant, having traversed the thirty labyrinthine miles of islands and skerries east of Stockholm, must complete a further eighteen miles of observed navigation through the island-studded lake before reaching Björkö. The island is so lonely and quiet under its birch glades today, its remains so mouldered in grassy earth, that it requires a strong effort of the imagination to see it as it was, a hub of traffic whose spokes reached out to England and Frisia in the west, Lake Ladoga and the Middle Volga in the east, Uppsala and the fur-bearing lands in the north, Gotland, Truso, Wollin, Hedeby, and all that lay beyond them, to the south. But such it was, one of the most important marts of viking Scandinavia. Its site is identifiably the so-called Black Earth area in the north-west of the island, darkened as this was by human habitation. It is difficult to determine when the town was established, but it was thriving and well known when Anskar made his visits there about 830 and 850. At first it appears to have been undefended, but in course of time its landward approaches were safeguarded by an earthen rampart, a 550-yard section of which, some 6 feet high and 20-40 feet wide, still runs along a low ridge east of the town. It is a fair assumption that this earthen rampart was surmounted by a wooden wall or palisade, and that its frequent gaps or openings were protected by formidable but now vanished wooden towers. The surviving eastern rampart was probably constructed shortly after 925. Close to the Black Earth, between south and south-west, on a low but in relation to the site commanding hill stood an oval-shaped fort, protected on the land side by a rampart of earth and stones, with three gateways, and seawards by steepdown 100-foot cliffs. Between fort, town, and lake there appears to have been a beacon site, which was later levelled off as the defences were strengthened and the need for garrison houses increased. The town was heavily built up between waterfront and rampart, save that a house-free boundary was left running inside the latter, possibly as a safeguard against assault by fire. Most of the houses were of wattle-and-daub construction, but there were a number of what their excavator Holger Arbman calls blockhouses, constructed of big vertical baulks of timber caulked with clay and moss. The abundance of weapons found in the area between fort and town, together with the absence of women's goods, suggests that the bulk of the garrison lived there, but a ring of blockhouses seems to have been built between the town and the town wall.

A seaside mart must cater for ships. The foreshore at Birka is gently sloping and was entirely convenient to the shallow ships of the time. In addition there is evidence of oaken jetties and breakwaters at several places inside the fortified area. Immediately to the north, and outside the rampart, are two natural harbours, Kugghamn, presumably named after the Frisian cog, and Korshamn, 'cross-harbour', or conceivably an earlier Kornhamn, 'corn-harbour'. Farther away, east of the town, is the artificial basin of Salviksgropen, which opened off a small lagoon which has now disappeared because of the slow rising of the land out of the water. This change of water-level has affected Kugghamn and Korshamn, too, which in viking times were more impressive and commodious than now.

North, east, and south of the Black Earth area, and south of the fort, are the main cemeteries of Birka, containing more than 2,000

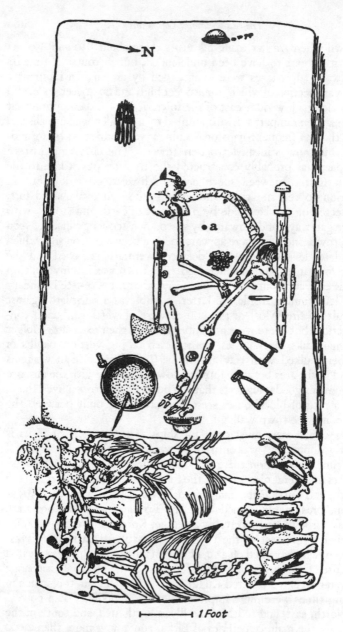

N

20. BIRKA GRAVE, NO. 581.

graves, most of them grassy barrows, large and small, but including many fine chamber graves also. The wealth of recoverable grave goods here is unparalleled in any other viking settlement. The richly furnished graves of chieftains, warriors, merchants, and their womenfolk have been excavated, to reveal the high standard of living here in the ninth and tenth centuries. In the grave illustrated (Birka 581) a fighting man has been laid to rest with everything he could require in the next world: two shields (one at his feet, one above his head), axe, sword, dagger, knife, two dozen arrows (we presume with a wooden bow), two spears, stirrups, and two horses, as well as a comb and bowl and other objects. A silver dirhem (*a*) found under the skeleton, which must have been minted 913–33, allows us to date the interment in the period 913–*c*. 980. Less splendid but equally revealing are the graves of merchants with their fine balances and weights, and the graves of men and women containing goods and coins indicative of the town's trade. Rimbert writes of its connection with Dorestad, and trade with the west is confirmed by the presence in Birka of handsome Rhineland pottery and glassware, scraps of high-quality woollen cloth almost certainly from Frisia, and coins from western Europe used for personal adornment. Holger Arbman has suggested that Birka had markets in winter as well as summer. There are men buried with ice-crampons on their feet, ice-picks are not infrequent, and skates made of bone are numerous. Progress into the north after furs may well have been easier in the winter, and certainly the pelts of bear, fox, marten, squirrel, beaver and otter, would then be in prime condition. Traces of all these, together with reindeer horn and walrus ivory, have been found in the town.

There seems to have been no very extensive manufactory in Birka—just indications that metal was worked for ornament or coins, and that objects of bone and glass (most likely beads) were produced—so with little agricultural land close by, the town's prosperity, indeed its existence, depended on the sale and transfer of goods, from any quarter and at all seasons of the year. But in practice Birka depended more on her eastern connection than any other, and more specifically on trade with the surprisingly accessible regions of the Volga. Graves containing Muslim coins are seven times more numerous than those containing currency from the west. Silver and silk came in by this same route, ornamented glass, rings and necklaces, and other luxurious appurtenances of a flourishing society. The Birka necklace of Plate 16 is a microcosm of the town's business interests. It is composed for the most part of beads of glass, crystal, and carnelian, but it is the additions, the inserted souvenirs or 'charms', which most excite our interest. Top left is a silver coin of the emperor Theophilus (829–42) from Byzantium; then two pendants culled from the Khazars of the lower Volga; after that come two silver wires threading one bead and five beads respectively, probably Scandinavian, followed by a fragment from an Arab silver bowl; then two more silver wires, each with one bead, and thereafter another silver wire coiled to make a disc, again probably Scandinavian, and yet another silver wire, this time strung with three beads; the next object, still bottom left, is an oblong book-mount brought from England, by what agency we cannot say; then come two round pendants, their centres hollowed, and finally a miniature silver chair.

But Birka's witness to the variety and extent of Viking Age

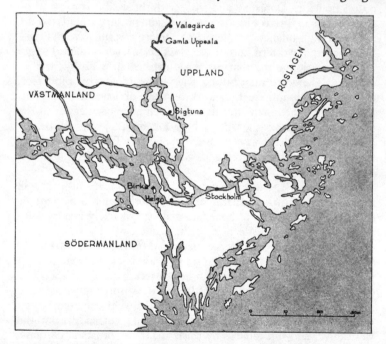

MAP 4. SWEDEN: THE EAST CENTRAL PROVINCES

trade is not its only claim to attention. We have earlier noted the significance of a combination of military power, an assembly for law, and a meeting-place for trade, in making possible the development of petty kingdoms in dark-age Denmark, and by implication elsewhere in Scandinavia. Birka is an example of this at a later stage of history. It is clear that it could not have come into being without royal approval. The island is small and thinly populated, and situated between the great royal estates of Uppland and Söderman-land. It could be reached only by traversing the royal lands and waters, and safeguarded by none but the royal power. Hardly less significant, the island lay at the meeting-point of three different herreds or hundreds, so that the problem of what law would be observed on Björkö was quickly an urgent one. The slender evidence provided by the old Västergötland law suggests that the various regions of Sweden were accustomed to look after their own folk better than the outsider. It was cheaper to compound the slay-ing of a man from another province, while men from abroad had no assured atonement at all. But if Birka was to attract merchants it must unequivocally guarantee their lives and property. We cannot doubt that the necessary changes in customary law came about on the initiative of the king of the Svea, though the laws themselves would be maintained by the Birka Thing. And, indeed, Rimbert informs us that at the time of Anskar's visits Birka was governed by a Thing under the leadership of a *præfectus regis*. There must have been a delimitation of authority as between king and townspeople, but a firm rule of law had such advantages for both parties that they may be assumed to have worked in harmony. We cannot feel assured that the so-called *Bjarkeyjarréttr*, the Law of Bjarkey or Björkö, was the law of Birka on Lake Mälar, but it is a likely supposition. The Frisian, Dane, German, Englishman, Finn, Swede, Balt, Greek or Arab (if he ever showed up) was offered safety and fair play; the townsmen and local traders could look to the peaceful pursuit of riches; and the king who safeguarded these processes enjoyed esteem, privilege, and profit. This personal hold on the Birka market brought much wealth to the Swedish king, and helps account for the strengthening of the monarchy and kingdom of central Sweden during the ninth and tenth centuries.

When Birka declined it declined rapidly. Its falling away may have been helped by the change in the water-level of Lake Mälar and its southern entrance in the late tenth century, but a more convincing explanation is the break in eastern trade which took place about 970 as a result of Svyatoslav's assaults on the Bulgars of the Volga Bend. There was no more kufic silver, no more coin from Islam. The men of Birka failed to adapt, and the indefatigable Gotlanders took over. There was no recovery, and at the beginning of the eleventh century trade moved northwards to Sigtuna.[1]

For Hedeby we are quite remarkably well informed. The town dates from the eighth century and seems to have developed from the growing together of maybe three small communities, each with its cemetery, one associated with the brook running immediately to the south of the (later) rampart, a second (rather less certain) with the still smaller stream north of the rampart (but south of the now tree-covered Hill Fort or Borghøjde), and the third with the rivulet which ran through the middle of the enclosed market-town and supplied it with fresh water. It grew rapidly in the early ninth century, and we read of it in connection with the political and mercantile ambitions of king Godfrey *c.* 800–10, and the missionary activities of Anskar in 826, 850, and 854. Thereafter the town is never out of sight. Seafarers like Ottar and Wulfstan refer to it, an exotic visitor like Al-Tartushi describes it, it experienced a Swedish interlude (see pp. 111–2 above) and a German, and was the scene of a Danish triumph under Svein Forkbeard in 983. In the mid-eleventh century its destruction by Harald Hardradi of Norway would be celebrated in verse exultant and durable.[2] Al-Tartushi was not

[1] The discovery in 1953 of rich finds covering a period of 600 years from the fifth (possibly the fourth) to the eleventh century on the island of Helgö, less than ten miles distant from Birka in Lake Mälar, has posed some so far unanswerable questions about the relationship between the two marts. Helgö dominates the water routes from the Baltic into central Sweden; it trafficked in luxury goods, and iron was smelted there. We assume it must have enjoyed a similar kind of royal patronage as Birka, which it outlasted, though its importance seems to have waned as that of Birka waxed. It certainly confirms that the Viking and pre-Viking Ages developed naturally and by steady process out of the centuries that preceded them.

[2] There are two memorial stones in the vicinity of Hedeby which make mention of a king Svein. The 'Danevirkesten' from Busdorf (Bustrup) records that 'King Svein raised the stone in memory of his housecarle Skardi, who had travelled west but now met his death at Hedeby.' The 'Hedebysten' records that 'Thorolf, Svein's housecarle, raised this stone in memory of his comrade Eirik who met his death when the warriors besieged Hedeby. He was a captain, a man of noble birth.' The likely candidates are king Svein Forkbeard (*c.* 983) and king Svein Estridsson (*c.* 1050), but it is not certain that both stones refer to the same king Svein.

overimpressed with it, and when we remember the elegance and
splendour of his native Cordoba, there is no reason why he should be.

Slesvig is a large town at the farthest end of the world ocean. Within
it there are wells of fresh water. Its inhabitants worship Sirius, apart

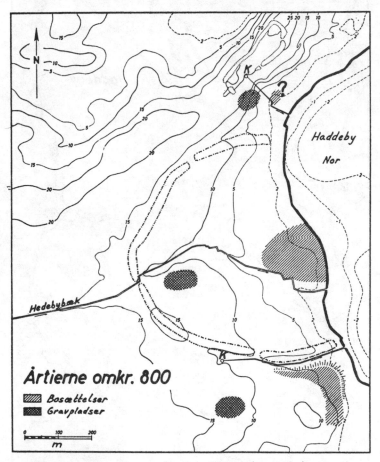

21. HEDEBY *c.* 800. THE SETTLEMENTS (*Bosættelser*) AND
THEIR CEMETERIES (*Gravpladser*)
The existence of the northern settlement and the dating of the
northern cemetery are somewhat uncertain. The town rampart,
of the early ninth century, is indicated by stipple lines. K. Spring.

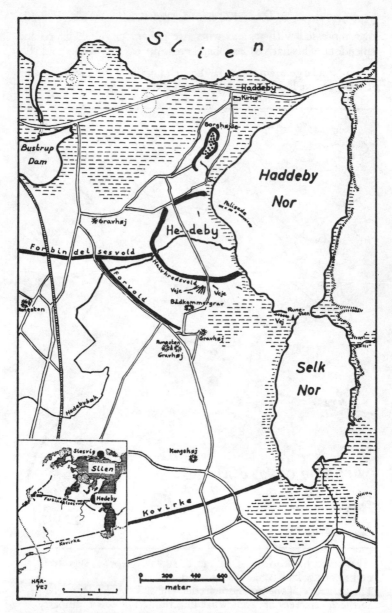

MAP 5. HEDEBY AND NEIGHBOURHOOD

from a few who are christians and have a church there. Al-Tartushi relates:[1]

They hold a festival where they assemble to honour their god and eat and drink. Anyone who slaughters an animal by way of sacrifice has a palisade [or pole] outside his house door and hangs the sacrificed animal there, whether it be ox or ram, he-goat or boar, so that people may know that he makes sacrifice in honour of his god. The town is poorly off for goods and wealth. The people's chief food is fish, for there is so much of it. If a child is born there it is thrown into the sea to save bringing it up. Moreoever he relates that women have the right to declare themselves divorced: they part with their husbands whenever they like. They also have there an artificial make-up for the eyes; when they use it their beauty never fades, but increases in both man and woman. He said too: I have never heard more horrible singing than the Slesvigers'—it is like a growl coming out of their throats, like the barking of dogs, only much more beastly.

This commentary of an observant Arab allows us an unforced transition to what we learn of Hedeby from the archaeologists of Germany. Al-Tartushi was right about the freshwater wells,[2] many of which have come to light with their skilfully contrived water-pipes. Once we allow that to worship Sirius means nothing more than being a heathen, he was right about the mixture of religions there, for graves both heathen and Christian and written sources confirm this. He was right in saying that much fish was eaten, the exposure of infants not forbidden, and that Norse women enjoyed far more independence than their sisters in the Muslim world. That both sexes used eye make-up to render themselves attractive is as open to belief or disbelief as John of Wallingford's complaint that the Danes in England combed their hair, took a bath on Saturdays, and changed their woollens at reasonable intervals to ensnare by these novelties our high-born English ladies. On the Slesvigers' throat for song and the Arab ear for music it is not for less favoured nations to comment.

[1] Al-Tartushi's relation is preserved in the 'Travel Book' of Ibrahim ibn Jakub, *c.* 975. See H. Birkeland, 'Nordens historie i middelalder etter arabiske kilder', in *Norske Videnskabs-Akademiets Skrifter*, II, Hist. philol. Klasse, 2, 1954, Oslo.

[2] Arne Hægstad, 'Har Al-Tartushi besøgt Hedeby (Slesvig)?' *Aarbøger for nordisk Oldk. og Hist.*, Copenhagen, 1964, pp. 82–92, suggests that by 'wells of sweet water' the Arab meant the local women, and that we cannot be sure his visit was to Hedeby and not to Wollin.

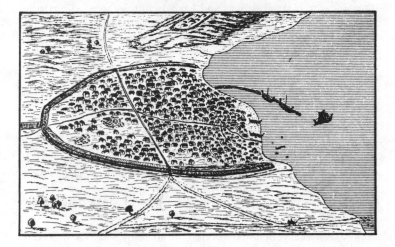

22. HEDEBY IN THE TENTH CENTURY (A PICTORIAL
RECONSTRUCTION)

For its day Hedeby was a well-built and well-organized town.
On three sides, north, west, and south, it was protected by a rampart roughly semicircular in shape and two-thirds of a mile long.
To the east it was bounded by the waters of Haddeby Noor, with
its notably shallow and therefore protective entrance from the
Schlei. This circumvallation had begun modestly enough as a yard-
high rampart with stockade and ditch, but successive developments
raised it during the tenth century to well over 30 feet, with a deep
moat and strong timber revetments. It had three gateways or
tunnels, one south and one north for the transit of men, horses, and
wagons, and one west at the point where the rivulet came in to run
quietly between its piled and strengthened sides down to the fjord.
The road tunnels were rather more than 6 feet wide, wedge-shaped
and planked, and the roadway beneath paved with stones to ease
the progress of horses' hoofs and cart-wheels. The area enclosed
between rampart and sea was a full 60 acres (Birka was 32), most of
it heavily built up, but with some open spaces left around the
cemeteries and alongside the stream, and an open flattish strip
alongside the water where ships and small boats could be beached.
Here, too, are traces of a slip for shipbuilding or repairing, important

trades in a mercantile and seafaring community. Running in a 480-foot arc from north to south-east out into Haddeby Noor was a strongly built wooden mole, which protected the foreshore from floods and offered ample opportunity for vessels to tie up to its massive bollards. Judging by the admittedly limited areas so far excavated, it was a well-made and agreeable place enough, though we shall not expect to find in a constantly developing town the constructional exactitude of the military establishments at Fyrkat, Trelleborg, or Aggersborg. The numerous dwelling-houses, workshops, store-houses, barns and stables, at first sight give the impression of being where they are for no better reason than that their first owners put them there. Even so the town was not too badly ordered. There were at least two good streets; the circumvallation never needed to be enlarged or drawn in; the town was well sited in the first place, and appears to have grown in a tidy progression westwards and inwards from the first well-developed area of settlement extending northwards from where the rivulet enters the sea. The 'craftsmen's quarter' was apparently earmarked as such. The size of the town's buildings varied from 22 feet by 54 to a mere 10 by 10. Some were stave-built with vertical planking, some with horizontal, and yet others were frame-built, with wattle-and-daub panels. The roofing was normally of reed-thatch. The doors were uniformly low, and the houses dating from the town's later development westward often had a sunken floor. When a house was rebuilt this took place on the old site. In general buildings were placed so that their gable end faced the street and their attendant outhouses stood behind them. The enclosures in which the houses stood were

23. HEDEBY: THE TOWN AND RAMPART (A PICTORIAL RECONSTRUCTION)

fenced or palisaded off, and many such enclosures were furnished with a well. Some Slesvigers gave house-room to cats and dogs.

The town seems not to have been deeply rooted in its countryside. Its geographical position at the head of the Schlei, within easy reach of the Baltic and, by way of Hollingstedt, handy to Frisia, western Europe, and the North Sea, ensured it a different destiny. To it, for sale and distribution, came the wares of many countries: ceramics and glassware and perhaps frankish swords from western Europe; millstones of basalt from the Rhineland, and

24. HOUSES AT HEDEBY (A PICTORIAL
RECONSTRUCTION)

from Norway pots and dishes of soapstone. From the Slav hunting-grounds came slaves, and from the eastern verges of the Baltic furs. Nor need we doubt that wine and jewellery moved through the town, with other luxury goods such as garments and fabrics. To this variety and abundance the town added its home-made quotas. One part of the town, though one must again emphasize how much remains to be uncovered, shows such evidence of manufacture that, as we have seen, its excavators at first called it the 'craftsmen's quarter', where the potter and weaver, jeweller and worker in bone and horn, plied their several skills. In the matter of workaday pots we can speak of something like mass-production. It was not the intention to rival the best imported goods: the Hedeby manufacturers aimed at the less wealthy buyer. Bronze and iron were worked there, and coins struck, but the site of the mint, like the site of Anskar's church, has not yet been discovered.

By the early eleventh century Hedeby had seen the best of its time, and it was not in its fortune to show vigour beyond the

Viking Age. Harald Hardradi burned it more or less to the ground in 1050, and there was a destructive raid by the Slavs in 1066; and eventually the town called by the Saxons Schleswig, 'the town on the Schlei', by the Danes Hedeby, 'the town at the heaths', and, on Ottar's authority, by the English *æt Hæþum*, 'at the heaths', fell into disuse and had its name and function usurped by a new Slesvig on the north side of the Sliefjord. But even more than the Swedish Birka, Hedeby presents the twentieth century with a surprisingly detailed picture of a viking town and mart from its modest beginnings in the eighth century to its brutal extinction in the mid-eleventh.[1]

[1] In addition to the fundamental studies of H. Jankuhn and Vilh. la Cour cited on p. 101 above, the reader is currently well served in respect of Hedeby by Helmuth Schledermann's two articles, 'Slesvig-Hedebys tilblivelse' in *Sønderjyske Årbøger*, 1966 and 1967, the first dealing with place-names, trade and routes, archaeological finds and topography; the second with royal power and its relevance to the town, the town's surroundings, and other Danish towns; the same author's 'Fra den Havn plejer skibe at udgå', in *Skalk*, 1963, nr. 3, pp. 15–26; Kurt Schietzel (recent leader of the excavations there), 'Neue Ausgrabungen in Haithabu', *Praehistorische Zeitschrift*, vol. XLIII-XLIV, 1965-6, pp. 303–7; the handbook of the Schleswig-Holsteinisches Landesmuseum für Vor- und Frühgeschichte, Schloss Gottorp, *Danevirke og Hedeby* (German and Danish versions), Neumünster, 1963; and in English the summary in Brøndsted's *The Vikings*, pp. 150–5.

For Birka see H. Arbman, *Birka, Sveriges äldsta handelsstad*, Stockholm, 1939, and *Birka, Untersuchungen und Studien I, Die Gräber*, Stockholm, 1943; and in English the relevant passages in H. Arbman, *The Vikings*, 1961; Brøndsted, *The Vikings*; P. H. Sawyer, *The Age of the Vikings*, 1971, more particularly pp. 177–86.

Kaupang: Charlotte Blindheim, *Kaupang, markedsplassen i Skiringssal*, Oslo, 1953, and 'The Market Place in Skiringssal. Early Opinions and Recent Studies', in *Acta Archaeologica*, XXXI, Copenhagen, 1960. Helgö: W. Holmkvist, B. Arrhenius, and P. Lundström, *Excavations at Helgö*, I and II, Stockholm, 1961 and 1964. Lindholm Høje: Th. Ramskou, 'Lindholm (Høje)'. Preliminary Reports in *Acta Archaeologica*, XXIV (1953), XXVI (1955), XXVIII (1957). Jomsborg: O. Kunkel and K. A. Wilde, *Jumne, 'Vineta', Jomsburg, Julin: Wollin*, Stettin, 1941. Grobin: B. Nerman, *Grobin-Seeburg, Ausgrabungen und Funde*, Stockholm, 1958.

Kurt Schietzel, *Berichte über die Ausgrabungen in Haithabu*, Neumünster, 1969ff; Sawyer, 1971, pp. 177–201; Charlotte Blindheim, 'The Emergence of Urban Communities in Viking Age Scandinavia. The Problem of Continuity', in R. T. Farrell (ed.), *The Vikings*, 1982; E. Roesdahl, 'The First Towns', in *Viking Age Denmark*, 1982.

2. Causes of the Viking Movement Overseas

BUT IT WAS NOT AS FARMERS OR TRADERS, NOR for their arts, industry, and domestic virtues, that the vikings most impressed the ecclesiastics recording the contemporary scene elsewhere in Europe. Of the five principal modes of making a northern living, by agriculture, fishing and hunting, following a craft, buying and selling, or robbing and fighting, it was the last which made the most spectacular impact on chroniclers abroad. And naturally enough, for the pain and grief of war incite the pen more than the tamer processes of trade. The movement of disturbed, needy, or merely warlike peoples southwards out of Scandinavia against their unwelcoming neighbours in what are today the British Isles, France, Germany, Spain, and Italy, had been taking place intermittently for almost a thousand years before the viking movement proper began towards the end of the eighth century. In the second century before Christ the Teutones and Cimbri had left their homes in Jutland to test the Roman power, and before the Age of Migrations was over Öster- and Västergötland, Skåne, Bornholm, and Vendsyssel would spawn with Goths, Langobards, Burgundians, and Vandals to add to the Empire's troubles. The southern wanderings of the Eruli during three centuries, the Geat attack on Frisia, and the Angles' share in the conquest of Britain have been referred to as illustrations of this northern overspill. But so far as we can tell, the seventh and most of the eighth century was a period of respite. For this there must have been good reason, part of which will be found in the close and unrelenting struggles for regional and national power both within and between the Scandinavian countries during this time, some account of which has been offered earlier,[1] the easing of their population and land problems brought about by the Migrations, and their preoccupation with the Baltic lands and the peoples east and north of them. Even more important was the question of means. The quick-in quick-out viking raids which began in the 790s, and still more the voyages of settlement to the lesser Atlantic islands which began somewhat earlier, were sea-borne and could hardly be undertaken until northern shipwrights had brought the sailing-ship to some such state of excellence as we observe in the vessels found at Gokstad in Norway and Skuldelev in Denmark. From all the evidence, pictorial and archaeological, the necessary command of techniques was attained about the middle of the eighth century.[2] It was then that northern sailors reaped the benefit of centuries spent traversing the leads and fjords of the Norwegian coasts, the belts and sounds and sandy entries of the Danish mainland and island-archipelago, the lakes and rivers of Sweden, and the crossing to Åland, Gotland and Öland, and all such training in seamanship as Skagerrak and Kattegat, Baltic and Baltic Gulfs provide.[3]

[1] More especially in the chapter on 'The Legendary History of the Swedes and the Danes' and the earlier part of 'The Historical Traditions of Norway to 950'.

[2] The classical early accounts of the viking ship for the English reader were those in Hjalmar Falk's chapter on 'Seafaring' in Shetelig and Falk, *Scandinavian Archaeology*, 1937; Brøgger and Shetelig, *The Viking Ships, Their Ancestry and Evolution*, 1950, new ed. 1971; and Thorleif Sjøvold, *The Oseberg Ship and other Viking Ship Finds*, 1959. Thereafter came the relevant chapters of P. H. Sawyer, *The Age of the Vikings*, 1962, revised ed. 1971, which among its other excellences summarized the views of Harald Åkerlund ('Áss och beitiáss', *Unda Maris*, 1955–6, and 'Vikingatidens skepp och sjøväsen', *Svenska Kryssarklubbens årskrift*, 1959); B. Almgren (ed.), *The Viking*, 1966; and Jacqueline Simpson, *Everyday Life in the Viking Age*, 1967. More recent studies, which have a far wider range of material to work on, including underwater wrecks, include D. Ellmers, *Frühmittel alterliche Handelsschiff-fahrt in Mittel- und Nordeuropa*, Neumünster, 1972, and numerous monographs and articles, e.g. Olaf Olsen and Ole Crumlin-Pedersen, *Vikingskibene i Roskilde Fjord*, Copenhagen, 1962–3, and *Fem vikingeskibe fra Roskilde Fjord*, 1978; A. E. Christensen, 'Scandinavian Ships from earliest Times to the Vikings', in G. F. Bass (ed.), *The History of Seafaring*, 1972; O. Crumlin-Pedersen, 'Skibstyper', in *KLNM*; 'The Ships of the Vikings' in *The Vikings*, Uppsala, 1978; 'Some Principles for the Recording and Presentation of Ancient Boat Structures', in S. McGrail (ed.) *Sources and Techniques in Boat Archaeology*, 1977; S. McGrail, 'Ships, Shipwrights, and Seamen', in J. Graham-Campbell (ed.), *The Viking World*, 1980.

[3] It is easy to overlook the obvious. Scandinavians were travellers by land,

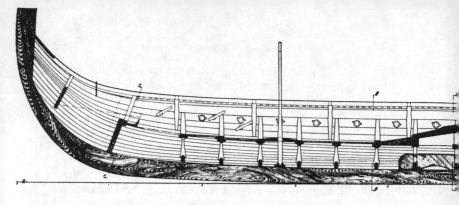

Section

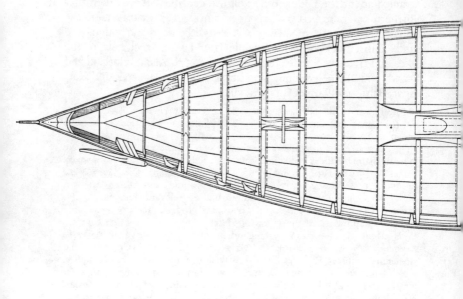

Section C—C.

General arrange
Sc

25. THE GOKSTAD SHIP (PLANS AND SECTIONS)

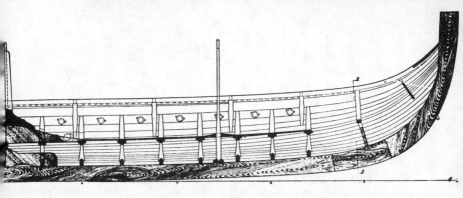

central line.

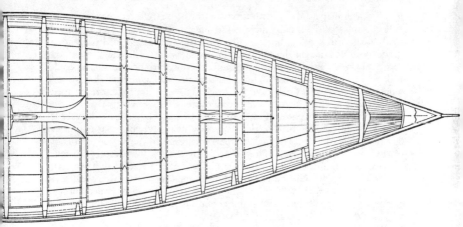

B—B.

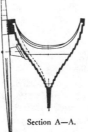

Section A—A.

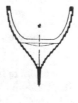

Section D—D.

of the Gokstad ship.
1 : 80.

If we take the Gokstad ship as our prototype (a fine vessel of the mid-ninth century), we might sum up the situation at the time of the early viking raids thus: around the year 800 a leader of rank and means could have at his command for ventures overseas a seaworthy and manoeuvrable sailing-ship, some $76\frac{1}{2}$ feet long from stem to stern, with a beam of $17\frac{1}{2}$ feet, and a little over 6 feet 4 inches from the bottom of the keel to the gunwale amidships. The Gokstad ship had a keel of 57 feet 9 inches, made from a single oak timber, and was clinker built of sixteen strakes of differing but carefully calculated thickness. The waterline strake was $1\frac{3}{4}$ inches thick, the nine underwater strakes and the three immediately above the

---

too. Their principal aid to locomotion was the horse, referred to on innumerable occasions in the literary sources, frequently in the historical, and found in abundance in heathen burials. The long trails of loose-roped pack-horses to be observed in the Icelandic countryside almost till the present day accurately represented the ancient Scandinavian habit. The northern peoples had a variety of carts and wagons for summer haulage, though few such workaday conveyances can have approached in splendour the ornate specimens, some of them of religious significance, discovered at Oseberg and Gokstad. They had sledges of different kinds, mainly but not exclusively for winter. Some scholars believe that the body of many carts or sledges was designed to work with wheels or runners according to the season, and could be transferred to a boat also. They knew the use of skis and skates (a number of these last, fashioned from pigs' shin-bones, have come to light at Birka and other places). The building and maintenance of roads, especially in swampy places or across streams and rivers, was a well-regarded form of community service. There are a number of runic stones commemorating men who built bridges or causeways, like that now in Fjenneslev Church in Zealand: 'Sazur raised the stone and made the bridge'; or that at Kallstorp in Skåne: 'Thorkel Thordarson made this bridge after his brother Vragi.' Interestingly enough, many of these inscriptions have a Christian flavour, like that on a rock at Södertalje: 'Holmfast had the ground cleared and a bridge built after his father Geir, who lived in Nasby. May God keep his soul. Holmfast had the ground cleared after his good mother, Ingigerd'; or the elaborate stone from Dynna in Hadaland, Norway: 'Gunnvor Thidrik's daughter made this bridge after her daughter Astrid. She was the most accomplished maiden in Hadaland.' Among the carvings on this stone are God (or Christ) and the Star of Bethlehem, and the journey of the Three Wise Men of the East. But the major works of this kind, like the causeway and river-bridge at Risby in southern Zealand, would be beyond private provision; and at Ravning Enge near Jelling a true bridge almost a kilometre long, built on at least 1700 strong wooden piles with maybe 800 angled posts, can hardly have been undertaken by any save Harald Bluetooth; and mighty engineering feat though it was, even that soon fell into disrepair.

waterline strake were precisely 1 inch; above this was the oar strake, $1\frac{1}{4}$ inches, and the two topmost strakes were just $\frac{7}{8}$ inch. The gunwale was substantial, $4\frac{1}{2}$ inches by $3\frac{1}{2}$. The strakes were joined together by round-headed iron rivets driven through from the outside and secured inside by means of small square iron plates. The caulking was of tarred animal hair or wool. The hull was kept in shape by nineteen frames and cross-beams. The decking of pine, in this case loose so that the space beneath could be used for storage, was laid over these beams. The strakes below the waterline were tied to the frames with spruce root lashings (in the Oseberg ship with narrow strips of whalebristle, in the Tune ship with bast), a device which contributed much to the ship's flexibility. This was still further increased by a carefully systematized trenailing of the above-water strakes to wooden knees and cross-beams or, in the case of the top two, to half-ribs secured to the strakes below and butted into the underside of the gunwale. The elasticity of this part of the ship was such that the replica of the Gokstad ship sailed across the Atlantic in 1893 by Magnus Andersen (a twenty-eight day passage from Bergen to Newfoundland) showed a gunwale twisting out of true by as much as 6 inches, yet was safe, fast, and watertight. With her mighty keel and flexible frame and planking the viking ship was an inspired combination of strength and elasticity. And this power to cross seas and oceans did not exhaust her excellence as a raider. An exceedingly shallow draught, rarely exceeding $3\frac{1}{2}$ feet, allowed her to penetrate all save the shallowest rivers, gave her mastery of harbourless shelving beaches, and facilitated the rapid disembarkation of men at the point of attack. By turning into the wind and making off by oar she was almost immune from pursuit by the clumsier sailing-ships of the lands she preyed on.

The ship was constructed almost entirely of oak. The sixteen pairs of oars were of pine, so regulated in length that they struck the water in unison. They were operated not by means of rowlocks but by closable holes in the fourteenth strake. The mast, too, was of pine, 26–35 feet tall, with a rectangular sail *c*. 23 by 36 feet, made of strips of heavy woollen cloth, strengthened it appears by a rope network, and hoisted on a yard some 37 feet long. The apparatus for bearing and supporting the mast was massive and strong. First there was the 'old woman' (*kerling*) or keelson, a prostrate block of solid oak resting on the keel over a span of four frames, with a cunningly designed socket to take the boot of the mast and assist its raising and lowering. Above the *kerling*, supported by the 'old woman' and no less than six cross beams, was another big block of oak, the mast partner, its forward section massive and closed, to take on three sides the pressure of the raised mast when the ship was running under sail and transmit the wind's power to the hull, its rear grooved to facilitate the mast's lowering. When the mast was raised this groove was filled with a fitting oak block or wedge. From the Gotland pictorial stones it appears that sail could be effectively shortened by the use of reefing lines, and recent opinion has inclined to the view that the viking ship could be sailed across and even near the wind. This was largely due to the use of the *beitiáss*, a removable pole or tacking boom whose heavy end was seated in a socket abeam of the mast while its lighter end was fitted to the forward leech of the sail to keep it taut and drawing when the ship was sailing on the wind.[1] She was steered by a side-rudder fastened to the starboard quarter, a singularly effective instrument pronounced by Magnus Andersen to be one of the clearest proofs of northern shipbuilding skills and seamanship. On his Atlantic crossing he found it satisfactory in every way, decidedly superior to a rudder on the sternpost, and manageable by a single member of the crew in any weather with just one small line to help him. Such ships would frequently be furnished with a ship's boat, some-times stowed on board, sometimes towed behind. Three such were found with the Gokstad ship, beautifully made and 32, 26, and 21½ feet long respectively, two with masts and all three equipped for rowing, but it is possible that the two bigger ones are not true ship's boats but grave goods. Bailing was by bucket and muscle-power; the anchor was of iron, and in general was served by a rope and not an iron chain. The ship could be tented for sleeping quarters by night. Finally it is worth re-emphasizing that the ship which carried the Norsemen overseas, whether to the British Isles, the Frankish Empire, or (self-evidently) to the Atlantic Islands, Iceland, Greenland and America, was a *sailing ship*: her oars were an auxiliary form of power for use when she was becalmed, in some state of emergency, or required manoeuvring in narrow waters, fjords, for

---

[1] The *beitiáss* has been reported on favourably by Captain Magnus Andersen, who crossed the Atlantic in a replica of the Gokstad ship; Captain Folgar, who in 1932 took a replica of a 60-foot knörr across the Atlantic by one of Columbus's routes and returned to Norway by way of Newfoundland; and by Captain C. Sølver, after his experience of the *Hugin* in 1949.

example, or rivers. This was true of raiding ships and carriers alike, though the ratio of men to space would naturally be higher in the raider. The ship of all work, the true ocean-goer, the *hafskip* or *knörr*, was in its general construction similar to the Gokstad ship, but broader in the beam, deeper in the water, and of a higher freeboard. This has always seemed clear from saga evidence, and was confirmed by the raising of Wrecks 1 and 3 from the waters of Peberrenden-Skuldelev in Roskilde Fjord, Denmark in 1962.

The study of the viking ship took a new turn in the fifties and sixties, when the developing science of underwater archaeology permitted the examination of a substantial number of vessels of different types and sizes which, unlike the early exemplars, were neither grave-goods nor of a sacrificial nature, but vessels built for a lifetime of hard work before finding their more or less natural end and resting-place. The picture is still far from complete, but what impresses at once is the hitherto undemonstrated variety of northern shipbuilding. The sagas preserve many names for warships, *skúta*, *snekkja* (taken into French as *esnèque*, the general word for a Norse pirate vessel, and into Russian as *shneka*), *skeið*, *dreki* (dragon-head), *karfi*, as well as the generic *langskip* (longship), and these between them represent a spread of from six to twenty oars a-side. Longships, levy-ships, or defence ships (*leið-angrsskip*, *landvarnarskip*), always assuming that this last is a genuine viking term, could be very big indeed and deploy much manpower, sometimes more than a hundred men. Olaf Tryggvason's *Long Serpent* is described as having thirty-four oars a-side, and Knut, we are informed, would build a longship of sixty benches, but we await the discovery of any such formidable monsters. The five Skuldelev ships now on display in their waterside museum by Roskilde suggest a comparable range on a more realistic scale in respect of the carriers of cargo. These ships were sunk in the channel there *c*. 1000, to prevent a seaborne incursion. Wreck 2 is a longship, 29 metres long and 4.2 wide, fully capable of moving 50–60 men over to England; Wreck 5 is a small warship, 18 m. by 2.6. But the real finds proved to be Wreck 3, oak-built, 13.3 m. by 3.3, and Wreck 1, built mainly of pine, 16.6 m. by 4.6. In these we discern a coaster and a deep-sea carrier respectively—the first of their indispensable kind to yield up their secrets to the shipwright and archaeologist. Students of the western voyages may well hold Wreck 1 in esteem as representative of the *knerrir* which maintained the Iceland–Greenland–Vinland routes, even if their beginning was with the Gokstad ship. With her open

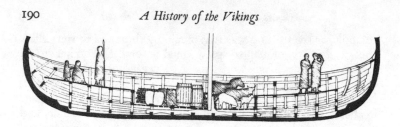

25a. LENGTHWISE SECTION OF SKULDELEV WRECK I, A
SEAGOING CARGO-SHIP WITH A HOLD AMIDSHIPS

carrying-space or hold amidships, her half-decks fore and aft
protective of further freight, she is estimated to have been able to carry
a cargo of 15–20 tons in a carrying-space of 30–35 cubic metres. With
her good design, sound construction, tractable sail and shallow
draught, this northern-type clinker-built, double-ended keel boat,
could carry her cargo to all marts, all coasts, and put it safely ashore.
The Gokstad ship, Skuldelev 1, and their kinds were the culmination
of a long process of experiment which began at least as far back as the
Bronze Age, can be charted with fair accuracy from the fourth to the
seventh century, and found the right answers, particularly in respect of
bow, stern, and keel, and the all-important business of mast and sail in
the eighth. When the Viking Age was over bigger ships would be
built, and the distinction between warship and merchantman would be
sharpened, but these are developments which concern us less than
directly.

The ship of all work, we have said, was the *knörr* (pl. *knerrir*), and
if we seek to understand the haven-finding art of the Norsemen it
must be with this sturdy craft in mind. It is generally accepted that
when the great Atlantic voyages of discovery and exploration took
place in the ninth and tenth centuries the North had neither compass nor chart. How then could a Norwegian, Icelandic, or Greenland
skipper in the year 1020 make his way confidently and accurately
from, let us say, Bergen in Norway to L'Anse-aux-Meadows in
northern Newfoundland? Clearly he had his sailing directions,
and some of these have been preserved in the passage from *Landnámabók* quoted on page 162 above. First and foremost he would
commit himself to a latitude sailing. This was no haphazard affair.
To begin with he would move thirty miles or so north of Bergen to
the landmark of Stad, because this had the same degree of latitude
as his landfall in Greenland. If now he sailed due west he would

find himself after the right count of days passing north of the Shetlands, and thereafter south of the Faroes at a recognizable and prescribed distance from them. On the same course he would next traverse the ocean well to the south of Iceland and know where he was not by the later measurement in miles but by observing the birds and sea-creatures associated with those waters. On a good passage, in clear weather, and with a following wind, this part of the voyage would have taken about seven days. It would take him almost as long again to sight the east coast of Greenland about eighty miles north of Cape Farewell. Now he must head south-west and reach the west coast of Greenland either by rounding the Cape or by threading Prins Christians Sund. From here on he would be following a well-described coastal route till he reached Herjolfsnes (the modern Ikigait), with its Norse farms and haven. Ahead lay the landmark of Hvarf, and thereafter many ports of call in the Eastern Settlement, in the region of the modern Julianehåb. He was now in the warm northward-setting coastal current of West Greenland and would progress with comparative ease and plenty of directions to the Western Settlement, in the neighbourhood of the modern Godthåb. From here we assume he would continue north by the familiar route to the northern hunting grounds, to the modern Holsteinsborg or the huge island of Disco. If from Disco he turned south-west for the eastern coast of Canada he would be conforming to a classic principle of Norse navigation, to make the shortest practicable ocean passage and use the clearest landmarks. He would also stand to benefit by the frequent northerly winds of the Davis Strait. From Disco or Holsteinsborg he would reach the southerly part of Baffin Island and know what kind of coast to expect there. He must now follow the land south, for an estimated number of days, passing the big inlet of Frobisher Bay and the entrance to Hudson Bay, till he sighted the forest land of Labrador, south of modern Nain. South of Hamilton Inlet he would be looking for the white beaches of the Strand and the distinctive keel-shaped Cape Porcupine (the Furdustrandir and Kjalarnes of the sagas), and so down past Battle Harbour till in time he sighted Belle Isle and thereafter the northernmost tip of Newfoundland and Cape Bauld. From here to Épaves Bay and the Norse houses by Black Duck Brook was a defined route without navigational problems.

This, inevitably, is a crude simplification of the sailing directions a skipper and his crew must carry in their heads as they sailed the coasts of West Greenland and Labrador. The knowledge of land-marks could be hardly less demanding on a sailor through the Norwegian skaergaard, or a newcomer threading the western islands of Scotland, though here the use of local skills might some-times be relied on. An immense sea-lore was indispensable, the lessons to be learned from cloud formations and the colour of water, marine creatures and birds, iceblink, currents, driftwood and weed, the feel of a wind. These sailors knew the sun and stars, the arts of rough and dead reckoning, and the use of a line to search the ocean's bottom. In a good day's sailing of twenty-four hours they could cover 120 miles and more.

But for the long Atlantic voyages between Norway, Faroes, Iceland, Greenland, America, the first requisite was the mariner's ability to fix his latitude. That the Norseman could do this is certain, though there is still doubt as to his method and instruments. We read, for example, of a detailed set of tables attributed to the Ice-lander Star-Oddi, which gave the sun's midday latitude week by week throughout the year, as he observed this in northern Iceland towards the end of the tenth century. This or similar information recorded on so simple an object as a marked stick would give the mariner an indication of his then latitude as compared with a known place. Any observation of the midday sun, or if need be of the Pole Star, even by so crude a method as the measurement of a shadow cast at noon or the calculation of the Star's height above the horizon expressed in terms of one's own arm, hand, or thumb, was a fair guide to latitude, which on the western voyages was much more important than longitude. Because if a storm-driven mariner (and there were many such during the early voyages of discovery and the ensuing period of trade) could get himself back to his correct latitude and sail in the desired direction he must, accidents and disasters apart, reach the place he was aiming for. The extreme casualness of thirteenth-century saga sources relating to sea-voyages is possibly thus explained. A ship leaves the Oslofjord for Breidafjord in Iceland, or Breidafjord for the Eastern Settlement in Greenland, or the Eastern Settlement for Leifsbudir in Vinland, or makes any such voyage in reverse, and the full extent of our information may be that it had a following wind, an easy passage, was much delayed, or blown about, and then arrived at its destination. The casualness would be still more understandable if we could be sure that in the Viking Age the Norsemen had learned to make use of the light-

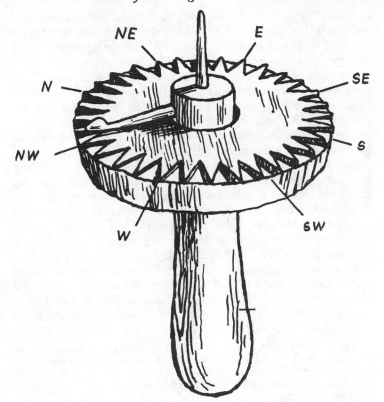

26. A NORSE BEARING-DIAL

polarizing qualities of calcite or Iceland spar (*sólarsteinn*, sun-stone), and could thus make an observation of the sun even when it was hidden from view.[1] It is reasonable to assume that they had bearing-

---

[1] *Flateyjarbók* and other Icelandic sources describe a phenomenon best explained by such a use of Iceland spar or something similar to make an observation of the sun. *Flateyjarbók* does so with a reference to St. Olaf of Norway in the first third of the eleventh century. The scientific principle of the polarization of light by Iceland spar was first formulated by Erasmus Bartholinus in Denmark in 1669, and in an indirect way led to the invention of the Kollsman Sky Compass, or 'twilight compass', *tusmørkekompas*, in use today by those civil airlines and air forces which ply the polar routes. It is certain that the Viking Age had no knowledge of the scientific principle

dials of a simple but effective kind, though the only indication of
this is the half of a round disc of wood marked with equidistant
notches discovered by C. L. Vebaek in 1948 at Siglufjord in the
Eastern Settlement of Greenland. Had it been whole the notches
would number thirty-two, offering a sophisticated division of the
horizon reminiscent of the late Middle Ages rather than viking
times, when an eight-point dial conforming to the eight named
points of the Old Norse horizon would appear more natural.[1]

Finally, even so cursory an account of the viking ship cannot be
left without one substantial qualification. The Gokstad ship would
presumably carry a crew of thirty-two to thirty-five; it is unlikely
that many raiding ships were bigger and carried more; the probability is that most of them were smaller. It is estimated that the
weight of the Gokstad hull, with all her fittings, was just over 20
metric tons; the *Viking* replica of 1893 was of just under 32 register
tons. It sounds less than large, but it was enough. Such vessels gave
a seafaring people an unchallengeable instrument of aggression.
The unexpectedness, the swiftness, and the savagery of the viking
raid on the monastery at Lindisfarne in 793 came as a bolt from the
blue not only to the monks surprised and slaughtered there but to
Alcuin over in Charlemagne's court.[2] 'It is some 350 years that we

---

involved. On the other hand, it will not take a man handling a piece of
Iceland spar long to hold it up to the light. At the moment the question of
viking use of the *sólarsteinn* is an open one, and it would be gratifying to have
it answered in the affirmative. See Thorkild Ramskou, 'Solstenen', in *Skalk*,
1967, nr. 2, pp. 16–17.

[1] The half-disc was found in a ruin thought to date from *c.* 1200. It has a hole
in its centre which could well be for a shaft, and this shaft might well contain
a shadow-pin and even a course-indicator. Not everyone accepts that the
half-disc is part of a bearing-dial, but it is hard to know what else it could be.
Similar but earlier finds would be useful. Carl. V. Sølver has argued convincingly for its nature and use in *Vestervejen. Om vikingernes sejlads*, Copenhagen,
1954, but is mistaken in describing it as a *sólarsteinn*. There is a useful description in English in Jacqueline Simpson, *Everyday Life in the Viking Age*, 1967,
pp. 94–5. The illustration on p. 193 is after Sølver.
[2] The date of the first Danish raid is rather loosely determined as during
Beorhtric's reign. He reigned from 786 to 802. The tone of the entry which
deals with it in the *Anglo-Saxon Chronicle* is markedly different from that for
793:
[789, for 787]. In this year Beorhtric took to wife Eadburh, daughter of
king Offa. And in his days came for the first time three ships of Norwegians

27. PERILS OF THE NORTHERN SEAS, I: THE
DEVOURING WHALE (OLAUS MAGNUS)

and our forefathers have inhabited this lovely land, and never before
in Britain has such a terror appeared as this we have now suffered
at the hands of the heathen. Nor was it thought possible that such
an inroad from the sea could be made.' Fifty years earlier he would
have been right; but now, within a period of five years, Norse free-
booters plundered and slew at Lindisfarne and Jarrow in Northumbria, Morganwg in South Wales, Lambey Island (Rechru) north
of Dublin in Ireland, in Kintyre and the Isle of Man, and at the
sacred island of Iona on the west coast of Scotland. In 799 they raided
various islands lying off Aquitaine in France. All this was a presage
of calamity which the future would not belie.

---

from Hordaland, and then the king's reeve rode thither and tried to make
them go to the royal manor, for he did not know who or what they were, and
with that they killed him. These were the first ships of the Danes to come to
England.

793. In this year terrible portents appeared over Northumbria and sadly
affrighted the inhabitants: these were exceptional flashes of lightning, and
fiery dragons were seen flying in the air. A great famine followed soon upon
these signs, and a little after that in the same year on the ides of January
[*read* June] the harrying of the heathen miserably destroyed God's church in
Lindisfarne by rapine and slaughter.

The reasons for this fresh stirring of 'tumultuary arms and numbers' were many. For Alcuin the sackers of Lindisfarne were God's instrument of wrath visited upon the sins of the people, but this, even if true (and Alcuin quotes Jeremiah 1:14 in support),[1] is not enough. The deeper causes of the viking movement overseas were rooted in human nature: the northern peoples had needs and ambitions, were prepared to make demands, and had the will, strength, and technical means to enforce them. They wanted land to farm, wealth to make life splendid, or bearable, and some of them wanted dignity and fame. Trade, colonization, piracy, and war would get them these things, and such could be practised only at the expense of neighbours near and far. The northern irruption surprised most contemporaries, but can surprise no one today.

A long tradition as well as the Migrations themselves testifies to recurrent overpopulation and land-shortage in Scandinavia. 'Each of these countries ("those peoples whom the northern pole aspects") was like a mighty hive, which, by the vigour of propagation and health of climate, growing too full of people, threw out some new swarm at certain periods of time, that took wing, and sought out some new abode, expelling or subduing the old inhabitants, and seating themselves in their rooms.'[2] A case in respect of the Viking Age proper was deployed by Johannes Steenstrup in his mighty *Normannerne*.[3] The limitations imposed on both crop and animal husbandry in parts of Scandinavia in early times by sea, mountains,

[1] 'Then the Lord said unto me, Out of the north an evil shall break forth upon all the inhabitants of the land.'
[2] Sir William Temple, 'Of Heroic Virtue', 1690, quoted from *Works*, iii, 363, 1814. The quotation, *populos quos despicit Arctos*, he takes from Lucan. Temple had canvassed northern matters with men as notable as Count Oxenstern (Oxenstierna) and Olaus Wormius, and shared their views and at times their errors. The bees and the hive he found in Jordanes.
[3] *Normannerne*, 4 volumes, Copenhagen, 1876–82. The two best-known examples of the tradition are Hengest's tale to Vortigern about the expulsion of surplus 'Saxons', best known through Geoffrey of Monmouth, *Historia Regum Britanniae*, vi, 10, Wace, and Layamon (the earlier stages of the tradition are discussed in K. Schreiner, *Die Saga von Hengist und Horsa*, 1921); and the emigration of the Gotlanders, as recounted in *Guta Saga*, ed. Pipping, Copenhagen, 1905–7. For a trenchant account of the latter, and the similar stories in Paulus Diaconus, *Historia Langobardorum*, Dudo, *Dudonis sancti Quintini de moribus et actis primorum Normanniae ducum*, and Saxo Grammaticus, *Gesta Danorum*, with a reference back to Herodotus, see L. Weibull, 'En forntida utvandring från Gottland', in *Nordisk Historia*, I.

28. PERILS OF THE NORTHERN SEAS, 2: THE
DEVOURING WHIRLPOOL (OLAUS MAGNUS)

latitude, and cold, especially in respect of Norway and upper
Sweden, were always constrictive, and at times severely so. Domi-
ciled in this circumscribed and vulnerable region was a vigorous and
fast-breeding race whose numbers increased considerably from the
seventh to the tenth century. Their social habits were shaped to
increase, though we must regard with caution the written evidence
for Norse polygamy. That men like girls, concubines, mistresses,
and that those who can afford them frequently acquire them, is not
a very particularized indictment. According to Adam of Bremen,
every Swede whose means allowed had two or three wives, while
the wealthy and high-born set themselves no limit. It sounds excessive, even for Swedes, while Ibn Fadlan's comments on the crude
sexual arrangements of the Rus in Russia (see p. 165 above) express
along with some truth the satisfaction of a man who manages these
things more elegantly at home.[1] On the most parsimonious count

[1] Their king, he says further, had forty women in his harem, and when he
wished enjoyed them in public, while his hirdmen were supplied with girls
for service and joy exactly like Harald Fairhair's champions back in Norway.
'Glorious is their way of life, those warriors who play chess in Harald's court.
They are made rich with money and fine swords, with metal of Hunaland and
girls from the east.' (*Hrafnsmál*, 8.)

Harald had nine sons who grew to manhood; his son Eirik Bloodaxe
had eight—and all needed a substantial patrimony. Great men had
wives by marriage-contract and, if they wished, by loose-bridal.
For any save the very poor a quiverful of sons was welcome. They
were proof of a man's virility, the extension of his right arm, and
along with poetry or a standing stone his best memorial to posterity.
They also manned ships and, in viking terms much the same thing,
filled armies. But they had to be provided for. Above all they had to
be fed. There were too many men at home, of chieftains' and farmers'
sons both, and 'Out they must, for the land cannot contain them'.
The tools of empire are younger sons, and throughout Scandinavia
these were in good supply.

It does not, of course, follow that their numbers were enormous,
as is sometimes argued for and sometimes contested. All they had to
be was sufficient. And this, in terms of far-reaching conquest or
permanent colonization, they often failed to be. Peoples can be too
numerous for their own meagre acres, yet not numerous enough
to fill and hold shires, provinces, and realms abroad.

For one particular category of men there was a second reason
why out they must. There must have been periods of violent disturbance in Denmark during the first thirty years of the ninth
century, while Godfred established his realm and cleared its coasts
of sea-kings, and later, when the sons of king Godfred fought the
sons of an earlier king Harald for supremacy; and, equally, a long
process of dynastic strife in the petty kingdoms of Norway during
the hundred years preceding the accession of Halfdan the Black *c.*
840. In wars of succession losers lose all, making a shift abroad
welcome to all parties. We know very little about the earliest Norse
incursions into the Shetland and Orkneys and thereafter the
Hebrides, but the first settlements, *c.* 780, appear to have been
peaceful and carried out by men concerned not with plunder but
with a search for pastureland where they could live the life and
reproduce the institutions they were used to. Vikings seeking a base
came later, nearer the middle of the ninth century, in part, one
suspects, because pressure was building up more strongly at home.
The main areas of colonization as opposed to conquest were explored
and taken over after 860. In the case of those dispossessed Danish
princes who found lands in Frisia, and the Norwegian vikings who
found themselves at loggerheads with Harald Fairhair, we have
indicative if not over-reliable information as to names and circum-

stance, and the record can be extended down through Gold-Harald in the one kingdom and Olaf Tryggvason in the other. Who led the first attacks on Northumbria, Scotland, and Ireland, we do not know, but it is a fair conclusion that many of them were made in a similar mould, men in trouble with a lord or lords stronger than themselves, men dispossessed, men banished, men who left their country for their country's good.

The contribution of pressures from outside Scandinavia to the viking movement has been variously assessed. So considerable an authority as Johannes Brøndsted will have nothing to do with it, on the grounds that there is no evidence for it, and that the early viking raids west and south-west bear no similarity to the great movements of the migration period.[1] But where no one cause seems sufficient we must clutch at every straw—and Charlemagne's Empire as it expanded northwards after *c.* 770 probably felt quite a heavy straw to those it drove against. Clearly this had nothing whatever to do with the Norwegian occupation of the Atlantic Isles and their first raids on the British Isles, but the strong Danish reaction against the Franks and Frisians and their Abodrit allies was an important part of the complex of motives and events characteristic of that first phase of the viking movement which may be held to have terminated at the end of the second decade of the ninth century. The disturbing influence of a great power acquisitively on the move was as marked in early times as in our own, and few survivors of the 1930s will feel that British and French politicians acted with more wisdom or courage then than did Godfred between 800 and 810. If Charlemagne's conquest of Saxony did nothing more to the north, it hardened Denmark militarily and drew its attention south; while the harm done to Frisia weakened the Empire's northern defences and established the most natural Danish raiding route south as the easiest and most assured. Soon, in any case, the political condition of the Empire, England, and Ireland would exert not pressure but an irresistible pull on all Norsemen to come down and exploit their exposed coasts, ill-knit territories, and their immense and ill-defended treasures.

We have mentioned trade, and trade's dark sister, piracy (pp. 166–7 above). Both were essential to the viking movement, for the vikings practised both, assiduously. When circumstance favoured they were happy to be merchants, but when seas were undefended and

[1] *The Vikings*, 1965, p. 25.

29. PERILS OF THE NORTHERN SEAS, 3: POLAR ICE AND
POLAR BEARS (OLAUS MAGNUS)

towns lay open they turned privateer. The first relevant entry in the
Anglo-Saxon Chronicle, that dealing with the Hordalanders who
encountered the king's reeve at Dorchester, and the amplified
account of the episode in the *Chronicon Æthelweardi*, is symbolic.
The unfortunate reeve thought they were merchants and directed
them to the royal manor for the customary preliminaries to trade.
But if merchants, they were rough-dealers, and for reasons which the
Chronicle does not explain they killed him. When Norwegians next
came to England they came to plunder. The process once started,
no mystery remains. Loot is loot in any language, and western
Europe was full of it. Ireland, England, France were the vikings'
Mexico, with learning, arts, wealth, and a civilization superior to
those of their northern *conquistadores*, and a similar inability to
defend themselves from a numerically inferior but mobile and
energetic foe. Report of the more accessible monasteries and
churches, the coastal marts and riverine towns, the defenceless
manor-houses and well-stocked farms, must have seeped through
the viking world like water through thirsty earth. There was still
a short delay: the Norwegians were taking over the sheep-pastures
of the Atlantic Isles and the Southreys; the Swedes were facing
east to the rivers and forests of Russia; and the Danes were at grips

with the Empire and each other. But the storm-bell was tolling and in 834–5 the breakers would come crashing in.

One other 'cause' of the viking movement invites comment. The northern peoples as the ninth century drew near had to be ready for it. Here, too, there is no mystery. Greed, self-interest, profit, advantage, describe or qualify it as one will, is endemic in human nature. Yet this is an unflattering way of describing the viking upsurge. That it was the expression of a heroic ideal is, on the other hand, all too flattering—and misleading. To see the viking movement in terms of heroic literature is like seeing the Italian Risorgimento in terms of grand opera, or the winning of the American West in terms of its equine equivalent. We have noted the three viking compulsions of land, wealth, and fame. Naturally these did not often operate separately or in isolation. They arose out of the northern way of life, and were pursued in the existing context of politics, geography, and economics. They indicate a not unusual way of thinking expressed in appropriate action. It was not even a matter of bravery, much less a heroic ideal: the vikings were no braver than the English whom they would eventually subjugate (with curious consequences for themselves), or the Welsh with whom they would fail. But by and large they were self-confident;

30. PERILS OF THE NORTHERN SEAS, 4: DRIFTWOOD AND WRECKAGE OFF GREENLAND (OLAUS MAGNUS)

today, tomorrow, or the day after they knew they had the beating, or it might be safer to say outmanoeuvring, of their enemy. Take selfconfidence and professional skill, add resource, cunning, no nonsense about fair play, a strong disregard for human life and suffering, especially the other man's, and you have a good soldier. Give a ship's crew or a mounted commando of such men a leader in whose intelligence, tactics, valour, profitability, and record of success they can trust, and you have a good unit. Multiply the units, find them a general like the famed Halfdan or Hastein, Ganga-Hrolf or Olaf Tryggvason, or a monarch like Svein Forkbeard or Knut, and you shake kingdoms. It is not surprising that the vikings prospered overseas as much as they did: the surprise is that they did not prosper more. For this, too, there were reasons, which will be discussed later. For the moment we may conclude that the viking's trade dovetailed well with the state of affairs in Scandinavia as the eighth century wore to its close. Fame, profit, change, adventure, land, women, danger, destruction, service, comradeship, command, irresponsibility, were all made realizable. And the North now had the ships.

As in Scandinavia, so at the receiving end in Europe the times were favourable to the art and practice of *viking*. From the beginning access, outrage, and escape were easy for individual and uncoordinated raiding parties. Till their sails notched the horizon of Scotland, Ireland, and the kingdoms of England, they moved in secrecy; in lucky conditions of weather and coastline they were on their prey with hardly an hour's warning; whether they strandhewed for cattle,[1] or plundered a monastery or coastal town, there would in their own phrase be 'little defence for the land'; and when the time came for them to row out and take the breeze in their sail they had soon vanished utterly. They held a comparable advantage on the national scale. Scotland, Ireland, England, Wales (and still less Russia in the east) were at no time kingdoms single and indivisible, and in 840 the Frankish Empire ceased to be such. In Scotland there was a medley of realms and races: Picts north of

---

[1] *strandhögg*, a shore-raid whereby vikings provided themselves with cattle, alive or slaughtered, and other stores. This was a practice eloquent of the ancient disunity of Scandinavia, where a man's loyalties were confined to his own patria, region, or petty kingdom, so that a Zealander would not plunder in Zealand (or his section of it), or a man of Sogn in Sogn, but felt free to help himself elsewhere. As the petty kingdoms were welded into larger units the custom grew displeasing to kings like Harald Fairhair and Harald Bluetooth. It had always been displeasing to those plundered.

Argyll and the Forth; Welsh in Strathclyde and Cumberland, and mingled with the Picts in Galloway north of the Solway Firth; Scots in their expanding kingdom of Dalriada (Argyllshire, Kintyre, and the islands of Bute, Arran, Islay and Jura); and Angles in Bernicia. In Ireland, true, there was a High King in Tara to whom the seven kingdoms of Connaught, Munster, Leinster, Meath, Ailech, Ulaidh, and Oriel did homage, but this was a unity more apparent than real. Between north and south there was the normal Celtic jealousy which no Golden Age contrives to charm away. Division in Wales was equally acute, and in England it was worse. In everything save material possessions Northumbria had long since declined from eminence and splendour, and the supremacy of Mercia, established in the eighth century by Ethelbald *rex Britanniae* and Offa *rex Anglorum*, broke in pieces within thirty years of Offa's death in 796. East Anglia regained its independence some time after 825 and Essex and Kent had hankerings of a similar nature. These two would submit in different degree to the emergent kingdom of Wessex under Ecgbert, though as late as 856 king Ethelwulf could be made to accept a division of Wessex which split off Kent and the provinces of the south-east. In the south-west the Welsh of Cornwall remained long unreconciled to an English yoke, and after 835 were briefly misled into thinking to exchange it for a Danish. Across the English Channel the death of Louis the Pious in 840 played straight into Danish and Norwegian hands. His eldest son Lothar, who had spent the last decade quarrelling with his father, now committed himself to quarrelling for another two with his brothers Charles the Bald and Louis the German. They defeated him heavily at Fontenoy, and the treaty of Verdun in 843 saw the end of Charlemagne's Empire. Lothar was still emperor, but his domain shrank to contain Italy, Provence, and Burgundy, and the lands running northwards to Frisia and the North Sea. All territories to the east of this Middle Kingdom went to Louis the German. They included Bavaria, Thuringia, Franconia, and Saxony, and brought him flush with the southern frontier of the Danes. To Charles went the territories west, roughly modern France between the sea and the rivers Rhône, Saone, Meuse and Rhine, and Spain down to the Ebro. Even here Brittany and Aquitaine had pretentions to independence. We may safely regard the increase of viking activity in the newly partitioned Empire as neither accident nor coincidence.

3. The Movement South and South-West to 954: the British Isles, the Frankish Empire, the Mediterranean

To follow in detail the viking onslaught on ninth-century Europe, whether nation by nation, decade by decade, or under the four generally accepted heads of individual raids for plunder, expeditions of political significance and intention, colonial ventures seeking new land for settlement, and enterprises whose main concern was mercantile and commercial, would be a big task—and in terms of this book a distorting one. It must be enough to trace it in general though one hopes indicative outline. We begin with Ireland in the 830s.

The Irish coast had suffered sporadically from Norwegian plunderers ever since the first raid on Lambey in 795, and sometimes the raiders had penetrated far inland. These were painful depredations,[1] but bearable, and left the character of country and people unchanged. But nothing could ever be the same again after the arrival of the famous Turgeis from Norway shortly before 840. Our knowledge of him, unfortunately, is at once inflated and diminished by the legendary material associated with him several hundred years after his death, when he had become a favourite receptacle for Christian indignation and alarm. But we can accept that he held command of a fleet, had ambitions and the energy to put them in train, came to Ireland at the right moment, and intended a prolonged stay. We first hear of him in the north, where he is said to have assumed the overlordship of all the foreigners in Erin, after

[1] And rhetorically recorded as such in the *Annals of Ulster* for 820: 'The sea spewed forth floods of foreigners over Erin, so that no haven, no landing-place, no stronghold, no fort, no castle might be found, but it was submerged by waves of vikings and pirates.'

which, helped by a civil war instigated by the priest-king of Munster, he spread his elbows to good effect throughout Ulster. By the capture of Armagh, at once a chief town of the north, the most important ecclesiastical centre of Ireland, and one of the holy places of western Christendom, he acquired wealth, power, reputation, and his place in Irish tradition. To him and his kind is attributed the establishment of harbour-strongholds at Anagassan, Dublin, Wexford, Waterford, Cork and Limerick, with important consequences for the subsequent history of both Norse and Irish Ireland. He is

MAP 6.   IRELAND AND THE IRISH SEA

reported to have intervened for gain in the civil war to the south of him; to have entered the Shannon and reached Lough Ree; the sack of Clonmacnois and Clonfert has been laid at his door, and the dispersal of their monks. Various of the Irish are charged with joining him, opportunists who reneged on Christianity and as Thor's men trooped into heathen temples which before Turgeis's time had been monasteries, churches, and abbeys. Few things in viking history sound less likely. These were the Gall-Gaedhil, Foreign Gaels or Foreign Irish, of whom the Irish complained that though the Foreigners were bad enough, the Foreign Gaels were worse.[1] Christian witness against Turgeis is unsparing for his desecration of holy places. Having expelled the abbot of Armagh, he sat himself down in the abbey as its heathen high priest, and at the altar of Clonmacnois his wife Ota (Aud) chanted spells and oracles. Possibly this was the way Turgeis chose to present himself to his people as leader, sustainer of sacrifices, and guarantor of good seasons, on the Norwegian model. More probably it is monkish invention. However, for the comfort of the Christian devout, there had been an ancient prophecy that Gentiles, Foreigners, would come from across the sea to confound the Irishmen for a period of seven years, and one of them would be abbot without pater and credo, without Irish, too, but only a foreign tongue.[2] The seven years were evidently now up, for in 845 he was taken prisoner by Mael Seachlainn, king of Meath, and drowned in Lough Owel, Westmeath.

A bad time followed for the Norwegians. By widespread raiding they still exacted a toll of misery and spoil, but a succession of defeats in the field reduced their strength and smirched their reputation.

[1] The Gall-Gaedhil would grow to considerable importance by 850, with their own social organization and their own armies under their own leaders. They began as a body of Irishmen who renounced Christianity and threw in their lot with the heathen Norse; but some are described as having been fostered in Norse homes and so inducted into a Norse way of life. There can be no doubt that a proportion of them were of mixed Norse-Irish parentage, sharing the culture, and blending (or muddling) the beliefs of Viking and Celt. This mongreldom of race, culture, religion, and political interest endeared them to nobody. During the 850s they fought battles against the Norwegians, against the Irish, and against the Norwegians and Irish combined. Expectedly they were earnest and heartless marauders. Their political power declined after 860, but they continued to contribute to the miseries of Erin. There was a parallel group of Gall-Gaedhil, Gall-Gael, Foreign Scots, in Scotland later, in Galloway, which received its name from them.

[2] J. H. Todd, *The War of the Gaedhil with the Gael*, 1876, p. 11.

Unless Ireland was to be left to the Irish—an unthinkable proposition for another thousand years—it was time for renewed foreign intervention. It was made by the Danes, and not out of love for their brothers the Finngaill, to whom they immediately offered war. In *c.* 850 their fleet put in to Carlingford Lough, on the southern edge of County Down; the following year they overran the Norwegian base at Dublin, making a big haul of treasure and womenfolk. The Irish preferred the newcomers to the old, but with a plague on both their houses. In 852 the Norwegians mustered for revenge and attacked the Danish fleet in Carlingford. St. Patrick favoured the Danes; a mere handful of Norwegians survived the three-day slaughter. The Danes, prudently, rewarded the saint with gold and silver; and the Irish, mistakenly, saw piety in the Danes. If so, it aided them little and not long. In 853 the Norwegians made a re-entry into Ireland with a royal fleet under the command of Olaf (Amlaibh), son of the king of Norway (Lochlann), though which son of what king is hard to determine.[1] The Danes and Norwegians, we are told, quickly recognized his authority and various of the Irish paid him tribute, including wergeld for Turgeis. Those Danes who had no stomach for a Norwegian master left for England, whence they had probably come in 850, and Olaf settled into Dublin. He then returned to Norway for reasons which can only be guessed at, leaving his brother Ivar in charge in Ireland. In 856–7 he returned to his Dublin kingdom and ruled it till 871,

---

[1] He has often, indeed generally, been identified with Olaf the White of Icelandic saga tradition. The identification is inviting but difficult. It rests mainly on the circumstance that each Olaf was said to have conquered Dublin and its neighbouring territory at more or less the same time. Otherwise their parentage is different, their wives are different, and their deaths are different. By way of complication Olaf-Amlaibh's brother Ivar-Imhar is sometimes equated with Ivar the Boneless (see p. 219 below), no Norwegian but a prodigy among the Danes. It makes the best of a bad job to postulate confusion in the Icelandic *Landnámabók*'s account of Olaf the White, to hold tentatively to Olaf-Amlaibh, whether he was at some time nicknamed the White or not, and to recognize Ivar-Imhar as his brother and a person distinct from Ivar the Boneless. (The Ragnar-complex has now been re-explored by A. P. Smyth, *Scandinavian York and Dublin*, I, 1975, II, 1978, and *Scandinavian Kings in the British Isles, 850–80*, 1977, who argues ingeniously for a military and dynastic presence and reality; and by R. McTurk, 'Ragnarr Loðbrók in the British Isles', *Proceedings of the Seventh Viking Congress*, Dublin, 1973, and reviews of Smyth, *Saga-Book*, 1977 and 1980, who argues, as I think, convincingly against.)

when he was again recalled to Norway and died in battle there. It was a restless reign, marked by shifting alliances, petty wars, harryings in Ireland which spared neither the homes of the living nor the graves of the dead, and in the period 865–70 by profitable expeditions against the Picts and Strathclyde Welsh in Scotland. Ivar lord of Limerick supported his brother Olaf in Ireland, and in 871 succeeded him as *rex Nordmannorum Totius Hiberniæ et Britanniæ,* which suggests that the Dublin kingdom had claims to authority over the Norwegians who had settled in the north-west of England. If so, this might explain Ivar's quarrels with the Danes of neighbouring Deira, which were offered as the justification for the attack on Dublin in 877 by Halfdan (we think) and the Danes of that kingdom. The attack failed and cost Halfdan his life up in Strangford Lough. With the principal Norse actors now off stage Ireland grew quieter, and more Irish. There was a falling-off in reinforcements from Norway, and Iceland was a new magnet in the west. An Irish king, Cearbhall of Leinster, Ivar's one-time ally, took what fortune offered. In 902 he seized Dublin from the Foreigners, and though he died soon afterwards Ireland enjoyed comparative peace for the next twelve years.

31. VIKINGS AT LINDISFARNE

Our reference to the Danish kingdom of Northumbria in the last quarter of the ninth century recalls us to England, the scene of the first viking raids *c.* 789 and 793, and even more pressingly to the

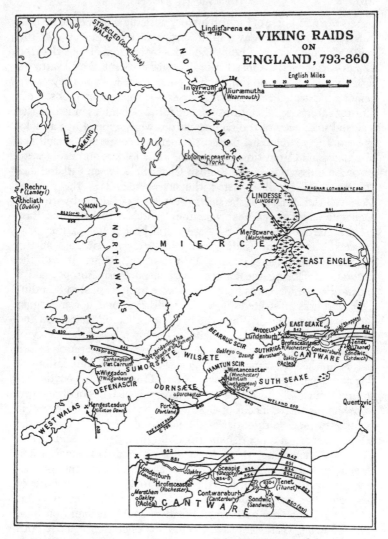

MAP 7. VIKING ATTACKS ON ENGLAND, 793–860

Continent. In Celtic Ireland the Norse incomers were predominantly Norwegian, in Teutonic England they were Danes. Under the year 835 (corrected from the *Chronicle's* 832) the *Anglo-Saxon Chronicle* ushers in a new phase of English history with the short notice that 'In this year the heathen devastated Sheppey'. It was in 834 after the temporary deposition of Louis the Pious by his unfilial sons that the Danes had moved against Frisia. The most recent Danish attacks against any part of the Empire had taken place in 820. These were minor and isolated events, but after 834–5, we appear to observe a sinister enterprise taken firmly in hand. In England, as in Frisia, the size and frequency of the raiding parties were stepped up; attacks present a less haphazard pattern, sometimes concerted, sometimes alternated, and from time to time the same leaders and fleets were in action either side of the English Channel. Between 836 and 842 strong Danish flotillas tested the defences, and in the case of Cornwall the loyalty, of the south-west coast of England with only moderate success; the next year they switched to Kent and East Anglia. Across the water they were still busier. In 834 they laid waste the important trading town of Dorestad, situated at the junction of the river Lek and an arm of the Rhine. It had the reputation of being the biggest mart in northern Europe, had a much-prized mint, coins from which were freely copied in Scandinavia, and was protected by water, palisades, and a Carolingian fortress. None availed. When the hand of the Carolingian grew too weak or too preoccupied to defend it, the town lay at the mercy of the Danes, and it was pillaged systematically for a generation before nature finished what man had begun when the tidal inundations of 864 overwhelmed large areas of the Low Countries, and by diverting the course of the Rhine in the direction of Utrecht destroyed once and for all the means of Dorestad's survival. After Dorestad it was the turn of Noirmoutier at the mouth of the Loire, a monastic site and centre of a flourishing trade in salt and wine; and in 836 Frisia again, and again in 837. In 841 it was the turn of Rouen, when Asgeir appeared from nowhere off the mouth of the Seine, headed upriver, sacked and burned the town, took a quick tribute of destruction and money from the countryside, and had his ships out and away before the gathering defenders could lay hand on him. The following year, 842, saw a combined operation against both England and France. 'In this year there was great slaughter in London, in Quentowic, and in Rochester.' Quentowic, directly across the Straits of Dover, rivalled Dorestad as a merchant town, and like Dorestad it had a mint. Its trade connections with England were close and profitable, and it was a bold and shrewd stroke of viking policy which sent the same fleet shuttling between them. Then in 842 the Norwegians made a well-documented appearance in French waters.[1] It would not be quickly forgotten. Sixty-seven ships of Westfaldingi, men from Vestfold, the historic region of Borre, Oseberg, Gokstad, and Skiringssal, but in all probability come now from Ireland, appeared unheralded off the Loire. Its horrors long past, this raid may be studied as a classic example of viking tactics and the conditions which ensured their success. Aquitaine was part of Charles the Bald's West Kingdom, but the rebel Count Lambert was ambitious to secure Nantes for himself. It is said that the vikings came at his invitation, and that it was French pilots who conned them through the sandbanks, shallows, and uncertain watercourses, which in high summer were judged an absolute protection from naval assault. The day was 24 June, St. John's Day, and the town was filled with devout or merry celebrants of the Baptist's feast. The Norwegian assault was of surpassing brutality. They slew in the streets, they slew in the houses, they slew bishop and congregation in the church. They did their will till nightfall, and the ships they rowed downriver were deep-laden with plunder and prisoners. This was maybe more than the Count had bargained for, but he did acquire Nantes. The Westfaldingi withdrew to Noirmoutier, whose monks had by now abandoned it, and contrary to Norse practice settled in for the winter. 'As if they meant to stay for ever', says the annalist ruefully. The island had much to recommend it. For a start it *was* an island, and therefore impervious to assault. It provided shelter for men and a haven for ships, where they could mend their wounded and ransom their prisoners. Further, Noirmoutier was a centre of the salt trade for the whole of western Europe, and to Noirmoutier came merchants for the good Loire wine. To it therefore, as wasps to honey, came the Norsemen.

This is the first time we hear of a viking force employing a winter base. Hitherto the leaders of expeditions had led their men out in late spring or summer and fetched them home in the autumn. *Viking* was seasonal employment: the winter did not lend itself so well to war and travel, whether by sea or land. So a man went home with his earnings to his parents, wife, and children, and if he was

---

[1] *Chronicon Engolismense* (Pertz, *MGH*, *SS* XVI, 486); *Chronicon Aquatanicon* (Pertz, II, 253); both *sub anno* 843. See F. Lot and L. Halphen, *Le Règne de Charles le Chauve*, Paris, 1909, I, 79 ff.

a bondi or a bondi's son saw to the roof, scratched the boar's back, whittled a toy sword, begat a new baby, and waited on the next call to service. But to stay abroad for the winter, as now in France and in 850 for the first time in England, gave *víking* a new emphasis. If one winter, why not two, and if two why not three? The winters were warmer down south, the seas never froze, the land was good, and was there to be taken. Why go back home at all? The small man got a smaller cut than his leader, but in kind it was the same. The Norwegians sailing west had occupied and farmed from the beginning. In Denmark where there was more cultivable land the same desires showed two generations later. Their wintering in Thanet, 850, and Sheppey, 855, was a portent. The year 845 was notable for a further development in northern tactics or strategy. The destruction of Hamburg that year was a royal undertaking (see p. 107 above), and not by the widest interpretation of the laws and customs governing international relations to be explained away as mere piracy or privateering. In the same year the daring of Ragnar's raid up the Seine to Paris and the helplessness of Charles the Bald led to a third and hurtful innovation. Ragnar, whom it is unnecessary to equate with his hairy-breeked namesake Ragnar Lodbrok (*loðbrók*),[1] entered the Seine in March, which it is fair to say was unexpectedly early, and made confidently for Paris. Charles collected an army against him, which he divided in two to guard both banks of the river. A viking operating in a partitioned empire knew how to deal with a divided army. Ragnar attacked the smaller Frankish force, heavily defeated it, and took 111 prisoners. These as a deliberate exercise in 'frightfulness' he hanged on an island in the Seine in full view of the second Frankish division. Beaten in arms and spirit, they could make no effective opposition. Ragnar went on upriver, and with the same cruel timing shown by the Westfaldingi at Nantes entered and plundered Paris on Easter Sunday, March 28. He was now more than 200 miles from his element the sea, and it would not seem past man's devising to have hindered his return. Instead Charles paid him 7,000 pounds of silver to depart in peace

[1] It is difficult to prove a negative, but there is little evidence of the existence of a historical Ragnar Lodbrok. True, he suffers more than most from the numbing disadvantages of a mythical saga and use as a heroic symbol, but even when these are set aside he is hard to locate in place or time. On a cautious estimate he must have been at least 150 years old when he died in his snake-pit and prime at York in the 860s. (And see p. 207, n. 1, above.)

and take his plunder with him. To anticipate a later term, this was the first 'danegeld', and Charles has been much castigated for it. But he is not without excuse. In theory Charles, like his brothers, could raise armies, build fleets, garrison towns, fortify coasts, bar rivers, and manhandle all vikings out of his realm—and who can doubt that he would have liked to? But theory and fact are different things. Charles had much to contend with: thrusting foreign foes, rivalry and enmity from his brothers, the veiled disaffection of great nobles, and the open rebellion of great provinces. He could be confident neither of the fighting spirit of his soldiers nor the patriotism of the counts who hung back from leading them. The vikings were a squalid nuisance, but their incursions must be seen in perspective. At times it must have appeared to Charles as though he was a man with a wolf at his throat and a wasp in his hair, and in this menagerie of menace the Danes were the wasp. To get rid of them, theoretically for good, in fact for six years, by payment may well have looked an act of statesmanship in 845, with trouble in the north and a Breton war looming in the west. Payment bought time, and time brought hope of amendment. Little enough time and little enough hope they seem to us now, but Charles was looking forward, not back. The sums paid out were weighty, on occasion enormous, but they came mainly from taxes, and the peasant taxpayer who carried the heavy end was in no position to protest. Between collection and payment there could even be a profit for the king.[1]

Another development of these same years was the viking contact with the Moors in Spain. This was ushered in by a raid by a fleet said to be 150 ships strong which entered the Garonne and plundered upriver almost as far as Toulouse. The area was in a state of civil war, the protagonists Charles the Bald and that young Pepin who sought to make himself an independent king of Aquitaine. Possibly the raid was made in support of Pepin; at any rate, Pepin's town of Toulouse was not assaulted, and the intact fleet went back down the river and is next heard of off the coast of the kingdom of the Asturias, in northern Spain. Opposition here was resolute and effective, the invaders were mauled by land and sea, and it was a depleted though still formidable fleet which escaped round Cape Finisterre and held

[1] The first recorded English payment was that promised to the Danes by the men of Kent in 865. Of the thirteen Danegelds levied in France we know the details of seven. These amounted to almost 40,000 pounds of silver plus, on occasion, meat and drink for the raiders.

south for Lisbon. After a fortnight's skirmishing and piracy there they pressed on to the Guadalquivir, and with a daring verging on folly went up the river and attacked the city of Seville. Except for the citadel it fell into their hands for a week; its men were put to the sword, its women and children carried off as spoils of war to the viking base on the island of Qubtil, today's Isla Menor, near the river's mouth. From here they raided the neighbouring country for the next six weeks. But the Moorish kingdom of Spain under Abd al-Rahman II was a different proposition from France under Charles the Bald, and once the period of surprise and unpreparedness was over the vikings for all their huddle of treasure and captives were in a position of much peril. To leave their headquarters was to invite attack by land and water; raiding parties were cut off, and several of their ships fired by a discharge of naphtha; and worst of all, the vikings lost thirty ships in a naval engagement at Talayata. The Moors took so many prisoners that the gallows of Seville did not suffice for them, and the city's palm trees bore strange fruit. Report of the Emir's victory was not entrusted to mouth and quill alone: he sent the severed heads of 200 vikings on a dumb but eloquent embassy to his allies in Tangier. However, the vikings had one asset left, their prisoners. The Moors wished to ransom them, and the captors struck a bargain. There was to be no more fighting, and the price should be worked out in food and clothes, not gold. Evidently the invaders had for some time been sealed off from sources of supply.

Some less martial conversation than this must have taken place between Moors and Norsemen, for the next year, 845, Abd al-Rahman sent an embassy under Al-Ghazal to the king of the Majus, with choice gifts for him and his queen. If the vikings of the Guadalquivir were Danes, we judge that the embassy was to Horik in Denmark, if Norwegians to Turgeis in Ireland. The northern king, whoever he was, dwelt on a big island in the ocean, gracious with gardens and flowing waters. Near by were other islands inhabited by Majus, and three days' journey away was the mainland or continent, and here, too, the king held power. The king's wife was named Nod, or Noud, and the gallant, graceful, and 50-year-old Al-Ghazal was delighted to find his wish for a beautiful friendship received in the same amiable spirit as it was offered. And how gratefully there must have fallen on an ear grown wary for an inrushing husband's unreason Noud's assurance that the Majus were too enlightened for jealousy and that northern ladies were free to leave their consorts at will. If the embassy had political or economic consequences, we are not informed of them, but it seems safe to assume that its main purpose was to encourage trade, more particularly in furs and slaves.[1]

These decisive years were followed by a long tale of depredation in Frisia and the West Kingdom, which need not be separately recorded, but is eloquently recalled by Ermentarius of Noirmoutier writing in the 860s. He exaggerates, no doubt, but who looks for measure in the cry of the toad under the harrow?

The number of ships increases, the endless flood of vikings never ceases to grow bigger. Everywhere Christ's people are the victims of massacre, burning, and plunder. The vikings over-run all that lies before them, and none can withstand them. They seize Bordeaux, Périgueux, Limoges, Angoulême, Toulouse; Angers, Tours, and Orleans are made deserts. Ships past counting voyage up the Seine, and throughout the entire region evil grows strong. Rouen is laid waste, looted and burnt: Paris, Beauvais, Meaux are taken, Melun's stronghold is razed to the ground, Chartres occupied, Evreux and Bayeux looted, and every town invested.

From this welter of harassment and destruction we pick one name, that of Bjorn Ironside, the *Bier costae ferreae* of William of Jumièges, son of Lothrocus king of Dacia (Denmark), otherwise Ragnar Lodbrok. Like his father, he is better known to legend than to history, but his day of glory (and he must have had one) extended from the mid-50s to 862. During the years 856–7 he was on the Seine, and some of the ill deeds listed by Ermentarius can be set to his credit. His name is associated with the vikings who established or took over a base on the island of Oissel (Oscellus), where they were at last strictly beleaguered by Charles the Bald. But as so often, the treachery of his noblemen, who invited Louis the German to enter the West Kingdom and 'help' his brother, an invitation too good to be declined, worked to the vikings' advantage and led to the raising of the siege after twelve weeks. The next development was the arrival of another viking band under the command of Weland, to whom Charles eventually offered 3,000 pounds of silver to rid him of their Oissel compatriots. For reasons profitable to both Charles and Weland the sum took a long while collecting. It

[1] For a translation of, and commentary upon, Ibn Dihya's account of this episode, see W. E. D. Allen, *The Poet and the Spae-Wife*, Viking Society, 1960.

involved a graduated tax on farms and land, on churches, and on merchants great and small. Eventually Weland received not 3,000 but 5,000 pounds of silver, and provisions of corn and cattle, too, and even then the royal accounts showed a balance. Weland kept his word, and the Oissel vikings were besieged a second time. They were not short of money, but soon ran out of food and paid Weland 6,000 pounds of silver to let them get away.[1] If they were Bjorn's men, they were released in time for one of the more spectacular enterprises of the century, the four-year cruise of Bjorn and Hastein with sixty-two ships to Spain, North Africa, and Italy, and possibly still farther into the Mediterranean. That they proposed to be out so long is unlikely: the two of their ships which were captured by the Moors off the coast of Spain were already laden with gold, silver, and prisoners. That the Norsemen would enter the Mediterranean eventually we see to be certain; Bjorn and Hastein were among the most famous of ninth-century captains and heedful of reputation; they may for some time have been considering a penetration of the Middle Sea in terms of glory as well as profit, or maybe their adventure grew in the undertaking. That they had begun to plunder at the earliest opportunity—well, what pirate ever passed by the prospect of easy gain?

We next hear of them at the Guadalquivir, where they seem not to have prospered. It is doubtful whether, as some Moorish sources say, they proceeded upriver as far as Seville. Soon they had passed through the Straits of Gibraltar, put in at Algeciras, plundered it, then made for the North African shore in the region of Cabo Tres Forcas. The local defence force panicked, and the vikings spent an unharrassed week rounding up prisoners for ransom, though some, probably negroes, they kept as *souvenirs de voyage*. These poor wretches, *fir gorm*, blue men, *blámenn*, black men (or merely men with dark skins), for the most part ended up in Ireland. The western Mediterranean was empty of armed Moorish ships, so they crossed back to Spain and harried the cost of Murcia. Their next landings

[1] Weland was not the first viking leader known to turn on his fellow Norsemen for money, and would not be the last; but he clearly improved the rate for the job. He was very much a businessman, and made no move against Oissel till his money was in hand. He filled in the intervening season by raiding in the south of England, in Wessex. Shortly after getting rid of the men on Oissel he entered the service of Charles the Bald and was baptized along with his family. It availed him nothing: he was challenged to fight by one of his pagan followers and killed.

were in the Balearics, which for the first time felt the northern scourge. Thence they held for southern France, put ashore at will in Roussillon and possibly sacked Narbonne. It was getting time to seek winter quarters, and these they found in accordance with viking practice on an island in the Camargue in the Rhône delta. It had been a wonderful summer of sunshine and blue water, of fabled coasts and storied islands. They had sailed by two great kingdoms, passed the Pillars of Hercules, and sojourned in classical Africa. They had a vast booty and many captives, their losses in men and ships had been light. They had shown the dragon-head and shield-wall in new havens, and were poised for fresh adventures. Meantime they were en-isled and safe.

Not so their French neighbours. Before they made the countryside too hot to hold them they had pillaged inland as far as Arles, Nîmes, even Valence, more than a hundred miles to the north. Then they took a beating from the Franks and judged it prudent to move on, so sailed east along the Côte d'Azur and Ligurian Riviera. Their movements from there on are largely unknown, but they found time to sack Pisa before heading farther south. They are spoken of as traversing the eastern Mediterranean as far as Alexandria; and Dudo of St. Quentin and Benoît of St. Maur have preserved the story of Hastein's 'Sack of Rome'. Naturally enough the man who regarded himself as the world's foremost viking was ambitious to sack the world's foremost city. So from the Rhône delta Hastein sailed on till he came to a city so big, so white, so splendid, so marbled, that what else could it be but Rome? But its defences were so strong that Hastein judged it impervious to assault. So the vikings hit on a ruse: they sent messengers to the city to tell how Hastein and his following were good men expelled from their own country and sea-tossed to this distant coast. They were weary and hungry, needed peace and provisions, and their sick chieftain lay at death's door. When next they came to town that door was passed; all he now required of this vale of tears was a Christian burial. The townsmen agreed to provide one; a long procession of sorrowing vikings followed the coffin to the graveside, where at the moment of committal the 'dead' Hastein rose in his coffin, drove his sword through the officiating bishop, and led his men on a riot of slaughter through the city streets.[1] His exultation knew no bounds,

[1] A similar (and similarly unlikely) ruse is recorded of Harald Hardradi and his Varangians (*Haralds Saga Harðráða.* 10).

till somewhat late in the day he discovered that the ravished city was not Rome at all, but Luna, whereupon he gave orders for the town to be fired and its menfolk massacred. Its women they spared. They would, they thought, have use for them elsewhere.

In 861 they were back in the neighbourhood of Gibraltar, where they were defeated by a Moorish fleet. The survivors escaped away north, their appetite for pillage unsated, and when they reached Navarre went inland and captured Pamplona. They collected an immense ransom for its prince, sailed north again, and next year one-third of their sixty-two ships were safely back in the mouth of the Loire. In saga-phrase theirs had been an enterprise 'at once profitable and honourable'. But without political consequence, and apart from the 'blue men' in Ireland we know nothing of the fate of their captives. Some had been ransomed, others less lucky had no doubt been disposed of to the Moors.

This was in 862. We have already seen the nuisance raids of individual leaders develop into big, well-organized expeditions which exploited local divisions and lived off the invaded country for lengthening periods of time. A new stage, that of conquest and residence, now followed. In 865 a big heathen host, or horde,[1] at a

---

[1] mycel hæðen here. The Anglo-Saxon Chronicle customarily designates a viking raiding party or army as a here. The term was that applied in the Laws of Ine to a substantial body of thieves. 'We use the term "thieves" if the number of men does not exceed seven, "band of marauders" (hloþ) for a number between seven and thirty-five. Anything beyond this is a "raid" (here).' (F. L. Attenborough, The Laws of the Earliest English Kings, 1922, pp. 40–1). The term used for the English forces was usually fyrd (fierd), army, force, levies.

In the light of this definition a 'big heathen horde' need not be all that big, and it is probable that contemporary records and modern historians alike have had inflated ideas of viking numbers. It is improbable that raiding ships ever carried more than 32–5 men, and the majority of them would carry less. P. H. Sawyer, The Age of the Vikings, pp. 124–5, has compiled a table of the numbers of ships mentioned in the Anglo-Saxon Chronicle before the end of the ninth century, and with his permission I reproduce it here:

789   3 ships of Northmen in Dorset.
836   35 ships; 25 in some versions.
840   33 ships; 34 in one version.
843   35 ships.
851   350 ships; 9 ships captured later that year.
875   Alfred fights 7 ships and captures 1.
877   120 ships lost at Swanage in a storm (or in a mist).
878   23 ships.

guess of 500–1,000 men, arrived in England to initiate a more sustained and coherent assault than had yet been attempted. Their leaders were Ivar (Yngvarr) called the Boneless, Ubbi, and Halfdan. Legend tells us that they were come from Scandinavia and Ireland to avenge the death of their father Ragnar, about whom we know nothing very much after his withdrawal from the Seine in 845 with 7,000 pounds of silver and the seeds of plague in his army, save that he was reputed to have come to England with two ships' crews and been defeated by king Ella of Northumbria, who had him thrown into a pit and stung to death by snakes.[1] Before he died he was heard to say prophetically: 'The piglings would be grunting if they knew the plight of the boar!' And suddenly here they were, snouting and tusking in England. First they got themselves horses in East Anglia, and the next year marched upon York. Northumbria was in its customary state of civil war; its people had just driven out their king Osberht and accepted Ella, a king not of the royal line. Too late the two kings joined forces, marched on York, which was by now in Danish hands, and suffered there an overwhelming defeat (867). Both kings were killed. The same legends which put Ragnar in the snake-pit now let his sons carve the blood-eagle on Ella's back.[2] The kingdom of Deira passed into Danish keeping.

---

882   Alfred fought 4 ships; 2 captured and 2 surrendered.
885   Alfred's fleet encountered and captured 16 ships, but was later defeated by 'a large force'.
892   The *here* crossed from Boulogne 'in one journey, horses and all,' in 200, 250, or 350 ships according to different versions of the annal.
892   Haesten came with 80 ships.
893   Northumbrian and East Anglian Danes collected 'some hundred ships and went south round the coast'. One version adds 'and some 40 went north round the coast'.
896   6 ships.
896   20 ships perished along the South Coast.

He fully sustains his argument that the viking armies should be numbered in hundreds, not thousands, and that even the Great Horde of 892 would hardly exceed 1,000 in number. Three or four hundred, one judges, would be a very substantial viking force. It is easy to find medieval exaggerations of the order of ten-, thirty-, even fiftyfold; the ninth century armies had to be kept in the field; and they were recruited from a limited manpower.

---

[1] See footnotes on pp. 207 and 212 above.
[2] This inhuman rite of cutting away the victim's ribs from his spine, then pulling out his lungs and spreading them like wings on his back, probably

This was only the beginning. After a sortie into Mercia, whose king half resisted and then bought peace, Ivar and Ubbi in 869 moved south into East Anglia, defeated the English levies, captured and cruelly executed king Edmund, a deed which lastingly impressed itself on the English imagination and did not pass unheeded in the north. The act itself and Edmund's sanctification were a reproach to the Danes to the end of the Viking Age; but in the short run nothing saved East Anglia from joining Deira in Danish hands.

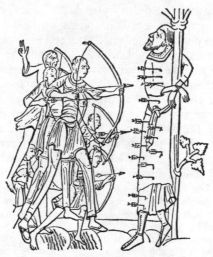

32. THE MARTYRDOM OF ST. EDMUND

'Hungry wolves take big bites.' In 870 Halfdan, accompanied by a second king and many jarls, led the Danes against Wessex, and seized and fortified the key town of Reading. 'During the year nine pitched battles were fought against the host in the kingdom to the south of the Thames, besides those frequent forays which Alfred the king's brother, and ealdormen and king's thanes rode on, which have never been counted.' The men of Wessex won one signal

had a moral or religious as well as a sanguinary significance for its perpetrator. It was unhappily no fiction—but owes its eminence in pseudo-lore almost entirely to fiction, from the exultant *Fornaldarsögur* to the *frisson*-seeking nineteenth century.

victory, at Ashdown, and before the year's end nine northern jarls and one king had died in battle. The Danes, though they won most of the battles, settled readily for a truce, and switched their effort to Mercia. But the most important event of the year was neither battle nor truce. Some time after Easter king Ethelred died and was succeeded not by his infant sons but by his brother Alfred. Alfred was Ethelwulf's fourth, or maybe fifth, son, and the fourth in line to inherit the kingdom. That he did so was the most remarkable accident in the history of the kingdom of Wessex.

Mercia had collapsed by 874, and now the Danish army, which had held together since 865, broke into two. Halfdan went back to Deira and from there made war on the Picts and the Strathclyde Welsh to secure his northern frontier, while Guthrum and two other kings departed for Cambridge in East Anglia. The actual occupation of English territory was about to start. In 876 Halfdan 'shared out the lands of Northumbria, and they [the Danes] were engaged in ploughing and in making a living for themselves'. The living seems to have included the profits of trade. The area partitioned was approximately that of modern Yorkshire. This decisive step taken, Halfdan follows his brother Ivar out of the light of history; presumably he set off against the Norwegians of Dublin and died in 877 (see p. 208 above). The autumn of 877 saw the second Danish distribution of English territory. Three years earlier the Danes had appointed 'a foolish king's thane' named Ceolwulf to look after the fallen kingdom of Mercia till they were ready to dismember it. Ceolwulf now received his wages in the form of half the kingdom; the rest was divided among the Danes who had fought for it. In short the great shires of Yorkshire, Nottingham, Lincoln, Derby, and Leicester had ceased to be part of the political realm of England, and maybe a belt of territory south of the river Welland as well. Danish settlement in this region was probably of two kinds, and did not involve a systematic displacement of the English. First in time and consequence there was a military settlement, but this appears insufficient to account for the number of Danes later to be found in the Five Boroughs, for example, often on virgin land along the lesser streams and tributaries and in districts of sandy or gravelly soil reminiscent of parts of the Danish homeland. It has been urged therefore that there were immigrants from Denmark quite apart from the fighting men, and that these colonized available areas behind the shield of the armies of the Five Boroughs, which for two

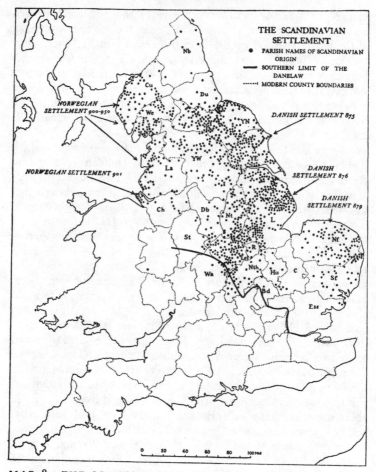

MAP 8.   THE SCANDINAVIAN SETTLEMENT IN ENGLAND

generations held Watling Street as the boundary between Danish
and English England.[1] But the degree and intensity of Danish
settlement in Mercia during the last quarter of the ninth century
awaits a full elucidation.

[1] The argument and some of its expression are those of K. Cameron,
*Scandinavian Settlement in the Territory of the Five Boroughs: the Place-Name
Evidence*, University of Nottingham, 1965, pp. 11 ff. and 22.

Guthrum meanwhile had twice probed at Wessex and been successfully countered. But in the first weeks of 878 he made a midwinter attack from his base at Gloucester which took the West Saxons completely by surprise. He occupied Chippenham without opposition, and with no West Saxon army anywhere in the field, and Alfred himself in flight to an island-refuge at Athelney west of Selwood, the subjection and consequent partition of Wessex appeared at hand. Extensive areas found it prudent to submit to Guthrum, and many West Saxons fled beyond the sea. But if Alfred despaired we do not hear of it. Small as his following was, he showed a hostile front to the Danes, and as the weeks went by the men of Somerset, Wiltshire, and part of Hampshire gathered to him. By valour and good fortune an attack on Devon mounted in South Wales, and in all probability led by the elusive Ubbi, had already been crushed. This cleared the threat to Alfred's rear, and seven weeks after Easter he felt strong enough to engage the Danish army at Eddington and pursue its defeated remnants to Chippenham. After a fortnight's siege Alfred and Guthrum came to terms: by the treaty of Wedmore Guthrum agreed to withdraw his forces from Wessex and himself accept baptism. On the lowest count he admitted one god more to his pantheon and allowed Christianity its full privileges within his dominion. But this is unlikely to be the whole of the story. He accepted the name Athelstan at his god-father Alfred's hand, and employed forms of it (Edelia, Edeltan) on the coins he had struck in the late 880s, and we can assume that his reign was an important stage in the Christianizing of the Danes in England. More immediately, in 879 he was back in East Anglia, to carry out the third Danish partition of English soil. The shires of Northampton, Huntingdon, Cambridge, and Bedford, together with Norfolk, Suffolk, and Essex, and (briefly) London itself, were to be made as Danish as the former English kingdoms that lay north of them. This considerable portion of eastern England, stretching from the Tees to the Thames, was the first delimitation of the future Danelaw (*Denelagu*; see Appendix 2, 'The Danelaw'), a kind of Denmark overseas, conquered, occupied, and organized by Danes, and clearly distinguishable from the rest of England by race, law, language, personal names and place-names, and not least by social custom. This was a political and military situation king Alfred had to live with; presently he and his successors would seek to contain and diminish it, then bring it back under English rule;

but to the close of the viking period Anglo-Danish and Anglo-Norman monarchs and law-makers would be forced to recognize the separateness and special circumstances of Danish England.

For the next fourteen years viking pressure on Wessex lightened. The new settlers of Northumbria, East Mercia, and East Anglia were not yet the men to beat their swords into ploughshares and pruning-hooks, but Wessex had proved herself a hard adversary, and had they not now estates to administer, land to farm, stock to care for, families to transport and settle into their new homes? The areas of plunder were asking for peaceful conservation, and the professional raiders, landless men, and members of war-bands must seek opportunities elsewhere. The Empire was prodigal of such, and England's respite till 892 marked the heyday of viking activity along the river-lanes of France and the Low Countries. Charles the Bald, as much maligned as he was unsuccessful, had died in 877, and his son and successor Louis the Stammerer survived him a bare eighteen months. The West Kingdom was thereupon divided between the Stammerer's two sons, and Provence hived off for Boso, admittedly a usurper, but the only effective candidate for it. Both sons were dead by 884, and the West Kingdom was taken over by Charles the Fat, who already was ruler of most of the so-called Eastern and Middle Kingdoms. But any hope that a reunited Empire would now rid itself of the viking nuisance (and Saracen menace) was illusory. Charles was not the man for the job. He had already given proof of his ineffectiveness when in 882 he not only allowed the beleaguered Danish army under Godfred, Sigfred and Orm, to depart unhindered from Elsloo, with 2,800 pounds of silver by way of inducement, but tried the dangerous expedient of establishing Godfred as the semi-independent ruler of part of Frisia. Godfred's limitations as a thinker saved Charles from the worst consequences of this blunder, and it even turned to his advantage after he had arranged for Godfred's murder in 885; but he had his subjects' confidence even less than his predecessors had. To list the depredations of these years would be a long business: Scheldt, Meuse, Somme, Marne, Seine, Loire, Maine, Aisne, Vire, and Oise were viking highways; Cologne, Aix, Trier, Liége, Rouen, Paris, Soissons, Bayeux, St. Lô were some of the places oppressed. The most celebrated event of these years was the siege of Paris, inaugurated in late November 885 and maintained with intermittent fury for a year. It was a year of destiny for Franks and Danes alike. Paris had been the capital neither of Charlemagne's empire nor Charles the Bald's kingdom, but now its decisive importance was revealed, both political and geographical. It was the key to France, and the archbishop of Rheims in his often-quoted letter to Charles the Fat did not greatly exaggerate when he warned him that if he lost Paris he would lose everything, for the enemy would command the Marne, Seine, and Yonne, and northeast the country would lie open as far as Rheims. For the Danes this attempt to force the passage of the Seine through the Paris bridges began with the hope of a huge booty, but by force of circumstance they came to accept it as a trial of strength. For their part the defenders of Paris, count Odo and abbot Joscelin, brought all the issues, political, religious, dynastic, under one head: they had been charged to bar the Seine against the Norsemen. The Danish offer to leave Paris in peace in return for a free passage was rejected; their bloody assaults of January 886 were repelled. By the use of engines of war, and with the help of the winter floods, the bridges were eventually so damaged that the river could be passed. Paris was invested and the great host set itself to plunder the countryside. But the city was now a magnet, drawing in the eastern Franks to attempt its relief, and eventually Charles the Fat himself. The Danish king Sigfred grew sick of the whole business and for the ridiculous sum of sixty pounds of silver agreed to pull out downriver, but the siege was not lifted. Abbot Joscelin died of sickness, but Odo stayed unflagging in the city's defence. He slipped out of the city to implore Charles to act quickly, then fought his way back in, to buttress the citizens with promises of the emperor's approach. This last was a clumsy and interrupted affair, but by October Charles was at Montmartre and in theory at least poised for the kill. But while Odo and his gallant defenders waited for the spear to go home Charles opened negotiations with the Danes, granted them the Seine passage against which the Parisians had fought so magnificently, gave them *carte blanche* to harry his not overloyal subjects in Burgundy, and paid them 700 pounds of silver to seal the bargain. This may have been the act of a statesman, but to the Franks it looked the act of a coward; they judged Charles not fit to rule and at the beginning of 888 deposed him. Once more Charlemagne's empire was shared out, and the new king of the west kingdom, Neustria, was Odo the defender of Paris. After a skirmish in 889 he paid the Danes the money promised them by Charles the Fat, and Paris never saw an invading fleet of Norsemen again.

Other parts of the Empire were not so lucky, but with a whole-sale change of rulers there was a new spirit of resistance in the land, and after their defeat on the Dyle near Louvain in 891 by that vigorous bastard of Carloman's, Arnulf king of the East Franks, the survivors of the great host got themselves west to Boulogne and from there crossed to Kent in England in 250 ships,[1] men, women and children, horses and all. Famine in the devastated areas as well as defeat in battle helped speed them on their way. Currently our old acquaintance Hastein, who was finding life difficult in Brittany, appeared in the mouth of the Thames with eighty ships. On the surface they found things little changed from when they were in England last, whether with the stalemated fleet which visited Fulham in 878–9 or the circumvented army which was driven from Rochester in 884. Yet change there had been, and this to the Danes' disadvantage. On the evidence of his coinage Ceolwulf had survived in English Mercia till after 880, but by 883 an uncompromising ealdorman named Ethelred held power there and threw his weight behind Alfred in his struggle with the invader. He became Alfred's son-in-law by his marriage to Ethelflaed, the king's eldest daughter, and his loyalty to the house of Wessex was unfaltering. In 886, the year of the siege of Paris, Alfred recovered London from the Danes and tactfully entrusted this Mercian town to the safe-keeping of Ethelred. In the words of the *Chronicle*, 'all the English people submitted to him [Alfred], except those who were under the Danish yoke'. That is, Alfred was now not only king of Wessex but of all free Englishmen. As such he negotiated the treaty of 886 with Guthrum the Dane, which by an agreed system of wergelds safe-guarded those Englishmen who were not free. It was a treaty bet-ween equal and consenting monarchs, but, as Alfred knew, no treaty on earth would stop the Danelaw helping its kith and kin if they returned from the Continent and embarked on a new harrying of England. So in 892 he took oaths for good behaviour from Northum-bria and East Anglia, and East Anglian hostages, but these, too, made no difference, and throughout the four-year war which now began the Danes of those kingdoms aided their compatriots with asylum and reinforcements, distractions in the field and strong support at sea. Without these forms of succour the great host and Hastein would have been sooner tamed. They found the English army more lively and mobile, for Alfred had gone a good way

[1] For P. H. Sawyer's table of ship-numbers see pp. 218–9 above, n. 1.

towards solving the worst problems of a peasant militia: its unwillingness to operate far from home or stay long on active service. 'The king', says the *Chronicle*, 'had divided his levies into two sections, so that there was always half at home and half on active

33. A NORSE SHIP
(The Town Seal of Bergen, *c.* 1300).

service, with the exception of those men whose duty it was to man the fortresses.' It was less than perfect, but made the levies more effective than they had been before. Second, he established a pattern of fortresses, strong-points, to protect every part of his realm. In these the people of a threatened district could take refuge; conversely it was their duty to keep them in repair and man the walls at need. Four men to a perch of stone-wall or earthwork was his

successor Edward's requirement, and each hide of local land must
supply one of them. Third, Alfred was building ships for defence,
big ships, 'on neither the Frisian model nor the Danish, but as it
seemed to the king himself they might be most serviceable'. These
sixty-seaters took no great part in the fighting war, but the ability
to hurt an enemy in his own element has always been a raiser of
morale. The general impression left by the *Chronicle*'s and Ethel-
weard's accounts of the campaigns of 892–6 is that the Danes enjoyed
their usual freedom of movement and in a harassed way kept the
initiative, but that the English counter-moves were well planned,
rapid, and cumulatively so effective that the Danes came to know
they could not win. Alfred and his lieutenants Edward and Ethelred
fought a defensive war, but in modern phrase it was the defence of
the counter-puncher who absorbs those of his opponent's leads he
cannot slip, then punishes him hard before he gets away. The
attacker, if not defeated, is usually glad to hear the bell.

So with the Danes. At times their two armies appear to have
acted in concert, sometimes they looked to their own affairs, and
between them they conducted a variety of local and long-range
forays from their various encampments. As always, they lived off
the country and collected booty, but on two occasions this last was
recovered from them, their camp at Benfleet was captured with the
ships, womenfolk, and children they had left in safe-keeping there—
an occasion when Alfred showed his great humanity—and several
times they were contained for substantial periods. Alfred was a
thoughtful student of war: in 893 he kept the Chester Danes out of
the Midlands by destroying all corn and cattle in their neighbourhood, so that they had perforce to remove into Wales; in 895 he
dislodged the Danes from their camp on the Lea, twenty miles
north of London, by blocking the course of the river, and defending
it with two forts, so that they might not move their ships out;
in 896, when the main fighting was over and the host withdrawn
into the Danelaw or overseas, he sent nine of his new ships after six
ships from Northumbria and East Anglia which were plundering
the coasts of Devon and Wight. In retrospect it appears a small, as it
was certainly a clumsy, engagement, but the *Chronicle* rightly made
much of it. In the first phase of the encounter the crews of two
Danish ships were annihilated, and only five men escaped on the
third. In the second phase two ships' crews were so crippled that
they failed to row past Sussex and were cast ashore there. When

they were brought before the king at Winchester he had them hanged out of hand, not as soldiers but as thieves and ruffians. A few badly wounded men on the remaining ship reached East Anglia with a tale of unmitigated defeat.

Three years later Alfred was dead, one of those who in the world's history best deserved his title, 'the Great'. From a Scandinavian point of view it was he who in the 870s denied the Danes the conquest of all England, with the consequences that must have flowed from it. He was the most effective opponent the vikings had met anywhere in Europe since the death of Charlemagne in 810. And he left a successor to continue his work. This was the energetic Edward, by-named the Elder, who before his death in 924 brought the whole of the Danelaw south of the Humber under English rule. He came to the throne at a time propitious for great deeds. Everywhere the tide of Norse aggression was running slack, in Ireland, in England, and in the territories of the disrupted Empire, though it was in this last that the Norsemen were about to achieve a considerable unexpected success. This was the cession of Upper Normandy, *in alodo et in fundo*, to Rollo and his following in 911, the latest and in its consequences the most impressive example of the intermittent Frankish device of enlisting one viking as watch-dog against the rest (and in this case against the Bretons, too). We cannot say for certain whether Rollo was a Norwegian or a Dane. Icelandic sources, late in time as usual, and including Snorri's *Heimskringla*, identify him with Ganga-Hrolf, Hrolf the Walker (so called because like Huiglaucus who ruled the Geats he was so big that no horse could carry him), the son of Rognvald earl of Moer, who in defiance of Harald Fairhair's ban plundered in the Vik, suffered outlawry, and after spending some time in Scotland proceeded to France, where he founded the dukedom of Normandy. Picturesque as this vignette is, it is probably accurate in its main aspect—his nationality. But Norman historical tradition is unaware of any such Norwegian Hrolf, save in so far as he gave his daughter a Norwegian name, Gerloc, i.e. Geirlaug.[1] On the scene of action itself Rollo was considered to be a Dane. Much of the evidence on both sides is obviously unreliable—the main 'Danish' authority is the notorious Dudo—but the nationality of the leader is less important than that of

[1] In accordance with a not uncommon Norman practice she had two names, Scandinavian and Frankish, Gerloc and Adelis. Similarly, the wife of duke Richard I was named Gunnor (Gunnvör) and Albereda.

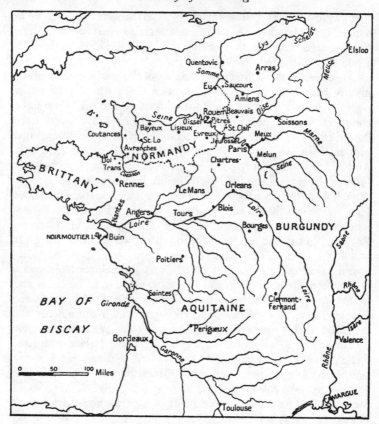

MAP 9. FRANCE AND NORMANDY

his army, which there is every reason to believe was predominantly
Danish.[1] Until 910 we are almost as much in the dark about Rollo's

[1] The problems here, and many of the answers, have been much clarified
by the fundamental study of J. Adigard des Gautries, *Les noms de personnes
scandinaves en Normandie de 911 à 1066*, Lund, 1954. The bulk of Rollo's army
was Danish. An appreciable number of them, especially among the settlers
between Bayeux and the Orne, had spent some time in north-eastern England
(for the evidence of an agrarian vocabulary see L. Musset, 'Pour l'étude des
relations entre les colonies scandinaves d'Angleterre et de Normandie', in
Mélanges F. Mossé, Paris, 1959, pp. 330-9). Others again had come from Ireland
or Scotland, and were presumably of Norwegian origin or affinity—they are
to be found in the Cotentin. The invaders brought very few women of their

movements as his ancestry, but he had evidently been operating in France for a number of years and had grown to prominence before the viking outburst of that year. In 911 he commanded the army which unsuccessfully besieged Chartres, and later is found back on the lower Seine. By now this was an area which the Danes had plundered bare and in practice controlled. Its one perdurable asset was its rich and orcharded soil, and this, after all, was what a Danish army by this time really wanted. Presumably the king of the West Franks made the overtures, while Rollo was clear-headed enough to welcome them. By the treaty of St. Clair-sur-Epte he was confirmed in the lordship of the spacious and strategically important territories whose modern titles are Seine Inférieure, Eure, Calvados, Manche, and part of Orne.[1]

But first Rollo did homage to king Charles the Simple and promised to defend the land entrusted to him. In 912 he was baptized, and though his followers must have varied considerably in their attitude to his new religion, the political wisdom of his decision is undoubted. Also, he had the Norse feeling for law and other men's observance of it, and quickly enunciated those general principles and specific regulations which ensure regard for a man's person and possessions. He strengthened the towns' defences and gave the countryside good peace. On all the evidence he was devoted to the interests of his fief. Its lands were shared out among the great ones of the army, and these re-apportioned their estates among the rank and file; but from the beginning Norman society had an aristocratic and incipiently feudal character lacking in Denmark and the Danelaw. Neither Thing nor hundred is heard of in Normandy. Its rulers early had their eye fixed on domination. The density of the Norse land-taking is proved not only by what history and tradition record of the actual turn of events, but by the hundreds of place-names (for example, with the suffixes -*bec* (ON. *bekkr*), -*bu* (*bú*), -*digue* (*dík*), -*tot* (*topt*, *toft*), and the like), and the numerous Norse personal names prefixed to the French suffix

---

own with them (just three northern feminine names as contrasted with more than eighty masculine), so intermarriage, if sometimes *more danico*, between Danes and French must have been common from the beginning. There is an admirable summary of these and related matters in L. Musset, *Les invasions: le second assaut contre l'Europe chrétienne (VIIe–XIe siècles)*, Paris, 1965, pp. 253-6.

[1] Norman territory would be substantially increased in 924 by the acquisition of Bessin and Maine, and in 933 of the Cotentin and Avranchin.

-ville. The settlers held on to their language for a generation or two, but everything was against its survival, and Dudo's interesting anecdote of Count William Longbeard of Normandy (*ob.* 942) sending his son from the court at Rouen to Bayeux to learn the tongue of his ancestors can be read two ways. But *dönsk tunga* would leave a residue of mariners' and fishermen's words behind it to sport in modern French like porpoises[1] in a surrounding ocean.

Not only in language but in institutions and modes of thought Normandy moved farther and farther away from her Norse origins during the tenth century. There was a brief attempt to put the clock back after the death of William Longbeard, but even in sentiment Normandy was casting off the ties that held her to Denmark, and the more brilliant exploits of the eleventh century, the conquest of Sicily and of England, though they arose in some measure through the same everlasting compulsions of politics, ambition, greed, national buoyancy, and overpopulation at home, were not a continuance of the Viking Movement.[2] They belong to the history not of northern but of western and southern Europe.

The years 910–11 which saw Rollo's translation from a viking chieftaincy to the overlordship of Normandy were significant for England, too. The first decade of the century had passed not too

[1] Fr. *marsouin* is the ON. *marsvín*, sea-swine.

[2] Material evidence left in the soil of France by her Norse invaders is scanty. A pair of oval bronze brooches of common Scandinavian type was found at Pitres, between Rouen and Paris. We assume they belonged to a soldier's wife who followed the wars in the late ninth century. There are a few swords and spears—surprisingly few. Of three known graves, that on the Île de Groix, opposite Lorient off the south coast of Brittany, is the most interesting and puzzling. The burial mound contains a ship-burial with cremation, certainly of a man, possibly of a woman, too. The man has been variously ascribed to Norway, Ireland, an army of the Loire, and Normandy. Grave goods include weapons and smith's tools, ornaments, a finger-ring of gold and beads of silver, an iron cauldron, gold and silver threads from a piece of interwoven cloth, various oddments, the rivets and nails of the burnt ship, and between ten and twenty bosses of the shields that lined her sides. One relic of the ship is unique—'a circular band 2 feet in diameter with movable leaflike ornaments round the outside and three rings inside. It can have had no practical purpose, and was evidently meant to be seen from both sides: it was not nailed on to anything else, for there are no holes. It seems most likely that this was the "dragon's tail", mentioned in the sagas, which balanced the figure-head at the bow. . . One of the Gotland carved stones (from Smiss in Stenkyrka) shows a very similar stern ornament.' (Holger Arbman, *The Vikings*, 1961, pp. 83–4.)

badly, though disfigured by the mutinous conduct of Edward's cousin Ethelwold, which included a defiance of the king, the abduction of a nun, and a flight to the Danes of East Anglia, whom he persuaded to go raiding in English Mercia and the north of Wessex. This cost him his life in 902. That the Danes should be so easily led to indulge in the old national pastime of destruction and plunder is a sad judgement on their political good sense. They had now been in possession of their English estates for over thirty years; they could be in no doubt as to the formidable nature of the English leadership in Wessex and Mercia and the kingdoms' strong defences. Their best policy would be to weld themselves together into a strong, durable kingdom of their own, accept authority, and consolidate the Danish interest in England. Could they but see it (and in time they would), the dual ambition of the English reigning house and the Norsemen of Ireland in the first quarter of the century made this their one hope of survival. Without the anchor of Northumbria the Danes of Mercia and East Anglia must soon be adrift—but the Northumbrians were as ill-judging as their southern neighbours, and in 910, convinced that the fighting strength of England had congregated with king Edward and his ships in Kent, they mounted an invasion of English Mercia which brought them at last to Tettenhall in Staffordshire, where they were overtaken and destroyed by the levies of Wessex and Mercia. So lightly was the anchor cast away, and the way opened to the subjection of the southern Danelaw. The death of the loyal Ethelred in 911 was no help at all to the Danes; he was succeeded by his wife, king Edward's sister, Ethelflaed the 'Lady of the Mercians', in whom the tenacity of purpose, strategic intelligence, and organizing power of her father king Alfred, are to be observed in fine flower. Along with Gunnhild Mother of Kings (Gorm the Old's daughter, sister of Harald Bluetooth, wife and widow of Eirik Bloodaxe, and mother of Harald Greycloak), and surely on a stronger foundation, she is the most remarkable woman we encounter in the western viking context. No one saw, or was brought to see, so clearly the importance of a well-sited fortress, or more clearly elicited the Danes' inability to cope with such. Her loyalty to Edward was as absolute as her husband's—and by this time Edward had a greater reality of power behind him.

His first move was to take over London, Oxford, and the lands belonging to them from Mercia into his own safe-keeping, then cover them by fortresses at Hertford and Witham. The next two years were spent in desultory fighting in the Midlands and the repulse of a powerful fleet of vikings from Brittany which entered the Severn and plundered extensively in the English border counties and South Wales before moving on to Ireland. But thereafter English pressure on the Danelaw was unremitting. By 916 brother and sister had established a double line of fortresses which not only secured the English frontier (against the Welsh, incidentally, and the Irish-Norse of the Wirral, as well as the Danes) but provided a springboard for the offensive campaigns of 917-18. Along the general line of Watling Street, from the estuary of the Mersey to Witham and Maldon in Essex, the army bases of the Danes were confronted by almost a score of fortresses which they could not subdue and might venture to pass only at their peril. Ten of these were Ethelflaed's work, Bremesburh, 910, Scergeat and Bridgnorth, 912, Tamworth and Stafford, 913, Eddisbury and Warwick, 914, Chirbury, Weardburh, and Runcorn, 915. Behind them stood Edward's constructions at Hertford, 911 and 912, Witham, 912, Buckingham (two forts, one each side of the river), 914, Bedford, 915, Maldon, 916. The use of these fortresses was an exercise in the logic of war. A strongly held fortress was practically irreducible, and the Danish attacks on Towcester, Bedford, Wigingamere, and Maldon, were all failures. It was the English good fortune that their own fortress system so consistently dominated the successive areas of advance that they could occupy Northampton, Huntingdon, Cambridge, Leicester, Nottingham, and Lincoln without need for storm. If the same was not true of Derby, occupied in 917, we may assume that the absence of the local Danish army on a foray farther south meant that it was weakly held. The English forces under Edward and Ethelflaed worked closely together and were following an agreed plan; the Danes, individualists as ever, had neither a united leadership nor a unified purpose. The 'raid' was becoming meaningless in terms of lasting advantage; they had no answer to fortress strategy, as would be demonstrated in the Western Empire also, and little heart for a sustained war. Without need for excessive bloodshed the English dealt them blow upon blow; their armies in East Anglia and southern Mercia disintegrated; and by the summer of 918 everything was ready for the final assault on the very heart of the Mercian Danelaw. By mid-June Edward had reached Stamford. Without delay he built his fortress on high ground south of the

Welland, thus dominating the Danish stronghold to the north. Once more the Danes submitted to the logic of the situation, Nottingham and Lincoln lay open to an English advance, but it was then, on 12 June, with the end of a long road in sight, that the Lady of the Mercians died, and her brother hauled back to secure the Mercian succession. For half a year he let her daughter Elfwyn hold a nominal authority before taking Mercia for himself. A minority of Mercian noblemen might be less than fully pleased, but none took action; the Welsh welcomed a monarch more benevolently disposed towards them than the long-hostile Mercians; and meantime the English fortresses kept the Danes helpless and unhappy in their attenuated territories. When Edward next turned in their direction they were sensible enough not to oppose him. In his triumph Edward bore himself calmly; he wanted the Christian Danes of the Danelaw as willing subjects who would find their interest best served when identical with his own. Besides, there was by now a new situation to deal with in the north, hardly less inimical to the Danelaw than to himself.

This had come about by reason of a considerable infiltration, or indeed invasion, of England north of the Wirral by Norsemen coming in the main from Ireland. The native Irish ascendancy immediately after the year 900 doubtless encouraged the movement, which is well attested by the place-names of north-west England and south-west Scotland and the sculptured stones of much of the area. Almost all detail is lacking till 915, but the political condition of north-west England and Northumbria in the 920s is witness to earlier Norse enterprise. We know of Ingimund (the Igmunt of the Welsh *Bruts* and Hingamund of the Irish *Three Fragments*) that he left Ireland after the fall of Dublin and sought land in North Wales, that he was driven away from there, and eventually turned up in the Wirral and still later attacked Chester. The Rognvald (OE. Raegnald), whose name is so prominent in Northumbrian history from *c.* 914 till his death in 921, and his successor Sigtrygg Gale (OE. Sihtric), were both immersed for a while in Irish affairs, the first as a marauder who had graduated from Scotland and Man, the other as the recoverer of Dublin, slayer of the high-king Njall, and king of the Liffey Norsemen. Both were of the stirring progeny of Ragnar, so regarded themselves as having claims on the Danish kingdom of Northumbria (i.e. the Old English Deira). The Irish-Norse migration into north-west England, the destruction of the

Northumbrian army at Tettenhall in 910, and the preoccupation of Edward and Ethelflaed with the southern Danelaw (and of the southern Danelaw with Edward and Ethelflaed), were circumstances favourable to Rognvald's bid to seize power at York, though he might count on the hostility of the rulers of the Scots, the Strathclyde Welsh, and the English of Bernicia (though some of these last, *robusti bellatores*, fought on his side), and, once more, Edward and Ethelflaed. In 919 he captured York and made himself its king. This was the resolution of a struggle between Danes and Norwegians which went back at least fifty years.

Its immediate consequences were not damaging to king Edward. He was alert to the danger of Irish-Norse incursion by way of the Mersey, and built or renewed several fortresses to prevent it. This did not inhibit the appearance of Sigtrygg Gale on the northern scene in 920, but Edward's subsequent fortification of the river crossing at Nottingham sounded a warning to Northumbria, while his new garrison fortress at Bakewell in the Peak of Derbyshire strengthened his hold on what he had already seized. And now, according to the *Chronicle*, his life's work was crowned when 'the king of the Scots and the whole Scottish nation accepted him as father and lord, and Rognvald and the sons of Eadulf, and all those who dwelt in Northumbria, both English, and Danish, and Northmen (Norwegians), and others; and the king of the Strathclyde Welsh and all the Strathclyde Welsh likewise'. This recognition of Edward's overlordship had a different meaning for each of its subscribers. Rognvald, for instance, was confirmed in his recently won kingdom and spared an Edwardian advance north at a time when the Danish and Christian part of his realm might wish to rise against him. In 921 Rognvald died and was succeeded by his kinsman Sigtrygg. When Edward the Elder died full of honour in 924 and was succeeded by his son Athelstan, it was Athelstan's wish to maintain the Northumbrian alliance by marrying his sister to Sigtrygg. A year or so later Sigtrygg died, and Athelstan was ready to act. The Northumbrians accepted Olaf, Sigtrygg's son by an earlier marriage, as his successor, and the boy's uncle Guthfrith, who had taken the Dublin kingdom after Sigtrygg, came to Northumbria to act as his regent. Athelstan promptly drove out the pair of them, Guthfrith to Scotland and Olaf to Ireland. Into the intricacies of the next ten years, and the embroidery of confusion woven by English and Icelandic historians during the next three hundred, there is no need to enter. The upshot of prolonged machination was the Norse-Celtic confederacy which faced Athelstan at Brunanburh in 937.[1]

It had not been too hard a-making. Athelstan's seizure of Northumbria was disquieting to many besides the defeated Norwegians from Ireland. Neither Scot nor Strathclyde Welsh wanted him for near neighbour, and among the Northumbrians themselves, even the English there, some held to the view that theirs had always been an independent kingdom, owing tribute to no southern king

34. 'THE SEAMEN STOOD READY, MANY VIKINGS EAGER FOR BATTLE'
Motif from a Gotland pictured stone.

before Athelstan. Guthfrith died in 934, and his son, yet another Olaf, was an imperious and ambitious viking who mobilized the considerable naval resources of the Dublin kingdom to regain, as he saw it, his rightful patrimony at York. So on the unidentified battleground of Brunanburh the army of Wessex and Mercia under Athelstan and his brother Edmund fought it out with the Norsemen of Ireland under Olaf, the Scots under Constantine, and the Strathclyde Welsh under Eugenius.[2] It was a long and fearful encounter

[1] The standard work is A. Campbell, *The Battle of Brunanburh*, 1938. We must accept the identification of the battle of Vinheid (*Vínheiðr*) in *Egils Saga Skallagrímssonar* with the battle of Brunanburh in English sources. However: 'The saga remains unsupported in practically all its details, and, in view of its frequent gross errors and confusions, cannot be used as a source for the history of the war of Æthelstan and Anlaf [Olaf Guthfrith's son]. If we abandon it, and abandon it we must, all hope of localizing Brunanburh is lost.' (Campbell, p. 80.)

[2] The Welsh of Wales, despite *Egils Saga*, took no part in the battle, though it had been an expressed Welsh hope, since the late 920s, that a Welsh and Irish-Norse alliance (*Kymry a gwyr Dulyn*, i.e. the Welsh and the men of Dublin) should rout the Saxons and drive them from Britain for ever. 'The Saxon hosts will not return.' See the *Armes Prydein*, lines 9, 131–2, 175.

before the northern and western armies broke and fled. Five young kings and seven of Olaf's jarls, together with Constantine's son and an unnumbered count of vikings and Scots, lay dead on the field. No need had that grey-headed scoundrelly Scot or the shamed Norseman to exult in their war-play with the sons of Edward.

Then the Norsemen departed in their nailed ships (*cnearrum*), bloodstained survivors of spears, on Dingesmere over the deep water to seek Dublin, Ireland once more, sorry of heart. The two brothers likewise, king and atheling both, sought their own country, the land of the West Saxons, exulting in war. They left behind them, to joy in the carrion, the black and horn-beaked raven with his dusky plumage, and the dun-feathered eagle with his white-tipped tail, greedy hawk of battle, to take toll of the corpses, and the wolf, grey beast of the forest. Never until now in this island, as books and scholars of old inform us, was there greater slaughter of an army with the sword's edge, since the Angles and Saxons put ashore from the east, attacked the Britons over the wide seas, proud forgers of war conquered the Welsh, and fame-eager warriors won them a homeland.

With these traditional embroideries of song the unknown poet of Brunanburh exulted over the enemy dead, and acclaimed the glory of proud England's arms. And indeed the flaxen-haired Athelstan was a glorious king, and his achievement, not only at Brunanburh, deserving of panegyric. His relations with the Scandinavian world were not all hostile nor limited to fighting the Irish-Norse claimants to York. He treated the Danelaw south of the Humber with consideration, many of Scandinavian descent and name attended his court as regional magnates or witnessed his charters, and, best of all, regarded themselves as his loyal subjects. He had raised Harald Fairhair's youngest son Hakon (*Aðalsteins fóstri*, Athelstan's foster-son) in his own court, and with Harald himself was at all times on cordial terms. His reputation at home, and in western and northern Europe, stood high. And yet it was so linked with his personal qualities that within a month or two of his death in the autumn of 939 Olaf of Dublin with his Irish Norsemen was back in York, and in 940 was raiding triumphantly through the Midlands. Athelstan's successor, his brother Edmund, had shown himself a resolute prince, but he was just 18 years old, and Olaf Guthfrith's son was a man who always took his chances. Edmund met him with an army at Leicester, but must have been at some unrecorded disadvantage, for there was no battle. Instead Olaf gained the whole of the modern shires of

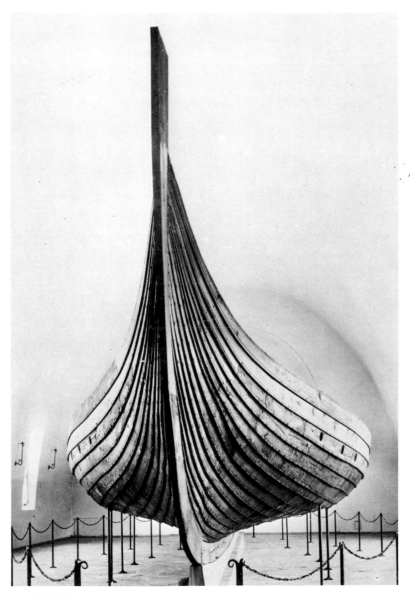

14. THE GOKSTAD SHIP

13. A PICTURED STONE FROM LÄRBRO, GOTLAND. For a description see page 343.

15. THE GRIMESTAD TREASURE, TENTH CENTURY, NORWAY

16. NECKLACE AND ARM-RING FROM BIRKA, GRAVE 632. For a description of the necklace see p. 172.

17. MEMORIAL STONE TO THE MOTHER OF ROGNVALD. 'She died in Ed, God help her soul. Rognvald had runes carved: he was in Greekland, was leader of a host.'

18. THE PIRAEUS LION, VENICE. The lion bears runic inscriptions of Swedish origin. (See pp. 267–8.)

19. THINGVELLIR, ICELAND. The site of the Althing. The white flagstaff, far centre, indicates the Logberg or Hill of Laws.

20. FLATEYJARBÓK. The passage begins with Tyrkir's claim to have found grapes in the land Leif Eiriksson therefore named Vínland, Wineland. It ends with the decision of Thorvald Eiriksson to undertake a voyage there.

Leicester, Derby, Nottingham, and Lincoln by a treaty arranged between the two leaders by the archbishops of Canterbury and York. This abandonment of the loyal Danes and English of the Danelaw to their traditional enemies the Norwegians was a humiliating setback for Edmund, and the cock-a-hoop Olaf wasted no time before turning north to the plunder and conquest of Northumbria beyond the Tees. A decisive test of strength seemed inevitable, but before it could take place Olaf died and his kingdom and army turned to the hand of that other Olaf, nicknamed Kvaran, Sigtrygg's son, whose destiny in England, brave adventurer though he was, was always to miss his chances. Within a year he lost to Edmund that part of the by now English-orientated and anti-heathen Danelaw which his namesake had just won. The redemption of the Five Boroughs was celebrated in a poem written not long after the event and incorporated in the *Anglo-Saxon Chronicle* under the year 942.

In this year king Edmund, lord of the English, his kinsmen's protector and loved wreaker of deeds, conquered Mercia as far as Dore divides, and Whitwell Gap, and the river Humber, broad stream of ocean—the Five Boroughs, Leicester and Lincoln, Nottingham and Stamford too, and Derby. For a long hard time had the Danes been forcibly subdued in bondage to the heathens, till king Edmund, Edward's son, protector of warriors, released them again by his valour.

For the next ten years the York kingdom of Northumbria presents a kaleidoscopic picture of change. Olaf Sigtryggsson was driven out by his subjects in 943, and a brother of Olaf Guthfrith's son named Rognvald (Raegnald) became king. In turn these both visited king Edmund and accepted baptism. Early in 944 Olaf Sigtryggsson was back again, but before the year was out Edmund forcibly expelled both Olaf and Rognvald. Till his death in May 946 Edmund was Northumbria's king, and was succeeded by his brother Eadred, king of England. But by 948, as we have earlier noticed (page 95), the exiled Eirik Bloodaxe, Harald Fairhair's favourite and most violent son, arrived in the kingdom of Northumbria, and by the magic of his name, lineage, and reputation commended himself to the Norsemen there and was made king. Eadred reacted strongly, under English pressure the Northumbrians abandoned Eirik, and in 949 Olaf Sigtryggsson was back yet again. Yet again he was expelled, and Eirik returned for a comparatively long reign of two years. Norse rivalries had never looked so senseless. The union of the kingdoms of Dublin and York was demonstrably an impossibility, but like puppets on a string the Dublin contenders came jerking across the Irish Sea. They seem hardly to have had time to strike the coins which are so eloquent a testimony to their royal pretensions, before they were on their way again. The best-known episode in Eirik's interrupted sojourn at York is in part apocryphal —the visit to his court of his mortal enemy, the Icelandic poet and fighting-man Egill Skallagrimsson, who cynically composed a panegyric on him and so ransomed his head from the Bloodaxe. Eirik's court at York was an anachronism, pagan and un-English. He was driven out for the last time in 954. He may well have been betrayed to his death at Stainmore. Odinn had always had high hopes of him, and he died gallantly. Valhalla stood open to receive him, and it was the Volsung heroes Sigmund and Sinfjotli who bade him enter. What heroes, they asked, attend you from the roar of battle? 'There are five kings,' said Eirik. 'I will make known to you the names of all. I am the sixth myself' (*Eiríksmál*).

With these meaningless permutations of the two Olafs, the second Rognvald, and the barbaric splendour of Eirik's death and memorial, a phase of viking history comes to an end. Harassed Wessex, partitioned Mercia, the subjugated regions which formed the Danelaw south of the Humber, and now at last that political quicksand the kingdom of York, had been made one kingdom. That kingdom would be free of Norwegian and Danish assault for almost thirty years, and when after the minor raids of the 980s a new threat to England grew apace, there were new actors on the scene, and a new sense of destiny in the northern air.

4. The Movement East:
The Baltic Lands, Russia, Byzantium

THE EARLY RISE TO POWER AND CONTINUING SUP-
remacy of the kings of central Sweden, lightly attested though
it is by documentary evidence, may well be the most decisive factor in the homeland history of Scandinavia throughout the pre-
viking and viking periods. In the eighth century the kingdom
based on Uppland, but including territories both north and especially south of it was unified, strong, and rich, and well placed for
colonial and mercantile ventures overseas. The natural direction
of these was east and south-east, to the island of Gotland and the
shores of the Baltic from the Gulf of Danzig to north of the Gulf of
Finland. Eventually their contacts with these profitable regions
would draw the Swedes further east till they came to the Russian
rivers and so by way of the Black Sea to the Caspian and Constantinople.

It would be hard to determine the date of the first Swedish incursions into the east Baltic lands. But they were certainly pre-
viking. Snorri in his *Ynglinga Saga* speaks of Swedish and other
northern kings raiding there, more particularly in Estland, the
country south of the Gulf of Finland, not long after the deaths of the
Uppland king Athils and the Dane Hrolf Kraki; and we long since
noted (p. 52 above), in Snorri's brief account of Ivar Vidfadmi
(*c.* 650–700?), the part-legendary Far-reacher or Wide-grasper, how
in addition to his fabled control of Sweden, Denmark, and Northumbria, he won for himself a large part of Germany and the entire
Austrriki, that unspecified eastern realm which included the coastal
lands of the east Baltic and the nearer parts of Russia in the area of
Lake Ladoga. Elsewhere we learn of Ivar that he drowned while on
an expedition to Russia. This at best comes to very little, and at

worst to nothing at all, nor is it significantly augmented by such other dubious references as can be culled from the *Fornaldarsögur*, Snorri's *Ynglinga Saga*, and Thjodolf's *Ynglinga Tal*. The documentary silence is, however, interrupted by Rimbert's *Vita Anskarii*, written about 870, which records of the Kurlanders, *Chori*, that they had in earlier times been subject to the Swedes, but had thrown off a yoke they found shameful. The Kurlanders defeated a Danish invasion *c.* 850, but Olaf, who was king in Birka, led a Swedish force against them, burned their fortress of Seeburg to the ground, and received the abject surrender of a second town, Apulia. The Kurlanders, we understand from Rimbert, who is echoed by Adam of Bremen, returned to their taxpaying.

The mention of these two towns in Kurland, the modern Latvia, sharply advances our story. It brings us to two famous sites of Gotlandic and Swedish settlement in the east Baltic, Grobin and Apuole, and assures us of Scandinavian interest there as far back as the mid-eighth century, and maybe a hundred years earlier. Gotlanders and Swedes, it appears, were there as partners, not rivals. Just when Gotland became auxiliary to or fully co-operative economically and politically with the kingdom of the Swedes is unknown;[1] her geographical situation *vis-à-vis* Denmark, Sweden, the eastern Baltic, the Slav peoples of the north German coast, and beyond these Russia and central Europe, had made her immensely wealthy, and at the same time highly vulnerable;[2] it was to be

[1] *Guta Saga* records that the first Gotlander to make a lasting peace with the Swedes was the legendary king Awair Strabain, who committed the Gotlanders to an annual tribute of silver. 'Thus the Gotlanders passed of their own free will under the king of the Swedes, so that they were enabled to visit any part of Sweden free and uncircumscribed, without toll, without charges. Similarly the Swedes had the right to visit Gotland freely, without corn-tax or other prohibitions. The king should give help and assistance to the Gotlanders whenever they needed or asked for it. Both king and jarl should send delegates to the general assembly of the Gotlanders (*Gutnalþing*), and collect the tribute there. These delegates had to proclaim the freedom of the Gotlanders to travel overseas to all such places as were subject to the king at Uppsala, and similarly and in like manner for those who had the right to visit here in Gotland.' (Ed. Pipping, p. 64.) Who Awair Strawlegs was, and when he flourished, who shall say? But it is likely that the saga here preserves a sound tradition.

[2] Of approximately 200,000 silver coins of the Viking Age so far discovered in Scandinavia, a half have been found in Gotland: Arabic 40,000, German 38,000, Anglo-Saxon 21,000. There is general agreement that the frequent and widespread burial of treasure indicates troubled times, and that very

expected that a strong and acquisitive Sweden would from early times have a covetous eye for her offshore neighbour, and eventually move against her. When king Alfred's informant Wulfstan sailed past Gotland in the late ninth century it 'belonged to the Swedes', and presumably had done so for a while. But at the time of the Grobin and Apuole settlement the Gotlanders, by virtue of their separateness and wealth, had a culture subtly differentiated from that of their Swedish neighbours, so that the archaeological remains of the two peoples are susceptible of distinction. Grobin today is a small town a few miles east of Libau (Liepaja). The old settlement is in many ways comparable with Hedeby and Birka. It was surrounded by an earthwork, and protected on three sides by the river Alanda. There are three adjacent cemeteries of considerable size. Some of the graves are of men from central Sweden, buried with their weapons and covered over with mounds; others are the graves of men and women from or at least connected with Gotland. The Swedish finds from the central cemetery have the unmistakable air of a military establishment, the Gotlandic of a civil community. Presumably the Swedes were there to secure an advantage which depended on a show of force—the exaction of tribute, for example; theirs was an arm freed for action. But the Gotlanders, we assume, sought neither piracy nor war: they had brought their wives with them, taken land and pursued a peaceful trade. The earliest burials may go back to c. 650, and cremations continued till c. 800. The precise relationship of Grobin to Seeburg is not yet established.[1] Twenty-five miles away to the south-east, in north-western Lithuania, is Apuole, Rimbert's Apulia, another large Scandinavian settlement, on the river Barte, with its attendant fortress, in whose ramparts was found a heavy concentration of non-Baltic and probably Swedish arrow-heads, in which some scholars are tempted to discern, a shade perilously one would think, a relic of the Swedish assault of c. 855. In the near-by cemetery is evidence that Gotlanders were in residence here, too, at roughly the same time as the Grobin settlement. There have been finds of Swedish material in other places in the Grobin area.

considerable quantities of money and ornaments were hidden, it was hoped temporarily, in the soil of Gotland to save them from vikings and pirates.

[1] The best account is B. Nerman, *Grobin-Seeburg, Ausgrabungen und Funde*, Stockholm, 1958.

Approximately a hundred miles down the coast, safely situated at the south-western extremity of the long, shallow, sand-barred lagoon of the Kurisches Haff, stood Wiskiauten. Here we seem to discern the familiar Scandinavian pattern of a market-town protected by a garrison. It must have been established more or less when Grobin ceased from active use, and persisted for another two hundred years, in large measure because its position near the river Memel secured it a share of ninth- and tenth-century trading from the Dnieper and the Black Sea. Eighty miles to the south-west, inside another vast lagoon, the Frisches Haff, and standing in much the same relationship to the great south- and south-eastern-running river artery the Vistula as Wiskiauten to the Memel, was Wulfstan's town of Truso, to be identified with the town of Elbing, now Elblag. At least we assume so, for to the present no true town has been found and excavated. Instead there have been finds of Norse weapons, and there is a large Viking Age cemetery near the modern town's railway station containing many Scandinavian graves, these, too, showing a Swedish-Gotlandic pattern. Further west, among the Slavonic Wends and Abodrits, it was the Danes and not the Swedes who would exploit the possibilities of trade, tribute, and plunder.

Clearly too much should not be read into the literary and archaeological record of a Swedish presence among the Letts, Lithuanians, and Slavs of the east Baltic littoral. There was such a presence, but it was less than dominant and very much less than imperial. Still, it was profitable, and wealth from these Slavonic lands poured first into Helgö, and with that town's waning into Birka till near the end of the tenth century. As evidence of Swedish power and enterprise the Baltic ventures are impressive in themselves, and still more so as an introduction to the Swedish entry into Russia now to be considered.

We begin with the many-times-quoted statement of the *Russian Primary Chronicle* (*Povest' Vremennykh Let*) concerning the 'Calling of the Varangians'.[1]

In the year 852, at the accession of the Emperor Michael, the land of Rus' was first named. We have determined this date from the fact

[1] Ed. E. F. Karsky, 1926, and V. P. Adrianova-Peretts (text prepared for publication by D. S. Likhachev), 1950; English translation of Karsky's text by S. H. Cross and O. P. Sherbowitz-Wetzor, *The Russian Primary Chronicle*, Cambridge, Mass., 1953. The work is frequently referred to as the *Nestorian Chronicle* or *Chronicle of Nestor*, because of an earlier belief that it was composed

that in the reign of this Emperor Russes attacked Tsar'grad [Constantinople], as is written in the Greek Chronicle . . .

(859) The Varangians from beyond the sea imposed tribute upon the Chuds, the Slavs, the Merians, the Ves', and the Krivichians. But the Khazars imposed it upon the Polyanians, the Severians, and the Vyatichians, and collected a white squirrel-skin from each hearth.

(860–62) The tributaries of the Varangians drove them back beyond the sea and, refusing them further tribute, set out to govern themselves. There was no law among them, but tribe rose against tribe. Discord thus ensued among them, and they began to war one against another. They said to themselves, 'Let us seek a prince who may rule over us and judge us according to the Law.' They accordingly went overseas to the Varangian Russes: these particular Varangians were known as Russes, just as some are called [*Svie*], others [*Nurmane*], [*Angliane*], [*Gote*],[1] for they were thus named. The Chuds, the Slavs, the Krivichians, and the Ves' then said to the people of Rus', 'Our land is great and rich, but there is no order in it. Come to rule and reign over us.' They thus selected three brothers, with their kinsfolk, who took with them all the Russes and migrated. The oldest, Rurik, located himself in Novgorod; the second, Sineus, at Beloozero; and the third, Truvor, in Izborsk. On account of these Varangians, the district of Novgorod became known as the land of

---

by the monk Nestor of the Pechersky cloister in Kiev soon after the year 1100. It is now more generally held that Nestor was either its first editor or just one of its compilers, and that the *Primary Chronicle* (*Nachal'naya Letopis'*) is based upon several earlier chronicles. The most important extant codexes are the Laurentian of the late fourteenth century and the Hypatian of the early or mid-fifteenth. For a compact account in English see G. Vernadsky, *Kievan Russia*, Yale, 1948, pp. 284–6, and for a fuller the Introduction to the Cross and Sherbowitz-Wetzor translation of the Laurentian text. *Povest' Vremennykh Let*, The Tale of Bygone Years, Book of Annals, Chronography, is the title by which the *Primary* (or *Nestorian*) *Chronicle* is normally referred to in modern Slavonic critical literature.

[1] Cross and Sherbowitz-Wetzor translate these as Swedes, Normans, English, and Gotlanders. Similarly they translate Liudprand's *Nordmanni* as Normans, meaning Northmen, Scandinavians, a customary Russian usage. However, in a book written for English readers 'Normans' is best kept for the inhabitants of Normandy. I would translate, with Vilhelm Thomsen, *The Relations between Ancient Russia and Scandinavia*, 1877, p. 13 (reprint in the Burt Franklin Research and Source Work Series, No. 77, New York, ?1964): 'They were called *Rus* as others are called *Svie* (Swedes), others *Nurmane* (Northmen, Norwegians), others *Angliane* (English, or Angles of Sleswick?), others *Gote* (probably the inhabitants of the island of Gotland).'

Rus'. The present inhabitants of Novgorod are descended from the Varangian race, but aforetime they were Slavs.

After two years, Sineus and his brother Truvor died, and Rurik assumed the sole authority. He assigned cities to his followers, Polotsk to one, Rostov to another, and to another Beloozero.[1]

This naive, well-meaning, and in its different redactions varied passage of legendary history relating to the origins of the (later) royal house of the kingdom of Kiev has been the subject of ency-clopedic exegesis. Yet for all the whittlings of folklorists, philolo-gists, historians, and chauvinists, and with full allowance for con-fusion, misunderstanding, and plain tendentiousness in the *Chronicle* itself, one irreducible fact remains: the tradition that the founders of the city states of Novgorod and Kiev[2] were men of Scandinavian stock, and drawn from such of them as were called Varangians or Rus.[3] We do not have to believe in the detail of three brothers

---

[1] Cross and Sherbowitz-Wetzor, pp. 58–60. There is a divergent account of Rurik's settlement in the Hypatian codex. 'They took with them all the Russes and came first to the Slavs (*Slovene*), and they built the city of Ladoga [the modern Staraja Ladoga]. Rurik, the eldest, settled in Ladoga, Sineus, the second, at Beloozero, and Truvor, the third, in Izborsk. From these Varangians the land of Rus' received its name. After two years Sineus died, as well as his brother Truvor, and Rurik assumed the sole authority. He then came to Lake Il'men' and founded on the Volkhov a city which they named Novgorod, and he settled there as prince, assigning cities . . .', etc. (op. cit., p. 233).

[2] The 'Varangian' passage of the *Povest'* quoted above continues: 'With Rurik there were two men who did not belong to his kin, but were boyars [chieftains]. They obtained permission to go to Tsar'grad [Constantinople] with their families. They thus sailed down the Dnieper, and in the course of their journey they saw a small city on a hill. Upon their inquiry as to whose town it was, they were informed that three brothers, Kiy, Shchek, and Khoriv, had once built the city, but that since their deaths, their descendants were living there as tributaries of the Khazars. Askold and Dir [Hoskuld and Dyri] remained in the city, and after gathering together many Varangians, they established their dominion over the country of the Polyanians at the same time that Rurik was ruling at Novgorod' (Cross and Sherbowitz-Wetzor, p. 60). Their principality was seized, and they themselves killed, in 880–2, by Rurik's successor at Novgorod, Oleg. 'Oleg set himself up as prince in Kiev, and declared that it should be the mother of Russian cities. The Varangians, Slavs, and others who accompanied him, were called Russes. Oleg began to build stockaded towns, and imposed tribute on the Slavs, the Krivichians, and the Merians' (op. cit., p. 61).

[3] I add a brief note on the by no means universally agreed meaning and derivation of Rus and Varangian. There has developed a consensus of Scandin-avian opinion, though with distinguished exceptions, that *Rús* comes from

coming over the sea (the number and relationship are a commonplace of founding stories), nor in that other commonplace, the invitation sent them by a troubled and comfort-seeking native people or peoples; it is of no particular importance whether or not we identify Rurik with the Rurik-Rorik who was active in Frisia and South

---

the Finnish name for Sweden, *Ruotsi* (cf. Esthonian *Rootsi*), which in turn goes back to the word represented in ON. by *róðr*, a rowing, rowing-way, waterway (cf. NE. 'roads'). The name *Ruotsi*, it is argued, arose from *róðsmenn*, men of the rowing-way, the people of today's *Roslagen*, the Rowing-Law, the coastal area of Swedish Uppland. In other words, the Finns named the Swedes after that part of the Swedish folk and realm they knew best; the name was carried by them north, east, then south to the area of Lake Ladoga, which was largely inhabited by people of Finnish origin when the Rus arrived, and from there spread by way of the Slavs through Russia and Byzantium. It was used only of the Swedes in Russia, never of the Swedes in Sweden. In course of time it came to include not only Scandinavians but those who lived under their sovereignty, including subject Slavs. E. Hjärne's suggestion, 'Roden, Upphovd och Namnet,' *Namn och bygd*, 1947, pp. 28–60, that *róðr* means ship, *róðsmenn* shipmen, and *Roslagen, Rodzlagen, Ropslaghin*, etc, means Ship-Law, provides an equally apposite origin.

Væringi, pl. *Væringjar* (Gr. βάραγγοι, Arab. *varank*), most probably derives from O.N. *várar*, pledge, oath, guarantee, together with the collective suffix *-ing*, and means men of the pledge, confederates. The Russian word *varyag* is used of itinerant pedlars, and it is tempting to assume that the men of the pledge were confederates in trading enterprises (cf. *vara*, wares), which fits in admirably with the Slav, Byzantine, and Arab designation of the general body of northern warrior-traders in Russia (not merely the Rus: the *Povest'* uses the term Varangian for Scandinavians 'from beyond the Baltic sea') as Varangians. The Baltic was *More Varjazhbskoie*, the Varangian Sea. The term Varangian seems not to have been known in Russia before the second half of the tenth century. A. Stender-Petersen (*Varangica*, Århus, 1953; 'Das Problem der ältesten Byzantinisch-Russisch-Nordischen Beziehungen' in *Relazioni, III, 165–88, X Congresso Internazionale di Scienze Storiche*, Rome, 1955) considers that the Væringjar were distinct from the Rus, and were a second influx of Swedes dating from Vladimir's conquest of the kingdom of Kiev in the 980s with a force recruited in Sweden. Further, the word *Væringjar* is of no very common occurrence, especially outside the description of the Varangian or Scandinavian contingent in the emperor's service at Constantinople as *Væringjalið, -lög, -seta*. There was possibly no need for it till the Rus had become substantially Slavicized and a new term came into use in Byzantium to denote men of Scandinavian origin.

The subject is a difficult one and the etymologies remain uncertain. The most readable 'Normanist' statement is still V. Thomsen's *Relations*. G. Vernadsky presents a summary of evidence for the 'anti-Normanist' view that the first wave of Scandinavians to reach southern Russia, in the early

Jutland in the 850s (see pp. 106, 109 above), and we cannot accept that there was no Rus activity in Russia before the 850s (there most emphatically was); but equally we cannot disregard the tradition itself, or lightly turn the first Rus into Slavs, Khazars, descendants of the Crimean Goths, or still less credible contenders for the title.

Evidence for Swedish activity in Russia before Rurik is of two kinds, literary and archaeological. But first we must take a look at the distribution of the non-Scandinavian peoples in Russia west of the Volga at the beginning of the ninth century. In Estland and around lakes Ladoga and Onega dwelt people of Finnish race, the Chud of the *Primary Chronicle*, and peoples of Finnish origin were early established around Rostov (the Meria) and Murom (the Muroma). With such or their like the Swedes had considerable acquaintance. At its other, southern, extremity Russia was bounded and contained by two great imperial powers, the Byzantine Empire dominating south-eastern Europe and the Black Sea region, and the Arab Caliphate with its capital Baghdad in control south of the Caucasus. The military strength, national wealth, political sagacity, and physical remoteness of these two powers made them immune to all save occasional excesses of Rus impudence. Their boundaries drew the line beyond which the south-eastern progress of the Swedes would make no headway. The two most important peoples north of them were the Khazars and the Bulgars. The first of these, a Turkic-speaking people of Asiatic origin, were all-powerful from the Caucasus and the northern shores of the Caspian through the lands enclosed by the lower Volga and Don, and exerted an often dominant influence between the Caspian and the southern Urals. The Crimea was also in their hands. Their capital was at Itil in the

---

eighth century, borrowed the name Rus from the Alanic *Ruxs*, in his *Origins*, p. 199. See further M. Vasmer, *Russisches etymologisches Wörterbuch*, Heidelberg, 1950–8, II, 551–2. There is an excellent review of the problems in Cross and Sherbowitz-Wetzor, pp. 35–50; and the chapters on 'Kievan Russia' in N. V. Riasanovsky, *A History of Russia*, New York, 1963, provide a just and balanced survey for the English reader.

Norse sources call geographical Russia *Svíþjóð hinn mikla*, Sweden the Great, and *Garðaríki*, the kingdom of (fortified) towns or steads. Most of these towns (villages?) were already in existence when the warrior-merchants of Sweden moved into Russia, and the name reflects their interest in the phenomenon. They call Novgorod *Hólmgarðr*, Island-garth, and Kiev *Kœnugarðr*, Boatgarth (?). *Serkland*, Silk-land, was the kingdom of the Muslims, Constantinople was *Mikligarðr*, William Morris's Micklegarth, the Great City.

Volga delta, near the modern Astrakhan. Their gift for trade and commerce, their unfanatical social and religious notions, and their geopolitical role as a buffer against such fierce nomadic Turkish tribes as the Petchenegs[1] made them so favoured of the Byzantines that in 834–5 the emperor Theophilus sent materials and engineers to construct for them the shining stone fortress of Sarkel, the 'White House', and so secure the Don portage and the east-west transit of goods from the Volga-mouth to Constantinople. West of the Khazars and north of the Byzantines was the western division of the Bulgars, a strong, aggressive folk often at war with the Empire. Modern Bulgaria preserves the names of these early invaders, but the native population was Slavonic and would absorb them completely. Split apart from these by the territories of the Khazars were yet other Bulgars, of Turkic origin, with a main encampment at Bulgar in the Volga bend. Bulgar and Itil were the two main trading centres of the Volga region. In the vast central area of Russia, now emptied of the Avars, dwelt several loosely organized Slavonic tribes, too independent of each other to form a confederacy strong enough to make impression on the khaganates of the Khazars and Bulgars, or to turn back the incoming Rus and frustrate their ambition to develop the river-routes from the Baltic to the Black Sea, from the Gulf of Finland to the Caspian.

We have reliable literary intelligence of the Rus in 839. Under that year the *Annales Bertiniani* report the arrival at the court of the Frankish emperor, Louis the Pious, of Greek ambassadors sent to him by the emperor Theophilus of Byzantium. They brought with them a letter and gifts, and Louis received them with honour at Ingelheim, near Mainz. They brought with them, too, certain men 'who said that they, that is their nation, were called Rhos (*qui se, id est gentem suam, Rhos vocari dicebant*), and whom their own king, Chacanus by name, had sent to him [Theophilus] in friendship, as they asserted'. Theophilus expressed a wish that Louis would arrange for these Rhos to continue their journey through his empire, for he could not allow them to return home by the route they had taken to Constantinople, so great would be their danger from rude and savage peoples. His curiosity stirred, Louis interrogated these

---

[1] Vernadsky, *Ancient Russia*, pp. 304–5, and *Origins*, p. 185, considers that Sarkel was built less against Petchenegs or Magyars than against the Rus, more especially those he places in the Azov region. It may well have been built against all three.

Rhos more closely about their appearance in his dominions, and learning that they were of Swedish nationality (*comperit eos gentis esse Sueonum*), and therefore linked with the hostile, plundering north, he decided to keep them with him for a while, till he was satisfied that they were honest men and not spyers-out of the Frankish realm. He sent intelligence to this effect back to Theophilus.[1]

The most delicate and at times contradictory shades of meaning have been extracted by scholars from the *gentem suam Rhos* and *gentis Sueonum* of this annal, but it is very much in accord with what the other literature and archaeology tell us about the Rus. The Rus who came to Louis's court were of Swedish origin or nationality, but they were not of Sweden itself. They had travelled south to Constantinople on a peaceful mission through the wild tribes dwelling about the Dnieper, and were now circuitously returning to that place in Russia where they had a settlement, colony, kingdom, call it what we will, with a leader strong enough and independent enough of the kingdom of central Sweden to style himself (or more accurately to be styled by the Greek emperor) Chacanus, the title borne by the khagans or kings of the Khazars and the Bulgars. Almost a hundred years later the Arab Ibn Rustah reports of the Rus that they have a prince who is called Khaqan-Rus.

The earliest significant archaeological evidence for the Swedes in Russia comes from the southern end of Lake Ladoga. Not on the lake itself, but in a typical protected position seven or eight miles up the river Volkhov, stood the town known in Norse sources as Aldeigjuborg and today identifiable on the map by the small modern town of Staraja Ladoga, Old Ladoga. It was of good size, almost a quarter of a mile square, surrounded by an earth rampart, and in part still further protected by the river and a ravine. The site was occupied long before the Swedes arrived, either by a Finnish or (less likely) a Slavonic community. These earlier inhabitants were friendly to the newcomers, no doubt because they benefited by the presence of traders and warriors in their midst. Evidence of a degree of Swedish occupation persists from the early ninth to the early eleventh century, and Snorri Sturluson mentions the place frequently. But the Finnish-Swedish heyday there was certainly the tenth century. Above the oldest layers of the town have been found the remains of squarish log-houses not likely to be Slavonic, and

[1] Ed. Waitz, Hanover, 1883, pp. 19–20. The reliable and well-regarded Prudentius bishop of Troyes was the author of this part of the *Annales*.

above these small Russian-style (Slav) one-roomed cottages with
the cooking-place in the corner. The final layer is unquestionably
Slavonic, and we may assume, as so often in parallel cases, that the
Swedes were eventually assimilated to the Finns and Slavs among
whom they had lived so long. The most dramatic viking remain
from Aldeigjuborg is a piece of wood, apparently from a bow, with
a runic inscription in complicated skaldic verse, showing the allitera-
tive pattern and obscure mythological reference typical of the high
flowering of such verse. It is of the ninth century.

35. PORTAGE ON RUSSIAN RIVERS, I (OLAUS MAGNUS)

A good deal about Aldeigjuborg will remain puzzling till the
early cemetery is found and excavated. Meanwhile we are aware of
a great many burial mounds in the Ladoga-Onega area, along the
rivers Volkhov, Sias, Pascha, Ojat, and Svir. The four hundred or so
of these which have been examined speak of Finnish and Swedish
traders and colonizers. The reason for their presence here rather than
elsewhere will be apparent if we follow in the track of those men who
set out from Sweden, Gotland, and Finland, to seek a profit, living,
even a home in the new land. The Swedes, Ålanders, and Gotlanders

were sailors, the Baltic and its sea-arms their roadways.[1] The simplest route east was to make use of the Gulf of Finland, from whose head a short, easy journey up the river Neva conducts to the wide expanse of Lake Ladoga. Soon our traveller would be at the confluence of the Volkhov, and soon thereafter at Aldeigjuborg. The majority of visitors would not stay long in the town. Some would acquire land outside it, to raise stock, crops, and families, but most had other things in mind. They were not farmers but merchants, and from Aldeigjuborg had a choice of routes to the rivers Dnieper and Volga, which were Russia's trade arteries. To reach the Dnieper our merchant, with others of his kind, would journey south along the river Volkhov to the town of Novgorod by Lake Ilmen, traverse the lake, and continue south along the river Lovat, and eventually by the use of smaller streams and a short and manageable portage reach the headwaters of the Dnieper. It was possible to make much the same connection by way of the Gulf of Riga and the southern Dvina,[2] or if a merchant chose he could return to the Baltic that way. If he sought the Volga, he had the choice of at least two more easterly routes, the better and more frequented out of Lake Ladoga by the river Sias, then by portage and the Mologa to the Volga north of Rostov, the other from Lake Ladoga by the river Svir to Lake Onega, and from there upstream to Lake Beloya, on whose southern shore stood the trading town of Beloozero, the patrimony of Rurik's oddly named brother Sineus, and so by way of the river Syeksna to the Volga itself. The area was one of rivers, swamps, and a great diversity of streams, and many of those who traversed it must have had their favourite routes, based

---

[1] The Ålands seem to have been part of the kingdom of central Sweden throughout the Viking period. Archaeological evidence shows a Swedish rather than a Finnish relationship, and suggests that the Ålanders took an active part in Swedish trade with Russia and the Muslim world. See Ella Kivikoski, *Finland*, 1967, pp. 132–4.

[2] As *Guta Saga* informs us. 'The exiled Gotlanders (see p. 196 n. 3 above) went forth into an island off Estland whose name is Dagaiþi [Dagö], and settled there, and built a fortified town which can still be seen. They could not maintain themselves there, set off up the waterway known as the Dvina, and up through Russia. So far did they go that they came to Greece.' (Ed. Pipping: Excerpt in *An Introduction to Old Norse*, O.U.P., 1957, p. 176.) For a discussion of a Dvina-Don-Donets route between the Baltic and Black Seas, and a markedly hypothetical case for the Varangians reaching the Azov *c.* 739 and borrowing the name Rus from the Antian Slavic tribes there, see Vernadsky, *Ancient Russia*, pp. 266–75, and *Kievan Russia*, pp. 333–4.

36. PORTAGE ON RUSSIAN RIVERS, 2 (OLAUS MAGNUS)

to some extent on the size of the boats they had with them and their arrangements for forwarding and transfer. The route south from Staraja Ladoga by way of Novgorod and the Lovat to the Dnieper could be used to connect with the Volga, too. There is convincing archaeological evidence of early Swedish and Finnish initiative along the river-routes from Lake Ladoga right down to Gnezdovo-Smolensk and from Lake Onega to Rostov and Murom.

By the closing decades of the ninth century the Swedes and the Rus were of considerable importance in Russian affairs. Over on the Volga they were active in trade and busily in contact with the khaganates of the Bulgars and Khazars; they were well known to the Muslims south of the Caspian, and having crossed that sea by boat from Itil would continue by camel train over the desert to Baghdad. Here and on the Volga bend they encountered merchants and trade goods from as far east as China, so that viking trade reached out eastwards to the confines of the known or rumoured world. Arabian silver, Persian glass, Chinese silk, narrow-necked bronze bottles from east of the Caspian, exotic purses from India, spices and wines, all these found their way to Novgorod, Gotland, and the homes and graves of Swedish Uppland, in exchange for slaves, weapons, honey and wax, and an odorous plenitude of furs. But on the Dnieper they

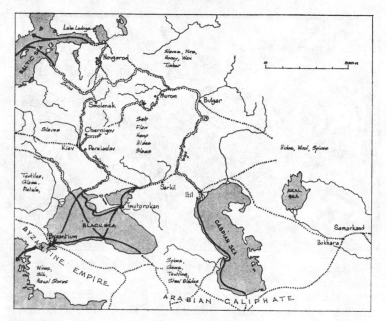

MAP 10. THE RUSSIAN RIVERS AND THE MOVEMENTS
OF THE RUS

were both traders and something more. Northwards they had their
city state of Novgorod and their base at Staraja Ladoga; along the
river they won a footing at Gnezdovo-Smolensk and Chernigov and
supremacy at Kiev, from which last they exploited and imposed
their will on the surrounding Slav population. Before the end of the
century Kiev under Oleg would be the main seat of Rus power in
Russia. From Muslim and Greek sources during the next hundred
years we acquire a good deal of picturesque (perhaps over picturesque) information about these Rus, 'whom we with another name
call Northmen (*Rusios quos alio nos nomine Nordmannos appellamus*)'.[1]

[1] Liudprand, bishop of Cremona, describing the peoples who dwell north
of the Byzantine Empire, *Antapodosis*, ed J. Becker, SSRG, Hannover, 1915, I,
11. Compare the same work, V, 15: 'There is a people dwelling in the north
whom for some bodily quality the Greeks call Rus; we however by reason of
the situation of their homeland call them *Nordmannos*.' Liudprand was an
envoy to Constantinople 948–50 and 968.

Ibn Rustah, writing in the first half of the tenth century, tells us how the Rus lived on an island (or promontory) in a lake, which was large, marshy, forested, and unhealthy. They were much busied with slave-hunting. 'They have no cultivated land but depend for their living on what they can obtain from Saqalibah's land[1] . . . They have no estates, villages, or fields; their only business is dealing in sables, squirrel, and other furs, and the money they acquire by these transactions they keep in their belts.' They journeyed and made war by ship, were excessively valiant and treacherous, were handsome, clean, and well dressed (Ibn Rustah notes the full baggy trousers gathered kneewards vouched for by Scandinavian picture stones and fragments of northern tapestry, though these may well have been influenced by Oriental fashions—the viking in general was *skartsmaðr mikill*, quite a dandy). They were hospitable and protective of their guests; were quarrelsome among themselves and frequently resorted to single combat (reminiscent of saga accounts of *hólmganga*) to settle disputes; but in the face of a common enemy they closed their ranks and fought as one man. They had priests and made sacrifices of men, women, and cattle to their god. The method of sacrifice was by hanging. They lived in a state of such insecurity and distrust that a man dare not go outside about his natural needs save with an armed escort. When one of their chieftains died they made a grave like a big house and put him inside, with his apparel and gold armbands, and an abundance of food, vessels with drink, and coins. Finally they put his favourite wife (woman, concubine) inside with him, still living, then closed the door of the grave, so that she died.

Ibn Rustah was possibly describing the Rus of Novgorod,[2] but his picture of a big trading-post maintained by force of arms among an alien community must be true of the other known centres of Rus

[1] That is, from the land of the Slavs. By the time Ibn Rustah secured his information there would have taken place a considerable fusion of the dominant Swedish-Rus and the general Slav population. At all time Rus military strength must have drawn substantially on Slav manpower.

[2] G. Vernadsky, *Ancient Russia*, p. 281 ff., and *The Origins of Russia*, pp. 189 ff., argues for Tmutorokan on the Taman peninsula, which is situated between the Black Sea, the Kerch Strait, and the Sea of Azov. He considers that Tmutorokan was early a military base of the Rus and their main centre of Oriental and Caucasian trade. In the middle of the ninth century its communications with the Rus of northern Russia were interrupted by the Khazars and Magyars (*Origins*, p. 209).

influence also. What he says of Rus burial customs is borne out by the wooden burial chambers at Gnezdovo,[1] Chernigov, and Kiev on the Dnieper, and by many wooden-chamber graves of Swedish provenance, including a number at Birka, some of them containing a man and woman, and sometimes a horse in addition to the other grave goods. On the Dnieper the women are never wearing Scandinavian brooches, so presumably they were women of the locality, living possibly in wedlock, but more likely in concubinage. This is consonant with Ibn Fadlan's chilling account of a slave-girl on the Volga being found to accompany her Rus master in death as in life.[2]

Our next informant as to the ways of the Rus is no less a person than the emperor Constantine Porphyrogenitus in his work *De Administrando Imperio*, written about 950.[3] He is concerned to tell of the convoys of vessels out of the Russian north which descend the Dnieper to Berezany on the Black Sea, and from there make their way to the imperial city itself. The boats from Further Russia (i.e. from beyond Kiev), he tells us, came from Novgorod, where prince Svyatoslav had his seat, the son of that Igor who had attacked Constantinople in 941, from Smolensk and Chernigov, Teliutza (Lubetch) and Busegrad (Visgorod), and they travelled downstream till they arrived at Kiev. Meanwhile the Rus of Kiev had been hard at work (their life, he says, *was* a hard one), for during the winter they were out on *poliudie*, that is, on their rounds, visiting the Slavonic peoples, Vervians, Dregovichians, Krivichians, Severians, and others who paid them tribute. Some paid in money, some in furs and other commodities, and there was always a use for slaves. In April with the thaw they returned to Kiev. The town stands on a

---

[1] Gnezdovo was admirably placed as a centre of trade, situated as it was by the Dnieper, and with access to the Dvina, and so to the Baltic, and that other important trade river, the Oka, leading east by way of Finnish Murom to the Volga, and so downstream to Bulgar on the Volga Bend.

[2] See Appendix 3. Yet it is probable that the evidence of the graves has been interpreted too favourably in respect of the Swedish presence. Many of the weapons, grave goods, and modes of burial are as likely to be Slav as Scandinavian, and more extensive archaeological investigation will probably diminish rather than enhance the Normanist claim. The many boat-burials, however, are certainly Scandinavian or show Scandinavian influence. L. Musset provides illuminating comment on this and related matters in his *Les invasions : le second assaut*, pp. 261–6 ('Problèmes Russes').

[3] Ed. G. Moravcsik and (trans.) R. J. H. Jenkins, I-II, Budapest, 1949–62.

series of bluffs on the river's west bank, and is unaffected by the spring floods, which raise the river's level as much as 16 feet, and increase its width from less than half a mile to five miles or even six. From April till June the Rus found it unnavigable, but after their return from their rounds they needed this length of time to transfer usable gear and parts from their old boats, hollowed out of a single tree, to the new ones prepared for them by the Slavs, and make all shipshape. By June the river was manageable; it still ran with more than its normal flow, but this served a purpose. The fleet now moved a short way downstream to the stockaded taxing-post of Vitichev (the emperor was writing at a time when the Rus of Kiev had absolute control of the Dnieper), and after a day or two all the boats sailed off 'to face the perils of the voyage together'. These were of two kinds: the natural hazards of the descent, which were worst at the rapids of the modern Dnjepropetrovsk, and the risk of ambush by the Petchenegs, which was at its most acute on the same stretch of river. The emperor is eloquent on the perils of the forty-mile succession of cataracts where the mighty river is compressed between walls of granite. It was to get over or past the rocks and boulders here that they needed the high water of the June season. Now the Rus go into the water naked, some feel the way with their feet, others ply their stout staffs at prow, amidships, and stern; now they unload their cargoes and use their slaves for a six-mile portage; now they appoint sentinels, lest the same fate befall them as befell prince Svyatoslav in 972, when the Petchenegs slew him near the rapids and made a drinking-cup of his close-shaven skull. The emperor has preserved the names of the seven cataracts he knew about, in their Slavonic and Scandinavian forms.[1] They are, these last, Essupi (*supa*), the Drinker, or Gulper, or (*ei sofi*), 'Sleep not!'; Ulvorsi (*hólmfors*), Island-force; Gelandri (gjallandi), the Yeller; Aïfor (*eifors*), the Ever-fierce, Ever-noisy, or Impassable, or (*edfors*), Narrow-force, or Portage-force; Baruforos (*bárufors*), Wave-force, or possibly (*varufors*), Highcliff-force; Leanti (*blæjandi, leandi*), the Laugher, or Seether; Strukun (*struk, strok*), the Courser—a piece of philological evidence as striking as it is unexpected. We read of one of these, Aïfor, on a runic stone at Pilgards in Gotland: 'Hegbjorn

---

[1] The difficulties of interpretation do not affect the Norse origin of the names. See Vilh. Thomsen, *Ancient Russia and Scandinavia*, pp. 52–67, 143–5, and K. O. Falk, 'Dneprforsanas namn i kejsar Konstantin Porphyrogennetos De Administrando Imperio', *Lunds Univ. Årsskrift*, 1951.

and his brothers Rodvisl, Osten, and Emund, had this stone painted in colours and raised. They also raised stones in memory of Hrafn, south of Rufstein. They went far into Aïfor. Vifil gave the order.' Hrafn evidently lost his life in that insatiable, boulder-strewn torrent.

37. THE FUR TRADE, I: MARTENS AND SABLES
(OLAUS MAGNUS)

Thereafter, continues the emperor, they come to St. Gregor's island with its giant oak tree, where they offer up sacrifice. And so in time they come to the island of Berezany on the Black Sea, its name, we think, a Rus remembrance of Birka and Bjorkö, the Birch Island in Lake Mälar, far north in the Uppland kingdom of the Swedes. And here on this Birch Island of the south an unknown Norseman named Grani cut runes in memory of his unknown comrade Karl—the 'farthest east' of this robust commemorative art.

But the stay of the convoys on Berezany would be a short one. By a treaty of 945 the emperor would make it clear he did not propose to see it become an island base: the Rus must go back home every autumn. Nor would the convoys be anxious to stay: the goal for so many of them was Constantinople, Tsargrad, the loveliest, most splendid, and richest of cities, on which the Scandinavian north was to bestow the simplest and most pre-emptive of titles,

Mikligarðr, Metropolis, the Great City. Everything that the archaeological sciences tell us about the settlements of the Swedes and the Rus, from Gamla Uppsala and Birka to Kiev, prepares us for the astonishment, admiration, and cupidity with which the Barbarians would first see the Queen of Cities riding the waters of Bosporus, Marmara, and the Golden Horn. For buyers and sellers this was an emporium beyond dreams; the Norseman could not fail to be impressed by the art, culture, 'politeness', and civilization he encountered here; while the visible manifestations of Greek permanence and power, the churches, towers, wharves, warehouses, fortifications (twelve miles of them), the palaces and statuary, to say nothing of its half a million inhabitants, were beyond his homeland imaginings. With their contribution to the ever-grinding mill of Byzantine trade, the Rus were welcome, even favoured, visitors, while politically it suited the emperor to have a khaganate at Kiev strong enough to restrain the turbulence of local tribes, but in the nature of things not strong enough to challenge the Empire with expectation of success.

Even so, relations between the Rus and Byzantium were not always peaceful. In the early 860s a fleet said to be under the command of Askold and Dir, the first rulers of Kiev, having already ravaged the shores of the Black Sea and the Propontis, appeared before Constantinople in the absence of the emperor, and was routed less by the overwhelming force the city could deploy than by prayers to the Virgin and the destructive storm that followed them. In 907 the Rus were back again, this time under Oleg, the uniter of Novgorod and Kiev, but what shall we say of a fleet of 2,000 vessels, a force of 80,000 men, and a stratagem which circumvented the chaining of the Bosporus by putting the ships on wheels and sailing them overland to Constantinople? Still, somewhere behind these accretions of fantasy may be found the reality of a Rus-Byzantine confrontation which led to the commercial treaty of 911–12, whose beginning, as recorded in the *Primary Chronicle*, is such a fanfare of northern nomenclature: 'We of the Rus: Karli, Ingeld, Farlof, Vermud, Rulov, Gody, Ruald, Karn, Frelav, Aktevu, Truan, Lidul, Fost, Stemid,[1] are sent by Oleg, great prince of the

[1] Karl-Karli, Ingjaldr, Farulfr, Vermundr. Hroðleifr, Góði-Guði, Hróaldr, Karni, Friðleifr, Angantýr(?), Thróndr-Thrándr, Leiðulfr, Fasti-Fastr, Steinviðr(?), are the normalized ON. forms. They point preponderantly to eastern Sweden, but some are Finnish.

Rus, and by all the illustrious and mighty princes, and the most noble boyars under his sway, to you, Leon and Alexander and Constantine, great rulers by the grace of God, emperors of the Greeks, for the maintaining and proclamation of the long-standing friendship between Greeks and Rus. . . .' What followed were regulations concerning killing and murder, theft, wreck and stranding, ransom and inheritance, and the like. Earlier, in 907, there had been mention of free baths and provisions and ships' gear reminiscent of deals and treaties far west in the Frankish Empire. There was now peace for thirty years, till prince Igor for no known reason came across the Black Sea in the early summer of 941 with a fleet said by the *Primary Chronicle* to consist of 10,000 ships, but certainly much overestimated by Liudprand of Cremona at 1,000. Whatever their number, they availed him nothing: a cruel reality underlies the tale of their destruction by outpourings of Greek fire. Vengeful and undismayed, he returned three years later with a horde of mercenaries and innumerable ships. This time there was no need of Greek fire. Greek diplomacy was just as effective. Igor was beguiled with gifts and promises; his Petcheneg allies departed with everyone's blessing to ravage Bulgaria; Igor led the Rus back home to Kiev, and in 945 a new treaty came into being which names no fewer than fifty Rus plenipotentaries, some with Norse but in contrast with the treaty of 912 many with Slavonic names. Once more there were legal stipulations, some renewed, some novel; they were allotted summer quarters in the suburbs of Constantinople, might not enter the city proper in detachments of more than fifty men, and these unarmed. The amount of silk they could purchase should not exceed the worth of fifty gold pieces, and this required a customs stamp before it left the city, no doubt by way of precaution against the local black market. The Rus were entitled to a month's provisions, free, and to food and equipment for their return to Kiev, which must take place every autumn. Finally, the Rus would fight the Bulgars and entreat the Khazars in accord with the needs of Byzantine foreign policy. When the Greek diplomats departed for home Igor gave them presents of furs, slaves, and wax.

These were not the only wars of the Rus, who, typically, were always prepared to vary the profits of commerce with those of martial arms. Al Masudi tells of a big viking raid in 912 across the Caspian to Baku and Azerbaijan. It ended disastrously. In 943 a large Rus fleet entered the river Kura south of Baku, reached the

38. THE FUR TRADE, 2: SQUIRRELS (OLAUS MAGNUS)

town of Berda on its tributary the Terter, and put a large number of the inhabitants there to the sword. In turn they were attacked within and without by Muslims and dysentery, and so brought to retreat, whereupon their adversaries dug up the corpses of the dead Rus and stripped them of the fine weapons they had taken with them into their graves—graves which also contained a wife or slave-girl, after the Rus (and it must be admitted, Slav), custom. This was in Igor's time. Igor's son Svyatoslav (his birth when his father was aged 75, and his mother, the famous Olga, 60, was a guarantee of wonders, some would say lies, to come) was a hardy campaigner against Khazars, Vyatichi, and Bulgars, and shortly before the Petchenegs took his head in 972 had behaved menacingly towards Constantinople itself. But not only in the un-Norse name he bore was Svyatoslav departing from his viking heritage. He rode without baggage, carried no kettle or cauldron, and supplied tent and couch by a saddle under his head. This was his appearance, as recorded by Leo Diaconus in 971, when he signed a treaty with the emperor Johannes Tzimiskes on the Danube:

Svyatoslav crossed the river in a kind of Scythian boat; he handled the oar in the same way as his men. His appearance was as follows: he was of medium height—neither too tall, nor too short. He had bushy brows, blue eyes, and was snub-nosed; he shaved his beard but wore a long and bushy moustache. His head was shaven except for a lock of hair on one side as a sign of the nobility of his clan. His neck was thick, his shoulders broad, and his whole stature pretty fine. He seemed gloomy and savage. On one of his ears hung a golden ear-ring adorned with two pearls and a ruby set between them. His white garments were not distinguishable from those of his men except for cleanness.[1]

A year or so later he was dead, and his three sons fought savagely among themselves to enlarge the third share of Kievan power he had appointed for each of them. Yaropolk slew Oleg, then perished in his turn, and it was the third son Vladimir who with the help of an army recruited, we are told, in Sweden succeeded to all the lands of the Rus. This Vladimir, as resourceful as he was ambitious, was born to do more than survive; he interfered victoriously in the affairs of various Slavonic tribes, made his presence felt in the north among the Ests and their neighbours, beat the Poles once and the Bulgars twice, and chastised the insolent Petchenegs. Then in 988 he accepted the Christianity of the Greek Church, and employed his enormous energy in building churches and christianizing his many-religioned subjects, no small number of them by immersion in the waters of the Dnieper. Like other Scandinavian princes (and his bonds with the North seem stronger than his father's and grandfather's), he had come to recognize the political and economic advantages of belonging to a monotheistic religion. He is not over-reliably reported to have taken an appraising glance at Islam, Judaism, and Rome, before settling on the faith of Byzantium. As part of the complicated and farsighted manoeuvre by which he brought Novgorod and Kiev into the community of Christian peoples he helped the emperor Basil II Bulgaroctonos put down a rebellion by Bardas Phocas, and was rewarded with the emperor's sister in marriage—an honour she tried hard to avoid, partly no

[1] G. Vernadsky, *The Origins of Russia*, p. 277 (Leo Diaconus, *Historiæ Libri decem*, ed. Haase, pp. 156–7). There is another translation in Holger Arbman, *The Vikings* (trans. Alan Binns), pp. 103–4. Professor Arbman continues: 'The description has many features (the hair lock, *osolodets*, in particular) of the Cossack *hetman* of the sixteenth century, and suggests how quickly the Rus were becoming Slavonic. Svyatoslav is not a Scandinavian name, and it is probable that he was in part of Slavonic descent.' In an earlier reference to Svyatoslav's birth Professor Arbman suspects that something has been lost of the Kievan family tree (p. 102).

doubt because of the eight hundred concubines and slavegirls he maintained in various Rus towns. Another far-reaching decision of his was to make the language of his new church Slavonic, not Greek or Scandinavian. This last, we assume, had long since ceased to be a possibility. But the influence of Byzantium, exerted through religion, education, culture and art, military alliance and commercial facilities, was great and increasing.

One more famous prince of the Viking Age was to succeed to the khaganate of the Rus after the death of Vladimir. This was Yaroslav, the best known of all Kievan rulers to northern historians. Like Svyatoslav, he was a man of inexhaustible energy, wide and calculating vision, and a sage awareness of what was needed to strengthen the kingdom of Novgorod-Kiev and enhance its prestige in the eyes of its neighbours. He was highly conscious of his Scandinavian connection, married Ingigerd the daughter of Olaf Skötkonung of Sweden, comforted and reinforced the dispossessed Olaf Haraldsson of Norway, gave refuge to the young Magnus Olafsson and to Harald Hardradi after Olaf's defeat at Stiklarstadir, found this latter employment in his army, and was recognized by him as his liege-lord and patron. Finally he gave him his daughter Elizabeth in marriage. Other daughters were bestowed on other monarchs, king Andrew I of Hungary, king Henry I of France. Four of his sons married into the courts of Byzantium and Germany. The arts of war and peace were equally dear to him. When in the 1030s he had ground down those ancient foes the Petchenegs he celebrated his victory and the God who gave it by building the first Russian cathedral, his church of St. Sophia, noble enough to have been long mistaken for a copy of St. Sophia in Constantinople. He asserted the Kievan power with similar success in the northern reaches of his vast dominion, brought the Chud back under control, and enlarged his boundaries to the west. Kievan hold on the Dnieper trade-route was now absolute; it was a time when the national coffers first bulged then overflowed; and the town, henceforth properly to be styled the city, of Kiev was the beneficiary. The heart of the city was walled about with an earthen rampart, with many bastions and gateways; churches arose there, other than St. Sophia, monasteries and schools. With the example of Constantinople before him, he knew that his capital city must not only be strong, but lovely and adorned, so he imported artists as well as architects, to provide frescoes and mosaics. Like king Alfred of Wessex a century and a half before, he brought in scholars to translate devout and necessary works into the Slavonic tongue; and like Alfred he sought to clarify and record the laws.

Yaroslav's achievement was a notable one. It has been remarked by many historians that under him the kingdom of Kiev moved and was seen to move within the European orbit. But it calls for special pleading to describe it in any meaningful sense as a Norse kingdom. There had been a steady process of assimilation to the native population for almost two hundred years: concubinage, inter-marriage, a change of language and religion, and the adoption of Slavonic customs had quietly eroded the Norseness of the Rus, and the massive influence of Byzantium carried the process ever farther. During Yaroslav's long reign (1019–54) he clashed only once with the Greeks, when he ill-advisedly sent his son to intimidate the capital in 1043. He lost his fleet, which was bad, and his illusions about the relative power of Kiev and the Empire, which was good. For Byzantium was by now essential not only to Kiev's prosperity, but to her purposeful survival. The absorption of Byzantine influence by the Kiev kingdom would prove one of its two main contributions to the future of Russia. The other was not the 'foundation of the Russian state' with which the Swedes are often overgenerously credited, but the creation or furtherance of durable trading towns, of which Novgorod, Beloozero, Izborsk, Polotsk, Rostov, Smolensk, Chernigov, and Kiev itself were the most important, and its decisive role in the development of a Slavonicized state extending from Lake Ladoga to the Black Sea. The foundation of the Russian state was a complicated and lengthy process in which the Rus played a memorable and effective, but not an only part. At what point in time the activities of the kingdom of Kiev ceased to be anything but marginal to viking history is open to debate. A hard answer might set it well back in the ninth century; an even harder might carry it back to the beginning and say it had never been anything but marginal. To the disengaged it may well seem that the Normanist case has been as overpresented by a majority of Scandinavian historians as it has been played down by a majority of the historians of Russia. Arguments for Scandinavian influence on Kievan law, literature, language, art, religion, coinage, customs, and social organization have not prospered; and it is a major presumption to take all Greek and Muslim references to the Rus as relating to men from Scandinavia, and to those alone. The

nations of the east Slavs played a far greater part in the foundation
and development of the Russian state than did the Norsemen. So
did Byzantium—and there is still a Muslim and a Turkic influence
to be added.[1]

In any case there was an emphatic break in Vladimir's time. The
conversion to eastern Christianity while Sweden was still heathen,
together with the encroachments of the Slavonic tongue, were
accompanied by an extraordinary decline in the import of Muslim
silver into Scandinavia.[2] This indeed was already marked in the
time of his ancestor Svyatoslav, and has been ascribed to the
interruption of Volga trade as a result of that king's warring against
the Bulgars of northern Russia, as well as to a silver crisis in Islam.
Either way, it is the fact rather than its cause which is important.
Scandinavia had grown used to silver, needed silver, and as supplies
from the Muslim world by way of Russia, and to some extent
Poland, dried up, they looked to Germany and England instead.
Silver from the mines of the Harz mountains came north by way of
loot and, increasingly, trade; and silver coins from England represent
successive payments of tribute till the country had been conquered,
when they represent the payment of northern soldiers in Danish
pay. The famous mart of Birka ceased to be of importance after
c. 970, such was its dependence on the Russian trade. It looks as
though the interests of Kiev and Sweden were by now less than

---

[1] These conclusions are confirmed by N. J. Dejevsky, 'The Varangians in Soviet
Archaeology Today' (a guide to the literature in Russian), *Mediaeval Scandinavia* 10,
1977, pp. 7–34.

[2] The incidence of kufic coins in Birka graves tells a clear story. The following table is
from H. Arbman, *Svear i österviking*, p. 135, by way of P. H. Sawyer, *The Age of the
Vikings*, p. 185.

Date of Coins	Number found in Birka graves
700–750	12
750–800	14
800–850	17
850–890	4
890–950	42
950–	1

I add Sawyer's comment: 'The presence of coins of the eighth century does not, of
course, mean that the graves can be dated to that time, for these older coins remained in
circulation for a long time in Scandinavia. Some of the older coins were in fact found in
graves along with later ones; for example in one grave a coin of 818–19 was found together with four from 913–32. Many of the other early coins may similarly have been
buried in the tenth century.'

complementary, and in some respects flatly opposed.[1] Increasingly the Rus looked first to themselves and next to Byzantium, and the gap between Svíþjóð and Svíþjóð hinn mikla, Sweden and Sweden the Great, grew wider. Yaroslav's northern sympathies and affinities obscure the estrangement, but hardly effect it, and after Yaroslav's death in 1054 nothing remains for our present chronicle.

Or almost nothing. The eastern Scandinavian connection with the famous Varangian Guard would not come to an end for another twenty years and more. That adventurers from the north would early take service with the Greek emperor was to be expected: it appealed to the age-old ambitions and compulsions which had enrolled men in the comitatus of Hygelac in the early sixth century, in Harald Fairhair's hird in the late ninth, and in Knut's Thing-mannalid in the eleventh. The sword-arm was a saleable commodity. And where could service be more honourable and reward more bounteous than in the sumptuous treasure-city of the Bosporus? So at times contingents, even small armies of the Rus, enlisted to do battle against the Emperor's enemies. There is a fair documentation of their campaigns throughout the tenth century; they landed in Crete and southern Italy, fought in Mesopotamia and Dalmatia, died in the sands neighbouring the Caspian. Their ships ploughed many waters. It was probably near to the year 1000 before the Varangians were organized as the emperor's personal guard. The 'axe-bearing barbarians' remained in the imperial service till the early thirteenth century, but after 1066 its composition was much changed. The sometimes glorious, occasionally monstrous, and all too often untestimonied exploits of Harald Hardradi between 1034 and 1042 suggest a guard still dominated by the Scandinavian connection, but after the Norman conquest of England numerous Englishmen and resident Danes left the country for military employment at Constantinople. They found many disaffected Normans and Frenchmen there already. Soon the guard would be more English than viking, a most curious consequence for an offshoot of the Norsemen in the east of the activities of an offshoot of the Norsemen in the west.

One other aspect of the Swedish movement into Russia has claims on our attention—the frequent runic inscriptions in the

[1] A good discussion in English of all these matters will be found in P. H. Sawyer, *The Age of the Vikings*, and more particularly in chapters 5, 'Treasure', and 8, 'Towns and Trade'.

motherland which record the journeys and deaths of her east-going sons. There is the stone at Ed in Uppland (Plate 17): 'Rognvald had runes carved for Fastvi his mother, Onæm's daughter. She died in Ed, God help her soul. Rognvald had runes carved: he was in Greekland, was leader of a host.' And this from Gripsholm, Södermanland: 'Tola had this stone raised for his son Harald, Yngvar's brother. They journeyed boldly, far afield after gold: in the east they gave food to eagles. They died in the south, in Serkland.' This was that Yngvar the Widefarer whose exploits in the east entered Norse legend—and Norse history inasmuch as twenty-five east Swedish memorial stones of the early mid-eleventh century tell of men who took the eastern road to Serkland and fell with Yngvar's host. Not all journeyed so far. A stone from Estaberg, Södermanland, records of Sigvid: 'He fell in Holmgard (Novgorod), the ship's captain with his crew'; and a stone from Sjusta, Uppland, tells of Spjallbodi: 'He met his end in Holmgard, in St. Olaf's church.' Not all were men of war: he was a peaceful trader to the Baltic lands whom a loving wife commemorated with a stone at Mervalla: 'Sigrid had this stone raised for her husband Svein. He sailed often to Semgali with his fine ship round Domesnes.' The memorial can be full and verse-adorned, like this to Thorstein at Turinge, Södermanland: 'Ketil and Bjorn raised this stone for Thorstein their father, and Onund for his brother, and the housecarles for their peer, and Ketillaug for her husband. These brothers were the best of men, at home and afield with a host. They kept their housecarles well. He fell in battle, east in Russia, leader of a host and best of men from this land.' Or it can be spare as the Timans stone in Gotland: *ormiga*: *ulfuair*: *krikiaR*: *iaursaliR*: *islat*: *serklat*: 'Ormika, Ulfair: Greece, Jerusalem, Iceland, Serkland.'

One of the most impressive of runic inscriptions relating to the Swedes in the east is preserved in a city they never troubled. Down past the Riva degli Schiavoni in Venice, outside the entrance to the Arsenal, stand four guardian lions. Two of them were brought to Venice from the Piraeus harbour of Athens in the late seventeenth century. The bigger of these (and the largest of all four) is a magnificent creature, 12 feet high, carved in white marble by a Greek artist seventeen hundred years ago. There he sits on his lean haunches, front legs braced, grave and regarding, and on his two shoulders displays worn and weathered runic scrolls inscribed there by Swedish soldiers in Greece in the second half of the eleventh century. But not deeply enough: they cannot be read, which, as Brøndsted says, is a pity. 'It would have been interesting to know what a Swedish Viking wished to confide to a Greek lion.' It is mere fancy to ascribe to the lion a message of Greek lastingness and Swedish transience in the context of Byzantium—but fronting him it is a fancy hard to dispel.

5. The Movement West: Iceland, Greenland, America

THE PRESENCE OF A VAST AND FOR THE MOST PART unsailed ocean to the west of Norway and the British Isles was a constant challenge to the land-hungry, wealth-hungry, fame-hungry vikings of Scandinavia. As soon as they had ships fit for its waters it was a challenge they accepted. The motivating force of the Norwegian sailings west, the colonization of the lesser Atlantic islands, and thereafter of Iceland and Greenland, and the attempted settlement in America, was a need for land and pasture. Fittingly enough, Iceland, whose soil the Norsemen made so devotedly their own, would prove the one lastingly successful 'pure' Norse colonial experiment overseas, and so deserves our special attention. But to its discovery and settlement, which dates from *c.* 860–70, the discovery of the Faroes was a necessary preliminary. In both countries the first men ashore were Irish religious, peregrini who had 'turned their back on Ireland' and sought hermitages across the northern waters. In his *Liber de Mensura Orbis Terræ*, written in the year 825, the Irish monk Dicuil has this to say of the islands surrounding Britain:

There are many other islands in the ocean to the north of Britain which can be reached from the northernmost British Isles in two days' and nights' direct sailing, with full sails and an undropping fair wind. A certain holy man [*presbyter religiosus*] informed me that in two summer days and the night between, sailing in a little boat of two thwarts, he came to land on one of them. Some of these islands are very small; nearly all of them are separated one from the other by narrow sounds. On these islands hermits who have sailed from our Scotia [Ireland] have lived for roughly a hundred years. But, even as they have been constantly uninhabited since the world's beginning, so now, because of Norse pirates, they are empty of anchorites, but full of innumerable sheep and a great many different kinds of seafowl. I have never found these islands mentioned in the books of scholars.

There is a general agreement that Dicuil is here speaking of the Faroes, Færeyjar, or Sheep Islands. In the same context he mentions Iceland.

It is now thirty years since priests [*clerici*] who lived in that island [i.e., Thule] from the first day of February to the first day of August told me that not only at the summer solstice, but in the days on either side of it, the setting sun hides itself at the evening hour as if behind a little hill, so that no darkness occurs during that very brief period of time, but whatever task a man wishes to perform, even to picking the lice out of his shirt, he can manage it precisely as in broad daylight. And had they been on a high mountain, the sun would at no time have been hidden from them. . . .

They deal in fallacies who have written that the sea round the island is frozen, and that there is continuous day without night from the vernal to the autumnal equinox, and vice versa, perpetual night from the autumnal equinox to the vernal; for those sailing at an expected time of great cold have made their way thereto, and dwelling on the island enjoyed always alternate night and day save at the time of the solstice. But after one day's sailing from there to the north they found the frozen sea.[1]

It would seem from this that Irish priests had reached the Faroes soon after the year 700 and lived there undisturbed till the first Norsemen arrived about a hundred years later and dispossessed them. Of these Norsemen we know practically nothing, save that the most important among them was Grim Kamban, who despite the testimony of *Færeyinga Saga* probably came by way of Ireland or the Hebrides rather than direct from Norway, and may have been a Christian. After his death, however, his fellow settlers are said to have worshipped him and offered him sacrifice. Presumably the economy of the islands was still based on sheep, which could graze the plains which diversify the steep hills, on fowling by net and pole along the precipitous cliffs, on fishing and whaling (the driving in, stranding, and slaughter of blackfish or ca'ing whales in the blood-red shallows of Midvagur or other beaches in August cannot have looked much different a thousand years ago from what it does

[1] Ed. Walkenaer, Paris, 1807, pp. 27–30.

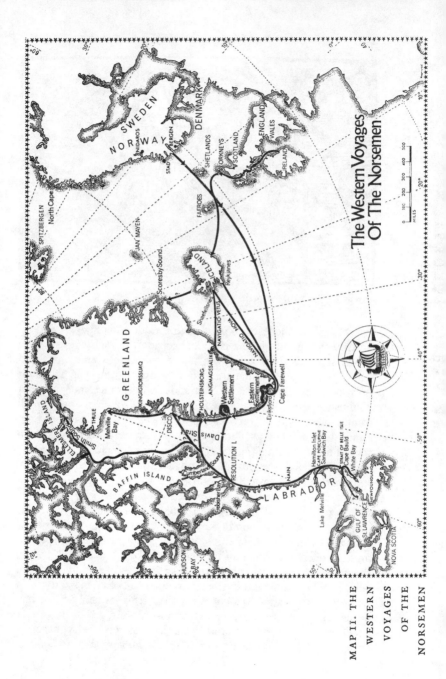

MAP II. THE WESTERN VOYAGES OF THE NORSEMEN

39. WHALE-FLENSING, FAROES (OLAUS MAGNUS)

today), and the modest profits of viking trade and piracy. The deep fjords which penetrate the islands, the tidal channels and rip-races which separate them one from another, the fogs and mists and storms of rain which afflict them at all seasons of the year, and their isolation (200 miles from the Shetlands, 240 from Iceland), had not diminished their attraction for religious solitaries and small communities, and in turn did not prevent the Norsemen from establishing a Thing at Thorshavn and from pursuing their known way of life, including the luxury of the blood-feud, everywhere.

It was intelligence gleaned in Ireland, the Western Isles, Orkney and Shetland, which led the Norsemen to the Faroes. Once Irish priests reached Iceland in the 790s news of this discovery must have spread rapidly. And none would more readily lend ear than the Norsemen, their minds on homes for their families, pasture for their animals, havens for their ships, and all such prospects of spoil or profit as offered. For men in the Faroes, Iceland lay to hand, and on the whole it is surprising that the first voyages of exploration were delayed till *c.* 860. Possibly the sharp outbreak of viking activity in western Europe after 830 contributed to this. Possibly there had been earlier voyages, unrecorded or unsuccessful.

Three names are associated with the first recorded voyages to Iceland, and it is worth noting that the *Íslendingabók*, or Book of the Icelanders (*c.* 1125), of the highly respected Ari Thorgilsson makes mention of none of them. Two of these pioneers are reported to have lighted on the country by accident of weather, the third with the help of three hallowed ravens—though it may be admitted that the use of birds as aids to navigation was a device anteceding the vikings. Two suffered the misfortune of a broken tow-line and lost their ship's boat with one or more members of crew aboard, all of them safely recovered later. Two of them climbed a mountain (a reasonable thing for newcomers to do) and were disenchanted with the view. All three gave the island a name. Three mariners, three voyages, three names: with these warnings against over-credulity belling in our ears, we may venture to sail in their wake.

The men named are Gardar Svavarsson the Swede, Naddod the Viking, and Floki Vilgerdason from Rogaland, both Norwegians. Sturla Thordarson's recension of *Landnámabók*, the Book of the Settlements, gives the credit of the discovery to Naddod, but a heavier weight of almost equally picturesque witness would ascribe it to Gardar. At the behest of his mother, a seeress (*Sturlubók*), or to lay claim to his wife's inheritance from her father in the Hebrides (*Hauksbók*), he set sail from his home in Scandinavia, was driven off course, and the gale and good luck helping raised Iceland east of the Eastern Horn. From here he sailed on round the land, wintered at Husavik in Skjalfandi, the Trembler, and the following summer discovered, or in the light of Irish intelligence confirmed, that it was an island, so with propriety named it Gardarsholm after himself, and on his return home praised it highly.

Of Naddod we read that he was *víkingr mikill*, a viking of note who seems to have made Norway and other Norse settlements too hot to hold him. His acquaintance with Iceland was entirely accidental. He was storm-tossed to Reydarfjord in the Eastfirths, where he climbed Reydarfjall in the hope of seeing smoke or other sign of human habitation. As he and his crew sailed away a heavy snowstorm enveloped the mountain, so appositely they named the land Snæland, Snowland, and back home in the Faroes they, too, praised it highly.

Floki Vilgerdason was likewise *víkingr mikill*, and sailed for Gardarsholm-Snæland as though intending to settle there. He took with him livestock, offered up sacrifice, and hallowed three ravens to show him the way, 'for in those days sailors in the Northlands had no loadstone'. He began by sailing to Shetland, where he lost one daughter by drowning, then sailed to the Faroes, where he lost a second by marriage. Then he sailed for Iceland with his three ravens. Some way out he loosed the first, which flew back to the land it had left. Then he loosed the second, which rose, surveyed the empty horizon, then prudently returned to the ship. Later he released the third, which flew straight ahead and so gave them a bearing for Iceland. They raised Horn from the east and sailed in Gardar's wake along the south coast and so to the northern shore of Breidafjord, to Vatnsfjord on Bardarstrand. Here they spent their time fishing and sealing, with no thought to the winter to come. But come it did, cold and snowy, so that their livestock perished for lack of hay. The spring, too, was cold, very cold, and when Floki climbed a mountain to check his prospects his discouraged eye beheld one of the southern arms of Arnarfjord stiff with ice. So he gave the island a third name, *Ísland*, Iceland, the one it has borne ever since. To add to his disenchantment he was late hoisting sail for his return. He failed to clear the Reykjanes headland in the teeth of the sou'-westerlies, had to turn and run for it, and spent the winter in Borgarfjord. His messmate Herjolf made what must have been a hair-raising crossing of Faxafloi in their parted tow-boat, but survived to tell the tale. On their return to Norway, Floki had nothing but ill to say of Iceland; Herjolf, whose impartiality is in the circumstances to be commended, spoke well of some things and ill of others; while a third man, Thorolf, undaunted by ice and haylessness, reported that butter dripped from every blade of Iceland's grass, for which testimonial to the land's benignity he was gratefully, or satirically, nicknamed Thorolf Butter.

In another decade the Age of Settlement had begun. Ari describes the arrival of the founding-father Ingolf [Arnarson] in seventy words which are the foundation-stone of Icelandic history;[1] *Landnámabók* enlarges the story after a fashion which makes it a pattern of Icelandic historiography. Thus. Towards 870 two foster-brothers back in Norway, Ingolf Arnarson (or Bjornolfsson) and

---

[1] 'A Norwegian named Ingolf is the man of whom it is reliably reported that he was the first to leave there for Iceland, when Harald Fairhair was sixteen years old, and a second time a few years later. He settled south in Reykjavik. The place is called Ingolfshofdi, east of Minnthakseyr, where he made his first landing, and Ingolfsfell, west of Olfus river, where he afterwards took land into his possession. At that time Iceland was covered with forest between mountain and seashore.' (*Íslendingabók*, cap. 2.)

Leif Hrodmarsson, were to fall out with their former allies and friends, the three sons of jarl Atli the Slender of Gaular, one of whom at a winter feast rashly swore to marry Helga, Ingolf's sister and the betrothed of Leif, or no woman else. This feckless vow cost him his life next spring, and within a year a second of jarl Atli's sons followed him violently into the grave. By way of penalty the foster-brothers were compelled to forfeit their estates, so without delay they fitted out a big ship and went off to find the land Raven-Floki had discovered and reported on. They made a reconnaissance in the Alptafjord area of the Austfirthir, wintered in Iceland, then went back home to plan a permanent settlement. Three or four years later they again came out to Iceland, with a ship apiece, their families, retainers, and some Irish slaves. On sighting the Icelandic coast the devout Ingolf cast his high-seat pillars overboard, vowing that he would make his home wherever Thor saw fit to bring them ashore. He spent his first winter on or near the lonely and command-ing fortress promontory of Ingolfshofdi, on the south coast, but Hjorleif (Sword-Leif: his name had been lengthened after he carried off a gleaming sword from an underground house or burial-mound in Ireland) was borne sixty miles further west to another such head, Hjorleifshofdi, where he and his fellow Norwegians were tricked and killed by their Irish slaves, who made off with the women, the movable goods, and the ship's boat to the fangy islands they could see in the south-west. There Ingolf caught up with them and killed them to the last man, which is why those islands, according to *Landnámabók*, got their name Vestmannaeyjar, the Isles of the Men from the West, the Isles of the Irishmen. Concurrently Ingolf's thralls found his high-seat pillars where Reykjavik stands today, and the following spring Ingolf arrived there, built himself a home, and took into his possession a patrimony bigger than many a Norwegian kingdom. Part of this he distributed among his followers, and so established at the very well-head of Icelandic history a pattern of land-taking and local lordship which would continue throughout the Age of Settlement and shape the Republic-to-be and its Constitution.

The colonization started thus summarily proceeded with vigour. In the south-east of the country, more particularly between the island of Papey and Papos in Lon, and further west in the rich grazing lands of Sida, the Norsemen found a scattering of *papar*, Irish monks and anchorites, but these solitaries had no wish to proselytize, and quickly went away. Otherwise the land was empty. There was no one and nothing to subdue—except the land itself, some five-sixths of which offered no support to human life. There were large areas devastated by volcanic action, with their debris of craters, lavafields, ash, and coarse black sand; there were screes, moraines and rocky outcrops, swamps and quags, geysirs and boiling mud; there were mountains, often barren, and icefields, always deathly. Fierce rivers poured from the island's centre to the sea, untameable as Thjórsá, or for long distances unfordable and unbridgeable as the northern and eastern Jokulsá. It was a sundered and barricaded land to which the land-takers came. Fire rose out of the ground, and sometimes the earth shook as though to rid itself of human encumbrance.

40. LAND OF FIRE AND ICE (OLAUS MAGNUS)

But this was by no means all the story. The habitable parts of the country proved attractive to men seeking sometimes a home, sometimes a refuge. Grass grew plentifully in long valleys, on broad plains or hillsides fronting the sea, and upland grazing on the *heiði* offered sheep a good living during the light bright months of summer. There was birchwood and scrub between mountain and seashore, and carpets of succulent blue berries in season, while the first generations, helped by a less extreme climate, grew a modest supply of corn. The lakes and rivers were filled with trout and salmon, the surrounding seas with fish and seals and whales, and the coasts and islands bred innumerable seafowl. And everywhere these creatures were at ease in the hunting-grounds, because men and men's ways were unknown to them. There were many catchment areas for driftwood. By *c.* 930 all suitable land had been occupied. The majority of settlers came from south-west Norway, from the viking breeding-grounds of Sogn, Hordaland, and Rogaland, most of them direct, but some by way of Scotland and her Atlantic isles, the Faroes and Ireland. From south-west Norway, too, came Iceland's law, language, and religion, and the predominantly Norse stamp of her civilization. Some of those who came from the western colonies were Christian, a few of them devout enough to inspire onomastic and homiletic anecdote in their post-Conversion descendants, like Aud the Deep-minded, who is reputed to have had Christian crosses set up at Krossholar, near Hvamm in Hvamms-fjord, and to have been buried in the salty no-man's-land below high-water mark, so that she might not lie in unconsecrated earth like her heathen neighbours; or the genial Svartkell from Caithness, whose grandson Glum, by the testimony of *Landnámabók*, still prayed to a Christian cross, with the words, 'A blessing ever on the old ones, a blessing ever on the young.' There were others less committed, like Helgi the Lean, who 'believed in Christ, and yet made vows to Thor for sea-voyages and in tight corners, and for everything which struck him as of real importance'.[1] But the vast majority of settlers were heathen. Here, too, some would be ardent, cast in the image of that Thorolf Mostrarskegg of later tradition who is said, not without exaggeration, to have made of Helgafell, Holy Mountain, on the southern shore of Breidafjord, so inviolate a sanctuary that neither man nor beast should suffer harm there unless they left it of their own accord, and no man should turn

[1] One can accept the proposition that there were Christians among the early settlers, and maybe a few among the late-comers, without being obliged to these minute particulars. The tenth-century Viking Age ship-grave excavated at Vatnsdalur, Patreksfjörður, in 1964, contained among its grave goods a Thor's hammer of silver, presumably worn as an amulet on a string of glass and amber beads; a piece of lead with an inlaid cross, apparently enamel-led; and a small fragmentary bronze bell, presumably Christian and brought from north-west England. It also contained a kufic coin, a dirhem. (See Thór Magnússon, 'Bátkumlið í Vatnsdal í Patreksfirði', *Árbók hins Íslenzka Forn-leifafélags*, 1966, pp. 5–32.

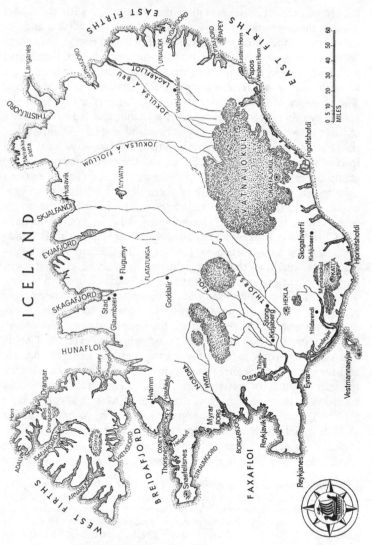

MAP 12. ICELAND

his unwashed face to it; but most were tolerant of their Christian neighbours, and could afford to be, 'for this [Christianity] rarely held good in their families, for the sons of some of them raised temples and sacrificed, and the land was altogether heathen for about a hundred years'.

Landnámabók records the names of some four hundred settlement-men. Estimates of the Celtic element among them have varied greatly, but that roughly one-seventh of them had a Celtic connection (often tenuous) is a not unreasonable guess. In addition there were many Celtic slaves and concubines in Icelandic households, some of them of good birth and standing. How far this Celtic, which predominantly means Irish, admixture of blood and manners affected the subsequent history and culture of Iceland has been long and inconclusively debated by historians, ethnologists, and literary critics. The most earnest protagonist of celticism cannot argue that the colonization of Iceland was anything but a Norse viking undertaking, though it is tempting to believe that it was the Irish infusion which most distinguished the Icelanders from the Norwegians and contributed in some measure to their literary achievement.

Iceland, we have said, was fully occupied by *c.* 930. We have this on the authority of the first great vernacular historian of Iceland, Ari Thorgilsson. The decades either side of the year 900 were propitious to colonization. It was a time when viking armies in the west suffered a series of reverses. Defeated in Brittany and on the Dyle, harassed and pounded in Wessex and Mercia, thrown out of Dublin, Anglesey, and the Hebrides, deprived of their leaders in Scotland and Orkney, they found their freedom of movement and prospects of gain sharply curtailed. Another bad development for the Norwegian viking was Harald Fairhair's welding of the kingdom back home. Icelandic tradition in the twelfth and thirteenth centuries was insistent that Iceland was settled mainly *fyrir ofríki Haralds konungs*, because of the tyranny of king Harald, and offered chapter and verse for it.[1] But we shall not be far from the truth if we conclude that the usual compulsions, land shortage, pressure of

[1] There were three main reasons for this: first, an external tyrant is an emotional necessity to small nations struggling for their independence; second, a search for 'holy freedom's laws' is a respectable reason for leaving one country for another; and third, for one's ancestors to have come out to Iceland after even a fictional opposition to Harald seems to have conferred the same kind of backward-looking prestige in one context as coming over with the Conqueror or the *Mayflower* in another.

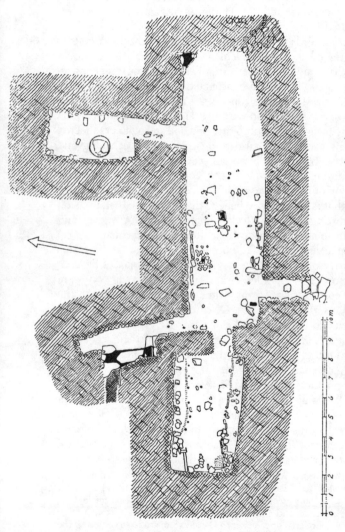

41. EARLY ELEVENTH-CENTURY FARM, GJÁSKÓGAR, THJÓRSÁRDALUR, ICELAND
The farm consists of four houses or sections; a hall 15 metres long, with a fireplace in the middle of the floor and sleeping-berths along both walls; a living-room with sitting-benches and a hearth; a dairy with an impression of a large vessel for milk or skyr sunk into the floor; and a privy with a groove running along one wall and opening out at the farther end.

population, restlessness, ambition or emulation, prospects of trade and hope of easy pickings, played a part in the colonization of Iceland, in addition to the special factors of the viking setbacks around 900 and the 'tyranny' of Harald Fairhair after Hafrsfjord. That Harald took an interest in the colonization, wished to exert a measure of control over it, and a degree of suzerainty over the colonists, is borne out by Ari Thorgilsson's statement that he set a tax on the head of Norwegian emigrants to Iceland, *Landnámabók*'s witness that to curb overextensive settlements and the quarrels these led to, he pronounced that no one should occupy more land than he and his crew could carry fire round in one day, and the curious story preserved in the *Sturlubók* and *Þórðarbók* versions of this latter authority about Uni the Dane, the son of Gardar the discoverer and circumnavigator, that he went out to Iceland at the bidding of king Harald Fairhair in order to make the land subject to himself or the king. Indeed, the kings of Norway would continue to keep a half-paternal, half-covetous eye on Iceland until the submission of the Republic to king Hakon Hakonarson in 1262–4.

Information about the settlers and their settlements is presented with unparalleled richness in Icelandic sources. Not all of it is credible, but the general picture is one we can rely on, of resourceful men crossing the northern seas in their tough and buoyant ships, making landfalls and getting themselves ashore, then exploring the empty countryside and exploiting its resources, appropriating land by strength and a first-comer's right, granting homes and holdings to their faithful followers, then settling down to an existence in which they called no man master and not many their peer.

Some of the settlers, we are told, built temples for the worship of their god, generally Thor, occasionally Frey, and more rarely Njord, Balder and Tyr. Odinn's followers were few, but in the next generation would include the magnificent Egill. The most circumstantial account of such a temple relates to Thorolf Mostrarskegg's so far undiscovered edifice at Hofstadir in Breidafjord.[1]

[1] 'He had a temple built—and a mighty edifice it was. There was a doorway in the side wall, nearer to the one end, and inside stood the pillars of the high-seat, with nails in them which were called the gods' nails. The area inside was a great sanctuary. Further in was a room of the same shape and order as the choir in churches today, where in the middle of the floor, like an altar, stood a pedestal, with an arm-ring without a join lying on it, twenty ounces in weight, on which men must swear all their oaths. The temple-priest was required to wear this ring on his arm at all public assemblies. On

Unfortunately archaeological research on the temple (*hof*) sites of Iceland has tended to nullify all such saga evidence. Most of them, if not all, owe more to nineteenth-century antiquarian enthusiasm than ninth-century religious zeal. It may be too early to say that Iceland (Scandinavia?) knew no such elaborate structures, but certainly the spade is proving no helpmeet to the pen. Probably the majority of places in Iceland where acts of worship, sacrifice, and sacral conviviality took place, were the homesteads of wealthy men, some of which may even have had a room earmarked for the purpose. The likeliest of such so far unearthed is the famous (and debated) site at Hofstadir in Mývatnssveit.

To maintain part of one's establishment for even occasional religious use, and to provide oxen and horses for sacrifice, was at once the privilege and perquisite of a man of means and authority. It arose out of, and contributed to, his strong position in the district, and he and his kind soon acquired the distinctive Icelandic title of the secular priest, godi (*goði*, godly one). Till 930 there was no central authority in Iceland, and in effect the godar (*goðar*) were its rulers. The office of godi was not coterminous with an estate or original land-taking; it could be acquired, shared, borrowed, or disposed of; but decidedly it remained a perquisite of the rich and powerful. Lesser men could transfer duty and allegiance from one godi to another; what they could not do was weaken the power of one without strengthening that of another. In other words, the institution itself could not be weakened, and when in 930 legislative and judicial power was placed in the hands of thirty-six leading men these were expressly and inevitably the godar. This attempt to provide Iceland with a constitution coincided with the end of the period of settlement. By this time it was apparent that men needed some form of machinery which would enable them to live together. The chieftains entrusted the introduction of a legal code for the

---

the pedestal too must stand the sacrificial bowl, and in it a sacrificial twig, like an aspergillum, by means of which the blood, which was called *blaut*, shall be sprinkled from the bowl. The blood, that is, which was shed when animals were slaughtered as a sacrifice to the gods. Around the pedestal in this same room were set the images of the gods.' (*Eyrbyggja Saga*, 4.)

This may be compared with Adam of Bremen's no less dubious account of the temple and god-images at Uppsala in Sweden, and with the fictional Gudbrand-temple near Trondheim in Norway, whose despoiling is recounted in *Njála*, 87. For a closer discussion of the *hof* or templum, see pp. 324–8 below.

whole country to Ulfljot of Lon, who returned to Norway, where
with the help of his uncle, Thorleif the Wise, he adapted the
Gulathing Law, the law of western Norway, to the needs of Iceland.
'And when he returned to Iceland the Althing was established, and
thereafter men had but one law here in the land.' Ulfljot's code has
been preserved in snatches only, and no great faith can be attached
even to these.[1] Certainly it started with first principles. 'This was
the beginning of the heathen laws, that men should not have a ship
with a figure-head at sea, but if they had, they must remove the
head before coming in sight of land, and not sail to land with gaping
heads and yawning jaws, so that the spirits of the land grow
frightened of them.' The thirty-six godar who controlled the
Althing or National Assembly elected a president or lawspeaker
(*lögsögumaðr*) for a renewable term of three years, whose duty it was
to recite one-third of the law to the assembled congregation every
year. Many famous men adorned this office, including Ulfljot
himself, the drafter of the constitution, Thorgeir of Ljosavatn, who
held office for seventeen years and though a heathen announced the
adoption of Christianity in Iceland, and Skapti Thoroddsson, who
held it for twenty-seven years, established the Fifth Court in 1005,
and made other far-reaching legal reforms. Later holders included
Snorri Sturluson and Sturla Thordarson, the historians.

The lawspeaker was the embodiment of the Constitution and a
repository of law, but he in no sense ruled the country or even the
courts. He could exert influence, but not wield power. That was
reserved for the godar. The Althing was unquestionably an
assembly for law of all free men who chose or were appointed to
attend it; but it was first and foremost the instrument of aristocratic
rule. It did not control the godar, but they it; and within their
home-districts their authority was absolute. Inevitably their
influence was strongly conservative. The reforms of 965 did nothing
to upset them. Iceland was now divided into four Quarters, North,
South, East and West, and the number of godar raised to thirty-
nine. In each Quarter there were assemblies for law in spring and
autumn; the spring Things proved highly successful in disposing of
minor suits. There were three such in each of the South, East and

---

[1] They are probably best regarded as antiquarian reconstructions by
learned men of the late twelfth or early thirteenth centuries of what they
judged such pre-Christian laws would be. See Olaf Olsen, *Hørg, Hov og Kirke*,
Copenhagen, 1966, pp. 34–49.

West Quarters, and four in the North. Three godar presided over each local assembly. The Althing was reformed in that its legislative and judicial functions became separate. The legislature was now called the Lögrétta or Law-righter, and consisted of no fewer than 142 members. This number was raised to 144 by the addition of the two bishops after the Conversion. The disproportion of the North Quarter was redressed by the co-option of three substitute godar from each of the other Quarters, making forty-eight in all. Each godi was attended by three advisers without power to vote. The Lögrétta alone could make new laws and interpret or amend old ones. It granted pardons, issued permits, and had some slight discretionary power in respect of various punishments. The judicature on the other hand now operated through four Quarter Courts which heard lawsuits from their own part of the country. Trial was made and judgement given in each court by a panel of judges or jurymen, probably thirty-six in number, and all of them appointed by the godar of the Quarter. The Quarter Court was expected to reach a unanimous decision on the cases submitted to it, unanimity being claimed if the minority vote did not exceed six. Naturally this was not always attained, and the need for a court of appeal was felt acutely till Skapti Thoroddsson established the Fifth Court (*fimtardómr*) c. 1005. This consisted of forty-eight judges or jurymen, appointed by the godar, whose number had been increased to forty-eight for this very purpose. This was the last significant change in the Constitution before the end of the Republic in 1262-4. Since the godar chose the lawspeaker, controlled the Lögrétta, administered the local Things, and appointed the judges to the Quarter Courts and the Fifth Court—and all this in addition to their religious office and the privileges of wealth and ownership of land in their home Thing-districts—it will be seen how completely they dominated Icelandic society from beginning to end of the Republic.

Much of the Republic's history lies outside the viking period. By summary assessment the Age of Land-taking or Settlement was over by c. 930, to be followed by the so-called Saga Age (*söguöld*), which lasted till 1030. During this period were enacted, or to it were attributed, the deeds we read of in the *Íslendingasögur*, the Sagas of Icelanders. This was followed after a period of consolidation by what may well be called an Age of Learning, which in its turn led to the Sturlung Age and the thirteenth century, known for two things above all: the ambitions and rivalries of the leading Icelandic families, which together with various economic and political factors ensured the loss of Icelandic independence to Norway; and the development and perfecting of the art of saga-writing which has remained the island's most distinguishing characteristic in the eyes of posterity. Two or three features of this cavalcade of history demand an all-too-brief attention.

Iceland's history began in heathendom, a circumstance of the first importance for its constitutional and literary achievements. But when Christianity moved into the north it moved into Iceland, too. The force behind the conversion was traditionally held to be the proselytizing zeal of king Olaf Tryggvason of Norway, but the exposure of Iceland to German and English influences was so considerable that the tradition may well be misleading. There would have been a conversion with or without such royal patronage. The first-named missionary, the German Thangbrand, was a muscular Christian after the fashion of Egino at Skara,[1] and the Englishman Wolfred at Uppsala;[2] he baptized a few of the leading men, took quarrels on his hands, was lampooned, killed two or three of his enemies, and departed homewards with a rough report of the contumacious islanders. A second mission followed, associated with the labours of a priest named Thormod (according to *Kristni Saga* he came from England, presumably the Danelaw); and this, by the witness of Ari's *Íslendingabók*, led to a confrontation at the Althing between a minority of Christians, including at least three godar, and a substantial majority of heathens. Both sides swore that they would not live together under the same law, and catastrophe seemed imminent.[3] 'Then the Christians requested Hall of Sida

[1] 'There he also broke to pieces a very highly esteemed image of Frikko.' (Adam of Bremen, IV, ix (9).)

[2] 'And as by his preaching he converted many to the Christian faith, he proceeded to anathematize a popular idol named Thor which stood in the Thing of the pagans, and at the same time he seized a battle-axe and broke the image to pieces. And forthwith he was pierced with a thousand wounds for such daring, and his soul passed into heaven, earning a martyr's laurels.' (Adam of Bremen, II, lxii (60).)

[3] Ari's chief informant was his tutor Teit, the son of Isleif, the first native bishop of Iceland. Ari's second fosterfather, Hall Thorarinsson of Haukadal, who lived to be 94, told him that he had been baptized by Thangbrand at the age of 3. In words reminiscent of Bede's (*E.H.*, V, 24), Ari tells us that he 'came to Hall when seven years old . . . and there I lived for fourteen years' (*Íslendingabók*, 9).

that he should proclaim that law which was right and proper for Christians; but he got out of this, in that he made payment to Thorgeir the lawspeaker that he should proclaim the law—even though he was still a heathen. And later when men had returned to their booths, Thorgeir lay down and spread his cloak over him, and lay quiet all that day and the night following, and spoke never a word. But the next morning he sat up and announced that men should proceed to the Law Rock. And once men had made their way there he began his speech.' It would be disastrous, he told them, if men should not have one and the same law, all of them, in this land. He thought it policy that they should not let those prevail who were most anxious to be at each other's throat, but reach a compromise. ' "It will prove true, if we break the law in pieces, that we break the peace in pieces too." And he so concluded his speech that both sides agreed that all should have that one law which he would proclaim.' Thorgeir's verdict, which must have been a surprise to the heathens, was that all men in Iceland should be baptized in water cold or warm, and become Christians. A few relics of heathendom were let stand: infants might still be exposed, horseflesh might still be eaten, sacrifice might still be carried out in secret. A few years later these survivals were abolished too.[1]

That Iceland was heathen from 870 till the year 1000 allows us to observe in considerable if disputed detail the founding and development of a Norse heathen nation. It meant, too, that a great deal of Icelandic literature, both the poetry of the ninth and tenth centuries and the family sagas written down in the thirteenth century, is concerned either directly or through antiquarian interest with aspects of the old religion. In addition Iceland preserved in the *Fornaldarsögur*, the Sagas of Time Past, a wealth of legend, folktale, tradition and pseudo-history, relating to Norway, Denmark, and Sweden. Saxo speaks rhetorically when he describes the Icelanders as 'devoting every instant of their lives to perfecting our knowledge of the deeds of foreigners [i.e. non-Icelanders]'—someone, after all, had to scythe hay and make butter, as well as practise the lordly northern art of living—but he is right to praise them for the

---

[1] *Íslendingabók*, cap. 7. It is customary to ascribe the Conversion to the year 1000, but Ólafía Einarsdóttir, *Studier i kronologisk metode i tidlig islandsk historieskrivning*, Stockholm, 1964, pp. 107–26, presents a good case for 999. Incidentally, any Icelandic written source which considers horseflesh the nonpareil at heathen feasts should be regarded with caution.

assiduity with which they 'culled and consigned to remembrance' the kind of historical and legendary information he so freely incorporated into his Danish History. Similarly their passionate concern for genealogy and family history made them proud to trace their descent from worshippers of Thor with the hammer, Frey with the phallus, and infrequently the High One, Odinn himself. In literature as in life their roots were in heathendom, and it is to a preservative as well as a creative impulse of Snorri Sturluson that we owe the survey of Norse mythology and skaldic art which we style his Edda. But it was equally important to the shaping of the nation that the Icelanders embraced Christianity when they did. Contacts with Europe were quickly both closer and more extensive; the detached stronghold of a disfavoured polytheism was now a full member of the Christian community. The colour of European learning in the ensuing centuries was Christian, and Iceland more than most countries stood to benefit. At first there were few priests, and these, as had happened in Scandinavia, tended to be foreigners, from the British Isles and Germany. Probably it was these men who introduced Roman script to Iceland. After one generation native priests emerged, the most famous of them Isleif, son of the chieftain Gizur the White.

Gizur was reputedly one of the first godar to accept baptism at Thangbrand's hands. The learned Isleif became Iceland's first native bishop (1056–80), and was succeeded in office by his son Gizur Isleifsson, who introduced tithes, made provision for the poor, carried out the first reliable census of taxable farmers, and was responsible for the change whereby two bishoprics were established in Iceland, one at Skalholt in the south-west, one at Holar in the north. Towards the end of his life, and possibly at his instigation, part of the law of Iceland was for the first time committed to writing. Two late contemporaries of his, Saemund the Learned, 1056–1133, and Ari Thorgilsson the Learned, 1067–1148, were the fathers of Icelandic historical writing, though the title is strictly reserved for Ari because he, unlike Saemund who wrote in Latin, used the vernacular. With Kolskegg the Learned, who died before 1130, they established a practice of responsible though far from scientific authorship which would persist until the thirteenth century produced Snorri Sturluson's *Heimskringla* and that blow-by-blow account of the last eighty years of the Republic which we know by the general title of *Sturlunga Saga*.

The thirteenth century, we have noted, was also the classical age of saga (i.e. family saga) writing. The hundred and twenty or more sagas (*sögur*) and short stories (*þættir*) provide us with a freely rendered and often fictional 'history' of most of the tenth century and the first third of the eleventh, revealed through the lives of outstanding men and women and the feud-ridden traditions of notable families, but much affected by the creative imagination of storytellers, authors and scribes, by the changes to which tradition is subject over a period of two to three hundred years, and the distortions inevitable when men of antiquarian interests and family pride portray one age partly in terms of another. The family sagas are both more and less than a history. The best, indeed the majority, of them rest on a foundation of history and antiquarian speculation, but the superstructure is often shaped by arbitrary assumptions as to the nature of history itself. The sagaman saw history in terms of men and women and human destiny, and in terms of a story. A saga was not the fixed and immutable record of known facts. It was an individual's version and interpretation of facts, and could undergo shortening, lengthening, interpolation of new material, deliberate change, accidental manipulation, plain misunderstanding. Thus *Landnámabók* ascribes the credit of the discovery of Iceland to different persons, and clouds its accounts of the first three voyages with such motifs of story as ships driven off course and parted tow-boats; and as we shall see, the two sagas which recount the Vinland voyages contradict each other at points where disagreement would seem harder than agreement. But when we consider the sagas as literature only, as examinations of human conduct within the conventions of prose narrative, *Njála*, *Eigla*, and *Grettis Saga*, to name the three masterpieces only, add a new dimension to the medieval literature of Europe.

The Saga Age was not an age of prose composition. Its literary glories were in verse. Poetry was a national industry during the Saga Age, and poets a national export. The most sublime of Eddic poems, *Völuspá* or the Sybil's Prophecy, was composed in Iceland *c.* 1000; the lifespan of the greatest of all skaldic poets, Egill Skallagrimsson of Borg, was *c.* 910–90; Kormak, Hallfred Troublesomeskald, and Gunnlaug Snaketongue with a highly suspicious similarity of story were love poets at home and court poets abroad; Einar Skalaglamm or Jingle-scale was Egill's friend and a poet of jarl Hakon of Hladir, who ruled in Norway till 995; Sighvat Thordarson was the friend, counsellor, and ambassador of St. Olaf as well as his poet; and Ottar the Black, Sighvat's nephew, practised his art at the court of king Olaf Eiriksson of Sweden as well as at St. Olaf's court in Norway. Thormod Coalbrow's-poet perished with Olaf at Stiklarstadir in 1030. After Eyvind the Plagiarist was silenced by loyalty to his dead lord, Hakon the Good, in the 960s, the office of court poet in Norway became the monopoly of Icelanders till the end of the thirteenth century. And there were plenty of poets at home, ranging from humble men who could turn a not too humble verse dignifying a local squabble to skilled practitioners like Thorarin the Black, whose verses are preserved in *Eyrbyggja Saga*, and Viga-Glum, whose verses, deceptions, and killings fill the pages of the saga which bears his name and purports to tell his life-story. We must not, of course, expect poets to be always telling the truth; the court poet, satirist, eulogist, have other important considerations in mind. Egill Skallagrimsson managed a twenty-verse *drápa* on Eirik Blood-axe which merely informs us that he was a brave soldier and free with his money. Nor are we always sure that we know what they are writing about, or whether the verses have been embedded in a proper prose context, or whether they are genuinely of the Viking Age. The time is past when a man could, like Finnur Jónsson, offer to go to the stake for the historicity of saga or skaldic verse, and remain unsinged. But the amount still astonishes, and we can but admire and wonder that this harsh and riven island whose population at no time exceeded 60,000 people, put forth from its scanty soil so rich and continuous a harvest of poetry, history, and saga. *Inopiam ingenio pensant.* 'They make good their impoverishment with their wits.' Saxo's adage carries less than the full truth, but if we accept the dictum that a nation's chief glory consists in its authors, then the poets of the ninth and tenth centuries, the historians of the twelfth and thirteenth, together with the story-tellers and saga-men, are Iceland's strongest claims to a high eminence among the peoples of medieval Europe, and it is they, rather than lawspeakers and administrators, heathen priests and Christian bishops, acquisitive chieftains and practitioners of feud, who made Iceland's most distinctive contribution to the viking and post-viking period.

And yet there was another sphere in which the Icelanders won an equally lasting fame. It was they who crossed the Atlantic ocean westwards to colonize Greenland and light upon the eastern coast of North America—and of all viking achievements it was this last which has most strongly impressed itself upon our modern imagination.

Effectively the story begins in 982, when a man named Eirik the Red, a native of the Jaeder in south-west Norway, who had already been outlawed from that country for manslaughter, and for the same sufficient reason been driven out of Haukadal in Iceland, received a three-year sentence of banishment at the Thorsnes Thing in Breidafjord for yet a third outbreak of killings. With Norway and Iceland barred to him he decided to sail east and fill in his time by finding and exploring a new land sighted some fifty years earlier by a Norwegian sailor named Gunnbjorn, when he had been storm-driven south then west of Iceland.[1] Judge, then, his satisfaction when after sailing from under the Snaefell jokul on the 65th parallel to the neighbourhood of Angmagssalik, and then coasting south, and so reaching the western coast of Greenland by way of Prins Christians Sund or Cape Farewell, he found himself in a land which in addition to its other attractions (and they were many) was empty of inhabitants. The rugged islands of the archipelago, the fjords and headlands, the hills right back to the Ice Cap, the rivers and lakes, and best of all the grassy slopes and scrub-strewn nooks, were his for the taking, and without loss of time he took them.

For three years he explored the region between Herjolfsnes (Ikigait) and Eiriksfjord (Tunugdliarfik), and with his crew marked the sites of farms and homes to be. Marked, too, that the land was rich in animals: bears, foxes, caribou; that the skærgaard bred sea mammals; and that wherever there was water there were fish. And everywhere birds that had never known the fowler's snare. So it was

---

[1] Gunnbjorn Ulf-Krakason on his involuntary journey into the west sighted some islands or skerries and the land behind them. The skerries were known as Gunnbjarnarsker (less frequently Gunnbjarnareyjar), and according to Ivar Bardarson in his mid-fourteenth century description of Greenland (*Det gamle Grønlands beskrivelse*, ed. Finnur Jónsson, Copenhagen, 1930), lay half-way between Iceland and Greenland (presumably the Norse settlements in Greenland, on the west coast). The identification usually accepted is with the islands east of Sermiligaq, near Angmagssalik, west across the Denmark Strait from Snæfellsnes in Iceland (so Gustav Holm, *Meddelelser om Grønland*, 56, 1918), and of late, a shade optimistically, with the rock-ribbed, grass-spattered island of Kulusuk. Gunnbjorn's family was later well represented in Eirik's part of Iceland.

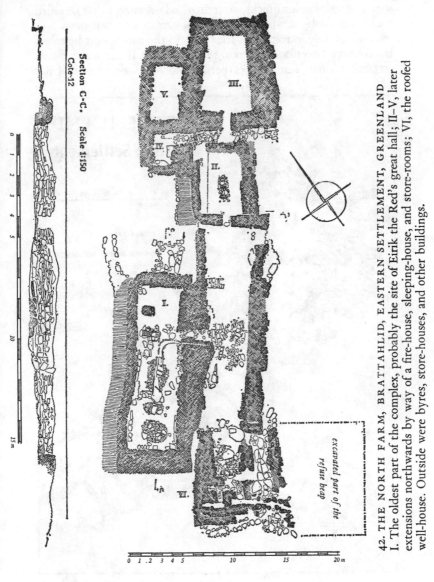

Section C-C. Scale 1:150
Cote-12

0 1 2 3 4 5   10   15 m

0 1 2 3 4 5   10   15   20 m

excavated part of the
refuse heap

42. THE NORTH FARM, BRATTAHLID, EASTERN SETTLEMENT, GREENLAND
I. The oldest part of the complex, probably the site of Eirik the Red's great hall; II–V, later
extensions northwards by way of a fire-house, sleeping-house, and store-rooms; VI, the roofed
well-house. Outside were byres, store-houses, and other buildings.

with a determination quickly to return and colonize it that he sailed
back to Breidafjord when his period of banishment was over. Not
too inaccurately in respect of the fjords of the south-west he called
the country Greenland, believing that no place is the worse for an
attractive name. Ten years earlier Iceland had suffered one of her

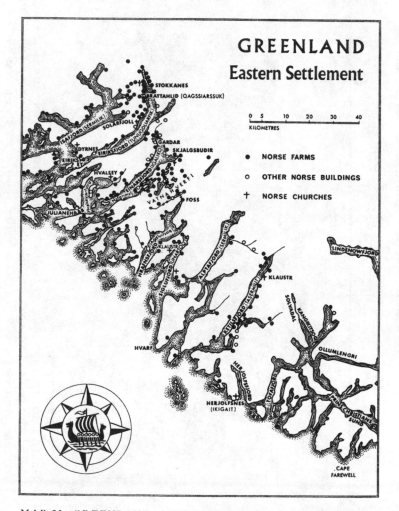

MAP 13. GREENLAND, THE EASTERN SETTLEMENT

cruellest famines, and in any case her habitable land had long since been taken up. There were rich and poor men alike facing a worsening prospect there, so when Eirik sailed again for Greenland in 986 he was accompanied by no fewer than twenty-five ships, fourteen of which arrived safely in the first settlement area. This was the region whose centre is the modern Julianehåb, the so-called Eastern Settlement, which would eventually number 190 farms, twelve parish churches, a cathedral at Gardar (Igaliko), a monastery and a nunnery. A decade or so later men had pushed on north as far as the modern Godthåb, and there by the fourteenth century the Western Settlement would come to number ninety farms and four churches.[1] Just north of the Eastern Settlement was a cluster of twenty farms round the modern Ivigtut. The colonization of Greenland began with perhaps 450 souls, almost all of them Icelanders, and eventually the population would number 3,000.

Quickly the Greenlanders had a constitution on the Icelandic model, a national assembly, and a code of law. They explored, hunted, traded, and prospered. For export they had furs and hides, ropes and cables, oil, woollens, and sea-ivory, and not least white bears and falcons. In return they needed corn, iron (including wrought weapons), timber, garments of European style, and assorted luxuries. Primarily these must come from Norway, and it was Norway who inherited when in 1261, just a year before the Icelanders, they surrendered their independence and became the farthest-flung and most perilously situated outpost of a fast-weakening, trouble-bound empire.

But the year 1000 was not a year in which Norsemen stood still, content with fixed horizons. Soon they were pressing north, for they needed more land, more grazing, more natural resources. 'Men', says the well-informed author of the mid-thirteenth-century *King's Mirror*, in his description of Greenland, 'have often tried to go up

[1] *Det gamle Grønlands beskrivelse* (1930); *Grønlands Historiske Mindesmærker*, Copenhagen, 1838–45, III, 228. In all some 400 Norse ruins have been discovered in Greenland, almost 300 of which are farms of varying size and different periods. The standard account of Norse finds to the beginning of World War II is Aage Roussell, *Farms and Churches in the Mediaeval Norse Settlements in Greenland*, MGr. 89, Copenhagen, 1941. For a later summary see Michael Wolfe, 'Norse Archaeology in Greenland since World War II', in the *American-Scandinavian Review*, xliv, 4, pp. 380–92, 1961–2. The verification of saga evidence in respect of Greenland is not without relevance to the same saga evidence in respect of Vinland. (Add Hansen, *Critical Account*, 1972.)

into the country and climb the highest mountains in various places to look about and learn whether any land could be found that was free from ice and habitable. But nowhere have they found such a place, except what is now occupied, which is a little strip along the water's edge.' So they looked north, and away beyond the Western Settlement found better hunting-grounds with good fishing and driftwood, from Holsteinsborg to the Nugsuaq Peninsula. These

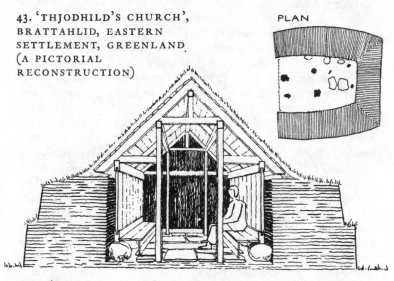

43. 'THJODHILD'S CHURCH', BRATTAHLID, EASTERN SETTLEMENT, GREENLAND (A PICTORIAL RECONSTRUCTION)

PLAN

were the *Norðrsetr, -seta*, the Northern Encampment(s) or Hunting Ground(s), where men took narwhal and walrus, ptarmigan, reindeer, and the prized white bear of Greenland. Still farther north, on the island of Kingigtorssuaq, near Upernavik, just short of latitude 73°N., the Eskimo Pelimut discovered in 1824 a stone inscribed with runes which tell that in 1333 three Norse Greenlanders had camped and wintered there. Earlier, in 1267, an expedition from the Eastern Settlement reached Melville Bay in latitude *c.* 76°N., observed traces of Skrælings in Kroksfjardarheidi (Disco Bay), and then got safely back home. These *Scraelinga*, says the thirteenth-century *Historia Norvegiae*, were small people (*homunciones*) who 'possess no iron whatsoever, but utilise walrus tusks for missiles and sharp stones for knives'. There may well have been voyages left unrecorded across the water to north-eastern Canada, but the few and tiny fragments of Norse origin so far found there (they include cloth and chain-mail sections) do not permit a safe conclusion as to how they came into Eskimo hands.[1] Also, such remote and inhospitable areas would not prove attractive to the solid settlement men whose first need was grassland for their stock, and this was to be found above all well up the fjords of the two major settlements. The most important area of Norse Greenland was that stretching from the head of Eiriksfjord by way of the head of Einarsfjord to Vatnahverfi. Here were the best farms, and here the best grazing, 'good and fragrant grass', as the *King's Mirror* describes it. Here lived Eirik the Red, his son Leif, and in time Leif's son Thorkell, and here a hundred years later lived the then leaders of the Greenland community, Sokki Thorisson and his son Einar. According to Ivar Bardarson, Greenland's chief officer always lived at Brattahlid in Eiriksfjord. At Brattahlid too Eirik's wife Thjodhild is said to have built the first Christian church in Greenland—maybe the turf-walled structure unearthed there with its graveyard during the 1960s—and a short sail and a short walk from Thjodhild's church are still to be seen the ruins of Greenland's one cathedral at Gardar. From Eiriksfjord, finally, would be mounted all the planned voyages of discovery and settlement to Baffin Island, Labrador and Northern Newfoundland, on the eastern shores of what is now Canada.

The first voyage which brought a European within sight of the North American continent was not planned. The man who made it, the Icelander Bjarni Herjolfsson, was therefore in line with Gardar, Naddod, and Raven-Floki in respect of Iceland, Gunnbjorn in respect of Greenland, and for what the evidence of *Eiríks Saga Rauða* is worth with Leif Eiriksson in respect of Vinland. All were storm-driven sailors lighting on lands unsought, though in the context of northern geographical speculation not entirely unsuspected. Bjarni Herjolfsson had spent the winter of 985-6 in Norway.

[1] P. Schledermann, 'Eskimo and Viking Finds in the high Arctic', in *Nat. Geographic*, 1981 (May); Robert McGhee, 'Norsemen and Eskimos in Arctic Canada,' in *Vikings in the West*, ed. Guralnick, Chicago, 1982. Patricia Sutherland (1977) has reported on a more intriguing find in a Thule period site on the west coast of Ellesmere Island, some 2000 kilometres north-west of the Greenland colonies. 'This hinged bronze bar is part of a folding balance, very similar to those used by Norse traders in weighing coins and other small objects' (McGhee, p. 49). Recent claims in respect of houses, cairns and artefacts farther south in the Ungava Bay region of Canada have not prospered. For the most recent and authoritative account of all these matters see R. McGhee, 'Contact between Native North Americans and the Mediaeval Norse: A Review of the Evidence', in *American Antiquity*, 1983.

The following summer he sailed to Iceland with a full cargo, intending to spend the winter with his father. But when he arrived there it was to hear the startling news that Herjolf had sold his estates and departed for Greenland on Eirik the Red's colonizing

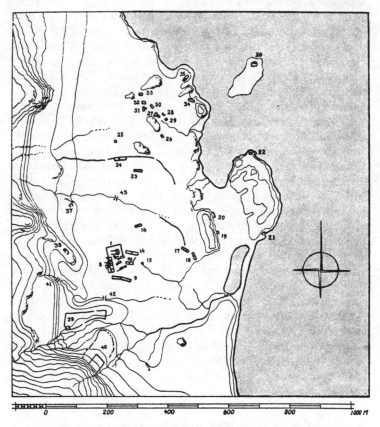

44. GARDAR, EASTERN SETTLEMENT, GREENLAND
'The place is now called Igaliko (the deserted cooking place). Survey map 1 : 10,000. 1: cathedral with churchyard; 8: episcopal residence; 9, 14: byres; 15: spring; 16: byre; 17–18: sheep-cotes; 19–22: storehouses; 23: enclosed garden; 24: byre and barn; 25: horse paddock; 26–35: "Thing booths"; 34–35, sheep-cotes; 36: storehouse; 38: sheep-pen; 39–40: large enclosures for domestic animals.'

expedition. He determined to follow him, no doubt collected all the information he could, and then with the consent of his crew he set off on what they all knew would be a risky journey, pilotless, chartless, compassless, for the south-western fjords of Greenland. Three days out, and the mountains and glaciers of Iceland whelmed under the horizon, they fell a prey to north winds and then to fog, and for many days had no notion which way they were going. Then the sun broke through, they took fresh bearings, hoisted sail, and journeyed for a whole day before sighting a land which was not mountainous, but well forested, with low hills. His crew, metaphorically speaking, were still all at sea, but Bjarni, if he did not know where he was, at

45. GARDAR (A PICTORIAL RECONSTRUCTION)
'This sketch of the episcopal residence at Gardar was made by Aage Roussell immediately after excavations were finished in 1926. The big building at the far left is the cathedral with a choir and side chapels. It is surrounded by a churchyard dyke. The long block in the foreground is the residence. To the right is the big byre, and the belfry may be seen above the house. The other buildings are storehouses, stables, smithy, etc.' (Compare the ground plan, no. 44 opposite.)

least knew where he was not. This could not be Greenland. So without going ashore, he held north along the coast for two days' sailing. The land here, they saw, was still well forested but flat. Again he refused to put in, and sailed with a south-west wind for three more days till they came to a land which was high, mountainous, and glaciered. A land in Bjarni's opinion good for nothing. So yet again he turned his prow from the land, and after four days' sailing before a strong wind he reached Herjolfsnes in Greenland.

In contrast *Eirik the Red's Saga (Eiríks Saga Rauða)* makes no mention of Bjarni, but in a section remarkable for confusion and irrelevance ascribes the honour of the discovery to Leif Eiriksson, the eldest son of the founder of the Greenland settlements. To Leif the *Greenlanders' Saga* assigns the credit of the first landings in the New World and the first sojourn in Vinland. There are good, though complicated, reasons for believing this to be right.[1]

For fifteen years the colonists of Greenland did nothing to improve on Bjarni's accidental acquaintance with the coast of eastern Canada. For one thing, they were too busy. There was no question of their not believing him. Medieval geography favoured the notion of more land to be found beyond Greenland, and, more practically, when men climbed the high mountains behind the settlements (as the *King's Mirror* informs us they did) they would see in the far distance either land itself or the cloud formations they associated with land. Out west, they knew, lay *something*. And so Leif Eiriksson enters the story. He sailed south from Brattahlid to

---

[1] The 'Vinland Sagas' are very important documents, and must be treated as such, though the need for care is evident. Thus, they were not written down for at least 200 years after the events they portray. They are prodigal of unlikelihood, contradictions and invention. They retail Old Testament reminiscence, Christian and heathen superstition, medieval pseudo-science, Germanic folktale and classical fable, and offer them as truth. But with it all they contain reliable information about how ships sailed on a traceable course out of Eiriksfjord in Greenland, north, west, then south, to northern Newfoundland, and maybe farther south again—certainly to the land-mass we now call North America, and certainly centuries before the voyages of Columbus. When scepticism has done its best, and blind belief its worst, enough of fact and rather more of tradition remains in the assorted witness of Gr.S. and ESR to direct us to persons, who are expendable, and locations, which are not.

The literature of the subject is enormous. The basic modern statements are those of Sven B. F. Jansson, *Sagorna om Vinland*, I. Lund, 1944; Jón Jóhannesson, 'Aldur Grœnlendinga Sögu', in *Nordæla*, Reykjavík, 1956 (trans. T. J. Oleson, 'The Date of the Composition of the Saga of the Greenlanders', in *Saga-Book*, 1962, pp. 54–66); Halldor Hermansson, *The Vinland Sagas*, Ithaca, 1944. Jansson and Jóhannesson established, *inter alia*, the greater age and reliability of Gr.S (c. 1200) as compared with ESR (c. 1265). There are useful presentations of the argument in Gwyn Jones, *The Norse Atlantic Saga*, 1964; M. Magnusson and H. Pálsson, *The Vinland Sagas*, 1965; G. M. Gathorne-Hardy, *The Norse Discoverers of America*, 1921, repr. 1970; Ólafur Halldórsson, *Grœnland í Miðaldaritum*, Reykjavík, 1978 (inclines to the beginning of the C13 for both sagas, but a post-1263 date for ESR is preferable); E. Guralnick (ed.), *Vikings in the West*, Chicago, 1982. The most recent bibliography, 'Norsemen in America' in *The Vikings* (ed. R. T. Farrell), 1982, is a selection from a forthcoming annotated list compiled by Louis A. Pitschmann.

MARKLAND AND VINLAND

→ Main route to VINLAND (Leif, Thorvald, Karlsefni).
⇢ Probable route of Thorvald and Karlsefni north-west from Leifsbudir-Straumfjord
E Indicate the approximate position of the native ESKIMO and INDIAN
I population c. 1000 A.D.

0 10 20 30 40 50 60 70 80 90 100
MILES

Cape Harrison
Hamilton Inlet
THE STRAND
Cape Porcupine
North West River
LAKE MELVILLE
English River
SANDWICH BAY
Goose Bay
L A B R A D O R
ALEXIS RIVER
ST. LEWIS RIVER
Battle Harbour
BELLE ISLE
ST. AUGUSTINE RIVER
Pistolet Bay
Sacred Bay
Great Sacred Island
Cape Bauld
Q U E B E C
LITTLE MECATINA RIVER
STRAIT OF BELLE ISLE
THORVALD'S MEN
HARE BAY
N E W F O U N D L A N D
WHITE BAY KARLSEFNI AND SNORRI

MAP 14.   MARKLAND AND VINLAND

meet Bjarni down at Herjolfsnes, bought his ship and enlisted some of his crew, and undertook a voyage of discovery. He sailed Bjarni's course in reverse and put ashore in three identifiable areas, on which he bestowed suitable place-names: Helluland, Flatstone Land, mountainous, glaciered, grassless and barren, which most students agree is the southern portion of Baffin Island; Markland, Wood Land, flat and forested, with extensive white sands and gently shelving beaches, thought to be Labrador south of the medieval tree-line (south of today's Nain); and finally Vinland, Wineland, a region whose identity has provoked considerable, and at times impassioned, debate, but whose northern extremity is almost certainly the northern extremity of Newfoundland. Here there was an island lying north of what appeared to be a mainland with a cape projecting northwards from it. Leif wintered in Vinland, at Leifs-budir, Leif's Booths, where day and night were of a more even length than in Iceland or Greenland, so that on the shortest day of winter the sun was visible above the horizon at about nine in the morning and three in the afternoon. He returned to Greenland the following summer, full of Vinland's praises, its sweet dew and frostlessness, its grass and grapes, timber and salmon. Eirik the Red was now dead, and Leif must take over his position and responsibilities. His sailing days were done. But they were a stirring family, and his brother Thorvald stepped forward with a scheme for exploring the new country more extensively. He sailed the known route to Leifsbudir in Vinland, and sent his men on a probe down the west coast. He himself headed back north past a cape he named Kjalarnes, Keel Ness, because he damaged his keel there, and into a big inlet leading west. Here they met the first natives to be encountered in America, and in the hostilities provoked by the Norsemen Thorvald was killed by an Indian arrow. Without other loss his crew returned to Leifsbudir, spent the winter there, and the following spring sailed for Eiriksfjord with their heavy news.

So far there had been no attempt at colonization. Bjarni had not so much as gone ashore, and Leif's and Thorvald's expeditions were literally intended to spy out the land. The next significant voyage was made by an Icelander named Thorfinn Karlsefni, who had sailed to Brattahlid with a cargo for sale, and while he was there married Eirik the Red's daughter-in-law Gudrid. The accounts of his Vinland expedition vary considerably in *Grænlendinga Saga* and *Eiríks Saga*, but both make it clear that he had in mind an extended or even a permanent stay. A number of his men took their wives along with them, and further, 'they took with them all kinds of livestock, for it was their intention to colonize the country, if they could do so'. The two sagas offer different accounts of their numbers and route. According to *Grœnlendinga Saga*, Karlsefni with sixty men followed the same route as Leif and Thorvald; he arrived at Leifsbudir, and there he stayed. *Eiríks Saga* is much more detailed, as it tells of Karlsefni's voyage with three ships and 160 men up the west coast of Greenland from Brattahlid in Eiriksfjord to an unidentifiable Bjarney(jar), Bear Isle(s), somewhere north of the Western Settlement. From there he crossed the Davis Strait with a north wind in two days to south Baffin Island, which we are told he named Helluland, and so proceeded south to the forests of Labrador, which he named Markland. Other place-names bestowed by Karlsefni's party were Kjalarnes, Keel Ness, to distinguish a cape where they found part of a ship's keel, and Furdustrandir, Marvel Strands, to denote beaches of such remarkable length that it took a remarkably long time to sail past them. That Karlsefni should give these place-names flatly contradicts *Grœnlendinga Saga*, and is assuredly wrong, but the author of *Eiríks Saga* had no choice but to say so. Having removed Bjarni Herjolfsson from the Vinland record, and transferred the accidental sighting of America to Leif Eiriksson (in the most perfunctory way, at that), and then having delayed Thorvald Eiriksson's voyage so that we now find him sailing in company with Karlsefni, he was left with no one who *could* have given place-names in America. Another major difference between the two sagas is that *Eiríks Saga* conducts Karlsefni not to Leifsbudir, but to two areas of settlement, the one named Straumfjord, Stream or Current Ford, which like Leifsbudir appears to be in the northern part of Newfoundland, and one further south called Hóp (the word means a landlocked bay or estuary). As before, the land yielded wild grapes, self-sown wheat, and tall timber, a snowless winter at Hóp (but a bitter one at Straumfjord), and natives of whom the colonizers fell foul. Thorvald Eiriksson was killed, as in *Grœnlendinga Saga*, by an arrow somewhere north and west of Straumfjord, though in more fanciful circumstances. Karlsefni's dealings with the native Skraelings (*Skrælingar*, a word of uncertain but uncomplimentary meaning, possibly 'screechers' or 'uglies') began with a surprise confrontation, proceeded to trade by barter, and ended in hostilities. Of their trading *Grœnlendinga Saga* has this to say:

After that first winter came summer. It was now they made acquaintance with the Skrælings, when a big body of men appeared out of the
forest there. Their cattle were close by; the bull began to bellow and
bawl loudly, which so frightened the Skrælings that they ran off with
their packs, which were of grey furs and sables and skins of all kinds,
and headed for Karlsefni's house, hoping to get inside there, but
Karlsefni had the doors guarded. Neither party could understand the
other's language. Then the Skrælings unslung their bales, untied
them, and proffered their wares, and above all wanted weapons in
exchange. Karlsefni, though, forbade them the sale of weapons. And
now he hit on this idea; he told the women to carry out milk to them,
and the moment they saw the milk that was the one thing they
wanted to buy, nothing else. So that was what came of the Skrælings'
trading: they carried away what they bought in their bellies, while
Karlsefni and his comrades kept their bales and their furs. And with
that they went away.[1]

---

[1] This is the witness of *Eiríks Saga*:

Then early one morning when they looked about them they saw nine [H. a
great multitude of] skin-boats, on board which staves were being swung
which sounded just like flails threshing—and their motion was sunwise.

'What can this mean?' asked Karlsefni.

'Perhaps it is a token of peace,' replied Snorri. 'So let us take a white
shield and hold it out towards them.'

They did so, and those others rowed towards them, showing their astonishment, then came ashore. They were small [H. dark], ill favoured men, and had
ugly hair on their heads. They had big eyes and were broad in the cheeks. For a
while they remained there, astonished, and afterwards rowed off south past the
headland.

Karlsefni and his men built themselves dwellings up above the lake; some of
their houses stood near the mainland, and some near the lake. They now spent
the winter there. No snow fell, and their entire stock found its food grazing in
the open. But once spring came in they chanced early one morning to see how
a multitude of skin-boats came rowing from the south round the headland, so
many that the bay appeared sown with coals, and even so staves were being
swung on every boat. Karlsefni and his men raised their shields, and they began
trading together. Above all these people wanted to buy red cloth [H. *adds* in
return for which they had furs to offer and grey pelts]. They also wanted to buy
swords and spears, but this Karlsefni and Snorri would not allow. They had
dark unblemished skins to exchange for the cloth, and were taking a span's
length of cloth for a skin, and this they tied round their heads. So it continued
for a while, then when the cloth began to run short they cut it up so that it was
no broader than a fingerbreadth, but the Skrælings gave just as much for it, or
more. (AM 557 4to, *Skálholtsbók*, with two variants from AM 554 4to,
Hauksbók.)

The outbreak of hostilities between Skrælings and Norsemen was decisive for the Vinland venture. The Norsemen had no marked superiority of weapons, their lines of communication were thin and overlong, and there was an insufficient reservoir of manpower back in Greenland. After three winters Karlsefni decided to get out. *Eiríks Saga* tells us there was by then jealousy and ill-feeling in camp over the women they had brought with them, and in any case Karlsefni was level-headed enough to recognize that for all the land's excellences 'there would always be fear and strife dogging them there on account of those who already inhabited it'. So home he went. *Grænlendinga Saga* makes mention of one more voyage to Leifsbudir, at the instigation of Freydis Eiriksdottir, sister of Leif and Thorvald. It was a bloody and melodramatic failure, as recounted. We conclude that all these voyages were over and done with by 1020 at the latest.[1]

But while there is general agreement that the Norsemen reached North America, agreement does not extend to how far south they reached. An increasing weight of opinion has now settled for southern Baffin Island as Helluland, Labrador south of Nain as Markland, but Vinland, Wineland, where the voyagers are said to have found

[1] There are important and trustworthy references to Vinland in Adam of Bremen, *c.* 1075, in the Icelandic Annals for 1121 and 1347, and in Ari's *Íslendingabók, c.* 1125 (quoted on p. 308); an unsatisfactory one preserved in connection with the no longer extant Hønen runic inscription found in Ringerike, Norway, and possibly of the period *c.* 1050; a number of casual ones in Icelandic histories and sagas of the thirteenth century; and what appear to be derivative mentions in some Icelandic geographical treatises of the fourteenth century. Adam of Bremen derived his information about Vinland from Svein Estridsson, king of the Danes, who died in 1076: 'He told me too of yet another island, discovered by many in that ocean, which is called Wineland from the circumstance that vines grow there of their own accord, and produce the most excellent wine. While that there is an abundance of unsown corn there we have learned not from fabulous conjecture but from the trustworthy report of the Danes.' (*Gesta Hammaburgensis: Descriptio insularum aquilonis,* IV, xxxix (38).)

There is also a less reputable but all too well-known body of evidence on offer for a Norse presence in North America. It comprises some 50 sites, 70 artefacts, and 100 or so inscriptions, among them the Newport Round Tower, the Kensington Stone, the Beardmore Find, a wide selection of weapons, mooring-holes and runic inscriptions, homely Follins Pond and the exotic Vinland Map, none of it to be given credence. (See T. C. Blegen, *The Kensington Rune Stone: New Light on an Old Riddle,* St Paul, 1968; B. Wallace, 'Viking Hoaxes', in *Vikings in the West,* Chicago, 1982.

grapes and wheat growing wild, is a different story.[1] The St. Lawrence Estuary, Baie de Chaleur, New Brunswick, Nova Scotia, New England, Massachusetts, Rhode Island, Long Island Sound, Virginia, Georgia, and Florida have been argued for with acumen and eloquence, and a single reliable archaeological discovery in any one of them could change the picture overnight. Maybe it was as a result of far-ranging voyages to coasts below the Promontorium that tales of grape-clusters, self-sown wheat, and kindly winters enriched the Norse tradition of Vinland; maybe longer voyages and later travellers blurred the outlines of Leif's landing and Karlsefni's

---

[1] It is a story reaching back to the great names of the Norwegian Fridtjof Nansen (1911), the American A. M. Reeves (1895), and the Danes Gustav Storm (1887) and C. Rafn (1837), but inasmuch as the long search has now homed in on the Norse remains at L'Anse-aux-Meadows and firmly established the northern extremity of Newfoundland as the ancient Promontorium Winlandiae, it must suffice to mention the more recent names of the Canadian Captain W. A. Munn (*Vinland Voyages*, St John's, Newfoundland, 1914, repr. 1946), the Finn Vaïno Tanner (*De gamla nordbornas Helluland, Markland och Vinland. Ett försök att lokalisera Vinlandsresornas huvudetapper i de isländska sagorna*, Åbo, 1941, and *Outlines of the Geography, Life and Customs of Newfoundland-Labrador (the eastern part of the Labrador Peninsula*, Helsinki, 1944), the Dane Jørgen Meldgaard, *Fra Brattahlid til Vinland*, Naturens Verden, Copenhagen, 1961, and the Norwegians Helge and Anne Stine Ingstad who conducted with American, Canadian, and Scandinavian help the excavations at the L'Anse-aux-Meadows site during the years 1961–8 whose results are recorded in *The Discovery of a Norse Settlement in America*, Vol. I, A. S. Ingstad, 1977, Vol. II, H. Ingstad, 1984, Oslo.

The Ingstads, overtaking and improving on the inquiries of their predecessors, have now not only identified a site of Norse habitation, but have excavated it, so that some eight or nine house-sites, with hearths, cooking pits, a smithy, bog-iron, boat-houses, a ring-headed bronze pin and a soap-stone spindle-whorl have come to light, some of which are quite certainly Norse and if not of the central date AD 1000 unarguably within the overall period of Norse activity in Vinland. The artefacts are few and not impressive; there are no human skeletons, no weapons, no conclusive evidence of farming or husbandry, not even a Thor's hammer or Christian cross. But the entire complex has undergone critical scrutiny by Scandinavian, Canadian and American archaeologists and workers in the ancillary disciplines, Eskimo and Indian as well as Norse, and while we await the final reports of Parks Canada, is at present just about universally accepted as authentic. Patently, such a demonstration of Norse saga-age habitation, however sparse or disjointed, in a saga-signposted area of the Promontorium Winlandiae has an importance far beyond any unrealized identification with a dwelling-site such as those attributed to Leif Eiriksson or Thorfinn Karlsefni.

The only other piece of tangible archaeological evidence that the Norsemen were in contact, somewhere, somehow with the Indians of the American continent is the Indian arrow-head identical with the quartzite of Labrador found by Aage Roussell in 1930 in the north-west corner of the churchyard at Sandnes in the Western Settlement of Greenland. It is the same kind of arrow-head as Jørgen Meldgaard found in the ancient Indian settlement by Northwest River at the inner extremity of Lake Melville in 1956, i.e. in the general area where we believe Thorvald Eiriksson was killed not long after the year 1000 by just such an arrow.

The 'Maine penny' much in the news of late is a genuine Norwegian coin of 1065–80 found in reputable circumstances and an acceptable archaeological setting, but the best opinion considers that the coin travelled south not in Norse hands but from the Dorset Eskimos of northern Labrador by way of northern Indians to the Indians of Maine.

Finally, this may be the place to add that attempts to replace Wineland (*Vínland*) by Grassland (*Vinland*), tempting though the rationalization is, are unconvincing.

settlement. Time will tell. Meantime it is prudent to hold on to the little we have. That Norse sailors arrived in the area of Belle Isle Strait is hardly to be disputed; that the northern tip of Newfoundland is the likeliest place to be the Promontorium Winlandiæ depicted on Sigurður Stefánsson's map of *c.* 1590, and Resen's of 1604, now seems handsomely confirmed; and that Thorvald Eiriksson sailed north from the Promontorium past the Strands (Furdustrandir) and Cape Porcupine (Kjalarnes) to meet his death up in Hamilton Inlet, where English River flows west into Lake

Characterum in hac mappa occurrentium explicatio ipsius Auctoris.

A *Hi sunt ad quos Angli per venerunt, ab anditæ nomen habent, tanquam irl solis vel frigoris adustione torridi et exsiccati.*

B *His proxime est Vinlandia quam propter terræ fæcunditatem et utilium rerum ubertim proventum, Bonam dixere. Hanc a meridie oceanum finire voluere nostri, sed ego ex recentiorum historiis colligo, aut freto aut sinum hanc ab America distinguere.*

C *Regionem Gigantum vocant quod ibi Gigantes cornuti sint quos Skrikfinna dixere.*

D *Orientaliores sunt, quos Klofina ab unguibus appellarunt.*

E *Jotunheimar idem est ac regio Gigantum mons: Frosorum, hic Regiam Geruthi et Gudmundi esse existimari licet.*

F *Sinum hic ingentem intelligimus in Russiam excurrentem.*

G *Regio petrosa, hujus in historia sæpe fit mentio.*

H *Hæc quæ sit insula nescio nisi ea forte quam Veneti ille invenit Frislandiamque Germani vocant.*

Autor hujus tabellæ Geographicæ perhibetur esse Sigurdus Stephanius Islandus vir eruditus, Scholæ Schalholtinæ quondam rector dignissimus, qui etiam alia nonnulla ingenii et eruditionis specimina edidit videlicet Descriptionem Islandiæ quam apud Serenissi: Regia Maj: Antiquarium Thormodu Torfæum vidisse me memini, nec non opusculum de Splotris, quod præteritu æstate ab amico quodam in Patria mecum comunicatum, penes me asservavi. Delineationem autem hanc suam, ex antiquitatibus Islandiæ maxima ex parte desumpsisse videtur. De Hellulandia Marclandia et Skrælinghialandia, videri poterit Arngrimus Jonas, qui ad Calcem opusculi de Gronlandia, Gronlandorum aliquot navigationes ad has terras annotavit, in terrarum etiam hyperborearum et ultra Gronlandiam delineatione, ubi Riseland et Jothinheima collocat, antiqui teftes quoq Islandicas secutum esse Autorem, ut scio, sed an authentica illæ sint dubito. Cum priore Gronlandiæ mappa Dñi Gudbrandi parum consentire hanc constat. Islandia hic justo majorem habet latitudinem, Promontorium etiam Winolfsnisk, in gentis continentis potius quam Isthmiæ vel promontorii speciem præsfert, ut cætera omittam, quod in ea curiositatis potius quam necessitatis ergo hanc mappam annotavi.

46. THE SKÁLHOLT MAP OF SIGURÐUR STEFÁNSSON, 1590

Melville, is consonant with the written sources and has (if only secondary) archaeological support. In these areas the Norsemen encountered two native populations, the aboriginal Indians and the Palaeo- (i.e. Dorset) Eskimos, both lumped together and described as *Skraelingar*. Thereafter, northwards in the Canadian Arctic lie argument and fantasy. Southwards in New England, or Maryland, lie speculation and hope. Not that there was no contact with Vinland after the great age of westward sailing *c.* 1000–20. Bishop Eirik (*upsi*) sailed there in a year variously stated to be 1112, 1113, 1117, and, most probably, 1121, with what result we do not know. As late as the middle of the fourteenth century men were still sailing there, presumably to fetch timber and furs. The Icelandic Annals record that in the year 1347 a ship with seventeen or eighteen Greenlanders on board was storm-driven to Iceland as they sought to return to their own country from Markland. But after that there was silence.

By 1347 dire events were happening in Greenland, presaging the destruction of the colonies there. In time they carry us far beyond the Viking Age; in every other sense they provide it with a poignant epilogue. Wise after the event, we can now see that everything about the Greenland settlements was temporary and marginal. Sailing the fjords or walking the pastures there today two things are immediately intelligible: how certain it was that men from Iceland would be attracted by the green and grassy oases of the south-west, make their homes and lodge their destinies there—and when events turned against them how likely it was that they could not survive. First, there was their geographical situation 'at the world's end', as Pope Alexander VI would later describe it; their dependence upon communications with Europe; the threat to existence from the constricting ice, the sundering ocean, and the worsening cold after 1200. Second, the Eskimo had been there before, and might he not return, far better equipped in the struggle for existence than the conservative Scandinavian? And, third, there were not enough of them to make good the wastage exacted by prolonged bad times. The settlements grew unmanned, unviable, and died out.

It is sometimes said that the surrender of independence in 1261 had deplorable consequences for the settlements' future. As a maritime power, true, Norway was entering upon a period of decline and would eventually be unable to maintain the long and dangerous sea-route to Greenland, while power politics in all three Scandinavian countries would operate to Greenland's disadvantage. On the other hand, where else could Greenland turn for succour when times grew hard and everything went wrong? What other course could save the Europeans there?[1]

As the stars in their courses fought against Sisera, so the revolving centuries fought against the Norsemen in Greenland. The great voyages of Eirik the Red, Leif, and Karlsefni all took place at a time when the northern lands and seas were enjoying a comparatively favourable climate. But after 1200 it began to grow colder, and by the middle of the fifteenth century it was very cold indeed. Over much of Europe the glaciers were advancing, the tree-line fell lower, vegetation and harvest were diminished by the cold, and the alpine passes were sealed for longer periods. The northern coast of Iceland grew increasingly beleaguered by drift ice; and off Greenland as the sea temperatures sank there was a disabling increase in the ice which comes south with the East Greenland Current to Cape Farewell, and then swings north to enclose first the Eastern and then the Western Settlement. By 1250 we have the testimony of the *King's Mirror* to the forbidding nature of the East Greenland Ice; a hundred years later Ivar Bardarson in his celebrated *Description of Greenland* tells how the old sailing route west has been abandoned as too dangerous because of the down-swinging polar ice, and men must now follow new sailing directions or 'never be heard of

---

[1] A series of recent publications by T. H McGovern, including 'The Economics of Extinction in Norse Greenland', in *Climate and History*, ed. Wigley, Cambridge, 1981, and 'The Lost Norse Colony of Greenland', in *Vikings in the West*, Chicago, 1982, has newly defined certain factors in the decline and extinction of the colony. The intense conservatism of the Norse Greenlanders has been noted by earlier students, but Dr McGovern has particularized this in two respects. First, the Norsemen seem to have learned nothing over three hundred years from the Eskimos' superior seal-hunting techniques; and second, he believes the colony came to suffer grievously from too inflexible and Europe-fixated an administration and too burdensome an ecclesiastical superstructure, which between them made unnecessarily heavy demands on the colony's dwindling economic resources and committed its man-power to tithe-collecting labours in the Nordsetur when it could have been more profitably employed nearer home. 'In the long run too much cultural stability may be as deadly as too little.' As the climate worsened, there is evidence that the unadaptive and therefore unsuccessful Norsemen found it necessary to devour their ever more debilitated farm animals, with dire and foreseeable consequences.

again'. For confirmatory evidence of the state of Icelandic waters we have Bishop Arngrim Brandsson's chilling account written some time before 1350. The voyage made in 1267 as far north as Melville Bay now sounds even more remarkable than at its first mention. For the growing cold was making sea-passages more hazardous—and had led to the reappearance on the west coast of the Eskimo or Skræling.[1] Soon after the middle of the thirteenth century they had penetrated the northern hunting-grounds as far as Disco, and seem increasingly to have hampered their use by the Norse Greenlanders. By *c.* 1340 they had reached the Western Settlement, and a little later Ivar Bardarson, who had been sent out from Norway to investigate the situation generally, could report that 'the Skrælings hold the entire Western Settlement'.[2] Even before the Eskimo arrived the Settlement was in trouble. It was more severely affected by a deterioration of climate than the Settlement further south, and it had grown harder to maintain constant touch with it. There is evidence that the pastures there had suffered from pest, while developments far away in Europe were helping destroy its economic viability. The increased trade in furs and hides out of Russia, the growth of the English and Dutch cloth trade as against Greenland woollens, and the preference of French workshops for elephant ivory over the inferior walrus tusk, helped price Greenland, and especially the remoter settlement, out of the market. But the Skræling would prove the last, unbearable burden. Unlike the white man, he had time and the climate on his side.

[1] When Eirik the Red and his comrades entered Greenland towards the end of the tenth century they found there traces of an earlier and, as they judged, non-European occupation. 'Both east and west in the country [i.e. at both the Eastern and Western Settlements] they found the habitations of men, fragments of boats (*?keiplabrot*), and stone artefacts, from which it may be seen that the same kind of people had passed that way as those that inhabited Vinland, whom the Greenlanders called Skrælings' (*Íslendingabók*). These particular Skrælings we assume were Palaeo-Eskimo people of the Dorset Culture, who vanished from south-west Greenland maybe as long as 800 years before. But the Skrælings who now began to make their presence felt in Greenland were people of the Thule Culture, who had made their way across northern Canada from Alaska, and from Ellesmere Island entered the Thule area of Greenland sometime before 1200. As the Inugsuk folk they proceeded to reoccupy the habitable strip of the western coast, and, though this is not to our purpose now, also went round the top of Greenland and spread far down the east coast, too.

[2] *Det gamle Grønlands Beskrivelse*, 1930, p. 8 and p. 29.

What happened to the Norsemen of the Western Settlement? Under the year 1342 the Annals of Bishop Gisli Oddsson state that, 'The inhabitants of Greenland of their own will abandoned the true faith and the Christian religion, having already forsaken all good ways and true virtues, and went over to the people of America (*ad Americæ populos se converterunt*).' However, in the first part of his statement (written in Latin *c.* 1637, though presumably based on earlier documents) the Bishop is demonstrably wrong—the Greenlanders had not abandoned the true faith—and it is not easy to decide what he meant by 'went over to the people of America'. It is as likely that by the people of America he meant the Skrælings of Greenland (who also lived in parts of Markland and Vinland) as the people living in America. That the Norse Greenlander had abandoned the Christian faith was to remain the most persistent and baseless piece of European information about them till the end of the fifteenth century. Some members of the weakened colony may indeed have thrown in their lot with the advancing Eskimo, or ceased to be European; but it is altogether more reasonable to assume that as many as could sought a refuge with their kinsmen and co-religionists down in the Eastern Settlement. From there rumour and dispossessed men filtered back to Iceland and Norway to tell their hearers of sinister happenings out in Greenland; but nothing would be done, in part because it was too troublesome to keep in touch with Greenland, in part because there was no profit in it. Greenland was falling out of sight, going over to the Skrælings. After *c.* 1350 the Norsemen survived in the Eastern Settlement alone.

They survived till *c.* 1500 and remained white, Norse, European, and Christian to the end. The so-called 'Middle Settlement' around Ivigtut disappeared by *c.* 1380; and the Icelandic Annals for the year 1379 record that 'The Skrælings attacked the Greenlanders, killed eighteen of them, and carried off two boys, whom they made slaves'. Soon the Skrælings would bypass the Eastern Settlement altogether and continue their odyssey south to Cape Farewell and from there up the eastern coast. All this while, too, communications grew more tenuous as trade grew less rewarding. Trade with Greenland was a royal monopoly, soon vested in the town of Bergen. But even in the thirteenth century Bergen had all the furs and hides it needed without having to fetch them from Greenland. And the town, like Norway itself, was headed for troubles enough of its own. Norwegian maritime supremacy was in rapid decline before the end of the century, and the day of the viking ship would soon be over. In 1349 the Black Death killed one in three of Norway's population. Bergen suffered worse than most. As though plague was not enough, the town was twice burned towards the end of the fourteenth century by the Victual Brethren, and twice sacked by Bartholomeus Voet in 1428–9. The Bryggen were three times almost totally destroyed by fire in 1322, 1413, and 1476. Finally, during the four-teenth century the Hansa merchants got a stranglehold on the town's trade, and by 1400 on that of all Norway. In all this, whoever stood to gain Greenland stood to loose. And lose she did.

Intermittently we have sight of the doomed colony. It was king Magnus Smek's intention to send a ship to its succour in 1355—but nothing seems to have come of it. The Greenland carrier or *Grænlands knörr* made the Greenland run at intervals till 1369, when she sank and was apparently not replaced. In 1385 Bjorn Einarsson Jerusalem-farer was storm-driven to the Eastern Settlement, where he spent two years. In 1406 a party of Icelanders arrived against their will and did not get away for four years. They found the Settle-ment entirely Norse and resolutely Christian. In 1448 we light on a papal letter of doubtful authenticity and muddled content relating to Greenland; and in 1492 a letter of Pope Alexander VI speaks of the church (cathedral) at Gardar and the grim condition of the Green-landers, short of food, beleaguered by ice, and as always in the un-knowing European mind guilty of apostasy. Certainly the last time a bishop set foot in Greenland was in 1377, but the flock proved tougher than its shepherds, and Christianity persisted. Among other visitors were a redoubtable pair of mariners, Pining and Pothorst, *c.* 1476, and an assortment of English skippers, most of them out of Bristol. Somehow even in the second half of the fifteenth century European garments and a few other goods found their way to Herjolfsnes, but the circumstances in which they did so are unclear.

Soon thereafter the Settlement was at an end, and here likewise much is obscure. What happened to the Norse Greenlanders, so that they vanished from history? Some have thought they died of physical degeneration and the mental debility that would accom-pany it. But the evidence used to support this theory (more particularly the skeletons found at Herjolfsnes) can be largely dis-counted. Others speculate that they were destroyed by plague, the Black Death, but the evidence for this is too slight to be forced to so deadly a conclusion. Did they, then, migrate to the adjacent parts of

Canada, the people of the Western Settlement *c.* 1340, and those of the Eastern *c.* 1500?[1] The evidence is negligible, and the circumstance unlikely. Were they carried off, willingly or unwillingly, by fishermen and pirates, to England? Once more the evidence is negligible. Did they so blend with the Eskimo that they disappeared as a separate race, though their blood and culture survived briefly and uncertainly in this diminishing form? In a few instances, no doubt, individual Norsemen did so come to terms with their environment, but as an explanation for the disappearance of the settlements this assumes the very thing it sets out to prove. Were they exterminated by the Eskimo? The supposition is strong, but the evidence is weaker than we could wish. Did they take to their unseaworthy boats and set off for asylum in Iceland? And did they go down, man, woman, and child, on the way? This would be a theory to end all theories—but a theory is all it is.

In the present state of knowledge—and it may not prove susceptible of much improvement—it seems safest to conclude that the Greenland colony died out for no one reason but through a complex of deadly pressures. Of these its isolation from Europe, the neglect it suffered from its northern kinsmen, the lack of trade and new blood, the worsening conditions of cold, and above all the encroaching Eskimo, were the most important. Even in theory they sound more than enough to bring down the curtain on this farthest medieval outpost of what had been the Viking and was now the European world, and extinguish it with all the trappings of an inexorable and heart-chilling doom.

[1] The far-reaching theories of Jón Dúason, *Landkönnun og Landnám Íslendinga í Vesturheimi*, Reykjavík, 1941–7, and Tryggvi J. Oleson, *Early Voyages and Northern Approaches*, Toronto, 1964, have won little support. See Gwyn Jones, 'The First Europeans in America', *The Beaver*, Hudson's Bay Company, Winnipeg, 1964, pp. 4–11.

IV. THE VIKING AGE ENDS

1. The Scandinavian Community, III: Culture and Image

Nothing was more characteristic of the northern lands than the Old Norse religion. Of the three homelands Denmark was the first because the best placed to receive Christianity, and the Conversion there was more or less completed in the last third of the tenth century. The effective christianization of Norway took place in the first third of the eleventh, but in Sweden heathendom outlasted the Viking Age. Heathen thought and custom, and some of its practice, persisted in the less accessible regions of Norway and Sweden till very much later. Iceland underwent a change of faith, formally, in the year 1000, and the conversion of the Greenlanders was begun the following summer. There is no reason to doubt the tradition that Shetland, Orkney, and the Faroes were won for Christianity between 1000 and 1005.[1] The main movers in all this were those with most to gain by it, native kings ambitious of a truly sovereign state, the missions from England and Hamburg-Bremen, and the policy-makers who stood behind them. But the conversion itself was inevitable, desirable, and beneficial.

It was an old-fashioned religion which had survived in the northern fastnesses so long, polytheistic, loosely organized, and seemingly

---

[1] As we have seen, the Norsemen were in general tolerant in matters of religion. A fair number of them underwent a minor form of baptism, *prímsigning* or *prima signatio*, when overseas in Christian parts. The sign of the cross was made over them, to exorcise evil spirits, they could attend mass without committing themselves to Christianity, and live in communion with Christians. 'This was a common custom of the time among traders and those who went on war-pay along with Christian men; for those who were prime-signed held full communion with Christians and heathens too, yet kept to the faith which was most agreeable to them.' (*Egils Saga*, 50.)

lacking a vocational priesthood. That it appears bare of theology and overfoliated with myth may be the effect of our ignorance, for the information which has come down to us is incomplete, hard to interpret, and frequently misleading. But it could be old-fashioned without being ineffective. He would be a supplicant hard to please who found no patron in its extensive pantheon, no convenience in its varied practice, no message in its myth and eschatology. It accounted for the creation of the world and charted the doom to come. It provided mysteries as transcendent as Odinn hanged nine nights on the windswept tree as a sacrifice to himself, and objects of veneration as crude as the embalmed penis of a horse. Like other religions it rejoiced the devout with hidden truth, and contented mere conformers with its sacral and convivial occasions. There was a god for those who lived by wisdom and statecraft, war and plunder, trade and seafaring, or the land's increase. Poet, rune-maker, black-smith, leech, rye-grower, cattle-breeder, king, brewer, each had a god with whom he felt secure; warlocks, men on skis, barren women, brides, all had a deity to turn to. Best of all, the powers, attributes, and functions of the gods overlapped so generously that Odinn's man, Thor's man, Frey's man, and the like, could expect to be looked after in every aspect of life and death.

Norse conceptions of how the world began and how it must end are preserved in two famous works, the verse *Völuspá*, the Sybil's Prophecy, probably composed early in the eleventh century, and the prose *Edda*, written by Snorri Sturluson about the year 1220. These are supported by passages in various mythological poems of the so-called Elder Edda, and present us in broad outline with the following. In the beginning, before men or gods existed or the world was made, there was a great void, Ginnungagap. North of the void was Niflheim, dark and misty, later to be known as the realm of death, with a well from which issued eleven rivers. South of the void was Muspell, fiery and hot, presided over by the giant Surt. The rivers of Niflheim froze, and from the cataclysmic union of hot and cold was born the giant Ymir, whose left armpit sweated offspring and whose one leg begat issue on the other. His nourishment was the milk of the cow Audumbla, which had emerged from the melting frost. She licked the salty ice-blocks for food and fashioned a being of human form, named Buri. Buri had a son called Bor, who married a giantess, and by her had three sons, Odinn, Vili, and Ve. These were the first gods. They killed Ymir, and from his body formed the world: sea and lakes from his blood, earth from his flesh, mountains from his bones, rocks from his teeth and jaws, clouds from his brains, and from his skull the sky. In the sky they set sparks as stars, created Night and Day to speed across the sky, and Sun and Moon to hasten unceasingly before the wolves who ceaselessly pursued them. The round disc of the earth was girt with a vast ocean, on whose farther shore lay Jotunheim, the home of the giants, with its stronghold Utgard. To protect Midgard, the world of men, the gods erected a palisade made from Ymir's eyebrows. Then they made the first man and woman, Ask (*Askr*, Ash) and Embla, from two trees, or a tree and creeper, which they found on the seashore, and gave them breath (or spirit), understanding, movement, and their five senses. Then in the middle of the world they built Asgard, the home of the gods. Here stood the residences of the gods, and here stood Valhalla (Valhöll), the Hall of the Slain, to which came all brave men who died in battle. Odinn was lord of the hall and lived there with his wolves and ravens and drank wine. Each day the armies of the valiant dead fought together on meadows outside the hall; then as evening came the slain rose up again, and victors and vanquished went indoors to feast on Odinn's pork and mead, taking their stoups of bright drink from the hands of the Valkyries, those maiden choosers of the slain who had earlier summoned them from the battlefields of earth. But those who died of age or sickness went 'northwards and netherwards' to the goddess Hel in Niflheim.

Central to this created world was the 'greatest and best of all trees', the World Ash, Yggdrasill, whose branches reach the sky and cover the earth, and whose three roots go out to the realm of the dead, the home of the frost-giants, and the world of men. It was on Yggdrasill (the name probably means Ygg's, i.e. Odinn's, horse, and Odinn's horse was a kenning for the gallows) that Odinn hung nine days and nights to win wisdom, and under Yggdrasill in Asgard was the holiest seat of the gods, where they assembled each day in council. Beneath its roots lay the wells (or well) of Fate and Wisdom, and by the well of Fate dwelt the Norns who tended the destinies of men, and whose names were Urd (*Urðr*, Fate *or* Past), Verdandi (*Verðandi*, Being *or* Present), and Skuld (*Skuld*, Necessity *or* Future). Each day they watered the tree from the well of Fate and refreshed it with the well's life-giving clay. No care was too good for it, for Yggdrasill bore up the universe, and on its well-being depended the welfare of the world. Living and sentient, it knew pain and decay like all living things. 'The ash Yggdrasill suffers harms,' says *Grimnismál*, 'more than men imagine.' In its branches perched an eagle with a hawk between his eyes, and the serpent Nidhögg was one of many snakes for ever gnawing its roots. Up and down the trunk between these two ran the squirrel Ratatosk and sowed mischief between them. Deer and goats devoured its shoots, and the huge trunk was invaded by rot. Of its origin we know nothing, but it would endure, aged and shaken, till the world's end.

The world's end was the Ragnarok, the Doom or Destiny of the Gods. It was so called because it had been destined from the world's beginning. Death which waits on every living thing waited on the gods, too, and on everything they had made. Immense forces of destruction surrounded them always; men and gods were deeply flawed; and the time must come when neither Odinn's wisdom nor Thor's valour could protect them any longer. In Asgard the death of Odinn's good and lovely son Balder, through the treachery of Loki, revealed to the All-Father that the last dread act was at hand. The punishment of that cunning, evil, and unnatural god set him irrevocably alongside the giants and his own monstrous progeny, and against all that was good and fair in Asgard. In Midgard the last phase would be preceded by an age of faithlessness and depravity: all ties and restraints would vanish between kinsfolk, fratricide and incest reign unchecked. There would be a long, dire winter (*fimbulvetr*), lasting three years with no summer-time between; then three years of war and discord: 'Axe-age, sword-age, storm-age, wolf-age, ere earth is overthrown.' Three cocks will crow, one in the gallows-tree, one in Valhalla, one in Hel; the pursuing wolves will swallow up both Sun and Moon, Earth's bonds will crack, the mountains fall. The wolf Fenrir, whose jaws stretch from heaven to earth, breaks his fetters; the Midgard Snake, spewing poison, rises from the sea; Naglfar, the Ship of the Dead, made of the uncut nails of dead men, breaks from her moorings down in Hel. The fire giants, led by Surt, come riding out of Muspell, and as they approach Asgard the rainbow bridge Bifrost cracks under their weight. Giant-home rumbles and the dwarfs whimper. Loki bursts free of his chains and advances to battle.

Meantime Heimdall, watchman of the gods, has blown his horn. Yggdrasill trembles. Odinn takes counsel at the well of Wisdom. The gods arm themselves, and the chosen of Valhalla, Odinn's

Einherjar, prepare for the fight from which none will flee and none rise up. Odinn leads them to the field, with his golden helm and spear. Thor has his hammer, Frey his sword—but not the good sword he gave to his messenger Skirnir. 'How fare the Æsir? How fare the Elves?' Odinn faces Fenrir, Thor the Midgard Snake, Frey faces Surt. Frey dies first, hewn down by a sword that outshines the sun. Thor kills the Snake, but when he has walked nine paces falls dead of the Snake's venom. The Wolf swallows Odinn, but Vidar, Odinn's son, takes vengeance when he stabs him to the heart. Tyr and Garm destroy each other, as do Heimdall and Loki. The sun grows dark, stars fall from the sky, the sea invades the land, Surt flings fire over all the world; heaven and earth, the whole universe are consumed, and Earth sinks into the sea.

But if the old order had gone for ever, a new order would arise. Another world would appear above the waters, green and pleasant with grass and self-sown corn. Two of Odinn's sons would survive the fire and flood, and two of Thor's. The blameless Balder and his blameless slayer Hod would join them from their place in Hel, and sweet and pleasant will be the life they lead, and stirring the tales they tell. Midgard likewise had two survivors who would replenish the dewy, fruitful earth, while the Sun's daughter, more radiant than her mother, measures the sky in her effulgent track.

That this Creation and Doom have features in common with other Indo-European systems of mythology, and are not uninfluenced by Christian conceptions, would become clearer if we had space to discuss their many details. The beliefs of the Hindus, Persians, Egyptians, Greeks, Romans, and Celts have all yielded striking comparisons, and the Norse gods display significant resemblances to members of other pantheons, though Dumézil's attractive division of the gods of both the Norse and what he considers the common Indo-European religion into three categories has found dissenters. In the first category are the dread sovereign, the ferocious master of magic and wisdom, like Odinn, and the milder sovereign who bestows law and justice, like (thinks Dumézil) Tyr. In the second are the warrior gods, like Thor, and in the third the gods of wealth and fertility, like the Vanir, whose chief figure is Frey.[1] Foremost of the Norse gods stands Odinn, strange and

[1] For Dumézil's brilliant though not always convincing thesis concerning the Old Norse religion, see his *Les Dieux des Indo-Européens*, Paris, 1952, and *Les Dieux des Germains*, Paris, 1959. His views are extensively referred to in

many-sided, demonic and frightening. It is his passion to know and understand, and for wisdom he has run many risks and made great sacrifices. For a draught from the well of Mimir (the Fount of Wisdom) he yielded up an eye; and for magic and its runes he hung nine nights on the windswept tree, wounded with a spear:

> They stayed me not with bread,
> Nor with the drinking horn;
> Downward I peered,
> Caught up the runes,
> Screaming I caught them,
> Fell back from there.

He was god of the gallows and those who died on it, god of war and those who perished by it, god of occult knowledge and master of the dead from whom this must be won. He was no Christ who hung on the tree for others. He sought his own gain—dominion and knowledge—and his suffering has more in common with shamanism than with Christianity. He was violent, fickle, and treacherous, apportioning victory by policy rather than desert, dashing down those who had most claim on his favour in the hour of their greatest need. Of heroes, Hrolf Kraki, Sigmund the Volsung, and Harold Wartooth were destroyed by him; of kings, Eirik Blood-axe and jarl Hakon Sigurdarson; among poets, Egill Skallagrimsson felt his chastening hand. Such were his proper worshippers: men who dealt in policy and power, spell-makers and rune-readers, they that knew the ecstasy of creation and the frenzy of war. Wotan, says Adam of Bremen—*id est Furor*. He had many treasures, his dedicating spear Gungnir, his gold ring Draupnir for ever dropping replicas of itself, his eight-legged steed Sleipnir, his hall Valhalla, his ravens Huginn and Muninn, Thought and Memory, who flew over the world each day and returned to tell in Odinn's ear all that was happening there. He had many names, relative to his many functions: All-Father, Lord of the Gallows, Ill-doer, Terrifier, Father of

---

E. O. G. Turville-Petre, *Myth and Religion of the North*, 1964, and in H. R. Ellis Davidson, *Gods and Myths of Northern Europe*, 1964. There is some useful comment in Ólafur Briem, *Vanir og Æsir*, Studia Islandica 21, Reykjavík, 1963 (with a summary in English, pp. 75–80). One would welcome an essay which approached the Old Norse religion by way of those good friends of man, the sun, ship, horse, and phallus.

Victory, One-Eye, Raven-God, Mimir's Friend, Fenrir's Foe. Victory in war was his gift, poetry his mead, his cup, his sea.

Aristocratic, perilous, incalculable, Odinn was no god for the ordinary man to meddle with. Such would be in every way better off with Thor. Irascible but kindly, boisterous but straight-dealing, a huge eater and drinker, here was a god with whom the peasant and other ranks could identify themselves. All those adventures of his, his travels, the way the giants made a fool of him—and the way he made a fool of them—this brought him home to the common man's bosom. But a god must be more than well loved: he must show the attributes of godhead, and this Thor did, abundantly. By name and quality he was the thunder-god, who rumbled in his goat-drawn chariot across the heavens and was armed with the thunderbolt in the shape of his short-handled hammer Mjollnir. Red-bearded, massive of frame, enormously strong, he was cast in a protecting role for Asgard and the gods, and by implication for Midgard and the race of men. Two of the eventual destroyers of the world had his special attention, the Midgard Snake and the frost- and mountain-giants, 'who know his hammer well when it comes through the air, for it has cracked many a skull of their ancestors and kindred'. He had two other treasures, the iron gloves which he donned to brandish Mjollnir, and the girdle of might which doubled his divine strength when he clasped it round his middle. It was Red Thor, not Odinn, who stood out against White Christ. It was the hammer, not the spear, which warded off the cross. In the later reaches of heathendom he was probably the most widely honoured of the gods, and it was Thor, not Odinn or Frey, who was set mid-most of them in Adam's description of the Uppsala shrine. In parts of Scandinavia he was the god of agriculture, too, but the lateness of manufacture of his famous hammer, together with the lateness of the written sources which tell of him, make it difficult to define his consecrative and fructifying role in heathendom. But he was a mighty god in the viking homelands, and in the colonies overseas he became the mightiest god of all.

Odinn and Thor were of the Æsir, Frey of the Vanir. These were a different family of gods whose chief figures were Njord and his two children Frey and Freyja. Male and female alike, they were representative of an earlier religion in the north, whom the Æsir figuratively overcame in battle, but failed to destroy or drive out. They were fertility gods. Njord's name and function connect him with the Germanic earth mother Nerthus, and whatever the explanation of this sexual divergence, ambiguity, or duality, we consider them the same deity. Her worship is described thus by Tacitus in his *Germania* 40:

None of these tribes [of north-western Germany] have any noteworthy feature, except their common worship of Ertha, or mother-Earth, and their belief that she interposes in human affairs, and visits the nations in her car. In an island of the ocean [a Danish island?] there is a sacred grove, and within it a consecrated chariot, covered over with a garment. Only one priest is permitted to touch it. *He* can perceive the presence of the goddess in this sacred recess, and walks by her side with the utmost reverence as she is drawn along by heifers. It is a season of rejoicing, and festivity reigns wherever she deigns to go and be received. They do not go to battle or wear arms; every weapon is under lock; peace and quiet are known and welcomed only at these times, till the goddess, weary of human intercourse, is at length restored by the same priest to her temple. Afterwards the car, the vestments, and, if you like to believe it, the divinity herself, are purified in a secret lake. Slaves perform the rite, who are instantly swallowed up by its waters. Hence arises a mysterious terror and a pious ignorance concerning the nature of that which is seen only by men doomed to die. (Trans. Church and Brodribb.)

This ancient Njörðr-Nerthus, with priest, wagon, island-grove, lake, sacrificed slaves, and reign of peace and pleasure, is hardly less a starting-point for exegesis than the lake and grove of Nemi; but we must rest content with a single paragraph about Njord's son. Frey was a god of fruitfulness and sexuality. His necklaced sister was his genial counterpart. His image at Uppsala was distinguished by its exaggerated phallus, and the similarly enhanced little statuettes found in Sweden must also be of him. His cult had its orgiastic occasions, which drew more disgust than information from Adam of Bremen and Saxo. To the Swedes he was God of the World (*veraldar goð*); his very name means Lord (*Freyr*). Another name of his was Yngvi, from which we conclude the Swedish royal house took its name *Ynglingar*. He is associated with stallions, owned a wondrous boar, and the skaldic poem most associated with him, *Skírnismál*, the Sayings of Skirnir, however distrustful one may be in general of interpretations of love stories, is an imperfectly concealed nature myth of the god of sunshine and fertility, Skirnir, finding his corn-bride Gerd (Gerðr, cf. Garðr), or the reflection in later verse of a ritual drama of the marriage of the impregnating sun and recipient earth. Men, animals, and crops looked to him for increase. He presided over rain and sunshine, and all the fruits of earth. He had a further significance, for death and fertility are closely related. It is this which gives meaning to those parts of Ibn Fadlan's account of the Rus burial on the Volga which describes how the friends of the dead man had sexual intercourse with the sacrificial bride or slave-girl (see Appendix 3). It adds meaning, and also confusion, to the widespread Scandinavian practice of ship-burial. From as early as the Bronze Age ships feature prominently in the fertility rites depicted on the rock faces of Bohuslän and other regions. Now the best of ships was Skidbladnir, and it was Frey who owned her. She was big enough to contain all the Æsir fully armed, but when not in use could be folded away in a purse. She always had a favourable wind. Like Frey's chariot, his ship may be seen as a symbol of death and rebirth. Love and begetting, seed-time and harvest, the breeding and nurture of stock thrive better in peace than war. But no leading god of the Bronze, Iron, or Viking Age could be entirely peaceful. Some of Frey's bynames show that he was a warrior, and at Ragnarok he would not flinch from Surt.

Odinn, Thor, and Frey were the gods most celebrated among the northern nations during the Viking Age. This does not mean that other gods, or goddesses, were not important. Tyr was a god equated by Tacitus with the Roman Mars, though his name is cognate with Greek Zeus, Sanskrit Dyaus; myth has the almost forgotten Ull contend with Odinn for supremacy; but by now both Tyr and Ull were gods in decline. The evidence of place-names would make Denmark the centre of the cult of the warlike but law-maintaining Tyr, central and south-eastern Sweden together with south and south-eastern Norway that of the once brilliant Ull. If these were representative of gods displaced, Balder, the son of Odinn and his wife Frigg, is an example of a god come fairly late to prominence. Good, beautiful, and beloved, he was killed by a mistletoe thrown at him by his blind brother Hod at the instigation of Loki. It is possible that the beauty and interest of Snorri's story of his death and funeral, the grief of the gods, and how Hermod rode down to Hel to beg that he be allowed to return, and how this was granted on condition that all things alive or dead would weep for him, and how all things did so weep save Loki, so that Balder stayed with Hel till after the Ragnarok, and only then returned to the world—it is possible that this, despite the violently different view of Balder presented by Saxo, has given him a prominence in the pantheon to which, considered in his character of god, he is not entitled. Heimdall, watchman of the gods, the killer of Loki, and in *Rígsþula* (see pp. 145-7 above) identified with Rig the father of all mankind, is another god of whom we could wish to know more. And so with the goddesses Idunn, Gefjon, and Frigg, and the lesser, tutelary, goddesses (*dísir*, sing. *dís*) associated with a district, a family, or sometimes an individual; with their festivals and sacrifices (*dísablót*); and so, on a lower level, with the elves, land-spirits, and dwarfs, and lower still the fetch or *fylgja*.

A religion needs more than a god. It needs ritual and places of worship. Concerning these we have a considerable amount of information in the literary sources, most of it late and some of it unacceptable, and by way of corrective the evidence of place-names and archaeology, in so far as this can be reliably interpreted. Inasmuch as we are dealing with many gods and a number of peoples over several centuries we can expect variation within any establishable pattern. Thus place-names with Odinn- are not infrequent in Denmark and southern Sweden, including Väster- and Östergötland, but are thin on the ground in Norway—though expectedly least thin in the south-east. In Iceland there are no Odinn- names. Names with Thor- are common everywhere, and especially in Iceland, where personal names with Thor- are likewise numerous, though it does not follow that his popularity in different countries rested on the same aspect of his divinity. Iceland has a few Frey-names in the east; they are known in Zealand, Fyn and southern Jutland; Norway has a good number in the south-east; and the abundance of Frey- names in Sweden confirms other evidence that until near the end of the heathen age his was the most important cult of that nation. The Tyr-names of Denmark and the Ull-names of Norway and Sweden locate the areas of their cults; but the subject is full of surprises. When the foremost authority of Norway, Magnus Olsen, listed the divine place-names of his country in viking times, they numbered as follows: names with Frey or Freyja 48, with Ull 33, with Thor 27, with Njord 26, with Odinn 12.[1] The second element of these divine place-names throughout Scandinavia relates sometimes to man-made features connected with the act of worship,

[1] *Hedenske Kultminder i norske Stedsnavne*, Christiania, 1915, I, pp. 63 ff.; *Nordisk Kultur*, XXVI (*Religionshistorie*), Copenhagen, 1942, pp. 60 ff.

like *hof*, house, *hörgr*, mound (shrine), *vé*, sanctuary (these meanings are a shade limiting and arbitrary), to natural features connected with worship and fertility, like *lundr*, grove, and *akr*, cultivated ground, and to a variety of landscape features, like *berg*, rock, *áss*, ridge, *ey*, island, *haugr*, mound. The first group is the most significant for the forms and places of viking religious observance.

It is remarkable that the Old Norse religion appears to have had no vocational priesthood. It was a function of the local leader or chieftain to act as intermediary between worshipped and worshipper. We have noticed about the 'secular priest', the godi of Iceland, that he was a priest only because he was a chieftain, and that his sacerdotal function depended upon his social status and, later, his authority and office as defined by the Constitution. There is no reason to believe things were different back in Scandinavia. The outstanding centres of religious observance would tend to be associated with the outstanding chieftains. It was the king of the Swedes who was responsible for the ceremonies at Uppsala, and the jarls of the Trondelag who maintained Hladir. It is true that the description of Thorolf Mostrarskegg's *hof* in Breidafjord, Iceland, speaks of a *hofgoði*, and *Vápnfirðinga Saga* 5 of a *hofgyðja* (*gyðja* the feminine equivalent of *goði*), just as Adam of Bremen speaks of *sacerdotes* attendant on the heathen gods at Uppsala; but it was the function of these 'priests' to offer sacrifices for the people, a role consistent with that of an officiating chieftain, and nothing more should be attributed to them.

The characteristic religious ceremony of the north was sacrifice (*blót*). With allowance made for local and chronological circumstance this was of two chief kinds. There was the votive offering, normally of a destructive nature, in which human beings, animals, weapons, boats, artefacts of all kinds, pass out of human possession into that of the god; and there was the convivial sacrifice where 'the worshippers collectively eat and drink the nourishment consecrated to the god. Our attention must focus on the convivial sacrifice, for this might presuppose the existence of buildings in which the ritual feast could be celebrated. Only late and unreliable sources record the ceremonial of the ritual feast (Snorri), but the impression conveyed by heathen poetry is that the slaughter of the sacrificial animal was in itself a ritual, the meat possibly being prepared by baking in an earth-covered pit lined with hot stones—an ancient method used primarily in cult ritual in the Viking period. In addition to the feast, the ceremony may have included singing, dancing, divination and the enactment of mythological scenes.'[1]

There remains the difficult question of where these sacrifices took place. By far the best known statement is that of Adam of Bremen in Book IV, xxvi–vii, of his *Gesta Hammaburgensis*:

That folk [the Swedes] has a very famous temple called Uppsala, situated not far from the city of Sigtuna or Birka. In this temple, entirely decked out in gold, the people worship the statues of three gods in such wise that the mightiest of them, Thor, occupies a throne in the middle of the chamber; Wodan and Fricco have places on either side. The significance of these gods is as follows: Thor, they say, presides over the air, and governs the thunder and lightning, the winds and rains, fair weather and crops. The other, Wodan [Odinn]— that is, the Furious—carries on war and imparts to man strength against his enemies. The third is Fricco [Frey], who bestowes peace and pleasure on mortals. His likeness, too, they fashion with an immense phallus. But Woden they chisel armed, as our people are wont to represent Mars. Thor with his sceptre [i.e. hammer] apparently resembles Jove. The people also worship heroes made gods, whom they endow with immortality because of their remarkable exploits, as one reads in the *Vita* of Saint Ansgar they did in the case of King Eric.

For all their gods there are appointed priests to offer sacrifices for the people. If plague and famine threaten, a libation is poured to the idol Thor; if war, to Wodan; if marriages are to be celebrated, to Fricco. It is customary also to solemnize in Uppsala, at nine-year intervals, a general feast of all the provinces of Sweden. From attendance at this festival no one is exempted. Kings and people all and singly send their gifts to Uppsala and, what is more distressing than any kind of punishment, those who have already adopted Christianity redeem themselves through these ceremonies. The sacrifice is of this nature: of every living thing that is male, they offer nine heads, with the blood of which it is customary to placate gods of this sort. The bodies they hang in the sacred grove that adjoins the temple. Now this grove is so sacred in the eyes of the heathen that each and every tree in it is believed divine because of the death or putrefaction of the victims. Even dogs and horses hang there with men, and a Christian told me that he had seen seventy-two bodies suspended promiscuously. Furthermore the incantations [songs] customarily chanted in the

---

[1] Olaf Olsen, *Hørg, Hov og Kirke*, p. 279. In this context I am heavily indebted to Dr. Olsen.

ritual of a sacrifice of this kind are manifold and unseemly; therefore, it is better to keep silence about them.[1]

Visual reconstructions of the Uppsala *templum* range from the improbable to the impossible. Certainly there were images of gods. Assuredly there was some kind of structure to protect them, but whether this was a mere four-cornered roof or something more elaborate due to the impact of Christianity and its churches we cannot say. Clearly the sacrifices were associated with the near-by grove and its huge evergreen tree rather than with the *templum*. Neither the literary nor the archaeological evidence suggests that the *templum* was a big one, and everything we know of Scandinavian buildings before 1070 convinces us that there can be no question of a *hof* big enough to contain a significant proportion of the large crowd assembled there. Also there is no trustworthy parallel to Adam's *nobilissimum templum*—which in any case he never saw. The scepticism of late expressed by archaeologists about the 'temples' here in Sweden, at Jelling in Denmark, at Hofstadir near Mývatn in Iceland, together with the higher criticism directed at thirteenth-century literary accounts in *Eyrbyggja Saga*, *Kjalnesinga Saga*, *Njála*, and *Heimskringla*, makes it prudent, perhaps imperative, to approach the subject another way.

The weight of evidence for the south Germanic peoples associates their religious practice with sites in the open air, and with groves and springs in particular. Early Christian laws in Norway, Sweden, and Götaland, the laws of Knut in England, and the Northumbrian priests' law of Danish provenance, point to the same state of affairs

---

[1] I have made two alterations in Tschan's translation. There are three relevant scholia accompanying the text:

Schol. 138. Near this temple stands a very large tree with wide-spreading branches, always green winter and summer. What kind it is nobody knows. There is also a spring at which the pagans are accustomed to make their sacrifices, and into it to plunge a live man. And if he is not found, the people's wish will be granted.

Schol. 139. A golden chain goes round the temple. It hangs over the gable of the building and sends its glitter far off to those who approach it, because the shrine stands on level ground with mountains all about it like an amphitheatre. [Cf. the temple of Solomon, II Chronicles, 3, 15–16.]

Schol. 141. Feasts and sacrifices of this kind are solemnized for nine days. On each day they offer a man along with other living beings in such a number that in the course of the nine days they will have made offerings of seventy-two creatures. This sacrifice takes place about the time of the vernal equinox.

among the north Germans. Men are forbidden to worship in or by
woods, mounds, stones, springs, sanctuaries, or holy places connected with heathendom, and the likeliest interpretation of such
injunctions is not that they reflect the general proscription of
heathendom but that they are directed against the places traditionally associated with it. Arab witness in respect of heathendom at
Hedeby (p. 177 above) makes no mention of a temple in connection
with the festivals there, though it does mention a Christian church;
while in respect of the Rus offerings to idols on the Volga it seems
that these wooden figures either stood in the open or under
unelaborate cover (p. 165). It is probable that the great majority of
buildings with the title *hof*, as they are mentioned in the sagas and
later antiquarian Icelandic tradition, were not temples dedicated to
a god, but by Olaf Olsen's definition were farms 'where cult meetings
were regularly held for more people than those living on the farm'.
In the northern climate it was useful to have a building where
convivial feasts could be held indoors, but for the rest of the time the
farm buildings would revert to normal use. The two well-known
Icelandic sites named Hofstadir, one in Mývatn, the other in
Thorskafjord, each with an oval pit for baking near at hand,
apparently much too large for the needs of one household, are the
likeliest examples of this.

A much older and wider-spread name for a holy place than *hof* is
hörgr, whose primary meaning is a pile of stones, whether natural or
man-assembled. Normally this, too, means a site in the open, but
from as far back as the Early Iron Age there are indications that an
image was sometimes set on a cairn, and it may be assumed that in
course of time it appeared natural to give these images some kind
of cover. But this did not convert the cairn into a temple: it remained
a shrine. The Viking Age knew shrines covered and uncovered, but
there is no trustworthy evidence that the *hörgr* was in any instance
a large or splendid building. As for the *vé*, we know little more than
that it was a holy place, and appears to have been in the open air.

Even the most fragmentary survey of the old religion must seek
to answer one more question. What did the Norsemen think about
death? To what heaven, hell, limbo, or nothingness did the dead
repair? And how did they make their way there? For once we have
not too few answers but too many. There are the statements
preserved in literature, more particularly by Snorri and the unknown
authors of the Eddic poems, but in a variety of sources besides.

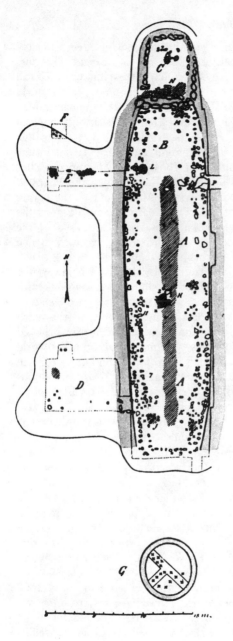

47. HOFSTAÐIR, MÝVATNSSVEIT, ICELAND
A large farmstead in northern Iceland, often called a temple-site. The large hall (A + B), is 36·3 metres long, 8·25 metres at its broadest, and narrowing at the gable ends. The outhouse (C) to the north is 6·2 by *c.* 4 metres, and is unlikely to be of any religious significance. The large hall was a banqueting-hall on occasions, and the oval pit to the south (G) may have been used for sacral cooking. (See p. 328.)

And there are the statements of the graves, which reveal widely differing beliefs about the nature and destiny of the dead. The most picturesque piece of literary evidence is the best known: that 'all the men who have fallen in battle since the beginning of the world have now come to Odinn in Valhalla'—though the same authority (Snorri's *Edda*) insists that Freyja takes half the slain into her hall Folkvangar. Women, too, came to Freyja, but virgins to the unvirginal Gefjon, whose name is reminiscent of Freyja's nickname Gefn or Giver. It is possible that those who worshipped Thor joined him in his hall Bilskirnir on Thrudvangar, the Plains of Might, and other deaths, other abodes. Antecedent to the viking Valhalla was the concept of Hel, which early received Sigurd the Volsung, the tigerish Brynhild, and in time Odinn's son, the blameless Balder. It was a concept which underwent much change for the worse when Loki's double-hued daughter Hel, half black, half flesh-colour, was thrown down there by Odinn with power over nine worlds, but with an obligation to share her provisions with men who died of sickness or old age. The wicked went to Hel, says Snorri, and from there into Niflhel, which is down in the ninth world. To what extent men in the ninth and tenth centuries believed in, or were fully aware of, this agglomeration of other-world destinations is hard to tell. Perhaps in trying to find out we are in the position of a post-nuclear inquirer establishing Christian notions of the after-life from a Jacobean translation of the Book of Job, a partial salvage of the Gospels, Traherne's *Centuries of Meditations*, and the hell-fire sermons of Mr. Spurgeon. Almost certainly no one man living at any one time did or could believe in the entire Norse eschatology as it has been preserved for posterity. Also, there is a good deal of literary evidence contradictory of the whole picture. Icelandic sources are rich in references to men who went into a grave and stayed there, or journeyed no farther than a near-by hill. Some of them kept benevolent watch on the neighbourhood, some, if disturbed, provided horrid company for the living. In general those evil in life stayed evil in death. On the other hand, the great northern wisdom-poem, the *Hávamál*, confines itself to this world and ignores the life to come.

On the whole we are safer with the evidence of the graves, though this, too, is not all of a piece, or always easy to interpret. Immediately we are impressed by the variety of funeral usage among the northern nations. They practised cremation as well as

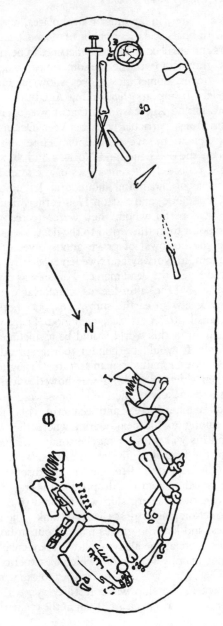

48. MAN'S GRAVE,
SÍLASTAÐIR,
KRAEKLINGAHLIÐ,
ICELAND
A man with his axe,
sword, shield boss,
knife, weights, and the
skeleton of a horse.

earth-burial, laid the dead to rest in mounds or level places, with or without grave goods, with boats real or symbolic or no boat at all, in big wooden chambers and small coffins, and sometimes in neither. There are single graves, graves for two (the one sometimes a woman slave), and communal graves. Sometimes graves show an inter-mixture of religious beliefs. It appears that Viking Age burial was strongly affected by pre-Viking Age customs, that it was open to local and regional distinctions, particularly as between Denmark, with its infrequency of cremation, save at Lindholm Høje, and its paucity of grave goods on the one hand, and Norway and Sweden on the other, and that it reflected different views of the after-life. The size and magnificence of the burial mounds at Jelling and Oseberg, as at Vendel, Valsgärde, and Sutton Hoo earlier, denote the importance of the persons for whom they were erected and furnished; but they also point from this world to the next.

Christianity forbade the bestowal of grave goods save of the simplest kind. Heathendom, in Norway and Sweden especially, did not. When means sufficed for it, the dead man or woman was given everything that could make the after-life as comfortable and honourable as that they knew on earth: ships, weapons, horses, wagons, adornments, utensils, toilet articles, even food. There was a fatalism in this: a chieftain in this world would be a chieftain in the next, a thrall a thrall. It would be helpful to the spread of Christianity that it did not perpetuate man's state throughout eternity. When a heathen chieftain or king was howed with his grave goods, the poets and makers of pictured stones were quite clear what next happened to him. We read and see pictures of heroes riding and, we think, sailing to the next world, where they are welcomed by Odinn and his valkyries, or maybe some other god. Ship-burials would seem the factual confirmation of this. The ship at Ladby in Denmark (the only one of its kind so far discovered there) had its anchor on board, ready to be dropped at the end of its lord's voyage. Conversely, the Oseberg ship was moored to a big stone. Probably the distinction matters less than we think. The big ships, like the small ones, and like the graves marked out in boat-shape by means of stones, were above all symbolical. They enabled the dead man's spirit, not his physical frame, which all experience showed must moulder wherever it was laid, to transfer to the world of the dead, and inasmuch as the ship was a fertility symbol, be reborn there. The evidence is nowhere clearer than in the cremation

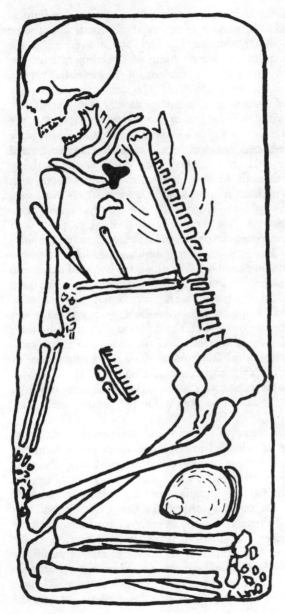

49. WOMAN'S
GRAVE,
HAFURBJAR-
NARSTAÐIR,
GULLBRING-
USÝSLA,
ICELAND
A woman with
her brooch, pin,
knife, comb,
beads, and large
shells.

graves at Lindholm Høje near the eastern exit of the Limfjord in northern Jutland. The sizeable cemetery there, consisting of some 700 graves, was in use from approximately the mid-seventh to the tenth centuries. It stands a little south of a settlement from the years 400 to 800; and a later settlement, of the eleventh century, overlaps part of the cemetery site. The cemetery was largely covered over by drifting sand and has recently been extensively surveyed. A majority of the graves are cremation type; but the dead bodies and their grave goods had not been burned in the place where they were buried, but elsewhere. The ashes were then carried to the cemetery, laid on a smallish piece of ground, and thinly covered over with earth. Many graves were then marked out with stones arranged in ovals, rounds, squares, and triangles. The ovals, *stensætninger*, are symbols of ships, and once they had served their immediate symbolic purpose the stones could be taken up and used for other and newer stone-settings. An interesting variation of ship-burial is that at Hedeby, where the ship was laid upright over a large wood-lined grave chamber containing the bodies of either two or three men who had their grave goods alongside them and three horses in a separate, much shallower, grave back under the stern. It is impossible to maintain that some boats in graves were not straightforward grave goods. In Iceland graves with boats are rare; the horse was the instrument of travel there, and more than two-thirds of known Icelandic viking graves show the remains of one or more horses buried with their master. Cremation was unknown there. Clearly no one explanation holds good for the many modes of northern burial, and no one notion for life beyond the grave.

Yet within this variety of concept and practice the old Norse religion was one. It belonged to the three Scandinavian countries and their colonies overseas, and belonged to them alone. The same is true of viking decorative art, which was homogeneous from the Trondelag to the Gulf of Bothnia, from Uppsala to the neck of Jutland. It had its roots in continental Germanic art, but was developing along distinctive lines as early as the fourth century A.D., and thereafter continued to do so, mainly because of the continuing devotion of Scandinavian artists to animal motifs for decoration, and their unwillingness to follow their European contemporaries into the intricacies of vegetation patterns. There is no question of their ability to do so, had they wished; nor were the minds of Scandinavian artists sealed to outside influences. War, piracy, trade, and purchase brought all kinds of beautiful objects back to Scandinavia, sword-handles, bookmarks and clasps, brooches, coins, chests, croziers, cups and goblets, statuettes, church plate, textiles. Irish, English, and Carolingian art strongly influenced northern practitioners, as to a lesser extent did the art of Russia. In other words, artistic impulses as well as artistic objects were part of the Viking Age intake; but it would be wrong to conclude that northern artists welcomed foreign arts because they felt themselves to be behind the times, naive, or provincial. It is every bit as likely that they welcomed them because they were assured in respect of their own tradition, the techniques they employed, and the clientele they served. Thus large quantities of gold and especially silver were melted down to provide the northern artist with the materials of his craft, while the undoubted foreign influences were skilfully absorbed into the native tradition, which they stimulated and helped reshape, but could not replace. The problem of native and foreign elements is even so a difficult one. For example, the Jelling style of decoration has been described as owing much to Irish (i.e. Hiberno-Saxon), Anglo-Saxon, and eastern art, while the latest study of the subject considers that most of its elements 'are derived from native Scandinavian traditions, which stem back to the beginning of the ninth century, when there may well have been some direct, or indirect, insular influences in Scandinavia'.[1] The problem is further complicated by the possibility of Scandinavian influence on some of the art which influenced Scandinavia. It is arguable that it took direct viking (probably Jelling) influence to produce the undated stone crosses in various east Yorkshire villages, and northern influence is undoubted for various monuments in those parts of England which were occupied by Norse armies and the settlers who followed them. The Ringerike style left its mark there in Knut's time; and in the days of those ex-vikings the Normans the last indigenous flowering of viking art, the Urnes style, achieved its final triumphs not at home but in England and Ireland. That Scandinavia should export as well as import art styles over many centuries, and be self-confident in using the imports, indicates the independent status of its artists. As artists will, they took what they wanted from the past and their

---

[1] D. M. Wilson and O. Klindt-Jensen, *Viking Art*, 1966, p. 116.

contemporaries abroad. What resulted was not bastard-Carolingian, or extra-Insular, but Viking art.

The development of this from pre-viking times till its eclipse in the twelfth century by Romanesque has been closely plotted in terms of styles: Oseberg, Borre, Jelling, Mammen, Ringerike, Urnes. Unfortunately the material is far from complete. We have the Oseberg ship with her wagon, and may wonder how many ships and wagons, now lost, received similar loving care. Few ship's vanes and standards survive, but they must have been made in hundreds; half a dozen Danish horse-collars with gilt-bronze moulds and panels are a meagre remnant of ancient plenty; little work survives in the Borre style, especially outside Norway, and the overlap of Borre and Jelling is obscured by the shortage of metal ornaments and an almost complete lack of evidence from architecture and furniture. It is troubling to know that bold primary colours were applied to both picture and rune-stones, when today we behold them all too anciently plain or freshly bedizened. But none of this forbids a verdict on the art of the northern nations as a vigorous, continuing, and triumphant activity, and an impressive manifestation of viking culture and civilization.

The Norsemen were excellent workers in metal, producing handsome weapons and agreeable ornaments for the person. However, in this they were at least matched by practitioners in other parts of Europe. Of their skill in cloth-making, costume, and tapestry we judge favourably on the strength of the little of their product which has survived. In architecture they showed skill in the use of turf, stone, and especially timber, and it is unfortunate that no examples of their kings' halls and farm-complexes have survived. To judge by late accounts and the evidence of archaeological excavation they surely produced buildings of much dignity, good proportions, solid workmanship, and high artistic finish—constructions, that is, in their own way matching the viking ships. But the distinctive achievements of viking art were in wood-carving and picture stones. To judge by what has survived, Norway was pre-eminent in the first and the island of Gotland in the second. Wood and stone were native materials, and it was in these that native artists excelled their contemporaries elsewhere.

Fittingly, the outstanding find of northern wood-carving comes from a ship-burial. If not queen Asa (see p. 85 above), it was assuredly a royal lady who was howed at Oseberg (Slagen) near

Tunsberg in the Vestfold. Only a royal house, we assume, could command the resources and artists needed for such a monument. Fortunately for posterity the burial took place in an area of blue clay which together with a peat cover preserved the ship and its grave goods for more than a thousand years till the excavation of 1904. Almost the entire find, carefully preserved and suitably restored, is now housed in the Viking Ship Hall at Bygdøy, Oslo, to provide an unparalleled exhibition of the northern wood-carver's art. Most notable are the ship's prow, the wagon, and three of the sledges. They are the product of a number of artists of the first half of the ninth century, whose work shows marked differences both in its inspiration and technique. One's first impression is of rich invention and vitality, in the long scrolls of interlaced animal-patterns on the ship's bows, the fantastic yet regulated groupings of gripping beasts and lugubriously comic human beings that enliven her prow or beak (*tingl*), the sculptured animal heads of the bed-posts (if stylized lions, to a layman somewhat equine lions), the skilled open-work at the rear of the wagon shafts, the narrative carvings on the wagon's front and sides, and the alarming animal-head posts on Gustafson's sledge. If the first requisite of art is that it should be alive, these have it. One is aware, too, of the luxuriance of fancy here: the proliferation of design, the intricate frames and borders with their gripping beasts, biting beasts, bird forms and serpentinings, the nicely differentiated human features, and the overall discipline which holds everything firmly in place. The Oseberg artists show differing degrees of sophistication, but their engagement, even their exultation, in what they were producing is discernible in each one. The gripping beasts of Oseberg are a good illustration of this. We have no certain indication of where this exciting little creature came from. Some give him an ancestry in Carolingian lion-forms; others derive all his features from earlier Scandinavian work. In either case he was a *lusus naturae*. Lion, dog, cat, bear are among his suggested constituents. The head is large, the eyes goggling, the nose blobbed, the mouth small. The forehead is baldish, and the back of the head carries a pigtail or scalplock. The expression of the full face can be at once fierce and comic. The body varies in width but the waist is thin; the thighs can be plump and pear-shaped. His paws (one would prefer to say hands and feet) give him his name: they are for ever gripping the sides of his frame, a neighbouring animal, some portion of himself, or sometimes all of these together. Two engaging little creatures on the bronze oval brooch from Lisbjerg in Denmark have spared one hand for a stranglehold on their own throats. This eccentricity aside, they look like grown kittens. Gripping beasts are to be found in great number throughout the ninth century. Their compactness and mobility allowed the artist endless variations: the more naturalistic of them recall without particularly resembling some well-known modern cartoon creations, and the young of the feline and ursine species in their most supple and strenuous postures. The less naturalistic achieve improbable feats of boneless contortion and wear looks of consternation. Grotesque, varied, ferocious, filled with energy, and lending itself to sallies of virile wit and humour, the gripping beast seems to have fascinated Scandinavian artists of the ninth century, who with all their interest in animal motifs had never found one quite so intriguing as this.

50. THE GRIPPING BEAST
Ornament of a brooch from Lisbjerg, Jutland, Denmark.

Some of the carving in the Oseberg find tells a story. On the front board of the wagon, over a band of fierce serpent forms is the picture of a man grappling with snakes, while a toad-like creature bites him in the side. Another man is fighting with a four-legged beast, and all around are other animals, snakes, and birds in a welter of combat. Possibly the chief figure represents Gunnar in the snake-pit. Similar fighting snakes and animals decorate the backboard. Down the sides is a wealth of animal ornament, the elongated beasts, seen mostly in profile, gripping and biting each other in a pattern at once violent and controlled. There is a dramatic insertion in the middle of the upper board on the right hand side, which has been interpreted in widely differing ways (Plate 4). It shows three human figures: on the right a man on horseback riding into the centre of the picture; in the middle another man, who has caught the horse's bridle in his left hand and holds a sword aloft in his right; behind him stands a handsomely dressed woman, wearing fine necklaces, and with a strenuous head of hair, who has caught the second man by his sword-hand. Whoever they are they meet in a tense and hostile moment. All three faces are filled with determination. The stance in each case is unyielding. A hint of rigidity in the human figures compared with the swirling menace of the creatures on the frieze below adds to the drama of their situation.

The elaborate animal heads topping the corner posts of the sledges probably served a practical purpose. They protected anyone sitting in the sledge by frightening off evil spirits. It has been conjectured that those set on the end of metre-long posts or handles were carried in processions, but this awaits proof. They have been ascribed to different artists, to whom descriptive titles have been given according to the style of their work: the Academician, the Carolingian, and the Baroque Master. They worked with varying degrees of mastery to produce these predatory heads, generally assumed to be leonine, and to enrich heads and posts with the most intricate and demanding ornamental patterns. The Academician's work is distinguished not only by the strong line of the gaping, blunt-toothed head, and the brilliant adaptation of his decorative patterns to its curves, but by the smooth neck and unfussed geometric ornament at the post's lower extremity. The Carolingian heads are clumsier and more barbarously decorated; those of the Baroque Master justify their name by the luxuriant richness of their ornament. Even the snout is enriched with a further beast-image, part animal, part bird, winged and horned; the protruding eyes are made more conspicuous with silver plates; the ornamenting of the head and neck, often deeply carved, is filled with twisting, inter-laced, and sometimes frenetic forms. All these animal heads are vivid, powerful creations in their own right, and doubly impressive in their context.

The Oseberg find consists of objects from the early Viking Age down to the middle of the ninth century. The main change in the tenth century was the movement away from the lavish modelling of the Oseberg styles to an emphasis on line and composition. Any such statement is a simplification, but the Jelling style is a very clear departure from Oseberg and Borre. The style is named after the

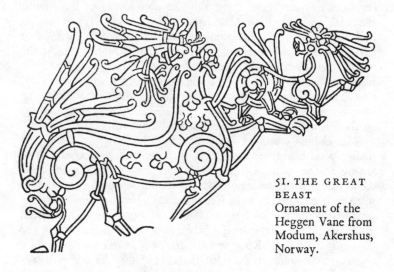

51. THE GREAT BEAST Ornament of the Heggen Vane from Modum, Akershus, Norway.

ribbon-like animal form (rather like an elongated S, and frequently crossed with another of the same shape) found in the grave chamber in the northern Jelling mound in 1820. It is *not* named after the 'great beast' depicted on the memorial stone erected at Jelling by Harald Bluetooth (see pp. 117 above). That, unfortunately for nomenclature, is an example of Mammen style, and its most important and influential example, with considerable consequences for Scandinavian and English art in the eleventh century. The stone, 'a semi-pyramidal boulder of red-veined, grey granite, some 8 ft. high and damaged slightly at the top' (to quote Klindt-Jensen's succinct description), was set up *c.* 980, and is the most imposing runic monument in all Scandinavia. One of its three faces is filled with all save the concluding half-dozen words of Harald's tribute to his father, mother, and himself. The second contains the representation of a big lion entwined with a snake, and the third a stylized picture of Christ bound and crucified, together with those few words of the runic inscription which refer to the conversion of the Danes to Christianity. Despite its border and interlace it is a simple and rather stiff composition, but of great interest because it is the first significant representation of Christ in Scandinavian art. The artist had evidently studied essays at the same subject by foreign artists.

The Mammen style is named after the find made at the place of that name in Jutland, which included a very fine iron axe-head inlaid with silver, and bearing on one side a prototypal image of a creature which is certainly an animal, and probably a lion, but whose head is not unlike a bird's. The Jelling lion is a more imperial beast, with a more heraldic stance, but close analysis shows much similarity in their detail. They are both portrayed with a double outline, there is an interlaced snake or snake-like band, they have rather small, cockerel-proud heads, spiral hips and a lip-lappet. Both have foliate features which suggest Carolingian or English influence. The great beast of the Jelling stone, strong, energetic, and elegant, would provide Scandinavian art with a dominant animal-motif to the end of the Viking Age. He would be copied more or less faithfully, with his bands, claws, pointed ears, and acanthus-leaf tail decoration, or he would be modified according to the inspiration and skill of the individual artist, till eventually we find him, in Ringerike style, featured on some of the most celebrated works of art of the late tenth and eleventh centuries, the Søllested horse-collar, the vanes from Heggen in Norway and Söderala in Sweden, the sarcophagus from St. Paul's churchyard now in the Guildhall, London, the Bamberg and Cammins caskets in Germany, rune-stones at home, and stone crosses abroad. In the full Ringerike development the design is distinguished by a quality of movement and the proliferation of graceful tendrils in place of the ears and tail. Sometimes the entire snake is expressed in Ringerike foliation. Sometimes the snake takes over, and either alone or with a colleague or two is the mainstay of many pleasing patterns on east Swedish rune-stones. Finally the great beast, astonishingly refined and literally thinned-down, becomes the new animal motif of the graceful Urnes style, as it is exemplified in the north portal of the Urnes stave church, the second and concluding glory of Norwegian woodcarving, and in manly delightful brooches, of which that from Lindholm Høje, now in Ålborg Museum, is probably the best known in Scandinavia, and that from Pitney, Somerset, the most beautiful in England.

There remain for separate mention the picture stones of Gotland. Hundreds of memorial stones were produced from the local lime-stone from the fifth century onwards, and in pre-viking and viking times (more especially during the eighth and eleventh centuries) they grew richly informative. General themes are easily recognized: ships on a journey, men fighting in battle or defending a house, a warrior being welcomed home or into Valhalla, often by a woman who offers him a drinking-horn, stories of gods and heroes. At the beginning of this book we described the rock-carvings of Bohuslän, Kivik, Simris, and their like, as the picture-galleries of the Bronze Age. The pictured memorial stones of Gotland are their counter-part for the Viking Age. We shall describe just three of them, all well known and readily available through photographs: Ardre VIII, Lärbro I, and Klinte Hunninge I. The first, about seven feet tall, with its sides inclining inwards to a 'neck', and with the normal

52. THE URNES BEAST
Ornament of the west gable of Urnes Church, Norway.

rounded top, is filled with narrative detail. In the upper field, i.e. that circumscribed by the rounded top edge and a decorative band across the neck, there is top-left a representation of Valhalla, a building with three arched entrances and seven apertures above them. Beneath it a group of people are carrying some kind of pole just above head-level. Most of the right half of the top panel is filled by Odinn's eight-legged horse Sleipnir, with the god on his back. The horse would seem to be galloping. Above Odinn there is a crumpled warrior, dead but still clutching his sword. In the much larger lower panel the top-left quarter is filled by a viking ship with its sail fully extended as it rides over high tip-curled waves. It has a look-out man in the prow, a steersman in the stern, complete with rudder, and a crew with swords in their belts. The rest of the stone is heavily loaded, but we recognize Loki in durance and his wife Sigyn with a horn trying to catch the venom from the snakes that surround him; likewise part of the story of Volund the Smith. There is his smithy with tongs and hammers, the headless bodies of Nithad's sons, and Volund in the shape of a bird flying away from Nithad's daughter Bodvild. Left of her are Thor and Hymir fishing for the Midgard Snake. Bottom centre is a building containing two men and a cow. A man outside has hold of the cow's halter. This leaves five small groups of figures unexplained and to the writer inexplicable. To the right of the stable, which has a paved floor, stands a dog.

The Lärbro stone is less complicated (Plate 13). The stone itself is narrower than Ardre VIII, and its sections are marked off with clear horizontal lines. In the topmost and semicircular panel a battle is taking place, with eagles and dead men. A mounted warrior has fallen to the ground. Two men apart in a building, their swords uplifted, appear to be taking an oath together. In the section below we see the eight-legged Sleipnir walking with a dead man on his back. Behind him, and facing in the opposite direction, are three men with down-turned swords. In the third section a warrior with a splendid shield rides proudly at the head of four armed men. He is greeted by a man holding a drinking-horn. The bottom panel (it fills half the stone) contains a big viking ship in full sail, her side lined with shields, her crew attentive to the rigging, with look-out man and steersman, and under her the familiar tall and curling waves. It is hard to say whether her prow and stern end in spirals or in animal heads, but probably the latter are intended.

The stone from Klinte Hunninge offers some interesting variations. The principal figures in the upper semicircular area are two
warriors fighting with sword and shield—it looks quite a formal
encounter—and a rider armed with shield and spear and accompanied by his dog. The middle panel has a stiff and awkward viking
ship under sail, over the usual stylized waves. Like the Ardre
(and Oseberg) ship she has a spiral at prow and stern. Immediately
thereunder is a portrayal of Loki plagued by snakes, with the

53. A DANISH STONE-CUTTER
The inscribers and carvers on stone
in pre-viking and viking times
seem not to have used a chisel but
a pointed hammer of the kind
displayed in the self-portrait of the
mason Gote above. Gjøl Church,
Jutland.

faithful Sigyn in attendance. But the intriguing picture is at the
bottom. Here two men are defending a gabled house with bows and
arrows, in a scene reminiscent of that relating to Volund and Egill
on the Franks Casket (Plate 3). As on the Ardre stone, a man outside the house has taken hold of the halter of the very large cow
standing within. Parts of the picture are difficult to interpret, but
the attackers seem to be getting the worst of it.

These and comparable scenes recur again and again on the
memorial stones of Gotland, and still wider throughout the viking
lands and colonies. The story of Sigurd the dragon-killer was a
particular favourite, and would persist in a different medium,
woodcarving, till well after the end of heathendom in Norway
(Plate 28). And there were other forms of pictorial art, for example
the scenes on the Oseberg wagon mentioned above, and the
processionals and depictions of hanged men on the Oseberg tapestry
(Plate 21). We read frequently of wall tapestries in great houses, and
sometimes of shields like the one a tipsy Egill Skallagrimsson spoiled
in the whey-tub at the Vidimyr bridal, pictured with old tales, set

with stones, and with twelve ounces of gold in the cross-pieces. But enough, one trusts, has been said to establish the distinction and distinctiveness of viking art.

All this while, along with religion and art, there was law in the northlands, pronounced and dispensed at the local Things, or courts, which grew up with the herreds or local communities they served; at the supra-Things associated with such large regional units as the Trondelag or Vestland in Norway, the demarcated spheres of Jutland and the Danish islands and possessions whose legal and administrative centres were towns like Viborg, Hedeby, and Ringsted, and likewise the main divisions of Sweden and Götaland, and the four Quarters of Iceland; or at such national assemblies for law as were established at Thingvellir in Iceland and, we think, at Gardar in the Eastern Settlement of Greenland. All such Things underwent the change from heathendom to Christianity (Gardar presumably came into being only in Christian times), and their laws were first committed to writing after this change. From the point of view of the student of the Viking Age this happened over-late. He has to wait upon documents of the twelfth and even the thirteenth century for a backward glance at eighth- to eleventh-century law, and this commits him to a highly subjective process of sheer speculation.[1] It was long held that a substantial body of custom and law could be recovered from saga sources, and indeed it can, but what is now very much in dispute is how reliable was the information transmitted to thirteenth- and fourteenth-century authors, how scrupulous were they in using it, and how far should we trust to them. The answer gets ever dustier. From *Konungsbók, Staðarhólsbók, Codex Regius, Járnsíða,* and *Jónsbók* we have a most detailed knowledge of Icelandic law in the thirteenth century.

---

[1] The literature is considerable. The following are important: K. Lehmann and Hans Schnorr von Carolsfeld, *Die Njáls-sage Insbesondere in Ihren Juristischen Bestandtheilen*, Berlin, 1883; Jón Jóhannesson, *Íslendinga Saga*, I, pp. 53–117, II, pp. 13–44, Reykjavík, 1956–8; Poul Jørgensen, *Retshistorie*, Nordisk Kultur, XVIII, 1933, and *Dansk Retshistorie*, Copenhagen, 1947; A. Taranger, *Udsigt over den norske rets historie*, Oslo, 1935. In English see L. M. Larson, *The Earliest Norwegian Laws*, New York, 1935; in French, Aa. Gregersen, *L'Islande, son Statut à travers les Ages*, Paris, 1937. The two close-packed works of Andreas Heusler, *Das Strafrecht der Isländersagas*, Leipzig, 1911, and 'Zum Isländischen Fehdewesen in der Sturlungazeit', *Abhandl. der K. Preuss. Akad. d. Wiss*, 1912, are rich in information, but draw some wrong general conclusions from it.

Sometimes the sagas in their portrayal of Söguöld Iceland (930–1030) agree with it, which tells us little, and sometimes not, which tells us still less, for it is no longer a tenable assumption that any saga whatsoever can be believed through thick and thin. Even if a saga is corroborated by other sagas or by a work of different intent like *Landnámabók*, we still have to satisfy ourselves that we are dealing with two independent sources rather than one source and a borrowing, and that the relevant portion of *Landnámabók* (or *Flateyjarbók* or *Heimskringla*) is itself open to proof or deserving of trust. This and similar considerations have played havoc with old-style romantic reconstructions of Viking Age law. Temple-law grows suspect when we doubt the existence of temples; warrior-law is unacceptable when recorded in sagas as unreliable as *Jómsvíkinga Saga* and *Hálfs Saga*; holmgang-law requires a hard look indeed as preserved for Iceland in *Kormáks Saga* and for Norway in *Egils Saga*. Court procedure as described in close detail in *Njáls Saga* is of the thirteenth century, not the late tenth and early eleventh, and so on.

Even so, we have a number of pointers to the place of law in Scandinavian life, including some from the Danelaw in England. It was associated with the Thing; it was the prerogative of all free men; and its operation was public. It would be naive to think that rank and wealth never swayed the courts or affected legal decisions. When the Danish invaders of Normandy were challenged from the bank of the river Eure and asked the name of their leader, they are said to have shouted back that he had no name. 'We are all equal.' Ganga-Hrolf's gloss on this has not been preserved—perhaps that equal they might be, but not all equally equal. But the free-born householder was sensitive to encroachment on his independence throughout the Scandinavian homelands and colonies, and never more so than in respect of his right to express his opinion in open assembly. It was his shout and clash of arms which gave validity to Thing-decisions. The law was very much in the public domain.

Areas of the law are easily guessed at. There must be regulations for establishing, conducting, and closing the Thing, and for discharging its business in due order and with proper safeguards. There were laws relating to frequent causes of civil dispute—boundary marks, hunting rights, flotsam and jetsam, the felling of trees and collection of firewood, infringement of grazing and the like; to libel, satire, calumny, the making of love songs, sheep-stealing, turning people's butter sour, and wooing their bees; to offences against the person, with an endless gradation of injury and penalty from cutting off a finger to cutting off a head. There were laws about the flouting of public morality, hurt to the community, and eventually about good old viking practices like *strandhögg* which had grown intolerable. There were laws dealing with fines, death, and outlawry. Increasingly there were laws about strangers and foreign nationals and the processes of trade. Religious observance, respect for holy places, the property of married women, and the huge and debatable sphere of manslaughter, self-defence, fair fight, burning indoors, killing under provocation, killing by night, in the king's presence, or in a holy place, unavowed killing, infamous killing, and murder most foul—eventually the law would have something to say about them all. The individual had his value, and the value could be fixed. Elaborate wergelds, sometimes counted in silver, sometimes in woollen, sometimes in cows, were the guarantee that a man might not be attacked with impunity in his person, family, property, or honour. Under all these heads the law spoke for the dignity of free men.

Literally spoke. Before the adoption of the roman alphabet the runic mode of northern inscription was not well suited to codex or chronicle (though one such codex is known: the *Codex Runicus*, AM 28 8vo), and the body of law must needs be carried in the memory. There was no mystery about this. First, there were private individuals knowledgeable in the law, and useful as advisers and consultants to those with a case to plead or defend. These, under one title or another, were lawmen. Second, in Iceland in particular we hear a good deal about the lawspeaker, an elected official whose business it was to hold the law in memory and recite one-third of it each year for three years at the main assembly. He was a speaking codex (no one, of course, would claim that he had no written aids to memory), the ultimate authority, and we know the names of those Icelanders who held the office from 930 to the end of the Republic in 1262–4. They make an impressive list. A grounding in law was part of a chieftain's education and contributory to his influence and power. And while the bondi depended on the law to make his life safer and easier, the law depended on the goodwill and participation of the bondi to make it operative. Theirs was a happy and mutually profitable partnership, still further improved when much of the law was christianized.

Legal procedure was far from perfect—but when was it otherwise? The enforcement of sentence was sometimes difficult, and occasionally impossible. There was a strong emphasis on the litigants themselves—too much depended on their private initiative and energy, and the backing they could command. There is evidence from Norway, Sweden, and Iceland that a litigant could appeal, literally, to the sword when he considered that the forms of law were inadequate in an affair affecting his honour. Yet on the whole the northern peoples were obedient to the rule of law, enjoyed its benefits in respect of their persons and property, and found it a stabilizer of their social order from king and chieftain to bondi and thrall. What might appear classic evidence of a wholesale flouting of law, legal procedure, and the Thing—namely, the tale of feud and blood-vengeance unfolded by the Icelandic sagas—on reflection proves to be nothing of the kind, first because of the fictional nature of a good part of it, and second because in any case the writers of sagas were not concerned with the law's successes and unspectacular benefits, but with its infrequent *causes célèbres*. In other words, even if we take saga evidence at its face value, our conclusion must be that the Icelanders were the same law-abiding and litigious people during the viking centuries that they are today. As for the Scandinavian peoples in general, their respect for law, their insistence upon its public and democratic exercise at the Thing, and its validity for all free men, together with their evolution of a primitive and exportable jury system, is one of the distinctive features of their culture throughout the Viking Age, eloquent of the value they set on the individual man and woman, and the enlightened pragmatism of their thinking.

And now, with three chapters on the Scandinavian Community, its geography, race, language, social structure, means of livelihood, religion, art, and law behind us, and some account rendered of the Viking Age at home and the viking movement abroad, the temptation is strong to offer generalizations about the viking himself, produce a 'typical' figure, and prop him against the museum wall with his catalogue number and descriptive label. It is a temptation to be resisted because of its limiting and misleading consequences. Harald Hardradi, who waged war from Asia Minor to Stamford Bridge for thirty-five years, was a viking; so was his father Sigurd Sow, who stayed at home and counted haystacks. Hastein, who led the Great Army of the Danes into England in the early 890s, was a viking; so was Ottar, who came peaceably to his lord king Alfred's court with walrus tusks and lessons in northern geography. The men who destroyed churches in England, Ireland, and France were vikings; so were the woodcarvers of Oseberg and the metalworkers of Mammen. The men who said 'With law shall the land be built up and with lawlessness wasted away' were vikings; so were the practisers and curtailers of blood-feud, the profit-makers and those who robbed them of profit, the explorers and colonizers, the shapers of verse-forms and makers of legends. The kings and their counsellors who brought the Scandinavian countries within the boundaries of Christian Europe were vikings. In short, the viking is the aggregate of this book and recalcitrant to summary.

However, most peoples and most ages nourish an image which they appear to prize, and by which posterity seeks to define their peculiar quality. There is no lack of mirrors for the Viking Age, held up by southern chroniclers and northern skalds and story-tellers alike. When Rognvald Kali, jarl of Orkney 1135–58, listed his personal accomplishments he versified within a tradition. 'I am a keen player at *tafl* ['tables', a hunt-game sometimes confused with chess]; nine skills I know; hardly will I make a mistake with runes, I have books and crafts constantly in hand; I can glide on skis, shoot and row, to meet any occasion; I am master of the two arts of harping and poetry.' It was an illuminating remark attributed to king Harald Hardradi of Norway about bishop Gizur Isleifsson of Iceland, that he was fit to be a king, a leader of vikings, or a bishop. As for manly virtue, the favourite themes of poets are valour, loyalty, open-handedness. When the greatest of northern poets, the Icelander Egill Skallagrimsson, set out to praise Eirik Blood-axe in his 'Head-ransom', he concentrated on Eirik's battles in Norway and abroad:

> Swordmetal pealed
> On rim of shield;
> Strife round him reeled
> Who ranged that field.
> Heard was the yell
> Of bladefury fell,
> Ironstorm's knell
> Past far sea's swell.

> King reddened sword,
> Came ravens a horde.
> Bright lifeblood outpoured
> As shafts flew abroad.
> Scots' scourge bade feed
> Trollwife's wolfsteed,
> Hel trod with her feet
> The eagles' nightmeat—

and drove the praise home with his twin refrains:

Bright fame he gat,   Eirik o'er sea
Eirik from that.   Paid the wolves' fee.[1]

In the paean to manly virtue which Egill composed for the friend of
his heart, Arinbjorn the hersir, it is his staunchness and good faith
he celebrates, along with his generosity:

There stood one   He's cruel to wealth
Staunch beside me,   Who dwells in the Firths;
Better than many   Dread enemy
A foe to money;   Of Draupnir's kin;
True friend of mine   And a stern foe
I'm free to trust in,   To bracelets stands;
Glorious grown   Fatal to rings,
In every counsel.   And treasure's bane.

Without qualities like these, and an attendant good fortune (for
'Good parts are one thing, good luck another'), it was hard for a man
to win good report, especially from the skalds. But the most
significant source of life's wisdom in the viking north will be found
not in narrative verse or public eulogy, but in the gnomic poetry of
the Poetic Edda, and there, chiefly, in the *Hávamál*, the Sayings of
the High One, i.e. Odinn. This is a fairly long poem of its kind,
containing 164 verses or stanzas, and although it passed through
several recensions before it was committed to vellum in the thirteenth
century, it is agreed that much or even most of it was transmitted
by oral tradition from heathen times. Its precepts are strikingly
unconsonant with popular conceptions of the Viking, whether as a
superhuman hero and devotee of Wyrd, hell-bent on doom and
destruction, and quitting life with a jest or laconic aphorism; as a
pure-blooded, clean-living, noble-thoughted nordic gentleman,
looking with innocent blue eyes on the tortuous corruptions of his
southern neighbours; or even a piratical, bloodthirsty, loot-laden
rapist, whose favourite tipple was mead quaffed from a dead enemy's
brainpan. The maxims, directives, warnings, and concealed pro-

---

[1] The rhymes here represent the rhyme-scheme of the original poem.
In Scandinavian court metre, *dróttkvæðr háttr*, rhyme and assonance are to be
found only within the line, the lines themselves being linked by alliteration
(see the verse on page 414). Rhymed verse, *runhenda* metre, would seem to be
Egill's own invention, *c.* 948, and may derive from the Old English rhymed
verse, and still more the rhymed Latin hymns (themselves owing something
to Irish-Latin hymns), which Egil presumably heard during his earlier stay in
king Athelstan's court. For a brief bibliography see my *Egil's Saga*, p. 15, n. 20.

verbs of early tenth-century Norway and Iceland, as they are preserved in the High One's wisdom, are above all prudential. The question is, How shall a man conduct himself so that his life may be reasonably happy and reasonably successful, reasonably blest with friends, reasonably useful to the community, and reasonably free of harmful entanglements? The freely but, I hope, reasonably rendered verses which follow are part of the answer.

Before proceeding up the hall, study all the doorways. You never know when an enemy will be present.

A guest needs water, towel, and a welcome, a warm word if he can get it, and the right sort of entertainment.

There is no better load a man can carry than much commonsense; no worse than too much drink.

A man of mark should be reticent, thoughtful, and brave in battle. Everyone should be happy and cheerful till he reaches the end.

Only a fool lies awake all night and broods over his problems. When morning comes he is worn-out, and his troubles the same as before.

Only a fool thinks all who smile with him are friends. He will find when he reaches the law-court how few real backers he has.

Better a house of your own, however small it be. Everyone is *somebody* at home. Two goats and a poor-roofed cot are better than begging.

Out in the fields a man should never be parted from his weapons. No one knows when a man in the open has need of a spear.

On the other hand, we must cultivate the good life, friends and company. We can do this and still keep our wits about us.

A man should not be grudging of the money he makes. Often what we intend for those we love is laid up for those we dislike. Matters frequently turn out worse than we expect.

Be a friend to your friend; match gift with gift. Meet smiles with smiles, and lies with dissimulation.

I was young once and walked by myself, and lost my way. I knew myself rich when I found a comrade. Man's joy is in man.

Generous and brave men get the best out of life; they seldom bring harassments on themselves. But a coward fears everything, and a miser groans at a gift.

Out in the fields I gave my clothes to two scarecrows. They thought themselves champions once they had trappings. A naked man is shorn of confidence.

A big gift is not necessary. Esteem can often be bought on the cheap. With half a loaf and a tilted bottle I have gained a companion.

A man should be moderately wise, never too wise. He who does not know his fate in advance is freest of care.

A man with few helpers must rise early and look to his work. A late-morning sleeper carries a heavy handicap. Keenness is halfway to riches.

Confide in one, never in two. Confide in three and the whole world knows.

Life is its own good. Take care to enjoy it and leave a good name behind. The best thing in life is to be alive and happy.

The lame can ride a horse, a man without hands herd sheep; the deaf can fight and prevail, it is better to be blind than burn [i.e. be cremated because dead]. A corpse is useless to everyone.

It is good to have a son, though he be born late, after the death of his father. Seldom will a memorial stand by the roadside unless kin erect it for kin.

Cattle die, kinsfolk die, we ourselves must die. One thing I know will never die—the dead man's reputation.

Praise no day until evening, no wife before her cremation, no sword till tested, no maid before marriage, no ice till crossed, no ale till it's drunk.

In view of the honourable position accorded to women in northern society, the *Hávamál* poet sounds less than cordial to them. Instead of the warm and often moving tributes to mothers, wives, sisters, on the runic stones, the brief utterances of love and loss, here are warning tugs at our sleeve.

No one should trust the words of a girl or what a married woman says. Their hearts have been shaped on a turning wheel, and inconstancy dwells in their breasts.

He who would win a woman's love must speak her fair and offer presents, praise the lovely lady's figure. It is the flatterer who carries the day.

Great love turns the sons of men from wise men into fools.

Be cautious, but not too cautious. Above all be cautious with ale or another man's wife. And, third, watch out that thieves don't make a fool of you.

And finally a curious injunction as to the gods:

Better no prayers than excessive offerings: a gift always seeks a recompense. Better no offering than excessive sacrifice. So declared Thundr (Odinn) before man's memory began.

These and the similar admonitions of *Sigrdrífumál*, *Reginsmál*, and *Grógaldr* are the work of realists. They come from men who drive their cows to a hard market. 'Don't argue with a fool, you have more to lose than he—Be patient with your kinsfolk, however exasperating they appear—Don't get involved with a married woman, and steer clear of female gossip—Never start a journey on an empty belly—A living dog is better than a dead lion—Marry a bargain, buy at a profit—Don't live to yourself, this makes you ingrown and uninformed.' There is no fine excess in any of this, no striking of attitudes. The *Hávamál* is a guide to conduct not to virtue. At best it commends enlightened self-interest. The absence of moral sanction has been many times noted; law and tradition are hardly mentioned; religion, as distinct from mythology, cuts little ice. A man is heard at the bar of public opinion; the verdict is that of a jury of neighbours. Folk wisdom, peasant cunning, mercantile caution, and the soldier's prejudice against being caught with his trousers down, have all contributed to the cool pragmatism of the gnomic poems. They are not the whole story, but serve as a corrective to high-flown sentiment and the heroic ideal, which also have their place. The northern ethos was the product of northern life and fully explicable in the setting of the Viking Age and viking movement, whose characteristics have now been set forth.

2. Svein Forkbeard, Saint Olaf, and Knut the Great

WHEN IN THE MILLENNIAL YEAR 1000 KING OLAF
Tryggvason in his scarlet cloak leapt from the gunwale of the *Long
Serpent* at Svold, and the kingdom of Norway broke from his hand,
the lords of three realms inherited. Olaf Skötkonung of Sweden
made the long-desired western advance into the former Gautish
coastal territories of Ranrike-Bohuslän and into the eastern districts
of the Trondelag. Jarl Eirik of Hladir, the magnanimous, temperate
son of that immoderate lover of gods, gold, and women, jarl Hakon
Sigurdarson, received the coastal provinces of the west from far-
away Halogaland beyond the Polar Circle in the north to the green
fields and early harvests of the Jaeder and Agdir in the south. To
Svein Forkbeard of Denmark, the shrewd and purposeful engineer of
the confederacy which destroyed the Norwegian Olaf, came the
traditional areas of Danish overlordship in the Vik. In fact, his gains
were more substantial than this. Jarl Eirik was his liegeman and son-
in-law, and while in the viking world it was not always safe to trust
to such relationships (Olaf Tryggvason was Svein's brother-in-law,
which helped him not at all), jarl Eirik's loyalty to Svein, as to his
son Knut after him, was as absolute as it was profitable. King Olaf
of Sweden entrusted part of his Norwegian territory to jarl Eirik's
brother Svein, and since Eirik seems to have been the ablest, as he
was certainly the most celebrated of all those brothers, it would
seem to follow that king Svein's influence throughout much of
Norway was strong indeed. And a firm hold there not only strengthened Denmark in a Scandinavian context; it made possible a
stepping-up of Svein's ambitions in respect of England.

After the expulsion of Eirik Blood-axe from York in 954, his
heroic yet somehow paltry death, and the seizure of Northumbria by

the English king Eadred, England was to enjoy a quarter of a century's freedom from Norse aggression. This fortunate period ended in 980. England's western neighbour Wales had enjoyed her respite earlier, from 918 till 952, when the death of one of the most renowned of Welsh kings, Hywel Dda ('the Good'), offered the Norsemen of Dublin and then of Limerick, too, together with their compatriots in Man, opportunities for gain and adventure they were prompt to make use of. The raids grew worse after 980; the cathedral of St. David's in Dyfed was sacked four times between 982 and 989; and Norse armies several times espoused a cause of profit on behalf of one scuffling Welsh prince or another. It is probable that they had more success in the southern half of the country during these fifty years than written history records, and, as in Ireland, fostered along the South Wales seaboard small marts and havens. In England as in Wales the renewal of Norse activity coincided with, or was inspired by, a change for the worse in rulers. The strong Eadred had been followed after the four-year interlude of Eadwig the All-fair by the strong Edgar in 959. Out of his strength he could treat the Danes in England at once generously and firmly. They need no longer be the alien people of a conquered province, but fellow subjects with the English of an English king. They would serve him in war and accept their lay and ecclesiastical lords at his hand. The king's peace would be as real in the Danelaw (it would shortly acquire this title) as in Wessex and Mercia, but their proved loyalty would be rewarded with an ungrudging recognition of Danish law and custom, and the right to manage regional affairs in their own way. On the face of it, self-interest if nothing better should make them a contented part of the English realm. Edgar died in 975 and was followed by his son Edward, of whom we know little save that he was young, unstable, resented by many, murdered in 978, and in time dubbed saint and martyr. He was succeeded by his 12-year-old brother Ethelred, from his accession to our own day one of the most fiercely reprehended of English monarchs. It was early in his disturbed, unhappy reign (978–1016) that the viking scourge again fell upon England.

The situation was a familiar one. In Denmark and the neighbouring north political change and material needs encouraged adventurers and restless men to try their hand at the old courses just when their natural prey invited assault by internal weakness and irresolution. But by now Normandy and the Frankish lands were closed to them, and the Danelaw was occupied by their own kith and kin; so the raids of the early 980s were almost all directed against the coast-line from Hampshire round to Cheshire, and were carried out by bands of limited size. But a change was heralded by Svein's succession to the Danish throne in 985 or soon thereafter. At what point in time Svein began to think of subduing England, as distinct from plunder-ing it, no one can say—whether the idea came to him slowly as he first heard tell of and then witnessed for himself the lack of will in England under Ethelred, or whether it was the destruction of Olaf Tryggvason in the year 1000 and the murder of his own sister in the St. Brice's day massacre of November 1002 which half led, half drove him to a course of action as gratifying to his ambitions as to his need for revenge. In any case the contrast between the calculating and purposeful Svein and the uncounselled and fitful Ethelred is as sharp as the differing fates of their peoples.

But first the young Olaf Tryggvason, trained in arms among the Rus of Novgorod and graduated to piracy in the Baltic, hung in the wings awaiting his tempestuous entrance upon the English scene. Trustworthy details of his early exploits there are lacking in both English and Norse sources. The battle of Maldon, where one version of the *Anglo-Saxon Chronicle* (A) puts Olaf (Unlaf, Anlaf) in command of the invading Norsemen, passed unmentioned in northern verse and saga. Byrhtnoth's brave but as it turned out foolhardy stand against overwhelming odds, his promise to glut the host with spear and sword and hard battle-play instead of the gold they demanded, found no remembrancer among the victors—and few imitators among the vanquished. Olaf's campaign over, he and Ethelred made a treaty together which offers valuable information about trade and shipping customs of the time (see p. 163 above), stipulates that all past offences between the peoples should be dismissed from mind, and concludes with an unadorned statement that 22,000 pounds of gold and silver have been paid to the vikings in exchange for peace.[1] The *Chronicle* under the same year speaks of a payment of 10,000 pounds. If there was one thing that everyone had learned by this time, whether payers or paid, it was that the truce resultant upon a forced tribute would be brief. Olaf Tryggvason is not heard of in England for a couple of years, but he would be back in 994, and in the meantime part of the viking force campaigned on, and two main

[1] Liebermann: *Gesetze der Angelsachsen*, Halle, 1903–16, I, 220 ff.

attempts to defeat them foundered on the treachery or cowardice of English leaders in the field.

Olaf Tryggvason, we have said, reappeared to plague England in 994. He had warships, warriors, and as ally king Svein Forkbeard of Denmark. The pattern of *víking* was changing when great kings and kings-to-be rather than the old-style captains brought their wave-stallions over the ocean's back to England. There are indications that already there were English noblemen prepared to take Svein as their king—men who could see no other remedy for the ineptitude of Ethelred. The martial glory of Alfred's line was now tarnished; in high places there was malaise where there should be judgement and valour; and the commonalty lost heart when half-heartedly led. But the storm of 994 was weathered, though at heavy price, because the alliance of Olaf and Svein was between two destined enemies and in the nature of things could not persist. Also, the men of London defended their city so bravely that the vikings failed in their attempt to burn it and suffered heavy casualties. Fetched up hard, they followed their usual practice, abandoned the siege, harried in Essex, Kent, Sussex, and Hampshire, found themselves mounts, and rode far and wide on errands of plunder and destruction. The English paid 16,000 pounds as the price of peace, and provisioned the host from the whole kingdom of Wessex. Olaf and Svein parted at once. The Dane returned home by way of Wales and Man, pillaging as he went. He was not the man to forget England, and would return. Olaf was baptized and left England for good. After 995 his fate lay in Norway.

While these two fleeting allies settled into their more natural role of enemies back home, the exploitation of English weakness continued. In the three years 997–9 a Danish army ravaged the coasts of Wessex almost at will, and one of the unhappiest entries in the *Chronicle* expresses the exasperation and dismay of the inhabitants there:

999. In this year the host again came round into the Thames, and so up the Medway to Rochester. They were opposed by the Kentish levies, and a sharp encounter took place: but alas! all too quickly they turned and fled, because they did not get the support they should have had, and the Danes had possession of the place of slaughter, and got horses and rode far and wide as they pleased, destroying and laying waste almost the whole of West Kent. Then the king with his counsellors decided to advance against them with both naval and

and levies; but when the ships were ready there was delay from day to day, which was very galling for the unhappy sailors manning the vessels. Time after time the more urgent a thing was the greater was the delay from one hour to the next, and all the while they were allowing the strength of their enemies to increase; and as they kept retreating from the sea, so the enemy followed close on their heels. So in the end these naval and land preparations were a complete failure, and succeeded only in adding to the distress of the people, wasting money, and encouraging their enemy. (Trans. Garmonsway.)

In the summer of 1000 the host crossed over to 'Richard's realm' of Normandy. Till 991 Normandy had been an ever-open point of repair for viking crews operating against England. That year Ethelred and Duke Richard I at the Pope's urging agreed not to comfort or harbour each other's enemies, but whether the agreement had much force or duration is open to question. There is no evidence that Duke Richard II received the Danes other than amicably in 1000. In 1001 they returned to Wessex on a course of depredation which ended only when Ethelred in the following year paid 24,000 pounds for the customary Danish pledge of peace. Within weeks he had married Duke Richard's sister Emma, probably out of a desire to improve his political relations with Normandy, but we have a hint that little improvement took place.[1] Norman sympathy for their not-so-distant blood-brothers in Scandinavia was natural and strong. Still, if Ethelred's Norman marriage brought no immediate balm to his hurt and griefs, it would in the long run provide him with a refuge. His other main deed of 1002 brought unrelieved disaster. This was his order for 'all the Danish people who were in England to be slain on St. Brice's day [November 13]', because he had been informed, says the *Chronicle*, that they were planning to kill him and his counsellors by treachery, and then seize his kingdom. Whether the report was fantasy, or the belated excuse for a vile and stupid deed, we cannot say. In any case the Danes of the Danelaw were practically immune from the possibility of massacre, but a massacre of kinds there was (we have a reference to such at Oxford), and among the victims tradition places king Svein's sister, the lady Gunnhild.

Svein's onslaught on England in 1003–5 was not aimed at securing a kingdom. It was his gesture of revenge, typically enough com-

[1] In William of Jumièges, who gives credit to a tradition that an English army shortly afterwards attacked the Cotentin.

bining the blood-feud with monetary profit. Exeter, Wilton, Salisbury, Norwich, and Thetford were among the towns sacked, and the only effective resistance came from the Anglo-Dane Ulfkell [Ulfcytel] Snilling, who fell upon the invaders after the sack of Thetford. Only English slackness in not carrying out Ulfkell's orders to cut to pieces the ships of the Danes saved the day for them, and 'they themselves admitted that they had never met with harder hand-play in England than Ulfcytel gave them'. So easily might the conquering course of Danish Svein have ended in death or ignominy. The Danes withdrew from England in the famine year of 1005, but were back in 1006 on a mission of challenge and bravado. The language of the *Chronicle* is ironic as it tells of the vikings' safe base in Wight, their well-stocked food-depot at Reading, of the great deeds threatened by the English if the host ever got as far as Cuckhamsley Knob on the Wiltshire downs, and how the host called their bluff not only by getting there but by insolently inviting attack, how they quickly put the levies to flight, and defying all prophecy rode back to the sea past the gates of Winchester, whose citizens beheld them, arrogant and confident, bringing provisions and treasures from more than fifty miles inland. This happened at midwinter, while Ethelred was meditating his Christmas fare in Shropshire. But he bestirred himself, and in 1007 paid the Danes a tribute of 36,000 pounds in return for peace, along with provisions and supplies gathered from all parts of the kingdom. With this prodigious addition to the booty they had already seized, the Danes were pleased to leave England.

The peace lasted two years. Ethelred took two steps to prepare for the next invasion, but as so often they went awry. He sought to stiffen his defences by appointing an ealdorman for Mercia, but chose the most notorious double-dealer of the age, Eadric Streona. And he tried to build a fleet strong enough to defeat anything the Danes could sail against him. According to the *Chronicle* every unit of 300 hides throughout the kingdom was to furnish the king with a warship,[1] and every unit of eight hides provide a helm and corslet. The fleet was ready early in 1009, assembled off Sandwich, and was quickly made ineffective by a grotesque combination of accusation, flight, selfishness, indiscipline, rivalry and self-mutilation. With

[1] For a discussion of what Earle called 'a tantalizing annal' see Earle and Plummer, *Two Saxon Chronicles*, II, 185-6. The variants are offered there, I, 138, and by Garmonsway, p. 138.

eighty ships burned and twenty defected, Ethelred, his ealdormen and counsellors, in the words of the *Chronicle*, 'went home'. The remaining ships were fetched to London, and the facilities off Sandwich abandoned to the Danes, who dropped anchor there on 1 August.

It was a formidable host which began in its confident way to harry the near-by countryside that same autumn. Unlike the armies of the sons of Ragnar a century and a half before, it was not composed in substantial measure of part-time soldiers hankering after a farm of their own. These were professionals. Their leaders in the absence of Svein were two famous brothers, Thorkell the Tall and Hemming, and a more shadowy figure, Eilaf the brother of jarl Ulf, who later (Ulf, that is) married Svein's daughter Estrid and became the father of king Svein Estridsson or Ulfsson and the progenitor of the royal line of Denmark to our own day. Here too we must mention that formidable and puzzling demonstration of kingly power in Denmark which till recently was held to bear closely on the contemporary Viking assaults on England: the appearance of timber-and-earthwork fortresses of a scale and model hitherto unknown there. Four such are known, at Trelleborg near Slagelse in West Zealand, at Aggersborg on the Limfjord in North Jutland, at Fyrkat near Hobro in East Jutland, and at Nonnebakken in the town of Odense on Fyn. All four are built to a pattern, and consist of a symmetrical grouping of wooden houses within a rampart. At Trelleborg there were sixteen such houses, arranged in groups of four, each four forming a hollow square, with the full count of sixteen forming yet another and larger square. Fyrkat and Nonnebakken likewise had sixteen houses, Aggersborg had forty-eight. There are differences in the size of the houses from fort to fort (all are based on the roman foot of 29.57 cm. modified to 29.33: Aggersborg, 110 such feet, or *c.* 33 metres; Trelleborg, 100 such feet; and Fyrkat, 96), but within each fort they are uniform.[1]

---

[1] Literature: P. Norlund, *Trelleborg*, 1956; C. G. Schultz, 'Aggersborg, vikingeleiren ved Limfjorden', *Fra Nat. Mus. Arbbejdsmark*, 1949; Olaf Olsen, 'Trelleborg Problemer', in *Scandia* 28, 1962; *Fyrkat. En jysk vikingeborg*. I. *Borgen og Bebyggelsen*, by Olaf Olsen and Holger Schmidt, etc. II. *Oldsagerne og Gravpladsen*, by Else Roesdahl, etc. *Nordiske fortidsminder*, 1977. There is an exposition of the 'very complicated issues' involving Harald, Svein, Trelleborg, Fyrkat, etc., by Olaf Olsen in *Skalk*, 1980, Nr. 3, pp. 18–26, and a discussion in Roesdahl, *Viking Age Denmark*, 1982, pp. 147–55.

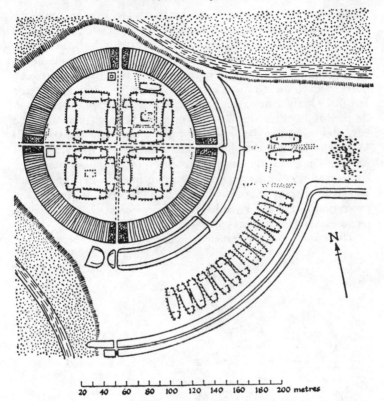

54. TRELLEBORG: A PLAN OF THE STRONGHOLD

Trelleborg, the first found and most extensively excavated of these forts, stands in a good defensive position on a piece of raised ground between two navigable streams, the Vaarbyå and Tudeå, which join here before flowing another two miles or so into the Great Belt between Zealand and Fyn. The site was improved by levelling and filling-in before building took place. The natural defences provided by the rivers and an expanse of swampy or flooded ground north, west, and south-west, were reinforced by a circular earth rampart, roughly 17 metres thick and almost 7 metres high, strengthened with palisades and traversed with stout timber. There were four gateways, set diametrically opposite each other, joined by roadways north by south and east by west (the orientation of Trelleborg is a little to the east of north, but the terms are convenient); these intersected at the centre of the house-blocks. The gateways were strengthened against earth-slip by a 6-metre-deep course of big stones throughout the width of the rampart. The outer face of the rampart was provided with various deterrent features. On the land side it had the additional safeguard of a wide, deep moat. But even this was not considered enough, and this same east and south-east land side was given an outer ward, with a lower rampart and a shallower ditch. Trelleborg today, with its ramparts in good trim, and the position of the house post-holes touched in with concrete, gives a strong impression of its former power, its domination of the land and quick access to the sea, the protection it afforded its ships from storm or sudden attack, the menace and mobility of its garrison.

The diameter of the fort proper, the inner ward, is 136 metres.

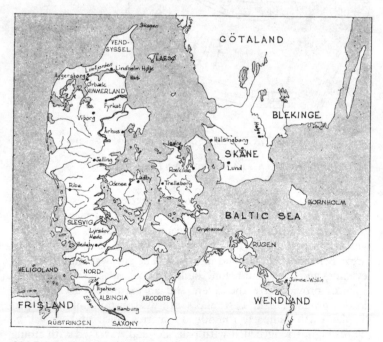

MAP 15.   DENMARK IN THE VIKING AGE

Most of this was occupied by the sixteen houses in their four hollow squares. A few smaller buildings, including what look like guard-rooms by the north and west gates, hardly affect the overall symmetry. The houses were stave-built of upright planks, and an outside row of slightly inward-leaning posts helped support the roof. The houses were boat-shaped, that is, with curved side-walls and straight end-walls, and internally were divided into three sections, the largest in the centre. There are further houses in the outer ward, thirteen of them set radially within the curved area (see plan), and two outside the inner moat and the eastern gate of the inner rampart. All these houses are of the same kind as the inner sixteen, except that the thirteen are not arranged in squares, and they are smaller by one-tenth, i.e. they are 90 roman feet in length, not 100. Outwards of the other two houses is the fort cemetery, parts of it older than the fort. A preponderance of skeletons were those of men of military age, which does not mean that they were all full-time military men. There were also a few old people and a few children buried there; and, significantly, a number of women. The grave orientations were east by west, but this in itself is not indicative of Christian practice. Grave goods were scanty but diverse. There were weapons (among them a longhorned axe-blade inlaid with silver, from around the year 1000), smith's tools, agricultural implements, women's jewellery and articles for spinning and weaving.

What, then, was Trelleborg? And, by analogy, what were Fyrkat, Aggersborg and Nonnebakken? Together with what has recently come to light about such great works as the Danevirke and Hedeby, the ambitious bridge-building at Risby and Ravning Enge, the Kanhave canal, and the anti-ship defences on Danish fjords and rivers, they invited a new assessment of Danish technical skills and the royal power necessary to exploit them *c.* 970–1020. Svein Forkbeard was an obvious candidate, and the four fortresses were seen as barracks and training-camps for soldiers bound for the English wars, and at the same time his guarantee against disorder, rebellion, even usurpation during his absence abroad (after all, had he not expelled his own father Harald Bluetooth from his throne and country no long time before?). Latterly the archaeological evidence has been re-assessed. There is no direct evidence of the fortresses' connection with the English wars, and they have been seen not as Svein's but as his father Harald's gesture of both benevolent and intimidatory power, controlling Denmark's interior lines of communication, housing the king's officers, moneyers, craftsmen, safeguarding his possessions, and by the strategic placing of their garrisons showing a protective arm to the loyal and a mailed fist to the disaffected. Whoever the royal architect, serious problems remain—not the least of them the very short period during which the strongholds were in use—twenty or thirty years at most, and the biggest, Aggersborg, not so much as completed. If they were overtaken by events, we can only guess, unconvincingly, at what those events were.

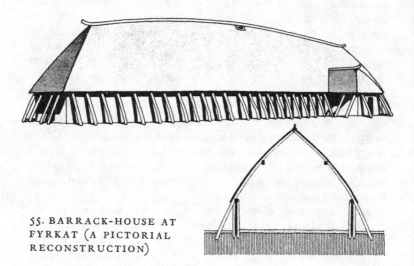

55. BARRACK-HOUSE AT
FYRKAT (A PICTORIAL
RECONSTRUCTION)

But to proceed with king Svein and his policy of warfare and profit across the North Sea. The 'profit' will bear underlining. We have seen (p. 265 above) how supplies of kufic silver were diminishing in the second half of the tenth century, and practically dried up at the beginning of the eleventh. The north needed silver in quantities, and the brigand-like commonsense of Svein told him where and how to get it: in tribute from a disorganized, disheartened, and immensely wealthy England. The process had started in 980, and in person or through his approval of other captains Svein was continuously involved in it from 994 till the day of his death in 1013. To attack the unhappy country was to be paid to go away, and to be paid to go away kept your army in being till you attacked again. The weight of tribute still astonishes: 16,000 pounds in 994, 24,000 in 1002, 36,000 in 1007, 48,000 in 1012: literally, England paid for her conquest with her own money. Not all the tribute took the form of minted coins. Brooches, arm-rings, torques, ingots—nothing came amiss so long as it was silver.[1] The men whose unrelenting arms levered away these vast and precious burthens were not all Danes; soldiers of fortune and mercenaries came in from every Scandinavian land. There are memorial stones in Sweden to warriors who campaigned and, some of them, died in England. There are five Swedish stones which tell of men who received tribute there, like that at Grinda in Södermanland raised to a brave father, Gudvi, who 'went west to England and received a share of the geld'; or that at Väsby informing us that 'Ali raised this stone in memory of himself. He received Knut's geld in England. God save his soul'; or the most famous and informative of all, the Borrestad stone from Orkestad in Uppland: 'Karsi and Gerbjorn had this stone raised after Ulf their father. God and God's Mother help his soul! But Ulf received danegeld three times in England. The first was that which Tosti paid. Then Thorkell paid. Then Knut paid.' Tosti has by some been assumed to be the Swedish father of that Sigrid the Haughty (Stórráða: see p. 136, n. 1, above) whom, if she existed, Olaf Tryggvason (we fear) spurned and Svein Forkbeard (we trust) married; Thorkell was Thorkell the Tall; and Knut was Knut the Great. The wealth thus extorted flowed back to all the Scandinavian lands, to the island of Gotland, mainland Sweden and Denmark, in smaller measure to Norway, and is not without trace in the Atlantic island dependencies.[2] The rapid increase of Anglo-Saxon coins in Scandin-

[1] It is not easy to restrict one's illustration to the English campaigns, because the island of Gotland is in every sense the most fruitful soil for such. Hoards discovered there up to 1946 contained more than 570 ornaments, many of them manufactured at home from foreign bullion; more than 2,300 pieces of silver in such forms as rods, bars, and rings; 93,000 whole coins and 16,600 fragments of coins, only three of which are not silver. All this came from abroad, most of it from the east, but it probably indicates the mixed nature of English and Frankish tribute, too. See P. H. Sawyer, *The Age of the Vikings* (1971) for an extended treatment in Chapter Three, 'Treasure'. New hoards continue to be found in Scandinavia.

[2] It has been suggested (Sawyer, 1962, pp. 98–9, and 1971, pp. 100–1), that the scarcity in Scandinavian hoards of English coins of the ninth century may be due to the circumstance that the money may have been used in England to acquire land for intending settlers. The idea has been well received in some quarters, but there is no positive evidence for it. The

avian hoards dates from the beginning of Ethelred's reign. At first the bulk of it represents tribute; but after Knut's conquest of the realm it represents the money raised in England to pay his soldiers' wages. The danegeld of 1018 reached the unparalleled total of 72,000 pounds over all England, plus a sum variously stated to be 10,500 or 11,000 pounds from the citizens of London. From 1012 onwards there was an annual tax or danegeld raised in England, and under Knut the army-tax (*heregeld*) took precedence of all other taxes. The *Chronicle* under 1040 informs us that the rate of pay in the naval force maintained by the Danish king was eight marks to a rowlock. While allowance for the differing sizes of sixteen ships is difficult (Knut is said to have had one showpiece of 120 oars), this would hardly have come to less than 3,000 pounds a year, and there were Knut's housecarles to be paid in addition. The flow of Anglo-Saxon coins into Scandinavia continued till 1051, when Edward the Confessor at last paid off his mercenaries.

Even though we abandon the silent witness of the four homeland fortresses, we have means enough to see the invading armies of Svein and Knut in fair perspective. First, there is the remarkably personal and emotive account of Anglo-Danish affairs given by the *Anglo-Saxon Chronicle* during the years of distress and mismanagement. Second are the large amounts of tribute and known rates of pay of the professional soldiers engaged in these impoverishing operations; and third, the contemporary influx of English money into Scandinavia revealed by the hoards discovered there.

Meantime the armies of 1009 were at work. Eastern Kent bought peace for 3,000 pounds, London showed its accustomed valour, repelling every attack, but thereafter the Danes cut swathes of destruction through the shires, burned Oxford, sacked Ipswich, and took heavy toll of the men of East Anglia and Cambridge at the pitched battle of Ringmere in 1010, where their old enemy Ulfkell Snilling stood firm, but the wretched Thurcytel with his 'mare's head' broke rank and saved life without honour by flight. Among the

---

Chronicle for 896 records how after the Danish defeats in 892–6 'the Danish host broke up, some to East Anglia, some to Northumbria, and those who were *feohlease* got themselves ships there and went south across the sea to the Seine'. It is unlikely that *feohlease* means 'moneyless', as Sawyer translates, with the implication that they sought money in order to settle; it is more likely to mean that they were without possessions or property in England, and so departed.

21. PICTURED TAPESTRY FROM OSEBERG. Apparently a procession. A depiction from not later than the mid-ninth century of costume, weapons, horses and their trappings, carts, birds and formal symbols.

22. FREY

23. THOR

24. A NORWEGIAN VIKING

25. ANIMAL HEAD (A LION?) FROM SHETELIG'S SLEIGH, OSEBERG. It has been suggested that these alarming heads were intended to frighten off evil spirits and give protection to those seated inside the four posts that bore them.

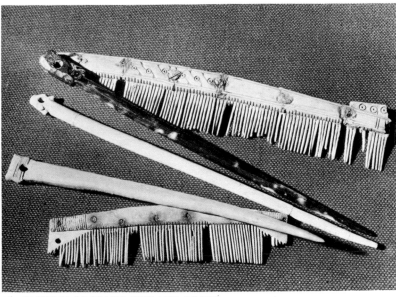

26. ARTICLES OF PEACE: PINS AND COMBS

27. ARTICLES OF WAR: AXE, STIRRUP, SWORD

29. TRELLEBORG TODAY. A view of the fort and its surroundings from the air.
The Great Belt in the background.

◀ 28. THE STORY OF SIGURD CARVED IN WOOD AT HYLESTAD. Reading from the
bottom right we see Sigurd and Reginn forging the sword Gram, the sword
breaking when tested on the anvil, and thereafter Sigurd using it to kill the dragon.
At the bottom left we see Sigurd roasting the dragon's heart while Reginn sleeps. He
burns his thumb and puts it, fresh from the dragon's heart, into his mouth, and at
once understands the language of the birds in the tree above him. Reginn is planning
to deceive him and secure for himself the dragon's treasure which we see loaded on
to Sigurd's horse Grani. He thrusts his sword through Reginn. After many disasters
Gunnar dies in the snake-pit, playing the harp with his toes.

30. THE DEATH OF ST OLAF AT STIKLARSTADIR

invaders, fighting under Thorkell the Tall's banner, was a thick-set young Norwegian, Olaf Haraldsson by name, of whom more would be heard later. The bitter fruits of Ringmere were that the Danes overran East Anglia, ravaged Thetford and Cambridge, and fared out with sword and fire to the shires of Oxford, Buckingham, and Bedford. There was hardly the show much less the reality of opposition. The *Chronicle* for 1010 depicts a country grown ripe for the taking:

Then they made their way back to the ships with their plunder; and when they were dispersing to the ships, then the levies should have been out, ready in case they should seek to go inland. Then, however, the levies were on their way home. And when the enemy was in the east, then our levies were mustered in the west; and when they were in the south, then our levies were in the north. Then all the councillors were summoned to the king, for a plan for the defence of the realm had to be devised then and there, but whatever course of action was decided upon it was not followed even for a single month. In the end there was no leader who was willing to raise levies, but each fled as quickly as he could; nor even in the end would one shire help another. (Trans. Garmonsway.)

The next year showed no improvement. When Canterbury and its archbishop fell into Danish hands in the autumn it was through treachery among the defenders. There had already been English overtures for a truce, but it was past Easter in 1012 before the full 48,000 pounds of tribute could be collected and paid over. For archbishop Ælfeah they demanded a separate ransom, which he would neither pay nor permit others to pay. The sequel was revolting. At an assembly of the army at Greenwich reminiscent or some drunken passage from the Fornaldarsögur of the north, they pelted him with bones and the heads of cattle till some more merciful ruffian crashed his axe against the old man's skull. Thorkell the Tall is said to have done his best to stop them, offering everything he possessed or might hope to lay hands on for Ælfeah's life— 'save only my ship'.[1] His failure to do so is thought to explain why on the dispersal of the Danish host later in the year he transferred his allegiance from Svein to king Ethelred, taking forty-five ships and their crews with him.

It has likewise been thought that Thorkell's defection was the

[1] Thietmar of Merseburg, *Chronicon*, ed. Holtzman, 1935, VII, 42–3.

spur which brought Svein to England the following summer. This does less than justice to Svein's cool-headedness. He had long shown himself a manipulator of men and events, and blest with a sense of timing. Danish pressure on England had been cumulative for more than twenty years, and between 1009 and 1012 it became intolerable. Given leadership, hope, and a cause, the English rank and file would have fought on doggedly, and maybe successfully; but all three were lacking. Despondency and defeat were in the air. The lesser Danish predators had completed their part of the 'Enterprise of England'; now it was the king's turn. The calculating Svein would be well satisfied to chastise Thorkell the Tall for desertion, or indeed ambition,[1] and bend him to his royal will, but this was not his main business, which was to make himself king of England. Nothing seems to have been left to chance. With a fleet reputed to have been as handsome as it was powerful, he set sail for Sandwich, proceeded from there to the Humber, then twenty miles up the Trent to Gainsborough in the heart of Danish England. It was his correct assumption that here he would be welcomed and safe. Earl Uhtred and all Northumbria submitted to him, likewise the people of Lindsey and the Five Boroughs, and soon afterwards all the Danes to the north of Watling Street. Leaving his ships and hostages in charge of his son Knut at Gainsborough, he took his mounted army through English Mercia, where for the first time they were allowed to harry, received the submission of Oxford and Winchester, and then attacked London. Here the ever-valiant citizens, strengthened by Ethelred's bodyguard and the crews of Thorkell the Tall, checked him heavily, but in the event to no purpose. Svein declined to batter his head against a fortified wall, and rode off to the submissive West Country. By the time he returned to Gainsborough the *Chronicle* records that the whole nation accepted him as full king. The Londoners' position had been rendered untenable; they sought terms and gave hostages, promised tribute and supplies. Ethelred, with no ally save Thorkell the Tall, sent his wife and sons

[1] A. Campbell, *Encomium Emmæ Reginæ*, Camden Third Series, 1949, p. lii, considers it highly improbable that Thorkell was ever in Svein's service or took any forces with him to England which could be considered part of Svein's army; but 'on the other hand, it is more than likely that his progress was regarded by Svein with disquiet, for the latter had himself long cherished designs upon England.' The *Encomium* is our most eloquent authority for the notion that Svein went to England at the persuasion of his warriors to chastise Thorkell's disloyalty (I, 2, pp. 10–11).

back to Normandy for safe keeping, and shortly after Christmas followed them there himself. Svein had arrived off Sandwich in late July, and now, five months later, he was master of all England.

Five weeks later he was dead. He was at most 55 years old when in the *Chronicle*'s impartial phrase he 'ended his days at Candlemas', 3 February 1014. He was one of the foremost viking kings. As a general and politician he had freed Hedeby from the Germans, increased Danish power in Wendland, gained authority over the Jomsvikings or whatever northern mercenaries gave rise to that contested name, disposed of Olaf Tryggvason and set jarl Eirik Hakonarson over those parts of Norway which he (and to a lesser extent the king of Sweden) did not rule directly; and finally he had conquered England. He favoured Christianity, but was tolerant of the heathen, and he brought wealth from abroad to enrich his dominions at home. Not least, he produced a son as able as himself, who would complete his work in England and Scandinavia, and it was not in Svein or any man of his time to know that this was a work which politically could not endure.

There was still a chance that England might be saved for Englishmen. Knut, to whom Svein's men now offered their allegiance, was at most 18 years old, his genius for management and opportunism immature, his experience of military command slight, and he had no lieutenant of stature at his side who could supply the unselfish support which the regent Guthorm gave to the 10-year-old Harald Fairhair or the tutelage which the 14-year-old Olaf Haraldsson received from Thorkell the Tall. And England, despite her twenty years' ravaging, was still strong and wealthy. For once the English acted quickly; they sent noblemen to Ethelred in Normandy inviting him to return and rule them again, more justly and wisely, and with a line drawn under the errors of the past. By April he was back and leading an army against the Danes and their allies in Lindsey. Knut, no doubt under advice, embarked his army and abandoned Lindsey to the resentful savagery of Ethelred. He sailed down the coast as far as Sandwich, where he mutilated his father's hostages before putting them ashore, and with this twofold legacy of horror and hatred behind him departed for Denmark. His elder brother Harald was king there, in succession to Svein, and friendship or self-interest induced him to help Knut win a kingdom of his own, elsewhere. An invasion force was assembled. It was Knut's good fortune to be joined by his brother-in-law jarl Eirik of Hladir, who as we have seen ruled so much of Norway by Danish permission. He was among the most seasoned warriors of the north, had practised viking early in Baltic waters, with his father was the victor at Hjorungavag, was credited with the sack of Aldeigjuborg in Russia, and according to Icelandic and Norwegian tradition played a prominent role in the sea-fight at Svold. By 1014 he had amassed considerable experience of men and state affairs. Content with his ancient title of jarl, loyal to the bonds of a profitable allegiance and kinship, he was the ideal *eaxlgestealla*, shoulder-comrade, of an ambitious but inexperienced young king. The enlistment of a second famous captain was more surprising. This was none other than Thorkell the Tall, who had gone over to Ethelred late in 1012 and given him faithful service ever since. After Ethelred's punitive expedition against Lindsey in 1014 Thorkell and his mercenaries were given a payment of 21,000 pounds, and it is hard to account for his prompt abandonment of a restored patron. It has been suggested that he had a slain brother to avenge upon the English, but Thorkell's mainspring was self-interest; he could read the times, and he never read them better than when he sailed for Denmark with the nine ships prepared to follow him and secured employment with Knut.

In the summer of 1015 when Knut's glittering menagerie of ships sailed for England those who should oppose him there had reverted to their normal malpractice. The sinister Eadric Streona for reasons unknown procured the murder of the two foremost noblemen belonging to the 'Seven Boroughs', Siferth and Morcar; king Ethelred abetted him by seizing their property and arresting Siferth's widow; Ethelred's son Edmund rescued the lady, married her in his father's despite, departed for the Five Boroughs, possessed himself of the property, and by consent of the inhabitants, equally resentful of Knut's desertion and Ethelred's revenge, made himself master there. At a time when unity was imperative the country was divided by ill feeling between Ethelred and his son and a feud between Edmund and Eadric. This may be the kind of situation Thorkell the Tall foresaw. In any case he was now on service with a compact, disciplined, and well-led army, which in September took the field in earnest. With treachery and distrust in the English air, they quickly made the weight of their arm known in Wessex and Warwickshire. The infamous Eadric came over to the Danish side with forty ships, and half the country was Knut's. Briefly Edmund combined with Uhtred of Northumbria to devastate Staffordshire, Shropshire, and Cheshire, but Knut carried the war northwards by way of Nottingham to York, and Uhtred had to submit. He was then murdered or executed and his earldom of Northumbria placed in the safe hands of jarl Eirik of Hladir. Knut next turned towards London, the hard knot of England, but before his ships came up the river Ethelred the Redeless died 'after a lifetime of much hardship and many difficulties', and the counsellors and citizens chose Edmund his son as their king.

A month later the Danes were besieging the city. It was an elaborate operation against a determined enemy, and though the city was invested on all sides, even to the extent that a channel was dug on the south bank of the Thames to permit the Danish ships to get up river, it failed. Edmund had already got away; he collected an army and waged what must have been a sensationally successful campaign to free Wessex, all of whose inhabitants, says the *Chronicle*, submitted to him. He then launched a vigorous and unexpected attack upon the army besieging London, driving it smartly back, but in doing so suffered such heavy casualties that he had to withdraw and allow them to renew the siege. London still held out in the face of the worst Knut could do; suddenly he abandoned the siege and having provisioned the host in East Anglia and Mercia sent his ships and the captured livestock to the Medway. The remounted host had arrived in Kent when Edmund caught up with it at Otford, put it to flight, and slew all he could overtake. The outlook for the Danes had so deteriorated that Eadric Streona changed sides again and joined Edmund, who took him back into favour. 'No greater error of judgement', says the *Chronicle*, 'was ever made than this'. And so it proved. For when the augmented army of Edmund encountered Knut's host at Ashingdon in Essex, 'the ealdorman Eadric did as he had so often done before; he and his men were the first to set the example of flight, and thus he betrayed his royal lord and the whole nation'. Knut won all England by his victory. Among the irreparable harms of the day were the death of Ulfkell Snilling, the defender of East Anglia, and the destruction of 'all the flower of the English nation'. Edmund Ironside survived and took refuge in Gloucestershire. Knut moved after him, but without more fighting a compromise was reached whereby Edmund should have Wessex and Knut the rest of the country. Among the honest brokers was Eadric Streona. It was a settlement loaded with the promise of future dissension. Neither Knut nor Edmund could leave matters so. But the death-struggle between them never took place. On St. Andrew's day (30 November) of this same year Edmund died at the age of 22, and in sorrow, necessity, and some relief, the whole realm of England chose Knut for its king. He was even younger than his rival.

With Knut as an English king we are not primarily concerned. But two events of 1017 invite attention. In that year Knut divided England into four parts, for administrative and military convenience. Wessex he kept under his own control, and he left jarl Eirik in charge of Northumbria. Thorkell the Tall received East Anglia, and no one could say that in one way or another he had not worked hard for it. To Eadric Streona went the whole of Mercia. But for a short while only. Within a matter of months Knut had him executed. Jarl Eirik held his earldom with honour till his death in *c.* 1023. Thorkell's course was more troubled. From 1017 till 1020 he appears to have been the foremost of Knut's lay subjects; we meet his name on charters, and he is named as accompanying the king on various important occasions. The most impressive witness to his standing during these first years is that he is the only magnate named in the statement of legal policy issued by Knut after his return from Scandinavia in 1020.[1] Then in 1021 he was outlawed; a reconciliation took place in Denmark in 1023 on terms which suggest that Thorkell was still a man of immense power: he was made Knut's regent in Denmark and the guardian of his son Hordaknut, but thereafter disappears from history. Knut's other action of 1017 was to marry Ethelred's widow Emma. In the *Chronicle*'s arresting sentence, he 'commanded the widow of the late king Ethelred, Richard's daughter, to be brought to him so that she might become his wife'. This was an admirable stroke of policy. It could hardly displease the English, promised well dynastically, and ensured the friendship of duke Richard II of Normandy. Knut already had an English consort, Ælgifu of Northampton, to whom he would remain warmly attached, and for whom (and her son Svein) he would make handsome provision in Norway as late as 1030; but Emma was his queen, and it was agreed that her children by Knut should take precedence over her sons by Ethelred and exclude the children of Ælgifu from the royal succession. It was a

---

[1] A. Campbell, *Encomium Emmae*, p. 75; Liebermann, *Gesetze*, I, 273–5.

'sensible arrangement', and for everyone except the Norwegians it worked out well. And unintentionally even for them.

In 1018–19 Knut's brother Harald, king of Denmark, died, and Knut crossed the North Sea to make sure of the succession. Thorkell the Tall remained in England, and perhaps it was now that certain earlier ambitions were reborn in him and led to his banishment in 1021. There is a complete lack of direct evidence, but one reading of Thorkell's shifts and vicissitudes is that he never quite gave up hope of some gigantic prize of his own, in England or Scandinavia, as opportunity offered. In other words he was a craggy and cunning survival of the old-style viking who looked after himself well until kings came in and spoiled the business. One explanation of Knut's placing his fleet off the Isle of Wight in 1022 is that he was safe-guarding the realm against some heavy stroke by the outlawed Thorkell.[1] At the reconciliation in Denmark of 1023 Knut seems to have brought one of Thorkell's sons back to England with him before trusting him with Denmark and Hordaknut. That Thorkell died within a year or two would be no grief to his royal master.

These were king Knut's first expeditions from England to Denmark and the north. Before he undertook his last he had given proof of himself not only as a good king of England but as a monarch of European stature. As a man he is hard to define, because we know so little about him,[2] but as a peace-bringer, legislator, administrator, statesman and politician, and as a patron of the Church we see him more clearly. In law he was less an innovator than a re-worker, and was as English as the English in the moral and improving ingredients with which he flavoured his law-making. Stenton justly describes Knut's legal code as one 'which in its length and varied detail gives him a high place among the legislators of the Dark Ages';[3] for the value of law lies very little in originality or ingenuity, but in its fair dealing between men, its assurance of rights, its practicality of

---

[1] It is difficult to get a clear picture of this year. During the course of it Knut is reported to have made a considerable naval demonstration in the Baltic, for the benefit of Jomsborg-Wollin, the restless Wends, and the inhabitants of Estland. It was after his return to Denmark from this show of strength that he was reconciled to Thorkell.

[2] *Knýtlinga Saga*, 20, tells us that he was tall, strong, fair-haired, keen-eyed, bountiful, valiant, and all-conquering. His nose, which was long, narrow, and slightly bent, somewhat marred his good looks. 'He was a man of great good luck in everything to do with power.'

[3] *Anglo-Saxon England*, p. 404.

enforcement, its power to settle argument, and forestall or compose strife. Further, for Knut law was a prop of kings, as was religion. We need not doubt his devotion to the Church, because he made use of the Church—as the Church made use of him. The links between Church and monarchy in England were close and strong; each had its duty to the other, for the glory of God and the good of the nation, and there is something magnificent about the way this young and alien conqueror accepted an English king's obligations in matters religious and ecclesiastical. His gains, properly, were enormous—nothing did so much to bring him within the comity of Christian Europe; he gained the blessing of the pope and the favour of the emperor;[1] he was seen by his royal peers to be a great monarch; he secured the support of the most powerful institution in England—but these were gains he well deserved, and behind the pomp and circumstance, the ceremonies of honour to St. Edmund and St. Alphege (Ælfeah), the restoring of monasteries and consecration of churches, the ostentation of the pilgrimage to Rome, he appears a man not untouched by humility before the Church in both her worldly and her sacred roles. He would be the last man to object to the worldly, he was so pragmatic a man himself.

In 1026 it was necessary for him to leave England and look to his Scandinavian interests again. Denmark had come under threat from Norway and Sweden, and to understand how this could be we must revert to the years 1014–16, when Knut so hurriedly withdrew from England that he might assemble a new army from Denmark and Norway and complete Svein's conquest. When again he sailed from Denmark jarl Eirik of Hladir sailed with him, and Norway was left in charge of Eirik's brother jarl Svein and maybe Eirik's son Hakon. This was the moment when a new Olaf, like Olaf Tryggvason a scion of the royal Yngling line, chose to make his bid for the partitioned kingdom. He was the thick-set young man we noted as fighting under Thorkell the Tall's banner at Ringmere in 1010, the

[1] To the pope he owed a reduction in the charges levied on an English archbishop when he went to Rome for his pallium. To the emperor and various rulers he owed a reduction in the tolls exacted from northern and English traders and pilgrims who passed through their dominions on the way to Rome. To the emperor Conrad he owed, as part of the wedding settlement between the emperor's son Henry and his own daughter Gunnhild, the return of Slesvig to Denmark and the recognition of the Eider as the German-Danish boundary.

son of a petty ruler in eastern Norway, and stepson of Sigurd Sow, the farmer-king of Ringerike, but destined to be the most famous Norwegian of his century, and of many centuries to come.

Olaf had been born *c.* 995 and set to viking at the age of 12 in charge of a tried ship's captain named Hrani. He harried in Denmark, Sweden, Gotland, Osel off the coast of Estland, and in Finland, too, where his good luck prevailed against the wiles of the local wind-brewers. Sometimes he raided, sometimes fought battles. By the time he met Thorkell the Tall, in the language of the skalds he had reddened nesses, sated the wolf's brood, roused the steel-storm, convened the Thing of arrows. In the language of plain men he had made an unmitigated nuisance of himself in northern waters.[1] As a member of Thorkell's company he made a warlike voyage past Jutland and Frisia to England, and in England fought at London, Ringmere, and Canterbury. When Thorkell entered Ethelred's service Olaf transferred his talents for destruction to France and maybe Spain. William of Jumièges knows him as *Olavus rex Noricorum* and puts him in the service of duke Richard II of Normandy. While in Normandy, *c.* 1013, he was baptized at Rouen. In Normandy, too, he appears to have taken service with Ethelred and followed him back to England. The sources agree that he fought further battles in England, but are divided as to which side he fought on. Chronology alone forbids us to think that he ever fought for Knut, for the absence of Knut from Denmark implied the absence of jarl Eirik from Norway, which gave Olaf the opportunity we know he was quick to lay hold of. In any case he arrived in Norway not later than 1015, and in all probability one year earlier. Concerning his thoughts, motives, plans at this time, save that he hoped to win Norway, we stand in the dark.

Nor are we much more enlightened in respect of the moves which brought him to power there. This is not the fault of Snorri

---

[1] Our most valuable sources for Olaf's life as a viking are the 'Viking Verses' (*Víkingavísur*) of Sighvat Thordarson and the 'Head Ransom' (*Höfuðlausn*) of Ottar the Black, both court poets of his in later life. Sighvat was Olaf's friend as well as his retainer and poet. He tells of thirteen set battles from Lake Mälar to the Guadalquiver, but exaggerates Olaf's importance in those of them we can identify from foreign sources. But cautiously interpreted the Viking Verses give a good generalized picture of a gifted young viking working his way up in his profession. See O. A. Johnsen, *Olav Haraldssons ungdom indtil slaget ved Nesjar*, Oslo, 1922, and G. Turville-Petre, *The Heroic Age of Scandinavia*, 1951, pp. 140-6.

Sturluson, who with an abundance of unverifiable detail brings him
to Selje south of Stad with two merchant ships and 120 men, lets
him dispose of jarl Eirik's son Hakon by a cunning but not unmerci-
ful viking stratagem, celebrates his golden oratory and persuasive-
ness, places his decisive confrontation with his enemies at Nesjar
off the western shore of the Oslofjord (this appears to have been
Sighvat the Skald's first attendance on Olaf on battle), and conveys
the victorious Olaf northwards to the Trondelag, which he saw
was the key to Norway. Jarl Svein's flight and death and young
Hakon's removal to England gave him the chance to establish
himself at Nidaros and keep an eye on those of his subjects likeliest
to cause him trouble. He rebuilt the town a second time, established
a residence there, and laid the foundations of a new church. From
the start it was his intention to attract traders to the town. There
were still chieftains like Erling Skjalgsson and Einar Thambarskelfir who would do him no service, and large areas like the remote
north and the interior stretches of the Trondelag which yielded
him no tribute, but by the end of 1016 in fact as in name he was
king over the immediately accessible provinces of Norway.

In most respects he was a good king, even a very good one.[1]

---

[1] He was not as good, of course, as hagiographical writing would make
him. No other king of the Viking Age was written about so extensively.
There is the anonymous 'First Saga', written in Iceland a little before 1180,
of which only fragments survive, and the big 'Legendary Saga' preserved in a
Norwegian manuscript of *c.* 1250; there are the numerous products of the
saint's cult, in prose and verse, latin and the vernacular (for example, the lost
Translatio Sancti Olavi, the *Acta S.O.*, and *Geisli*); there is much skaldic verse
by a number of skalds, including Sighvat Thordarson, Ottar the Black, and
Thormod Coalbrow's-skald; northern historians from Ari and Theodoricus
downwards speak of him, and he is occasionally referred to in foreign sources;
and clearly there was a rich oral tradition concerning him. Finally there is
Snorri Sturluson's *Óláfs Saga Helga*, written as a separate work, but later
incorporated in his *Heimskringla*, where it is a third of the whole. The Olaf
material consists of hagiographical and lay tradition and invention, king's
life and saint's life, closely and troublesomely blended. Among many
important studies are Sigurður Nordal, *Om Olaf den Helliges Saga*, Copenhagen,
1914; O. A. Johnsen and Jón Helgason (ed.), *Den store saga om Olav den hellige*,
Oslo, 1941; and Bjarni Aðalbjarnarson, *Heimskringla*, II, Íslenzk Fornrit,
Reykjavík, 1945. There is an excellent brief survey in 'Kongekrøniker og
kongesagær' by Th. D. Olsen in *Norrøn Fortællekunst*, Copenhagen, 1965.
The English reader is well served by G. Turville-Petre, *Origins of Icelandic
Literature*, 1953 (chapter VII, 'Historical Literature of the Late Twelfth
Century', especially pp. 175–90).

Most remarkable of all for a man of his early training in rapine and slaughter he gave his subjects peace and security. That he could be hard and merciless goes without saying, but except in matters of religion he reserved this side of his nature for those who disturbed his peace or challenged his authority. Like Knut over in England, he had a strong feeling for law. The law-meets and assemblies, the Things, kept their former dignity and power, and may have been strengthened inasmuch as Olaf worked through farmer aristocrats of his own choosing rather than the old-style local kings. Like Knut he relied a good deal on the legal enactments of his predecessors. Snorri tells us that he often had recited in his presence the laws which Hakon the Good had prepared for the Trondheim region, and some of these, in consultation with the wisest men he could gather at court, he amended, 'taking away or adding as seemed best to him'. Neither rank nor riches could bend the law; Olaf was immune to threats or bribery; and we have said that he could be merciless. Not all the laws known in later days as 'king Olaf's Law' were his; members of the lordly families of old who bore justice on their sword-points did not disappear in a generation; but Olaf's reign saw an impressive development of the notion of law in a national context. Sighvat's poetic compliment, while excessive, was not entirely undeserved: 'King, you can establish the nation's law, which stands firm among all men.'

His most renowned work for Norway was to make her Christian. This had implications beyond a change of gods and forms of worship. It brought Norway out of the past into the present, lessened her isolation, and inducted her, partly at least, into the fuller European civilization of the time. Much progress had already been made; in places where Danish influence was strong, like the Vik, there had been proselytization since the conversion of Harald Bluetooth; Hakon the Good, Harald Greycloak, and Olaf Tryggvason had toiled for the faith in their different degrees; but the remoter areas of the interior and the northern coasts stayed benighted. Olaf's methods were uncompromising; he executed the recalcitrant, blinded or maimed them, drove them from their homes, cast down their images and marred their sacred places. However, baptism and the king's friendship were always on offer. But baptism was one thing: a state church for Norway was another and a harder undertaking. His success in organizing this was remarkable. His right-hand man and counsellor was Grimkell, to judge by his name a Norwegian. It was with Grimkell and other priests that he worked out a framework of church law at Moster. He used priests and missionaries from England, too,[1] but because of Knut's rule there it was to Bremen that he sent Grimkell and other priests for their consecration. The Christian law formulated at Moster was of prime authority; it was read out at the different Things, and there are confirmatory references to it in the oldest Gulathing Law. Olaf had many churches built in Norway, and we assume that parts of the Moster law were concerned with their upkeep, administration, and their place within the Church as a whole. There is a shrouding overlay of pious propaganda in much medieval writing about Olaf, but one thing is clear: by the time he died Norway was a Christian country, and no relapse into heathendom was possible.

It helped in this respect that his downfall was followed by his sanctification. It helped, too, that his downfall was due to king Knut, another determined Christian.

For ten or twelve years Olaf's foreign policy had been favoured by Knut's preoccupation with his realm of England, while the rivalry of the jarls of Hladir had been providentially removed by Eirik's transfer to Northumbria, Hakon's capture and oaths, and the defeat and death of jarl Svein. This left Sweden and the Atlantic Islands. These last, Faroes, Orkney and Shetland, in their different

[1] The English share in the conversion of the Scandinavian lands was considerable, from Willibrord's mission in the first half of the eighth century to the time of Knut and Svein Estridsson in Denmark; under the two Olafs and Harald Hardradi in Norway; and so far as we can judge at various times in Sweden. England supplied missionaries, priests, bishops, saints, and martyrs, and influenced ecclesiastical terminology and epistolary usage. See A. D. Jørgensen, *Den nordiske Kirkes Grundlæggelse og første Udvikling*, Copenhagen, 1874–8; Ellen Jørgensen, *Fremmed Indflydelse under den Danske Kirkes tidligste Udvikling*, Copenhagen, 1908; K. Gjerset, *History of the Norwegian People*, I, 1915; H. G. Leach, *Angevin Britain and Scandinavia*, Harvard, 1921; Oluf Kolsrud, *Noregs kyrkjesoga*, Oslo, 1958; and for Iceland, Jón Helgason, *Islands Kirke fra dens Grundlæggelse til Reformationen*, Copenhagen, 1925. There is further bibliographical reference in F. E. Harmer, 'Epistolary Usages of Scandinavian Kings' in *Saga-Book*, XIII, pt. III, 1949–50. For a useful survey of the Christianization of the north, see Lucien Musset, 'La Pénétration chrétienne dans l'Europe du Nord et son Influence sur la Civilisation Scandinave', in *Settimane di studio del Centro italiano di studi sull'alto medioevo*, XIV, pp. 263–325, 527–35, Spoleto, 1967.

ways acknowledged his overlordship, though Olaf's court poet Ottar used the language of eulogy when he assured the king that before his day no warlike Yngling laid such a yoke on the isles in the west. Against Swedish encroachment he stood firm from the beginning. When the king of Sweden sent his tax-gatherers across the mountains into Gaulardal and Orkadal we are told that Olaf had twelve of them hanged on a ridge as sport for the raven, a warning to the Swede, and a joyful spectacle for Norwegian passers-by. It is easier to believe that in the disputed territory of Ranrike he had the Swedish king's two officers put to death and replaced them with a nominee of his own. Here, too, he built the town of Sarpsborg and fortified it with a moat and rampart to hold the Swedes at bay. As always, information about Sweden is hard to come by. There had been a Christian mission to Sweden after the death of Olaf Tryggvason whereby king Olaf Eiriksson, Sköt-konung, was converted to the new faith, but only a small minority of his people followed his example. Eventually Olaf of Norway married his Swedish namesake's daughter Astrid. We are given to understand that Olaf of Norway was the prime mover in the settle-ment. It was he who sent embassies through the desolate interior, using for the purpose his court poet Sighvat. The *Austrfararvísur*, or 'Verses on an Eastern Journey', of this Icelandic emissary between the kings of Norway and Sweden, and more particularly those relating to his adventures in the horse-foundering, man-rejecting heathen hinterland, are as entertaining as they are informative. Time and again the poet and his comrades knock on a door for shelter; time and again they are sent packing. One house was hallowed and heathen, another hag-ridden and elf-ruled; three in a row were inhabited by farmers named Olvir, and all three drove them away; at the next all they got was a surly stare from the closing doorway. But this was grist to the poet's mill: he seems to have very much enjoyed it, and certainly we enjoy his wry humour and mock-complaints at the forestlands and Gautland. Whether this rough terrain and its rough inhabitants belonged to Swede or Dane we do not know; we presume it was to the former. In any case Sighvat and his comrades re-traversed it, a marriage was arranged, and its terms bargained for. Common interest and fear of the Danes brought about an alliance of Norway and Sweden. Somewhere about this time the Swedes grew so dissatisfied with Olaf Sköt-konung, in part because of his newfangled religion, that they compelled him to share his rule with his twice-named son Onund Jacob; Olaf died in 1022, and it was with Onund that Olaf of Norway made a compact at Konungahella to attack Denmark. Happy the king who has no foreign policy. This led to Knut's third expedition to Denmark in 1025–6, which in its turn led to the reversal of Norwegian Olaf's fortunes.

One wonders why Knut had not moved before. The reasons seem to be that he had plenty to occupy him in England, and that England was a far richer prize than Norway; that his situation in both England and Denmark imposed caution on him; and that so long as Norway and Sweden stayed on bad terms he had little to fear from either. It is unlikely that Knut had a theory of empire impelling him to add Norway (and some say Sweden) to his realms of England and Denmark. But he would be sensitive to the threat to English and Danish trade and security posed by an unfriendly king in Norway and the Atlantic islands; if either opportunity or compulsion arose he was the man to act upon them, and the middle 1020s offered both. We postulate the death of Thorkell the Tall soon after 1023, but the succession of Knut's brother-in-law jarl Ulf as regent in Denmark led to fresh doubts and dangers. We are far from clear who jarl Ulf was—he has been furnished with Danish, Swedish, Gaulish, Jomsborg, and English antecedents—but on the most charitable count he showed less than full loyalty to king Knut. There was the dubious transaction when by means of a stolen seal and a forged instrument he sought to make Knut's young son Hordaknut king of Denmark (*Fagrskinna*, written by an Icelander in Norway shortly after 1220, implicates queen Emma in this); he provided no worthwhile opposition to the first hostile moves of Sweden and Norway, but retreated to Jutland; and there was Ulf's disputed role in the disputed battle at the Holy River in the disputed year of 1025–6–7.[1] Knut, it is clear, had much to see to, and was aware that some of it was happening behind his back. Not that he was entirely idle in respect of Norway. There must be some disaffection after an enforced change of religion and a paring down

---

[1] The *Anglo-Saxon Chronicle* (E) puts the battle in 1025, but this is too upsetting to the chronology supplied by Scandinavian sources to be acceptable. The known facts of Olaf's last years point to 1027 (a date skilfully defended by Campbell, *Encomium Emmae*, pp. 82 ff.). But if we believe that Knut's pilgrimage to Rome took place in 1027, we are forced to assign the battle to 1026.

of the kingly families of old. His bribes and promises had already begun to move north.

When Olaf with sixty ships sailed to harry Zealand, and Onund with a much bigger fleet began to harry Skåne, Knut moved north in person with a fleet from England to Limfjord in Jutland, where he was joined by a second fleet recruited at home. The news of his coming gave heart to all Denmark, and when he stood out into the Kattegat with his combined force Olaf judged it prudent to leave Zealand. Swedes and Norwegians then harried the coasts of Skåne together, a feeble gesture in kings who had sworn to conquer Denmark, and even here their opportunities dwindled as the Danish fleet drew near. They retreated to a defensive position in the mouth of Holy River, Helga-á, on the east or Baltic coast of Skåne, and here Knut fought with them. Some early writers awarded the victory to Knut, others to the confederates. Jarl Ulf is reported as playing a decisive role on both sides. Details of the fight are more than usually unreliable. But something may be deduced from its immediate consequences. Onund headed off home with as whole a wagon as remained to him, and almost at once his alliance, though not his friendship, with Olaf broke down. Knut retired to Denmark and settled his score with jarl Ulf: he had him murdered in Roskilde church, then compounded the scandal with generous endowments of land. Olaf's position was more difficult. The first whiffs of treachery were reaching his nostrils; he had to get back home, but, remembering the fate of Olaf Tryggvason, dare not risk an ambush in the Øresund; there was nothing for it but to abandon his ships and take the overland route to Sarpsborg. There was a short period of peace during which Olaf could do little save grow increasingly uneasy, while Knut increased his chances of a bloodless conquest of Norway by enhancing his prestige throughout the north by the spiritual and temporal benefits of his pilgrimage to Rome. Meantime, because a wolf in its lair never wins a ham, nor a sleeping man a victory, his agents were suborning Norwegians great and small. 'I have never', says the *Hávamál* poet, 'found a man so generous and hospitable that he would not take a present, nor one so free with his money that he would be displeased with an award if he could get one.' Some held their hands out for money; others of the ancient hersar aristocracy craved esteem. Knut dispensed both. Before the year's end he was sure of Harek Thjotta, Thorir Hound, Einar Thambarskelfir, and Erling Skjalgsson. When Knut arrived off

Norway with a powerful fleet in 1028 he was unopposed. Olaf tried to rally men to his drooping banner, to no avail.[1] His one small victory ended in the murder of Erling Skjalgsson, to whom he had promised quarter, and lost him more than he gained. Kalf Arnason deserted him, and with a few trusted companions he crossed the mountains to Gudbrandsdal and passed by way of Sweden to find sanctuary with his kinsman Yaroslav in Russia. But the all-conquering Knut made a triumphal progress up the Norwegian coast. Wherever he put ashore he was hailed, or maybe tolerated, as a deliverer, and when he reached Nidaros was accepted as Norway's lord and king. Yet again a king who had lost command of the sea had lost his kingdom as a consequence, and Knut, who held that command, inherited. He proclaimed his son Hordaknut king of Denmark, and having set Hakon Eiriksson of the Hladir line of jarls to govern Norway on his behalf, sailed by way of Sarpsborg, where he was acclaimed king over Vik, to Denmark and so to England. There had been many inflated claims to glory on behalf of earlier Scandinavian kings, but with the description of Knut as *Rex totius Angliae et Dennemarchiae et Norregiae et partis Suavorum* there can be little quarrel.[2] Even if we accept that *Suavorum* should read *Slavorum*, the ruler of Skåne, and maybe of Blekinge, suffers no very crippling diminution.

The following summer the situation in Norway changed. Jarl Hakon drowned in the Pentland Firth; he was the last effective representative of a family comparable in dignity and esteem to the Ynglings, and there was no Norwegian with a pre-emptive claim to succeed him. Knut seems to have made promises to both Kalf

[1] A number of scholars have held that Snorri was misled by his knowledge of thirteenth-century Norway when he portrayed its eleventh-century chieftains in rebellion against king Olaf. It is arguable that he had more support in parts of the country, in Uppland and the Vik for example, than Snorri allows for, and that his opponents were not so much politically allied against their sovereign as disaffected for more personal reasons, including loss of land or status, change of religion, family grievances, and private quarrels with the king.

[2] It is found in his letter of 1027 to the English people, a translation of which will be found in D. Whitelock, *English Historical Documents*, 1955, pp. 416–18. A number of coins bear the inscription *Cnut rex sv*, and that *sv* can refer only to Sweden is proved by the attribution on the coin's reverse: *Thormod on Siht*, 'Thormod in Sigtuna'. Thormod was a moneyer of the Swedish king Onund-Jacob. The inscription may be taken at its face value or, more convincingly, as evidence of a Knytling aspiration.

Arnason and Einar Thambarskelfir; he continued to handle them skilfully if trickily, but announced that Norway would be ruled by his son Svein. With his English mother Ælfgifu, who would be known to Norse historians as Alfifa (*Álfífa*), Svein set off for Norway, probably from Denmark, and mother and son arrived in the Vik from the south at much the same time as an overlooked but natural contender, the recently expelled king Olaf Haraldsson, crossed into Trondheim province from the east. As in the year 1000 the pieces were on the board for a further famed encounter of the Viking Age.

We assume that it was news of Hakon's death which quickened Olaf's resolve to win back Norway, but he would have made the attempt sooner or later. Early in 1030 he began his preparations, travelled the frozen Russian rivers to the coast, and when the sea-ice broke up sailed with 240 men to Gotland. Here he had confirmation of Hakon's death, and with rising hope went on to Sweden, where Onund was not slack in well-doing, but with an eye to Knut, not overzealous neither. He supplied his former ally with 480 men and leave to recruit what others he could. With these he headed into the forestlands of Dalarna, where he was met by his half-brother Harald (Hardradï) and other of his kinsmen with their following. But if his friends in Norway were aware of his movements so, too, were his foes. While Olaf pressed on through the forests and mountains of the interior, the war-arrow was borne through northern and western Norway. Harek of Thjotta and Thorir Hound came down from the north with their men; the lords of Agdir, Rogaland, and Hordaland fared from the south, and the sons of Erling Skjalgsson moved a covering force east from the Jaeder. In Trondheim at the centre of preparations stood Kalf Arnason. Those great chieftains who had accepted bribes and office at Knut's hand had everything to lose if Olaf returned to power; but strikingly enough the farmers great and small were equally opposed to him. The army that eventually defeated him at Stiklarstadir was reckoned the biggest ever assembled in Norway, of one hundred hundreds, or 14,400 men. As a figure it looks suspiciously large and round. Olaf could muster not more than 3,600, made up of Norwegians from his own south-eastern part of Norway, Swedes, and an assortment of unidentifiable riff-raff, many of them heathens. He also had three Icelandic poets in train, including Thormod Coalbrow's-skald, who would die of his battle-wound at Stiklarstadir, but his faithful

Sighvat was on pilgrimage to Rome. These poets Olaf is said to have brought within his shield-wall, bidding them mark the event well and immortalize it later.

From their verses and such other traditions and legends as were associated with the battle Snorri composed one of his consummate narrative pieces. For once his natural pragmatism is tempered by sympathy with Olaf. To a cold eye it might appear that Olaf set death or victory on a desperate throw, and it is interesting to find that tradition, in general so favourable to him, shows him returning to his kingdom with everything he had formerly reprobated, a part-alien and part-heathen army of mercenaries. Against him, we read, were none but Norwegians. But in all likelihood the battle reflected the permanent realities of Scandinavian politics: pressure and inter-ference from Denmark and Sweden, and the Norwegians divided in factions. The traditional date of the battle is 29 July 1030, but there was an eclipse of the sun visible at Stiklarstadir on 31 August, and the two dates were not unnaturally confounded. Details of the battle are lacking,[1] but when the day ended Olaf was dead, and once more Norway had broken from a Norwegian's hand to the hand of a foreigner.

Medieval historical works are eloquent that Norway at once had cause to regret it. But the partiality of their witness is patent. Understandably for skalds like Sighvat the hillsides which had smiled

---

[1] Snorri's account is deliberately heroic and highly fictitious. The day, he informs us, began in epic style. Olaf woke early and called on Thormod to recite a poem to rouse the host. This was the old *Bjarkamál*, which told of the doomed stand of Hrolf Kraki and his champions at Lejre. Their courage whetted, Olaf's men advanced to the place of slaughter. Olaf wondered whether his half-brother Harald was not too young and weak for what lay ahead: Harald replied that if nothing else would serve, his hand should be tethered to his sword-hilt. The armies were harangued by their leaders, and the leaders harangued each other. Then to a shout of '*Fram, fram, bóandmenn!*' ('On, on, farmer-men!') in the one army and '*Fram, fram, Kristsmenn, krossmenn, konungsmenn!*' ('On, on, Christ's men, cross-men, king's men!') in the other, the unequal struggle began. The weather was bright and the sun shone from a clear sky, but as blows were struck and the dead men fell, sky and sun grew red, and before the battle ended it was dark as night. The king fought with exceeding valour and no thought of flight. Two of his poets, his standard-bearer, and his marshall fell near him. In turn the king was brought to bay by broad-axe and spear and died of three fearful strokes. Some say Kalf Arnason dealt him his last wound, some say a different Kalf. The king's sanctity was revealed forthwith by the miracles wrought by his blood.

in Olaf's reign grew dark and louring, but it is hard to believe that Ælgifu and Svein would promptly set out to punish their friends and supporters, crop the chieftains' power, and impose burdens on the free householder. Almost everything the synoptic historians say under this head sounds a note of national and hagiographical propaganda. Had Norwegians, they seem to ask, destroyed a king of their own blood to burden themselves with a bad Dane and a worse Englishwoman? Their mulctings are recounted, their acts of oppression noted in detail, taxes, legal disabilities, enforced services, but there is no good reason for believing in any of it. They are the secular counterpart of the carefully fostered legend of the dead Olaf. Men talked, or it was said that men talked, of the maimed or blind or dead made whole by his blood; and when permission was granted to exhume his body, foreseeably it was found to be uncorrupted. Foreseeably bishop Grimkell declared him a true saint, and had him translated to that St. Clement's Church in Nidaros which Olaf had founded twenty years before. The miracles increased in scope and number, legends grew, stories spread, and it was right and proper for good Norwegians to believe in them. They strengthened the Church and they enhanced the native monarchy. The cult of St. Olaf, so swiftly born, so straitly based, spread to many countries and proved long-lasting. King Olaf died against a rock at Stiklarstadir; St. Olaf continued his work long beyond the Viking Age as *perpetuus rex Norvegiae*, 'Norway's eternal king'. Some of the changes affecting Norway would become apparent only during the course of the century, but two were quickly made plain: that Norway had become a Christian country, and that the days of foreign kings and their regents were over.

When Olaf set out on his death-journey in the heart of winter from a frozen Russia he left behind him at Yaroslav's court his young son Magnus, borne to him by his *frilla* Alfhild, and named, we are told, after Charlemagne (Karla-Magnus) on the initiative of Sighvat the Skald. He was now the best hope of the Norwegian party, and thought was given to his return and restoration. There may have been another candidate, a self-styled son of Olaf Tryggvason who sailed to Norway from England in 1033. He sounds a creature of folk-tale, and is described as an impostor and son of a priest. In the battle which proved fatal to his hopes he hurled spears with both hands at once, crying, 'Thus my father taught me to say Mass!' If he ever lived he was thereupon killed. Norwegian emissaries left for Russia, met Yaroslav and Magnus Olafsson there, and brought the boy back and had him made king. The Danish ascendancy was in heavy regression, and in the autumn Svein sought refuge with his brother Hordaknut in Denmark. A month or two later, on 12 November, king Knut died in England and was buried at Winchester. The death of this great king who had briefly controlled the North Sea, Skagerrak and Kattegat, the Sound and the southern Baltic, and been lord of so many peoples, was a happy accident for Norway. The unpopular Svein likewise died, Hordaknut could not risk leaving Denmark in face of the threat to Danish interests in Norway, and this in turn led to the election of his half-brother Harald Harefoot first as regent then as king of England. The Anglo-Scandinavian empire, if it ever existed, had fallen apart, and by their muddled lives and early deaths the sons of Knut ensured that the Anglo-Danish monarchy would soon follow its example. The Viking Age was ending, though harsh throes were still to come. Meantime of the Scandinavian kingdoms Norway was the chief beneficiary of change.

3. The Viking Kingdoms to the Death of Harald Hardradi, 1066

THE VIKING AGE DID NOT END SUDDENLY, AND IT MAY appear an arbitrary fall of the axe which terminates its story in 1066–70. Many phenomena of the Age, particularly religion and kingship, had experienced change by 1030–5, which saw the death in battle at Stiklarstadir of Olaf Haraldsson, king and saint, *perpetuus rex Norvegiae*, and the death by sickness in England of king Knut the Great, the Mighty, the Old, *rex totius Angliae et Dennemarchiae et Norregiae et partis Suavorum*; but all such change is more clearly defined after 1066, the climacteric year which saw the death at Stamford Bridge of Harald Hardradi of Norway and the conquest of England by William of Normandy. The twenty years before 1050, and the twenty after, show an obvious shrinking back upon itself of the viking world, though much of the evidence has a clearer message for posterity than for men living at the time. Thus there was a heavy setback to Norse aspirations in Ireland in 1052, when Diarmaid of Leinster seized the Dublin kingdom—but the Norsemen there had suffered setbacks before and been returned to power. The death of Yaroslav in 1054 was the end of Norseness in the Kievan kingdom of Russia—but this only confirmed what thinking men had long known to be a political and economic fact. The greatest of the Orkney jarls in might, wisdom, and magnanimity, jarl Thorfinn, who had greatly extended his realm, died in 1065, to the comfort of Malcolm Canmore king of Scotland—but Orkney, Shetland, Man, the mainland and islands of Scotland were well used to permutations of local power. Jomsborg-Wollin was destroyed in the early 1040s—but it had burned before, and who could say it would not rise again out of its ashes? Hedeby was destroyed by pillage and fire *c.* 1050, but there would soon be a new mart north of the Sliefjord. For every town that was falling away a new town was being built up. The Vinland venture had been concluded, unsuccessfully, thirty years since, but trade there had never amounted to much and land-taking to nothing at all. Besides, Greenland and Iceland were doing well, apart from an infrequency of drinking-parties in the one and an occasional famine in the other, and had not the 'well-informed prince of the Norwegians', Harald Hardradi, shown that the old spirit of exploration for gain was still alive by attempting the Frozen Sea? Not too successfully—'After he had explored the expanse of the Northern Ocean in his ships, there lay before their eyes at length the darksome bounds of a failing world, and by retracing his steps he barely escaped in safety the vast pit of the abyss.'[1] But it made for talk of the right kind.

In most of this there was nothing to convince the ordinary man of the mid-eleventh century that it was well an old age was out and time to begin a new. As in the legendary sixth century and the viking heyday he continued to go about his business, and it was the same business. The land was farmed with love and diligence. The long flat Danish landscape, the high Norwegian valleys, the clearings of the Swedish forests yielded corn or fragrant grass; sheep grazed the pastures of a thousand islands between the Ålands and the west Greenland archipelago, and on the mainlands went up to the seter and the heiði in spring and fattened there till the first cold nights of autumn. Northwards in Norway and Sweden the Norseman and his animals contended for grazing with the bright-clad nomads and their migratory herds; in Iceland the bondi widened his homefield, so that a greener grass encroached on the livid wilderness. There and in Greenland even more than at home he must select beasts to be brought through the winter and slaughter the rest in September. They were small animals by today's standards, the sheep springy, the cattle multi-coloured and unshapely, yielding less meat and milk, but easier to transport on voyages of colonization. In general horses were exempt from this autumnal slaughter; they were clever at finding food and survived all save the savagest weather.[2] Between 750 and 1100 life on the land changed comparatively little: peasant and franklin stayed deeply conserv-

[1] Adam of Bremen, IV, xxxix.
[2] One can still see these sturdy little *útigangshestar*, or out-grazers, in Iceland today, their wise and melancholy eyes surveying the prospect of spring through a veritable shako of forehead-hair and mane.

ative. Great lords came and went; some were good, others were bad; you took up arms for or against them only if you had to. The Norwegian farmers who defeated and killed king Olaf were content to see him sanctified. The English, including the Danes of England, who had followed Knut followed Edward. The Danes of Denmark obeyed in turn their own Hordaknut, Magnus the Norwegian, and Svein Estridsson, and would not have jibbed at Harald Hardradi. True, there was a new religion to be observed, and soon wise men would be writing down the law, all very important, no doubt, especially for kings and jarls and bishops and zealots, but for the most part not bearing too hard on the farmer scything hay in Gudbrandsdal or Borgarfjord, the fisherman dropping his nets off the Lofotens or Jutland, and the cold-fingered fur-hunter spearing and trapping in wildernesses from the Gulf of Bothnia to the verges of Baffin Bay. Merchants whose interest was in profit continued to sail the trade-routes of Baltic, Sound, and Kattegat, lay-to by night in the leads of western Norway, or turned their laden ships south and south-west to Frisia, France, and the British Isles. Hucksters with a packhorse penetrated fjords and crossed mountain passes. Smiths and craftsmen were traffickers to dwellings great and small, with pots, lamps, and brooches for the womenfolk, tools, weapons, and drinking-vessels for the men. More of life's amenities were distributed over a wider territory.

Similarly in the towns there was no great outward change. Birka might die slowly and Hedeby be swiftly extinguished, but on the narrow roadways of Sigtuna, Nidaros, and Slesvig, amid the jostle of carts and animals, gadding women and gossiping men, or down at the waterfront watching the transfer of wares from ship to cart, and hearing the tap of the shipwright's hammer, a nordic Rip van Winkle from a century or two earlier would not feel significantly out of place. Certain outlandish additions to masculine costume, especially those long, full baggy trousers copied from Serkland, and too many women flaunting a linen petticoat instead of the good old woollens—but they still built the houses the same way, the ships looked the same, as did the carts and sleds and the beasts that drew them; there were the same-shaped saddles laid over the same-shaped horses, and much the same bridles and stirrups. And the weapons, in look and hoist, very much the same. And if you looked in through the opened doorways the same loom and wheel, spit and cooking pot, dish and spoon, the same unsilenced women contradicting their menfolk, the same children. Dogs, too—a cur was always a cur, all teeth and tail. If you were a religious man you would, of course, notice a degree of change, and probably regret it. If you were a Swede you would find it a novelty that a Norwegian now lorded it over the Danes. And if you were a wise Swede you would doubt that it could last.

Nor would it, and the Norwegian-Danish treaty of 1064 which recognized that each country was independent of the other is not the least pointer to the end of the Age. From its beginnings till the proclamation of Magnus Olafsson as king in 1035 Norway had been subjected to Danish influence, and the succession of events which made Magnus king of Denmark after Hordaknut's death in 1042 was without parallel in earlier Scandinavian history. But it led to a new imbalance, and it was not until the restoration of a Danish king to Denmark in 1047 and Norway's recognition of him in 1064 that the scales hung steady between the neighbours. The cancellation of the Norwegian claim to the throne of England in 1066 and Svein's virtual abandonment of the Danish in 1070 were likewise events of terminatory significance.

Before the death of Harald Hardradi in 1066 there had been further developments in the slowly changing social order of the Scandinavian homelands. They can be followed most clearly in Norway, where they affected all four classes, the king, the aristocracy, that ubiquitous body which included 'all husbandmen, those too who worked in the forests, and salt-men, and all takers of prey by sea and land', and, finally, the thralls. In the century after the death of Harald Fairhair no Norwegian king died peacefully in his bed and was succeeded by his son. Eirik Blood-axe was driven out and killed in England; Hakon the Good was killed by Eirik's sons at Fitjar; Harald Greycloak was enticed to Denmark with Norwegian help and killed in the Limfjord; jarl Hakon was deserted by his subjects and killed in the Trondelag; Olaf Tryggvason was killed at Svold by a confederacy including jarl Eirik Hakonarson; jarl Svein was driven out and died in Sweden; Olaf Haraldsson was driven out and on his return killed at Stiklarstadir. Most were rulers who had themselves seized the throne by violence, usually by sea-borne invasion. But in 1035 Magnus became king by the invitation of his subjects, and later made a peaceable arrangement with his uncle Harald Hardradi when he, too, sought dominion in Norway. Harald's death in England owed nothing to his subjects, and his sons, grandson, and great-grandsons succeeded him in due order. Not less remarkable, his immediate descendants solved the problem of a double, even a triple kingship, without resort to assassination or civil war.

Clearly the monarchy was on a new footing. In the main this was because it had either broken or contained the power of the regional chieftains and changed the nature of the aristocracy. The viking captain with a hird and a fleet, thriving on civil war at home and plundering expeditions abroad, was departing the scene. The new chieftains were landed men, concerned with stability and peaceful development. A bondi aristocracy worked more closely with the king, and proved better for the country's prosperity, than a viking aristocracy with recurring military ambitions. The ruthless reign of Harald Hardradi was good for Norway; his long wars with Denmark were the ugly backside of his determination to be master in his own house. The king-breakers and king-makers whom he had inherited along with the kingdom, like Einar Thambarskelfir and the Arnorssons, he destroyed without scruple as opportunity arose. Only one private army would be tolerated: the king's. And this everyone would tolerate, the new-style chieftains, usually landed men and overseers, who attended to regional needs between royal visitations; the bishops whose interests were bound up with the king's, and who brought to his support not only their spiritual authority in Norway but the strength derived from their active membership of an institution which had taken Christendom as its parish, besides the organizing and administrative ability distinctive of the Church and so necessary to an emergent kingdom; and the free men likewise who looked to the king to implement law and justice. The only time the bondis need fear the hird was when they fell short in their duty to the king. During Harald's long reign this happened particularly in respect of Uppland, which he was determined to bring into full obedience. An improved relationship between the Norwegian king and his franklins great and small knit the kingdom more firmly together, and was matched south of the Skagerrak by the attachment of the Danes to Svein and his realm of Denmark.

Other social changes followed from the dying down of *viking*. Slavery was enfeebled as an institution as the supply of slaves came to an end. Emigration overseas fell off when there were no new lands to settle, no old ones from which to dispossess English, French, or Irish householders. Younger sons must now make do at home, break the soil's surface wherever this was possible, seek higher or more northerly grazing, or, commonly, settle for a smaller farm, a straitened tenancy, and increasingly as time went on for hiring out as labour. This had important consequences at home, and immediately apparent ones overseas, in that the most sensational manifestation of Scandinavian history and civilization as it is recorded in other than Scandinavian sources, that is, the Viking Movement, the excursus abroad, was grinding to a halt. Viking incursions into the kingdom of the Franks (but not the Germans) had ended early in the tenth century with the creation of the duchy of Normandy, and after the death of Knut the ancient West Saxon dynasty pre-emptively reinherited England. Earlier still, on the principle that if one has a farm and a manor house one lives in the manor, Knut had settled to be king of England rather than Denmark, and sent his vikings back home. Apart from the fact that the viking aristocracy was in decline, with the arguable exception of Harald Hardradi's exploits in Byzantium and the north there were remarkably few viking opportunities left. And hardly any vikings. Instead there were Danes, Norwegians, Swedes, though the extent to which they were aware of their separateness from each other is hard to say, and across the water the Norse of Dublin, those of the sea-sundered region between Orkney and Man, the Icelanders by now become a people apart from Norway and the Western Islands, and the Greenlanders far out on the rim of the world. Even if 'vikings' now existed and had their ancient longings, where could they fulfil them? Alas for private enterprise and the rights of free men! Monarchs had taken over the business of war. Harald Hardradi's expedition to England, Svein Estridsson's baffled action there in 1069–70, and if they can properly be counted, the abortive plans of king Knut II (St. Knut), and the three west-ward sorties of Magnus Barelegs at the end of the century, were all royal and therefore at least quasi-national undertakings. There were still great blood-lettings, from Clontarf in 1014, by way of Lyrskov Heath in 1043 (where most of the blood was Wendish), to Gate Fulford and Stamford Bridge in 1066; service in the king's hird was still a hook drawing brave men to riches and regard; but the once-esteemed profession of arms with piracy offered fewer openings and ever-scantier opportunities. As for home waters, the seizure of cattle, food, and booty, *strandhögg*, *nesnám*, and *herfang*, were under ban. The viking was become an anachronism at home and abroad.

It is indeed curious to observe how by 1066-70, after two and a half centuries of ardent expansion overseas, the viking peoples, with the significant exception of their remote Atlantic colonies, were in large measure back inside their original boundaries. For this there were four good reasons: the constant struggle for territory and dominance in and between the three homeland kingdoms; their general inability to propagate elsewhere their political, social, and religious systems; the fact that they must encounter nations and peoples, the Franks and English, the Empire, Byzantium, the Caliphates, and in the long run the Slavs, richer or stronger, and altogether more absorbent and self-renewing than themselves; and, most important of all, their lack of manpower. These reasons are not always separable one from the other, and are capable of subdivision. But it is manifest that the wars at home for some kind of Scandinavian imperium, or even the welding of a kingdom or extension of a patrimony, persistently handicapped Norse ambitions abroad. Olaf Tryggvason and Olaf Haraldsson, Svein Forkbeard, Magnus Olafsson, and Harald Hardradi (to say nothing of Svein Estridsson) were all kings whose plans for Scandinavia delayed or terminated their operations in the west,[1] and the list could be lengthened with the names of leaders as famous as Godfred, Horik, Olaf-Amlaibh, and even Thorkell the Tall. The viking peoples, even under Knut (who, it must be remembered,

---

[1] There is confirmatory evidence from the buried hoards of Scandinavia. '[The] relationship between disturbances and hoards is well established for historical times both in Scandinavia and elsewhere and the best explanation for the large number of hoards from certain periods seems to be that those were unusually disordered. It has long been recognized that in Norway there are many hoards from the disturbed reigns of Olaf Tryggvason (died 1000), St Olaf (died 1030) and Harald Hardradi (1046-66), while there are few from the more peaceful reign of Magnus the Good (1035-47).[55] Similarly in Denmark there are many hoards datable to the period 1050-65 when there was extensive fighting between Harald and Svein Estrithson.[56] The same is true of England: the reign of Edgar has yielded very few hoards and the five years that saw the Norman Conquest, 1065-70, produced more hoards than the preceding five decades.' (P. H. Sawyer, *The Age of the Vikings*, p. 105, with references to [55] A. W. Brøgger, 'Et mynt fund fra Foldøen i Ryfylke, fra xi Aarhundrede', in *Aarbøger for Nordisk Oldkyndighed og Historie*, 1910, pp. 239-82; [56] R. Skovmand, *De Danske Skattefund fra Vikingetiden og den ældste Middelalder indtil omkring 1150*, Copenhagen, 1942, pp. 192-6; [57] R. H. M. Dolley, *Anglo-Saxon Coins*, pp. 163-5.

increasingly identified himself with English interests) never settled to a common purpose—and it was impossible that they should. Under the second head it might be argued that Iceland and the Danelaw show that viking polity and custom could be exported; but Iceland was a country devoid of inhabitants, save for a few *papar*, and therefore a special if not unique case; while the strong flavour of Scandinavia in the Danelaw and its various influences back home cannot hide the readiness with which before the time of Brunanburgh it looked to England rather than to Denmark or Norway. The Norsemen there had gratified their desire for land, and wanted to farm it, not go on fighting for ever, and they came to find their heathen Norse brothers less congenial than their Christian English cousins. The religious view was everywhere important. In England, Normandy, and Kiev, the rejection of Æsir and Vanir in favour of Christ ate deep into the Norse sense of separateness, as back in Scandinavia heathendom had helped sustain it. And almost everywhere their numbers were too small, and their presence subject to erosion. At their western extremity it was this which led them to abandon Wineland the Good, and in course of time fail where the Eskimo would succeed, in Greenland; and in the east, in Russia, they were submerged completely. Even the improvements that were taking place in Scandinavian agriculture, and the new soil being brought under cultivation, led to fewer men going overseas. When, as we must, we set aside the exaggerations of Christian chroniclers from Ireland to Byzantium, with their tale of hundreds and thousands of ships, and tens of thousands of warriors distinguished by superhuman strength and subhuman destructiveness, and think instead on the realities of manpower and logistics, it is imperatively borne in on us that as colonizers or conquerors the vikings were too few for the many and varied causes they bore in hand. And this told more and more against them as their initial advantages of surprise and mobility were whittled away.

Paradoxically, in the light of all this, in two areas overseas they appear to have been too successful for their own good, in that they established colonies which became independent of the homeland, went their separate ways, and rendered further immigration impossible. The first of these was Iceland, whose ties of affection with south-west Norway were not more heartfelt than their devices for avoiding the pressures of Norwegian royal power. Remote and conservative, its habitable areas soon occupied, it became a country of its own, and by virtue of the administrative enactments of 930 and 965 a republic answerable to none but its own folk. The second was the duchy of Normandy, which so cut free of its Danish-Norwegian apron-strings that long before the Viking Age closed it was French in language, culture, and political institutions, Christian in religion, and committed to a future in western Europe, without regard for the medieval north it had deliberately turned its back on. It does not do to forget that the Icelander and the Norman were blood-brothers, and that the enterprise and energy shown by the one in mastering his sea-girt, stony province, developing its arts and constitution, and mounting the voyages of exploration and colonization to Greenland and North America, were the counterpart of the organizing ability, statecraft, and military zeal which made the duchy of Normandy so formidable a newcomer to the comity of western Europe, and led in course of time to the Norman conquests in England and Sicily—though the two states' differing destiny in the post-viking centuries affords one of the more striking illustrations of geo-political determinism in the history of our continent.

In earlier chapters we have concluded the viking story in respect of the eastern progress to Kiev and thence south to Byzantium, the westward progress to Iceland, Greenland, and the fronting coast of North America, and the founding by Hrolf and his Danes of the duchy of Normandy. Before we return to Norway and Denmark, with the reference this entails to England, the tangled course of Norse affairs in Ireland demands a brief mention. Here, and still more in the viking colonies and conquests in Scotland and the islands from Man to Orkney, the practice of *viking* died hard. But much of what happened in these latter areas, though fascinating in itself, and amply if often creatively recorded in northern saga, was hardly central to viking history. Ireland was different. The Norsemen (part Danes, part Norwegians) had established a number of important trading towns in the southern half of the island, Dublin, Wexford, Waterford, Cork, and Limerick, and it was in petty kingdoms in and around these that leaders great and small maintained the viking tradition of a military aristocracy based on sea-power and comitatus, and sustained by the profits of trade, tribute, and war. The nature of this society was little changed by an acquaintance with unpeaceful Christianity or intermarriage with the unpeaceful Irish; and the evidence of the graves, especially in respect of weapons, still points to a life tumultuous, decorative, and lordly. The Irish triumph of 902, which gave them Dublin, proved short-lived. The Norsemen were back in 914, recovered Dublin, captured Limerick, held the overlordship of Waterford, and initiated another century of intermittent strife. For a while the affairs of the Norsemen in Ireland were bedevilled by their ambitions in northern England, which brought them brief glory, but helped the Irish kings contain their territorial ambitions. No doubt each lurch of Norse policy seemed meaningful at the time to men like Guthfrith and his son Olaf, to Sigtrygg Gale and Olaf Kvaran, and the various Ivars, Rognvalds, and Sigtryggs who span the century between the return of the grandsons of Ivar of Limerick and the battle of Clontarf. There was the dream of a maritime confederacy both sides of the Irish Sea, there were the encircling Irish, and the never-slackening demand for plunder and tribute to reward their hirdmen. But the hyperbole over events and the emphasis on romantic personalities in the documents which record their deeds, bring them too closely into line with the murky-glittering heroes of the Sagas of Old Time to engage our full belief. The stock of Ragnar continued to breed sowers of gold and feeders of ravens, but no one of them, whatever his valour and triumphs, gave his countrymen in Ireland a prospect of dominance and permanency. Olaf Guthfrith's son died in the north of England in 941, seemingly on the very brink of success, but it is unsafe to conclude that had he lived he would have held his own with the resolute Edmund. Olaf Kvaran not only abandoned hope of securing Northumbria in 951, but at the end of his long reign in Ireland lost Dublin and died a straw-death in Christian Iona. Thereafter the Norsemen found no one to match Mael Seachlainn Mor in the centre and Brian Boru in the south, and it was only the normal intractability of Irish politics which prevented their being bundled into the sea in the heyday of these two kings. But Ireland of the priests, the story-tellers, and the high kings, remained even after Clontarf in that state of dis-unity which made viking entry safe and survival easy.

Clontarf is one of the incantatory names of viking history, a foreign counterpart of Hafrsfjord, Hjorungavag, Svold, and Stiklar-stadir. Like them it was too important to be left to historians, so passed into the legend-maker's hand. Soon it was not merely a battle for an exceeding prize between armies, with the exceeding profits of Norse traders and carriers decorating the background, but the formal assembly of heroes pursuant of doom. Between Liffey and Tolka, within a mile or two of Dublin Bay, there gathered on behalf of Ireland in April 1014 the high king Brian with his son Murchad and grandson Tordelbach, Mael Seachlainn and the southern O'Neill, and Ospak of Man. Opposing them, with their backs to the sea, stood jarl Sigurd the Stout of Orkney, Brodir of Man, Maelmordha with his Leinstermen, and the Dublin vikings under the command of Dubhgall, brother of Sigtrygg Silk-beard. It was an alignment which set brother against brother, father-in-law against son-in-law, Irishman against Irishman, viking against viking, and the skalds and sagamen did it justice, weaving many remarkable personalities, motives, and incidents into their tragic tapestries. There was Gormflaith (Kormlod), mother of Sigtrygg Silk-beard, sister of Maelmordha, widow of Olaf Kvaran, divorced consort of Mael Seachlainn, deserting wife of Brian, impossibly promised as a prize of victory to both Sigurd of Orkney and Brodir of Man, with the Dublin kingdom for dowry. At a far extreme there was Thorstein the Icelander, son of Hall of Sida, who knelt and tied his shoelace, calmly, as men fled after the fall of jarl Sigurd. The pursuing Irishmen asked him why he was not running away like the rest of them. 'Because I can't get home tonight,' said Thorstein, 'for my home is out in Iceland.' He was spared, that his answer might be known—or invented. Omens, wonders, and miracles multiplied, to foretell or confirm the fall of princes. On the Irish side Brian was cut down as he prayed for victory in 'Tomar's Wood', his son Murchad was killed even as victory came in sight, and his grandson Tordelbach, hunting victims by the river-mouth as a seal hunts salmon, was drowned near the Weir of Clontarf. Along with their leaders died 4,000 Irishmen. Of Vikings and Leinstermen the slaughter was worse, for when they fled it was to the hardly attainable refuge of their ships or the viking stronghold over the Liffey. Sigurd died bravely, Brodir gruesomely (if we may trust to *Njáls Saga* 157), and with them 7,000 men. Thereafter it was clear that Ireland would never fall under a Norse yoke, but it also happened that the Norsemen were neither now nor later expelled from Ireland. They remained important to the country's trade and the development of its towns, had kings here and princes there, survived the military disasters of 1052, and were still royally led at the coming of the English in the 1160s and '70s.

We said, at the end of our preceding chapter, that the chief beneficiary of the changes consequent upon the death of Knut and his sons was Norway. A more cynical opinion might limit the benefits to her king, Magnus, and his eventual partner and successor, Harald Hardradi (*Harðráði*, Hard Counsel, Hard Ruler, Harald the Ruthless). At his death in 1035 Knut left three sons, two by his mistress Ælgifu, that Svein whom we have seen expelled from Norway upon the return of Magnus Olafsson, and Harald nicknamed Harefoot, and the third, Hordaknut, the issue of his marriage to Emma, widow of the ill-starred Ethelred. It was Knut's intention that both England and Denmark should be ruled by his one legitimate heir, Hordaknut, but even if all parties, factions, kingdoms, mothers, and half-brothers had been in full agreement, this was impracticable. Hordaknut already bore the title king of Denmark and was resident there. It was to him that the discredited Svein, Ælgifu's son, fled for refuge in the autumn of 1035, and it was at Hordaknut's court that he died a few months later. This still left Harald Harefoot, then resident in England. In the normal course of events Hordaknut would have come straightway to England to be hailed as her king; but this he could not do. The resurgence of Norwegian interests in Norway, accompanied by hostility to Denmark and the sudden prestige of Magnus, kept him so to speak on the frontier. To leave Denmark was to invite invasion. Still, something had to be done, and over in England an English habit prevailed. There was a compromise of interests: the election of a king was postponed, Harald Harefoot was made regent, and Hordaknut's mother Emma remained in charge of Knut's treasure-chest and some of his house-carles in Winchester. But the arrangement was not intended to last, or even to work. Ælgifu's maternal ambitions, thwarted in the case of the dead Svein, were intensified on behalf of Harald; Knut's treasure was seized, a 'king's party' rapidly and efficiently established, Emma's chief supporter, earl Godwine, suborned or otherwise brought over, and Emma's son by Ethelred, Alfred the Ætheling, betrayed and so horribly ill-treated that he died of his blinding. In 1037 Harald was recognized as king of England, and Emma driven from the country to seek refuge with Count Baldwin in Flanders.

And still Hordaknut could not move. It was not until 1038 that he and Magnus reached the agreement which permitted him to gather an invasion force to recover his rights in England. First he went with ten ships to consult with his mother in Bruges. Possibly he had intelligence that all was not well with Harald Harefoot's health, for he was still in Bruges when his half-brother died of an illness on 17 March 1040. Three months later he reached Sandwich with a fleet of sixty-two ships, and 'was at once received by both English and Danes, though afterwards his councillors made a stiff recompense for it when they ordained that [Hordaknut's] sixty-two ships should be paid at the rate of eight marks a rowlock'. In 1041 this fleet-tax produced the monstrous sum of 32,000 pounds of silver for Hordaknut and a commensurate grievance for his subjects. He had Harald's body disinterred from its tomb at Winchester and thrown into the Thames, made peace with earl Godwine for his share in the Ætheling's death in return for a resplendent warship equipped for eighty men, harried all Worcestershire to avenge the killing of two of his tax-collectors, basely betrayed earl Eadwulf of Northumbria, and in the opinion of the C version of the *Chronicle* 'never did anything worthy of a king so long as he reigned'. This was for a period of two years, and in its entry for 1042 the same authority records how 'this year Hordaknut died as he stood at his drink, and he suddenly fell to the ground with a horrible convulsion; and those who were near thereto took hold of him, but he never spoke again, and passed away on 8 June'. The thrones of Denmark and England stood without an incumbent, and the feeble progeny of Knut was exhausted. Svein had failed in Norway, Harald and Hordaknut in England. The Norwegians already had a king of their own ancient

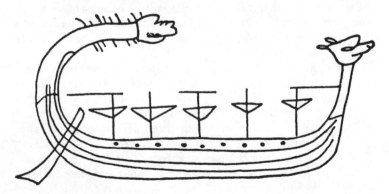

56. A NORSE SHIP

line, and so now would the English, when immediately and by acclamation they chose Hordaknut's half-brother Edward, son of Emma and Ethelred, and finished with Danish kings (though not with Anglo-Danes) for ever. The problem of succession in Denmark was more complicated, and to understand it we must look back to the train of events in Denmark and Norway after the accession of Hordaknut and Magnus Olafsson.

At the time of his return from Russia to Norway in 1034 Magnus was 11 years old. Hordaknut, when he became full king of Denmark, was 17. Both must have relied on their mentors, and we are unclear as to the advice these gave them and the course of action that ensued. A weight of testimony, Danish, Norwegian, and Icelandic (the *Chronicle of Roskilde*, Saxo, Theodoric, *Agríp*, *Morkinskinna*, and *Fagrskinna*, as well as *Heimskringla*), speaks of a 'treaty' between the two kingdoms; but Adam of Bremen speaks of war. The treaty, we are told, was negotiated on an island at the mouth of the Göta-elv or Göta-river, a water-boundary between the kingdoms, at which Magnus and Hordaknut took each other for foster-brother and pledged everlasting peace. If either died without a male heir, the survivor should take his lands and subjects. The twelve highest-born men of each country swore confirmatory oaths that this peace should be enforced so long as any one of them stayed alive. The death of Hordaknut when king of both Denmark and England would give any such arrangement momentous consequences. If, on the other hand, we trust to Adam, who has Magnus invade Denmark during the absence of Hordaknut in England (in this particular Adam is astray), defeat Svein Estridsson, to whom Hordaknut had entrusted his fleet, and seize the Danish kingdom on Hordaknut's death, this was a conquest whose consequences would prove equally fraught with destiny.

But if Magnus was the man in possession, there were other possible contenders. The first of these was another Harald, son of a doughty father, Thorkell the Tall, but he was murdered within the year by Magnus's brother-in-law Ordulf, son of duke Bernhard of Saxony. This left another Svein, sometimes called Ulfsson after his father jarl Ulf, whom Knut cut down in his pride and treachery in Roskilde church, and sometimes Estridsson after his mother, Knut's sister. By blood he was Hordaknut's true heir, with a realistic claim to the throne of Denmark and a theoretical one to the throne of England, where he spent his youth as a hostage for his father's good faith while regent of Denmark. He had lived a further twelve years in Sweden in the service of king Onund Jacob. He was a personable and wealthy young man, with a limp, considerable natural gifts, a subtle sense of political manoeuvre, inexhaustible determination, and patience without end. But Magnus had four weighty and on the whole unanswerable advantages: his prestige (he was a winner of victories, Svein was a loser; he had a saint for father, Svein an unavenged traitor); there was his agreement with Hordaknut and the Danish aristocracy, or maybe his simple right of possession; his deep purse; and his speed of action. And these advantages rested on or were reinforced by his superior fleet. Before Svein could rally his supporters, Magnus crossed from Norway to Jutland and was proclaimed king at the Viborg Thing.

In the circumstances Svein Estridsson judged it advisable to come to terms with Magnus. Once more a Dane met Magnus at the Göta-elf, and this time he promised allegiance. In return Magnus set Svein as jarl and regent over Denmark, like his father Ulf before him. This was more than Svein could have hoped to achieve by force of arms, and he returned to Denmark well placed, as he thought, to exploit the indignation caused by the murder of Harald son of Thorkell the Tall, and so further his own advancement. Soon afterwards he betook himself to Viborg Thing, where the Danes are said to have paid him the same homage due to a king they had recently paid to Magnus. But any satisfaction Svein felt would be short-lived. Magnus moved with his usual speed and energy, and Svein had little to set against the powerful fleet with which he sailed for Denmark. Prudently he departed for Sweden and the court of Onund Jacob, and played a spectator's part in the stirring events which next took place in Denmark.

When Svein was appointed regent of Denmark it was 'for the protection of the land' against the increasing activity of the peoples and settlements of the south Baltic coast, more particularly the Slavonic Wends. In the event Magnus had to discharge the task himself. Either immediately before Svein's disaffection or soon thereafter he moved against Wollin, whose inhabitants, by now predominantly Wendish, but no doubt still retaining a Danish element more sympathetic to Svein than to any Norwegian, had thrown off their allegiance. In 1043 he took the town by storm, burnt its fortifications, and ravaged the surrounding districts. Snorri, for what his word is worth, describes Magnus's attack as against the Wends in Jomsborg, and the skaldic verses incorporated in his narrative (they are by Arnor Jarlaskald) make no mention of vikings, only of Wends and heathens. Adam of Bremen (*schol. 56*) has Magnus besiege Jumne, 'richest city of the Slavs'. At any rate, the Jomsborg vikings, creatures of legend for the best part of a century, now disappear from our sight for ever.

Magnus now turned to deal with a Wendish invasion of southern Jutland. Continuing Slavonic pressure westwards through the north German plain was the most serious menace to Danish security at home since the northward-looking ambitions of Charlemagne, and a sharp threat to Danish trade. The outlook was equally perturbing to the Saxons, and Magnus and his brother-in-law Ordulf joined forces to save their peoples from the common danger. But clear though the situation was, and urgent the need, there were complications. There were Norwegians who judged it politic to let the Danes clear their own southern boundaries and weaken themselves in the process. There were Danes who wished to see the Wends defeated but grudged the glory of a Christian triumph to a Norwegian, while supporters of Svein were less than happy to aggrandize the popularity of his rival. But with his usual incisiveness Magnus brought his fleet to Hedeby and disembarked his men in the rear of the Wends, who were harrying farther north. This permitted him to join with Ordulf and the Saxons. The question now was whether to fight, and it seems to the modern observer, as it seemed to Magnus and Ordulf in September 1043, that there was only one answer. So the Norse-Saxon army moved into position on the flat expanse of the Lyrskov Hede north-west of the modern Schleswig, and there, if it had not already done so, legend took over from history. That night the Christians slept, as good Christians should, in their armour under their shields. The king prayed and was wakeful, but slept long enough to see his father St. Olaf in a dream and learn that the morrow would be rough on the heathen. And so it proved. As dawn grew to day the northerners heard the ringing of a bell on high, and those who had been in Nidaros thought it sounded like the pealing of the great bell Glad which St. Olaf had presented to the Church of St. Clement there. If the Wends heard it too, the circumstance went unreported. It was Michaelmas Eve. All Christian sources stress the superiority in numbers of the Wendish host, but in the light of St. Olaf's assurance this could not dismay the land's defenders. It is told of Magnus that, fortified by faith and vision, he doffed his mail-shirt and fought in a kirtle of red silk swinging the battle-axe Hel which had been St. Olaf's own. The foremost of the Wends fell in waves, those in the rear fled and perished like cattle, the entire heath was strewn with their dead. Adam of Bremen ventures a total of 15,000 Wendish corpses, Snorri leaves it with the statement that in Christian times no such carnage was ever wrought in the north as that among the Wends on Lyrskov Heath. That the Wendish army was shattered in Jutland and the Wendish threat to Denmark removed is not to be doubted. Both conclusions are unaffected by the inconsistencies, even the contradictions, to be found in the early sources.[1]

Magnus had still to deal with the threat to his authority in Denmark posed by Svein Estridsson. He had also to make a gesture in respect of England, which by his treaty with Hordaknut he considered should now belong to him, not to Edward the Englishman. The English took his claim, as they should, seriously, for he disposed of the naval strength of two great seafaring kingdoms, but his preoccupations at home, first with Svein and then with his maternal uncle Harald Hardradi, prevented his ever mounting an expedition for England, where he knew he could look for a united opposition, save for the eccentricities of queen Emma and maybe bishop Stigand of Elmham.[2] To Svein Estridsson's inquiries about

---

[1] Our doubts extend far beyond the discardable hagiographical and propagandist details. Skaldic verses by Thjodolf Arnorson and Arnor Jarlaskald preserved in *Morkinskinna* but not used by Snorri Sturluson in *Heimskringla* point to there being two big engagements, one on Lyrskov Hede and the other by the Skotborgará, Skotborg river, near Ribe, a good way farther north. Snorri evidently considers the Skotborgará to be a river traversing Lyrskov Hede (*Hlýrskógsheiði*). *Knýtlinga Saga* 22 would have Svein Estridsson take part in the battle, on the Danish side, invoking to this end a probably misquoted verse by the skald Thorleik the Fair. With comparable rashness *Ágrip* makes Svein fight for the Wends. *Morkinskinna, Fagrskinna,* and *Heimskringla* preserve the likely tradition that Svein, having reneged on his treaty with Magnus, could take no part in the struggle. Adam of Bremen makes no mention of his royal friend and patron Svein, but ascribes the victory 'on the heath near Hedeby' to Magnus. For a concise summary, see Bjarni Aðalbjarnarson, *Heimskringla*, III, pp. xi–xii and 42.

[2] There is little evidence that Magnus seriously considered the conquest of England. Also it is hard to credit Adam of Bremen's twicemade assertion that Edward of England promised Svein Estridsson that he should be his heir (II, lxxviii, and III, xii). Sture Bolin suggests (*Scandia*, V, 214–21) that Adam's words may be interpreted to mean that Edward had made this promise not to

help against Magnus, England returned an unhelpful answer. In 1045 and again in the following year Edward stationed a fleet off Sandwich in readiness for a Norwegian attack; early in 1047 he and his councillors refused Svein's request for fifty ships to serve with him in northern waters. But for the moment we must stay with the year 1045.

Svein was not the only monarch-to-be who ate Onund's meat that winter, for 1045 saw the re-entry into the northern arena of the last of the part-historical, part-legendary viking heroes, Harald Hardradi, the 'thunder-bolt of the north', as Adam of Bremen described him. We saw him last at Stiklarstadir, young, untried in war, most valiant, fighting alongside his half-brother Olaf. That was fifteen years ago, when he was 15 years old. The man who now returned to Sweden from the east was 30, in the prime of his strength, the flower of his fame and ambition. His valour and skill at arms were legendary, as were his deeds and reputation as a captain of armies. Brought off the field after Stiklarstadir, and healed of his wounds in a lonely farm-house, he thereafter crossed the Keel into Sweden, and from there proceeded into the service of king Yaroslav in Russia, taking part in the Polish campaign of 1031. Three years later, with a personal following of 500 warriors, he sailed to Byzantium and entered the imperial service. It would be imprudent to insist on the details of the campaigns with which his saga credits him during the next ten years, but we can be sure he spent most of the time with harness on his back, and became a commander of the Varangians. He was a professional who fought in any theatre of war to which his employer sent him, including the Greek islands, Asia

---

Svein but to Magnus. It may be granted that Adam was much misinformed by Svein in various contexts concerning himself and Magnus. In the mid-1040s Edward had not the slightest need to placate Svein, but he and his councillors felt unease about Magnus. That the arrival of Harald Hardradi's son Magnus in the Irish Sea in 1058 with a view to conquering England should be related to Edward's promise of the succession to Magnus the Good some twelve years earlier is a possibility, but nothing more. His expedition is noticed in Welsh and Irish sources (see the reference in B. G. Charles, *Old Norse Relations with Wales*, Cardiff, 1934, p. 48, n. 4) and, very sparely, in the *Anglo-Saxon Chronicle* (see Earle and Plummer, *Two Saxon Chronicles*, II, p. 248): 'In this year came a naval force from Norway: it is tiresome to relate how it all happened.'

Minor, the Caucasus, Palestine, Sicily, Bulgaria.[1] With every allowance made for the subsequent growth of his legend, he showed himself during these years fierce, resourceful, cunning, resilient and enduring, and when occasion called for it, double-dealing, vengeful, and cruel. In brief, the epitome of the viking who lived by rapine and war, believed in fame, riches, and power, and employed fair

[1] *Haralds Saga Sigurðarsonar*, 2–16, offers a highly coloured and far from acceptable account of Harald's exploits while in the service of Byzantium. It much exaggerates his importance in Byzantine affairs, informs us that the empress Zoe wished to marry him, confuses Asia Minor with Africa, credits him with various time-worn stratagems for the reduction of cities, and offers some eccentric information about palace politics. We can accept that the Varangians played an important part in the events of 1042 which led to the blinding and deposition of Michael Calaphates; but *Heimskringla*'s insistence that Harald personally gouged out the emperor's eyes is made suspect by its choice of Constantine Monomachus in the true victim's stead.

The comparable Greek source, the anonymous 'Book of Advice to an Emperor', *c.* 1070–80 (ed. Vasilievsky and Jernstedt, in *Cecaumeni Strategicon*, St Petersburg, 1896) has this to say of Harald: 'Araltes [Harald] was son to the king of Varangia, and had a brother Julavos [Olaf] who inherited his father's kingdom after his death and made his brother Araltes next after him in the kingdom. But while he was still young he decided to go on his travels and pay his respects to the blessed emperor Michael Paphlagon and acquaint himself with Byzantine administration. He had with him too a company of 500 valiant soldiers. Off he went, and the emperor received him as was seemly and proper, and dispatched him together with his company to Sicily, because the Byzantine army had a war on its hands in that island. And he went there and achieved mightily. And when Sicily had been conquered he returned with his troop to the emperor, who appointed him *manglavites* [belt-wearer, a mark of honour]. After this it befell that Delianos began a revolt in Bulgaria, and Araltes and his company went campaigning with the emperor and achieved mightily there against the enemy, as befitted a man of his lineage and valour. The emperor returned home once he had subjugated Bulgaria. I too fought for the emperor as best I might. And as soon as we reached Mesina (?) the emperor appointed him *spatharokandates* [troop-leader, a rank of honour] as a reward for his services. After the death of the emperor Michael and that nephew of his who succeeded him [Michael Calaphates], Araltes sought to obtain permission in the time of Monomachus to return home to his own country, but he was not given leave for this, but instead difficulties were put in his way. Even so he got away by stealth and became king over his country in place of his brother Julavos.'

This associates him with the Sicilian campaign of 1038–41 and the Bulgarian campaign of 1041, and shows a less than sensational rise in the service. For a general discussion, see Sigfús Blöndal, 'The Last Exploits of Harald Sigurdsson in Greek Service', in *Classica et Mediaevalia*, I, 2, 1939, pp. 1–26.

means and foul to obtain them. If the Viking Age went out with
Harald Hardradi it ended with a foremost kemper, albeit a shade
new-style.

Meantime he had not returned home by way of Kiev, Novgorod,
and Aldeigjuborg through any sentimental longing for his native
land and tongue. He had heard how Magnus was ruler over two
kingdoms since the death of Hordaknut, and wanted his share of
Norway—to which he considered himself entitled as Olaf's half-
brother and one who had shed blood for the cause while Magnus was
still a child in Russia. Since Svein wanted something from Magnus,
too, it was natural for them to lay their heads together in Sigtuna
and plan a demonstration against what they regarded as the most
lightly held part of Magnus's dominion. This led to the ravaging of
Zealand and Fyn, but an alliance between Harald and Svein was
based on the merest expediency: the game of power politics in
which they were engaged with Magnus was three-cornered, not a
straight fight. Harald's aim was a kingdom or half-kingdom in
Norway; Svein wanted Denmark; Magnus wanted Norway and
Denmark, but could afford to settle for half of the one so long as he
held on to the whole of the other. Nothing could illustrate more
clearly the status of a 'kingdom' as the personal property of its then
ruler, whether by inheritance, donation, or conquest. Nation it was
not. Nor, in speaking of the kingdom of Norway should we forget
how remote in miles was the north, how remote in spirit the inland
provinces, and how little national sentiment obtained in either.
This was hardly less true of Sweden.

In circumstances which early sources do little to clarify, Harald
made contact with his not unwilling nephew, and Magnus agreed
to a division of his Norwegian territories. 'The kings were now
merry'—but not for long. The situation was still three-cornered
when Magnus died of accident or sickness, by land or water, in
Jutland or Zealand, in the autumn of 1047. Svein had fled to Skåne,
but promptly returned. He was acclaimed king at Isøre Thing on
Zealand and (for the second time) at Viborg Thing in Jutland, and
king he remained over Denmark till his life's end in 1074.

A long and pointless struggle now ensued between Harald and
Svein, characterized on Harald's side by viking raids and punitive
expeditions, on Svein's by battles lost and resistance renewed. The
Icelandic historians exerted their full powers of memory, rearrange-
ment, and invention to shed splendour, even humour, on what is

essentially a sorry narrative of coasts raided, farms burned, husbands killed, and womenfolk carried off. The skalds, too, did their best. The stag of billows, kelpland-courser, still bore ring-sarked oaks of Odinn to the Thing of arrows, where they fed the wolf, gave meat to the raven, shed wound-dew on the waters. But by now we have heard it all before; the limitations of the style are becoming exposed; and it is gifted amateurs like Harald himself with his four-lined contrast between sailors anchored in the hostile Randersfjord and husbands lullabied a-bed by their night-linened wives,[1] or the unnamed sailor who sang of burning Hedeby, that suddenly catch our fancy, not Harald's versifying public-relations men. There were two main periods of Norwegian aggression against Denmark, separated by a ten-year interval during which Harald most resolutely stabilized his boundary with Sweden, drove hard ecclesiastical and economic policies at home and abroad, and strengthened his personal authority by ruthlessly, and often basely, getting rid of various of his enemies and friends, including the four great lords of the Trondelag and Uppland: Einar Thambarskelfir, whom he made 'kiss the thin lips of the axe', along with his son Eindridi; Kalf Arnarson, whom like a northern Uriah he saw advanced into the forefront of battle that he might die of an undefended back; Finn Arnarson, an unwitting tool in his brother's destruction, who fled to the Danes; and Hakon Ivarsson, great-grandson of jarl Hakon of the Trondelag, who fled to the Swedes. The earlier attacks on Denmark were concentrated in the three or four years following upon Harald's accession to the throne of all Norway in 1047, the later came to a climax after 1060. The first series was distinguished by the destruction of the town of Hedeby, the second by the sea-fight at the Nissa in Halland.

The destruction of Denmark's main mart may appear a self-mangling exercise for a man ambitious of the Danish throne. But burning towns came naturally to Harald. Besides, they were of timber here up north, and easily rebuilt; and if we can trust to Snorri the expedition of 1049 had terror and loot as its primary objectives. The congested wooden houses inside their confining rampart made a splendid blaze. An unknown man of Harald's army, with a turn for verse and arson, records how he had stood the previous night *á borgar armi*, on the stronghold's arm, no doubt the

[1] The verse has also been attributed to Thjodolf Arnarsson, and may be of still later provenance.

rampart's northern extremity, and watched the flames climb high over the houses. It was a gallant deed, he opined, and calculated to make Svein as well as Hedeby smart.

The wasteful campaigns that thereafter sought to make two unwilling kingdoms into one dragged on till 1064, when even Harald must recognize that everyone was sick of them. The fight at Nissa itself, which emptied seventy ships of the Danes, settled nothing. Svein was back in Denmark the following winter with undiminished revenues and the approbation of his people. During the winter of 1063–4 messengers passed between the two rulers and a peace meeting was arranged at the Göta river in the spring. The two kings arrived for negotiations which for a while went as uncordially as a modern peace treaty, and for much the same reasons of pride, greed, revenge, and embittered memory. Then wisdom prevailed. Harald should have Norway, Svein Denmark. The ancient boundaries were left undisturbed; there would be no compensation paid or exacted; the line was drawn as of that day, and the peace should last their lifetimes. Harald, winner of battles, carried his banner, the famed Land-Waster, back to Norway, disciplined Raumarike and Heidmark, and fiercely chastised the tax-withholding Upplanders. Svein, loser of battles, returned to Denmark and bound up the nation's wounds. Always defeated, constantly in flight, invariably returning, he had outlasted Magnus and would outlast Harald by eight good years.

And now the Viking Age was moving to its close. Its last and

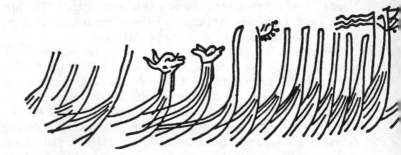

57. A NORSE FLEET
'With sharp keel they ploughed the crest of the foaming deep and sailed in a swift course between skerries and capes till they

consummatory figure had just two more years to live before he died his splendid and unnecessary death at Stamford Bridge near the city of York, drawn there by the never-failing viking compulsions of land, wealth, and fame overseas. His first battle had been at Stiklarstadir back in 1030; next came the great arc of sacks and sieges, sea-fights and land-battles, from Poland through Russia by way of Asia Minor and Bulgaria on to Sicily; then his bid for a kingdom in Norway, wars throughout Uppland and along the Swedish border, and seventeen years of hostilities against the Danes. Now, his fiftieth year safely behind him, he would please himself and gratify his chroniclers by challenging fortune once more, in a greedy, royal, and aesthetically satisfying way. He would undertake an expedition west-over-sea and meet his doom in a holocaust reminiscent of the fabled encounters of old. He would fail to win England, but would ensure its conquest by another and remoter branch of the Nordmanni, the Normans of Normandy. This was the last effective viking intervention in the affairs of western Europe; the manner and extent of Harald's disaster, and its consequences for three nations, made it culminatory.

It was on 5 January 1066 that Edward king of England died of age and sickness, and was succeeded one day later by Harold Godwinson, his *subregulus*. Harald of Norway was never the man to forget that he, too, had a claim to a land as rich as England. One of his first actions after he became sole king of Norway had been to dispatch envoys of peace there. (Svein, typically, asked yet again

reached the town and laid their prows up to the pier in the presence of a great crowd (Bergen).'

to be sent a fleet of fifty ships, and yet again was denied them). But no emphasis on Harald the viking abroad should obscure that he was a hard-headed king at home. The early years of his reign were no time for an Enterprise of England, and thereafter he was too deeply engaged with Svein, though maybe the western expedition of 1058 conducted by his son Magnus shows that he was keeping his ambitions warm. By the winter of 1065–6 he was at long last free to plan a course of action in the light of the significant news coming in from England, Flanders, and Normandy. The legality of his claim, its strength or weakness compared with the claims of others, would not worry him. The thing that mattered was could it be enforced? Clearly he thought it could, and that Svein's claim as the nephew of Knut could not. We would give a good deal to know what was said in Trondheim that winter and the following spring about Harold Godwinson the Englishman and William the Bastard of Normandy and *their* claims. One thing we can be sure of: Harald of Norway judged he had the beating of them both. The emissaries who came to him from Harold's brother Tostig, the deposed earl of Northumbria, and from the stirring hive of Orkney with pleas and counsel would be of the same opinion. Even so he must plan carefully, move unannounced, strike hard and true. It is difficult to believe that so shrewd a calculator as William knew nothing of Harald's interest, particularly in view of the Scandinavian connection, but we have no evidence that he was aware he was planning a full-scale invasion. Harold Godwinson was taken entirely by surprise, so perhaps we should attribute the silence of Norman and English sources before the event to the Norwegian's skill in mounting an expedition and, when the moment came, his speed in delivering the blows. It helped that Harold and William had much on their minds, and it is a legitimate speculation that Harald Hardradi had over the years assembled so many and such large fleets for inter-Scandinavian operations (he took 180 ships into battle at the Nissa) that no one in Normandy and England could be sure that the 200 or so ships assembling in the Solunds were not intended for the same purpose. In the autumn the fleet set sail, with Northumbria as its ultimate destination. By the time it was joined on the other side of the sea by its reinforcements under Tostig and the Orkneyers it is said to have numbered 300 ships and 9,000 men. It could hope for the support of Tostig's former earldom, and rely on the goodwill of the Scots.

Possibly Harald knew that the wind which carried him down the coast of Yorkshire, ravaging in Cleveland, Scarborough, and Holderness on the way, would keep the Norman invasion fleet in port and immobilize Harold Godwinson, condemned to wait upon William's initiative. But speculation serves no purpose: once Harald entered the Humber and, moving behind the few and retreating English ships, followed the Ouse to Riccall, three miles below the conjunction of that river with the Wharfe, where he disembarked his men, he was committed to winning a kingdom or a grave on English soil, whatever the course of events down south. Northumbria was not to be acquired without a battle, and one which though somewhat neglected in history and story compared with the battle of Stamford Bridge, played a vital part in deciding the issues of the year. The small English fleet lay a few miles up the Wharfe at Tadcaster; ten miles north of Riccall stood the city of York, and Harald advanced upon it without delay. Barring his road was the army of Edwin earl of Mercia and Morcar earl of Northumbria. The earls had taken up position at Gate Fulford on the Ouse, two miles south of York, and here they fought with Harald and Tostig on Wednesday, 20 September. It was a hard and close-locked engagement for most of the day. When the Englishmen broke they had suffered losses which would affect the issue at Hastings, while Norwegian mortality helped decide Stamford Bridge.

Meantime, though Harald of Norway did not know it, Harold of England was riding north with his housecarles, and the invasion coast stood open. This was a calculated risk of the English king's, a course imposed on him by the kingdom's need and his own temperament. A change of wind could prove him wrong, without proving his critics right.

For Harald Hardradi the road to York lay open, as did York itself. He had everything to gain by moderation; it was not treated as a hostile town, and once he had taken hostages for good behaviour and provisions for his troops, he retired to his ships at Riccall. At this same time he offered the citizens of York a treaty whereby they would become his allies and march south with him 'to conquer this realm'. But habit demanded that he secure hostages from throughout the shire, and we assume that it was to receive these that he now marched the main body of his army to Stamford Bridge on the Derwent, twelve miles from the ships at Riccall, and eight miles north-east of York. It was a good centre of road communications, well suited to his purpose. Harald's movement away from his ships was eloquent of self-confidence—and ignorance of the man he had to deal with. A forced march had by now brought Harold Godwinson north to Tadcaster, where he met with the English ships and spent the night of the 24th. Incredibly, Hardradi was still unaware of his movements. On the morrow, Monday, 25 September, Harold moved rapidly north through an undefended York, and at the end of a seventeen-mile march came upon the unsuspecting Norwegians at Stamford Bridge.

We know very little about the battle itself. The Norwegian position was on the east bank of the river, but possibly because of their leisurely overconfidence and subsequent surprise they seem not to have set a strong enough guard about the vital bridge. 'A very stubborn battle', says the *Chronicle*, 'was fought by both sides.' It was an encounter which moved northern historians to compile a magnificent story, complete with omens, accidents, confrontations, gnomic rejoinders, berserk fury, and the casting away of armour, but story, alas, is all that it is.[1] In numbers and quality, weapons and armour, the armies were well matched. In skill, valour, and

---

[1] There are thoroughgoing discussions of the northern historical material relating to the battles of 1066 in Bjarni Aðalbjarnarson, *Om de Norsk Kongers Sagaer*, Oslo, 1937, and in his many-times cited edition of *Heimskringla*. See also G. Indrebø, *Fagrskinna*, Kristiania, 1917, and most recently Svend Ellehøj, *Studier over den ældste norrøne historieskrivning*, Copenhagen, 1965. The i ... ant parts of *Hemings þáttr* have been translated by Jacqueline Simpson, *The Northmen Talk*, 1965; and *Orkneyinga Saga* may be read in G. W. Dasent's version, Rolls Series, 88, 1894. It is interesting that *Morkinskinna* (the oldest of the three), *Fagrskinna*, and *Heimskringla* omit from their rather stereotyped set of portents attendant on Harald's expedition, as well as on the battlefield itself, the 'haired star', Halley's Comet, whose appearance so deeply impressed the compilers of the *Anglo-Saxon Chronicle* and the Bayeux Tapestry. Of confrontations the one we set aside with most regret produced the promise to Harald Hardradi of seven feet of English ground, 'or as much more as he is taller than other men', and Harald's comment on his English namesake: 'A small king that, but he stood bravely (*var.* well) in his stirrups.' The only English contribution in any way comparable is the *C-Chronicle*'s twelfth-century conclusion. 'The Norwegians fled from the English, but there was one Norwegian who stood firm against the English force, so that they could not cross the bridge nor clinch victory. An Englishman shot with an arrow but to no avail, and another went under the bridge and stabbed him through the coat of mail. Then Harold, king of the English, crossed the bridge and his levies went forward with him; and there made great slaughter of both Norwegians and Flemings.' (Trans. Garmonsway.)

experience it would be hard to choose between them, and each had an imperative need of victory. They fought on foot, and with the advantages of surprise and preparedness resting with the English, so far as we can tell they slogged it out till the day turned irrecoverably against the Norwegians. Harald, says tradition, was struck in the throat by an arrow and fell. There can have been few survivors from his bodyguard: a new generation of soldiers had to grow up in Norway before an overseas adventure could be undertaken again. When their frightfully punished army at last took to flight the survivors were harried over a dozen bloody miles to Riccall. There was to be no residual menace in the north when Harold Godwinson sped south again. But at Riccall he stayed his reddened hand and gave the *wēalāf*, the sorry remnant, quarter. Of the battle and its aftermath the *Anglo-Saxon Chronicle* (D) has this to say: 'Then Harold our king came unexpectedly upon the Norwegians, and met them beyond York at Stamford Bridge with a great host of Englishmen, and that day a very stubborn battle was fought by both sides. There were slain Harald Hardradi [MS. Fairhair] and earl Tostig, and the remaining Norwegians were put to flight, while the English fiercely assailed their rear until some of them reached their ships: some were drowned, others burnt to death, and thus perished in various ways so that there were few survivors, and the English had possession of the place of slaughter. The king then gave quarter to Olaf, the son of the king of the Norwegians, to their bishop, to the jarl of Orkney, and to all those who were left aboard the ships. They then went inland to our king, and swore oaths that they would ever maintain peace and friendship with this land; and the king let them sail home with twenty-four ships.'

This Olaf was Olaf Kyrre, the Gentle or Peaceful, who ruled at first with his brother and then alone over Norway till 1093 without strife or bloodshed. It was well for the Scandinavian kingdoms that he was spared. He sailed for home by way of Orkney, and one wonders how soon he learned that within days of the truce at Riccall the victorious Harold Godwinson had made a second forced march, this time south to his death at Hastings, and that the Normans had achieved what their northern kinsmen had missed, the conquest of England.

One year after Stamford Bridge Harald Hardradi's body was brought from England to Norway. He was buried north in Nidaros, in St. Mary's church, which he himself had founded. When that huge skull, with its sweeping moustaches and mis-aligned eye-brows, and that stupendous frame which for thirty-five years was 'never free of turbulence and war', were laid away in the presence of his peace-loving son, the Viking Age was over.

Symbolically if not factually. For in 1069 Svein Estridsson, made hopeful by unease and rebellion in the northern half of England, dispatched a strong invasion fleet to that country. It had no success off Kent and East Anglia, but at York won a victory ominous for the Normans. But in their viking greed for prisoners and money its leaders allowed king William to win back the initiative his captains had lost, devastate the north and the north Midlands, and when Svein crossed in person to the Humber in the spring of 1070 it was to find the situation so unpromising that by summer-time he made peace with king William and sailed his fleet home again to Denmark. Old habits die hard, the Danes briefly, and the Norwegians till the skirmish at Largs in 1263, would again lead their lank steeds of ocean into western waters, display the dragon-head, but these were the spasmodic efforts of stragglers in a race already run, whose principal figures had long since quit the field and, save for the winners of fame, been hooded in darkness for ever.

And so the Age ended.

> *þverra nú, þeirs þverrðu,*
> *þingbirtingar Ingva,*
> *hvar skalk manna mildra,*
> *mjaðveitar dag, leita,*
> *þeira's hauks fyr handan*
> *háfjöll digulsnjávi*
> *jarðar gjörð við orðum*
> *eyneglda mér hegldu.*

Minish they now who diminished
Dawnfire of meadfoaming horn;
Now vanish the heroes, time-vanquished,
War's flaunters, the thingmen of Ingvi.
Who now shower limbeck's snowsilver
As guerdon past earth's sea-isled girdle?
Or fill high hawkfell of my hand
With skald's reward for skilled word?

This had been Egill Skallagrimsson's lament for Arinbjorn the hersir, when he learned of his death alongside Harald Greycloak of

Norway at the battle by Hals in the Limfjord, *c.* 974. A century later it can serve as an epitaph for those last strong props of the Viking Age—the unknown fighting-men who watched Hedeby blaze and covered the retreat at Stamford Bridge, great lords like Einar Thambarskelfir and the Arnarsons, and the monarchs themselves—who died with the reigns of Harald Hardradi and Svein Estridsson, and brought the Age to its rough-hewn, mortuary conclusion.

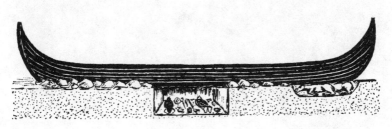

58. 'THE RIDERS SLEEP, HEROES IN THE GRAVE'

APPENDIXES

I. Runes

The first runic alphabet is thought to have originated either a little before or a little after the beginning of the Christian era. It consisted of twenty-four letters or phonetic symbols, organised in three *ættir* or families of eight, and with minor variations in the shape of some of the letters was common to all the rune-using Germanic peoples. For convenience the runic alphabet is known as the *futhark*, from its first letters (just as our present alphabet is sometimes called the ABC). Each letter had its proper and significant name: for example ⼘, f, was Gothic *faihu*, ON. *fé*, OE. *feoh*, cattle, property, wealth; ⼚, þ (=th), Gothic *þauris*, ON. *þurs*, giant (but OE. *þorn*, thorn); ⼞, w, Gothic *winja*, ON. *vin*, pasture, or Gothic *wunja*, OE. *wynn*, joy; ⼝, h, Gothic *hagl*, ON. *Týr*, OE. *Tiw*, the god. The entire alphabet may be set out thus:

ᚠ ᚢ ᚦ ᚨ ᚱ ᚲ ᚷ ᚹ ᛬ᚺ ᚾ ᛁ ᛃ ᛈ ᛇ ᛉ ᛊ ᛬ᛏ ᛒ ᛖ ᛗ ᛜ ᛚ ᛟ ᛞ

f u th a r k g w h n i j p E R s t b e m I ng o d

The language represented by these phonetic symbols is the Old Norse common to the Scandinavian peoples during the first six or seven hundred years after the birth of Christ. But both alphabet and letters were undergoing modification and the *futhark* of the Viking Age proper, *c.* 700–1050, was one of sixteen letters, thus:

ᚠ ᚢ ᚦ ᚬ ᚱ ᚴ ᛬ᚼ ᚾ ᛁ ᛅ ᛋ ᛬ᛏ ᛒ ᛘ ᛦ With the three later dotted runes ᛁ ᛂ ᚽ

f u th ǫ r k h n i a s t b m I R   e g y

These are the Danish forms, normal over Denmark, Skåne, much of Sweden and Norway. There was a further Swedish-Norwegian series with substantially reduced branch-strokes, and a second Swedisl refinement, the so-called Hälsinge runes. However, the reduction from twenty-four to sixteen letters, which meant that one rune must now serve for more than one sound, raised problems. Three dotted (*stungne*) runes were added to the sixteen during the eleventh century, and eventually Scandinavia would enjoy a complete runic ABC on the Latin model.

Where and how the runic alphabet originated is still a subject of debate. That roughly a third of the long *futhark* derives from Latin capitals is self-evident; but other alphabets, Greek, Etruscan, and north Italian, have been brought into the account, as have the Celts, Goths, Marcomanni, and Eruli. Where so much is uncertain, it may be enough to conclude in general terms that the *futhark* was in part based on one or more southern European alphabets, among which the Roman predominated, and in part invented. The shape of its letters based on vertical and diagonal strokes, and avoiding horizontals and curves, suggests this was an alphabet designed for use on wood. The earliest dateable runic inscriptions are to be found in Denmark, but this does not disprove a contemporary usage among the Goths north of the Black Sea. A majority of scholars stress the magical significance of runes, and runes were undoubtedly used in a most special way for spells and magic. But runes were an all-purpose alphabet and were used increasingly for non-magical (i.e. gnomic, commemorative, recording, identifying) purposes. The range and number of runic inscriptions during the Iron and Viking Ages is impressive: from Greenland to the Black Sea, from the Isle of Man to Athens; they are rare in Iceland, plentiful in Denmark (about 500) and Norway (about 750), and most abundant of all in Sweden, which has some 3,000, including 1,000 or more in the province of Uppland. Brief Bibliography: O. von Friesen in *Nordisk Kultur*, VI, 1933; A. Bæksted, *Runerne, deres Historie og Brug*, Copenhagen, 1943; S. Bugge, *Norges Indskrifter med de ældre Runer*, Christiania, 1891–1923; M. Olsen, *Norges Innskrifter med de yngre Runer*, Oslo, 1941–51; L. Jacobsen and E. Moltke, *Danmarks Runeindskrifter*, Copenhagen, 1942; S. Söderberg, E. Brate, E. Wessén, R. Kinander, etc., *Sveriges Runinskrifter*, Uppsala, 1900–. R. W. V. Elliott, *Runes, an Introduction*, Manchester, 1959; L. Musset, *Introduction à la Runologie*, revised ed. Paris, 1976; R. I. Page, 'Rune-Masters and Skalds', in J. Graham-Campbell, *The Viking World*, 1980.

II. The Danelaw

The Danelaw was by name and definition that part of England in which Danish, not English, law and custom prevailed. It comprised the Danish conquests and settlements in Northumbria, East Anglia, the Five Boroughs of Stamford, Leicester, Derby, Nottingham, and Lincoln, and the south-east Midlands. Its southern boundary was established by the treaty made shortly after 886 between king Alfred and Guthrum of East Anglia. It followed the estuary of the Thames upstream to the confluence of the river Lea, just east of London, a town which remained in English hands, then up the Lea to its source near Dunstable, whence it led north to Bedford. From Bedford it followed the Ouse westwards to where it was crossed by Watling Street at Fenny Stratford. Northwards of this irregular line lay English Mercia and the territories won by other Danish armies. The effect of the treaty then was to bring about the threefold division of England into Wessex, English Mercia, and the Danelaw; and though the Danelaw's political independence lasted fifty years at most, its separate, i.e. Scandinavian, quality was recognized not only by Alfred and his English successors, but by the laws of Knut in the early eleventh century and by Norman law-givers after the Conquest.

The Danelaw (its name had no currency before the time of Knut) was, we suspect, at no time fully homogeneous, but internal variations in respect of race, density of Norse settlement, political allegiance and social organization, counted for less than its separateness from English England. The evidence of personal coins and moneyers is indicative, and that of language, vocabulary, and place-names compulsive, that there was a rapid and heavy settlement of parts of the Danelaw by Scandinavians 'representing little less than a migration' (K. Cameron, *Scandinavian Settlement in the Territory of the Five Boroughs: the Place-Name Evidence*, 1965, p. 10), and recent attempts to minimize the Norse element have been unconvincing. Scandinavian vocabulary penetrated every domain of language, as the following groups of words indicate: *law, by-law, outlaw*; *riding, wapentake*; *husband, fellow, husting*; *awkward, happy, ill, loose, odd, seemly, ugly, weak, wrong*; *calf, leg, skin, skull*; *bull, egg, kid*; *bank, brink, booth, down* (i.e. birds' down), *knife, race, rift, thrift, trust, window*; *they, them, their*, (and the pronominal adjectives *both* and *same*); *sister*; *to call, crawl, cut, drown, lift, reef, scare, take, want*; *birth* and *to die. Dönsk tunga* was spoken in parts of England long after the end of Danish rule there, and in parts of Scotland even later. But the main interpenetration of tongues had taken place before the death of Knut. The evidence is so abundant that, reinforced as it is by such place-name elements as *-by, -beck, -breck, -fell, -gill, -keld, -mel, -rigg, -scale, -sough, -skeith, -thwaite, -thorp*, and *-toft*, it points to a considerable number of northern speakers in the Danelaw.

Of place-names those in *-by* and *-thorp* are the most significant. Cameron calculates that of the 303 names in *-by* recorded in Domesday Book as being in the territory of the Five Boroughs, at least 87 per cent are Scandinavian compounds. The evidence of the *-thorp* names (they number 106) is likely to prove not less decisive. Yorkshire and Lindsey in Lincolnshire show a Scandinavian division into 'ridings' (i.e. thridings, thriding, ON. *þriðjungr*, 'a third part'); Yorkshire and the counties of the Five Boroughs were subdivided not into English hundreds but into wapentakes, a curious development from the ON. *vápnatak*, the 'weapon-taking' or brandishing of weapons which denoted approval of decisions made at the Thing—not that the word was ever used in Scandinavia for a legal or administrative unit. In the Five Boroughs arable land was commonly divided not into English hides but into ploughlands, which in turn were subdivided into eight oxgangs—a ploughland representing a unit of land which could be worked by an eight-ox plough-team in one year. Norse words for classes of men persisted in the Danelaw after Domesday Book, including the hold (ON. *höldr*) or free land-owner, who in Norway could be buried next to the *lendrmaðr* or *hersir*, and in Northumbria had a wergold of 4,000 thrymsas, double that of a thane, equal to that of a king's high-reeve, and half that of an earldorman or bishop; the sokeman or superior landowning peasant, owing fair duty to his lord's estate, but participant in that highly relished privilege of free men everywhere —responsibility for the payment of his own taxes to the king; the dreng (ON. *drengr*, 'brave, worthy man'), a shade better off in status than the attached peasant, and surviving the Conquest on the royal manors between Mersey and Ribble; and, finally, the bonde and the thrall.

The Scandinavian basis of law and legal custom in the Danelaw was frequently and handsomely acknowledged by the law-makers of all England. No doubt there were variations of legal practice amongst the Danelaw's different regions, but these again were less significant than the overall difference from Wessex and English Mercia. This was not just a matter of terminology, though such Scandinavian or anglicized Scandinavian terms as *lahslit*, 'breach of law', *lahcop*, 'purchase of law', *sammæle*, 'agreement', *botleas*, 'unatonable', *festerman*, 'surety', *sacleas*, 'innocent', and the like, bear witness to concept as well as vocabulary; but the notion of law itself was at times distinct from that of England. Thus, a Danelaw wergeld was related to the dead man's rank rather than his lord's, and offences against the king's peace were more sternly penalized than in England. But the most striking example of Danelaw legal usage will be found in the Wantage code of Ethelred the Unready, which describes the legal assemblies or courts of the Five Boroughs: first, the court of the Five Boroughs considered as a unit, presided over by an ealdorman or king's reeve; second, the court of each separate Borough; and, third, the wapentake court. All this is strongly reminiscent of the supra-Things and local Things of Scandinavia and Iceland; but the resemblances do not end there. In each wapentake there were twelve leading men, thanes, with a special responsibility for law—the so-called jury of presentment. These twelve were required to take oath on holy relics that they would neither accuse the innocent nor shield the guilty, after which they were empowered to arrest any of ill fame then at odds with the reeve. In Stenton's words: 'The sworn jury is unknown to pure Old English law, and it is safe to follow the long succession of scholars who have seen in the twelve leading thegns of the wapentake an institution derived from the juries of twelve familiar in the Scandinavian north. Although the fate of the suspects was settled by the ordeal, and not by the judgment of the thegns who had presented them, there is reason to think that these thegns formed what may be called an upper bench of doomsmen within their wapentake. A later passage in the codex runs: "Let the judgment stand on which the thegns are agreed; if they differ, let that stand which eight of them have pronounced, and let those who are outvoted each pay six half-marks." On general grounds it is highly probable that the thegns of this passage are identical with the thegns on whom the wapentake relied for the presentment of evil-doers. In any case, the passage is interesting as an illustration of the climate of thought which lay behind the practice of the Danelaw courts. It is the first assertion in England of the principle that where opinions differ that of the majority must prevail' (*Anglo-Saxon England*, pp. 503–4. For the Danelaw in general see the same work, pp. 494–518). Finally there are the lawmen (*lagemanni*), familiar to us from Scandinavia, and more especially Iceland, mentioned in connection with Cambridge, Stamford, Lincoln, York, and Chester, where they appear to have constituted a judicial body (normally of twelve) who gave verdicts in appointed cases.

Despite the basic research of Cameron and Jensen in place-name studies, and of Dolley in numismatics, problems remain. But there is no need to wait on a general conclusion regarding the Danelaw. 'The Scandinavian impact on England resulted in a thorough enrichment of the community. Intensification of agrarian effort brought it about that by 1066 Lincolnshire, Norfolk and Suffolk ranked high among the prosperous shires of England. Scandinavian contribution to the political life of the country had been great at all levels, from the monarchy itself, where Cnut ranks as one of the most successful of English rulers, to the minor administrative divisions of the Danelaw and the hustings and courts of doomsmen of London, York, and Chester. The opening up of the North Sea to regular commerce proved permanent and was not disrupted by the Norman Conquest. Above all the impact of these active seafaring northerners on the early life and stabilization of the towns of north and eastern England was tremendous. York appears in saga stories as an impressive town where the Scandinavian language and institutions were fully familiar. [For York see A. Hall, *Viking York and the North*, 1978; and the York 'The Vikings in England' Catalogue, 1981–2.] The importance of the Scandinavian element in London has probably been underestimated.' When to this we add the blending of English and Scandinavian art, especially the sculpture in stone, and the Scandinavian share in the English language, the historian's final sentence is a just one. 'Regionally and generally the influx of the Scandinavians made a vital contribution to the inner nature of the English communities of the Middle Ages.' (H. R. Loyn, *The Vikings in Britain*, pp. 136–7.)

The importance of the new Danelaw to the Norsemen back home, save as a temporary outlet of population, awaits a full determination: i.e. its part in christianizing first Denmark and then Norway and Iceland; its influence on visual art in Scandinavia; on coinage and currency, and on such military and quasi-political institutions as the *leiðangr* and *hirð*; and on the concept of monarchy itself. Its influence may well have been considerable in these and other spheres.

III. A Rus Ship-Burial on the Volga

[During the years 921–2 the Arab Ibn Fadlan served as secretary of an embassy from the Khalif of Baghad to the Bulgars of the middle Volga. About one-fifth of his account of his journey (the *Risala*) relates to the Rus whom he met at the camp and trading-post, later the town, of Bulgar. We have already noted his witness to certain of their social and trading habits (pp. 164–5, 197 and n. 2 above). His account of a Rus funeral is the most celebrated part of the *Risala*. It is here quoted in the version of H. M. Smyser, which takes account of the translation into German of Ahmed Zeki Validi Togan and that into French of M. Canard. The passages in roman type are based on·the manuscript of the *Risala*, probably of the eleventh century, discovered at Meshed in Iran in 1923 by Zeki Validi. Those in italics are based on Amin Razi's version of the *Risala* (AR), of 1593, which is thought to derive from a good early MS. and to preserve many valuable details not found in the Meshed MS. (see the references to A. Zeki Validi Togan, Canard, and Smyser on p. 164 n. 2 above).]

87. I had heard that at the deaths of their chief personages they did many interesting things, of which the least was cremation, and I was interested to learn more. At last I was told of the death of one of their outstanding men. They placed him in a grave and put a roof over it for ten days while they cut and sewed garments for him.

If the deceased is a poor man they make a little boat, which they lay him in and burn. If he is rich, they collect his goods and divide them into three parts, one for his family, another to pay for his clothing, and a third for making *nabīd* [an intoxicating drink, perhaps beer], which they drink until the day when his female slave will kill herself and be burned with her master. They stupefy themselves by drinking this *nabīd* night and day; sometimes one of them dies cup in hand.

(AR: They burn him in this fashion: they leave him for the first ten days in a grave. His possessions they divide into three parts: one part for his daughters and wives; another for garments to clothe the corpse; another part covers the cost of the intoxicating drink which they consume in the course of ten days, uniting sexually with women and playing musical instruments. Meanwhile, the slave-girl who gives herself to be burned with him, in these ten days drinks and indulges in pleasure; she decks her head and her person with all sorts of ornaments and fine dress and so arrayed gives herself to the men.)

When a great personage dies, the people of his family ask his young women and men slaves, 'Who among you will die with him?' One answers, 'I'. Once he or she has said that, the thing is obligatory; there is no backing out of it. Usually it is the girl slaves who do this [i.e. volunteer].

88. When the man of whom I have spoken died, his girl slaves were asked, 'Who will die with him?' One answered, 'I'. She was then put in the care of two young women, who watched over her and accompanied her everywhere, to the point that they occasionally washed her feet with their own hands. Garments were being made for the deceased and all else was being readied of which he had need. Meanwhile the slave drinks every day and sings, giving herself over to pleasure.

89. When the day arrived on which the man was to be cremated and the girl with him, I went to the river on which was his ship. I saw that they had drawn the ship on to the shore, that they had erected four posts of birch wood and other wood, and that around it [the ship] was made a structure like great ships'-tents out of wood [Canard: and that around these posts they had arranged some kind of great scaffolding of wood]. Then they pulled the ship up until it was on this wooden construction. Then they began to come and go and to speak words which I did not understand, while the man was still in his grave and had not yet been brought out. (AR: *The ninth [ZV; Canard: tenth] day, having drawn the ship up on to the river bank, they guarded it. In the middle of the ship they prepared a dome or pavillon à coupole (kunbad) of wood and covered this with various sorts of fabrics.*) Then they brought a couch and put it on the ship and covered it with a mattress of Greek brocade. Then came an old woman whom they call the Angel of Death, and she spread upon

the couch the furnishing mentioned. It is she who has charge of the clothes-making and arranging all things, and it is she who kills the girl slave. I saw that she was a strapping old woman, fat and louring.

When they came to the grave they removed the earth from above the wood, then the wood, and took out the dead man clad in the garments in which he had died. I saw that he had grown black from the cold of the country. They had put *nabīd*, fruit, and a pandora in the grave with him. They removed all that. The dead man did not smell bad and only his colour had changed. They dressed him in trousers, stockings(?), boots, a tunic [*qurṭaq*], and caftan of brocade with gold buttons. They put a hat of brocade and fur on him. Then they carried him into the pavilion [*qubba*] on the ship. They seated him on the mattress and propped him up with cushions. They brought *nabīd*, fruits, and fragrant plants, which they put with him, then bread, meat, and onions, which they placed before him. Then they brought a dog, which they cut in two and put in the ship. Then they brought his weapons and placed them by his side. Then they took two horses, ran them until they sweated, then cut them to pieces with a sword and put them into the ship. They took two cows, which they likewise cut to pieces and put in the ship. Next they killed a rooster and a hen and threw them in. The girl slave who wished to be killed went here and there and into each of their tents, and the master of each tent had sexual intercourse with her and said, 'Tell your lord I have done this out of love for him.'

(AR: *The tenth day, they brought the deceased out of the ground and put him inside the pavilion* [qubba] *and put around him different kinds of flowers and fragrant plants. Many men and women gathered and played musical instruments, and each of his kinsmen built a pavilion* [qubba] *around his pavilion* [qubba] *at some distance. The slave-girl arrayed herself and went to the pavilions of the kinsmen of the dead man, and the master of each had sexual intercourse once with her, saying in a loud voice, 'Tell your master that I have done the duty* [or exercised the right] *of love and friendship.' And so, as she went to all the pavilions to the last one, all the men had intercourse with her. When this was over, they cut a dog in two halves and put it into the boat, then, having cut the head off a rooster, they threw it, head and body, to the right and left of the ship.*)

90. Friday afternoon they led the slave-girl to a thing that they had made which resembled a door frame. She placed her feet on the

palms of the men and they raised her up to overlook this frame. She spoke some words and they lowered her again. A second time they raised her up and she did again what she had done; then they lowered her. They raised her a third time and she did as she had done the two times before. Then they brought her a hen; she cut off the head, which she threw away, and then they took the hen and put it in the ship. I asked the interpreter what she had done. He answered, 'The first time they raised her she said, "Behold, I see my father and mother." The second time she said, "I see all my dead relatives seated." The third time she said, "I see my master seated in Paradise and Paradise is beautiful and green; with him are men and boy servants. He calls me. Take me to him." ' Now they took her to the ship. She took off the two bracelets which she was wearing and gave them both to the old woman called the Angel of Death, who was to kill her; then she took off the two finger rings which she was wearing and gave them to the two girls who served her and were the daughters of the woman called the Angel of Death. Then they raised her on to the ship, but they did not make her enter into the pavilion.

Then men came with shields and sticks. She was given a cup of *nabid*; she sang at taking it and drank. The interpreter told me that she in this fashion bade farewell to all her girl companions. Then she was given another cup; she took it and sang for a long time while the old woman incited her to drink up and go into the pavilion where her master lay. I saw that she was distracted; she wanted to enter the pavilion, but put her head between it and the boat [sic.] Then the old woman seized her head and made her enter the pavilion and entered with her. Thereupon the men began to strike with the sticks on the shields so that her cries could not be heard and the other slave-girls would not be frightened and seek to escape death with their masters. Then six men went into the pavilion and each had intercourse with the girl. Then they laid her at the side of her master; two held her feet and two her hands; the old woman known as the Angel of Death re-entered and looped a cord around her neck and gave the crossed ends to the two men for them to pull. Then she approached her with a broad-bladed dagger, which she plunged between her ribs repeatedly, and the men strangled her with the cord until she was dead.

(AR: *After that, the group of men who have cohabited with the slave-girl make of their hands a sort of paved way whereby the girl, placing her feet on the palms of their hands, mounts on to the ship. After that, they give her a hen, which she throws into the ship after tearing off its head. Then she drinks a cup of an intoxicating drink and pronounces many words, and, thrice standing on the palms of the men, she comes down and mounts again to the ship and recites many things [Canard: sings some snatches]. She goes into the pavilion [qubba] in which her husband [Mann; mari] has been put, and six of the relatives of her husband go into the pavilion and unite sexually with this wife in the presence of the dead man. When they have finished these duties of love, the old woman who, according to the belief of these people, is the Angel of Death arrives and lays the wife to sleep beside her husband. Of the six men, two seize the legs of the slave-girl, and two others her hands, and the old woman, twisting her veil, puts it around her neck and gives the ends to the two other men so that they can pull it so tight that the soul escapes from her body.)*

91. Then the closest relative of the dead man, after they had placed the girl whom they have killed beside her master, came, took a piece of wood which he lighted at a fire, and walked backwards with the back of his head toward the boat and his face turned (toward the people), with one hand holding the kindled stick and the other covering his anus, being completely naked, for the purpose of setting fire to the wood that had been made ready beneath the ship. Then the people came up with tinder and other firewood, each holding a piece of wood of which he had set fire to an end and which he put into the pile of wood beneath the ship. Thereupon the flames engulfed the wood, then the ship, the pavilion, the man, the girl, and everything in the ship. A powerful, fearful wind began to blow so that the flames became fiercer and more intense.

92. One of the Rus was at my side and I heard him speak to the interpreter, who was present. I asked the interpreter what he said. He answered, 'He said, "You Arabs are fools" ' 'Why?' I asked him. He said, 'You take the people who are most dear to you and whom you honour most and you put them in the ground where insects and worms devour them. We burn him in a moment, so that he enters Paradise at once.' Then he began to laugh uproariously. When I asked why he laughed, he said, 'His lord, for love of him, has sent the wind to bring him away in an hour.' And actually an hour had not passed before the ship, the wood, the girl, and her master were nothing but cinders and ashes.

Then they constructed in the place where had been the ship which they had drawn up out of the river something like a small round hill, in the middle of which they erected a great post of birch wood, on which they wrote the name of the man and the name of the Rus king and they departed.

Supplementary Booklist in English, 1984

I. *Scandinavia and the Movement South-West*: K. Cameron, 'The Significance of English Place-Names', Proceedings of the British Academy, 1976. *Place-Name Evidence for the Anglo-Saxon and Scandinavian Settlements. Eight Studies*, English Place-Name Society, 1975. G. Fellows Jensen, *Scandinavian Settlement Names in the East Midlands*, Copenhagen, 1978. R. A. Hall (ed.), *Viking Age York and the North*, 1978. H. R. Loyn, *The Vikings in Wales*, 1976; *The Vikings in Britain*, 1977. Else Roesdahl, *Viking Age Denmark*, 1982. P. H. Sawyer, *Kings and Vikings. Scandinavia and Europe AD 700–1100*, 1982. Th. Andersson and Karl I. Sandred (eds), *The Vikings*, Uppsala, 1978.

II. *The Movement East*. H. R. Davidson, *The Viking Road to Byzantium*, 1976. K. R. Schmidt (ed.), *Varangian Problems*, Scando-Slavica Supplementum, Copenhagen, 1970.

III. *The Movement West*. Eleanor Guralnick (ed.), *Vikings in the West*, Chicago, 1982. 'Historical Evidence for Viking Voyages to the New World' (Gwyn Jones); 'The Lost Norse Colony of Greenland' (Thomas H. McGovern); 'The Discovery of a Norse Settlement in America' (Helge Ingstad); 'The Norse Settlement at L'Anse aux Meadows' (Anne Stine Ingstad); 'Norsemen and Eskimos in Arctic Canada' (Robert McGhee); 'Viking Hoaxes' (Birgitta Wallace). H. M. Hansen, *A Critical Account of the Written and Archaeological Sources' Evidence concerning Norse Settlement in Greenland*, MoG, Copenhagen, 1972. A. S. Ingstad and H. Ingstad, *The Discovery of a Norse Settlement in America*, Vol. I, *Excavations at L'Anse aux Meadows, Newfoundland*, Vol. II, 1984, Oslo. Jón Jóhannesson, *A History of the Old Icelandic Republic: Íslendinga Saga*, trans. Haraldur Bessason, Winnipeg, 1974.

IV. *General*. R. T. Farrell (ed.), *The Vikings*, 1982. J. Graham-Campbell (ed.), *The Viking World*, 1980. D. M. Wilson (ed.), *The Northern Lands*, 1980. Reviews and articles in *Saga-Book* of the Viking Society for Northern Research, London, and in *Medieval Scandinavia*, Odense, *passim*.

Select Bibliography

The Bibliography is presented in six sections: 1, A short list of books in English, introductory to the subject; 2, General and national Scandinavian history; 3, Pre-viking Scandinavia; 4, The vikings overseas; 5, The Scandinavian community; 6, Sources.

The lists are alphabetical, except that books in English precede those in other languages.

The sections are not exclusive of each other.

I. *An introductory list of books in English:*

1. Bertil Almgren (ed.), *The Viking*. 288 pp. C. A. Watts. 1966. A general survey, impressively illustrated with plates and drawings.

2. Holger Arbman, *The Vikings*. Trans. Alan Binns. 212 pp. Thames and Hudson. 1961. Brief but authoritative, with an emphasis on archaeology and art. Handsomely illustrated.

3. Johannes Brøndsted, *The Vikings*. Trans. Kalle Skov. 347 pp. Penguin Books. 1965. Excellent on the background and life in the Scandinavian homelands. Light on political history and the vikings overseas.

4. R. W. Chambers, *Beowulf. An Introduction to the Study of the Poem*. With a Supplement by C. L. Wrenn. 628 pp. Cambridge University Press. 1959. The classic statement in English of the Geat-Swedish and other heroic problems.

5. Gwyn Jones, *The Norse Atlantic Saga*. 246 pp. Oxford University Press. 1964. The Norse voyages of discovery and settlement to Iceland, Greenland, and America, with a translation of the more important early documents.

6. T. D. Kendrick, *A History of the Vikings*. 412 pp. Methuen. 1930, repr. 1968. A full-scale history in English of the Vikings at home and abroad. Comprehensive and stimulating, but needs revision.

7. Axel Olrik, *Viking Civilization*. 246 pp. Allen and Unwin. 1930. A translation by J. W. Hartmann and H. A. Larsen of Olrik's *Nordisk*

Aandsliv i Vikingetid og Tidlig Middelalder, revised after the author's death by Hans Ellekilde.

8. P. H. Sawyer, *The Age of the Vikings*. 254 pp. Arnold. 1962. Informative, important, selective, severely critical. Revised ed. 1971.

9. Haakon Shetelig and Hjalmar Falk, *Scandinavian Archaeology*. Trans. E. V. Gordon. 458 pp. Clarendon Press. 1938. A brilliant and humane survey from the earliest times to the end of the Viking Age, appropriately illustrated.

10. Haakon Shetelig (ed.), *Viking Antiquities in Great Britain and Ireland* I–VI. Oslo. 1940–54. Includes 'An Introduction to the Viking History of Western Europe', 164 pp (1940).

11. Jacqueline Simpson, *Everyday Life in the Viking Age*. 208 pp. Batsford. 1966. A well-judged survey, tellingly illustrated with plates and drawings by Eva Wilson.

12. E. O. G. Turville-Petre, *Myth and Religion of the North*, 340 pp. Weidenfeld and Nicolson. 1964. The standard work in English on the ancient Scandinavian religion, but stronger on the literary side than the historical or archaeological.

13. G. Vernadsky, *The Origins of Russia*. 354 pp. Clarendon Press. 1959. An admirable survey, which sets the Scandinavian-Rus contribution to early Russian history lower than most Scandinavian scholars do.

14. David M. Wilson and Ole Klindt-Jensen, *Viking Art*. 173 pp. Allen and Unwin. 1966. A good general survey, effectively illustrated.

15. P. Anker, *The Art of Scandinavia*, I, 452 pp. Hamlyn. 1970. Authoritative, and splendidly illustrated.

II. *General and National Scandinavian History:*

See Almgren, Arbman, Brøndsted, Kendrick, Sawyer, under I.

P. G. Foote and D. M. Wilson, *The Viking Achievement*, 1971.

K. Gjerset, *History of the Norwegian People*, I–II, 1915. (Somewhat dated.)

K. Larsen, *A History of Norway*, Princeton, 1948.

L. Larson, *Canute the Great and the Rise of Danish Imperialism during the Viking Age*, New York, 1931.

E. Oxenstierna, *The Norsemen*, 1966.

G. Turville-Petre, *The Heroic Age of Scandinavia*, 1951. (An excellent introduction, strong on the written sources.)

I. Andersson, *Skånes historia till Saxo och Skånelagen*, Stockholm, 1947.

E. Arup. *Danmarks Historie*, I, Copenhagen, 1925.

J. Bjernum, *Kilder til vikingetidens historie*, Copenhagen, 1961. (A simple, clear, reliable introduction.)

J. Bjernum and Th. Ramskou, *Danmarks Sydgrænse*, (Copenhagen, 1948.)

S. Bolin, *Skånelands historie*, Lund, 1933.

Sture Bolin, *Ur penningens historia*, Lund, 1962.

A. E. Christensen, *Vikingetidens Danmark*, Copenhagen, 1969.

V. La Cour, *Danevirkestudier*, Copenhagen, 1951. (Chapters on Swedish, German, and Danish rule in Denmark.)

P. V. Glob, *Ard og plov i Nordens oldtid*, Århus, 1951.

G. Hafström, *Ledung och marklands indelning*, Uppsala, 1949.

A. Holmsen, *Norges Historie, Fra de Eldste Tider til 1660*, Oslo-Bergen, 1961.

Bjørn Hougen, *Fra seter til gård. Studier i norsk bosetning-historie*, Oslo, 1947.

H. Jankuhn, *Haithabu. Ein Handelsplatz der Wikingerzeit*, 4th ed., Neumünster, 1963. (Chapters on social and economic history in Scandinavia.)

A. O. Johnsen, *Fra ættesamfunn til statssamfunn*, Oslo, 1948.

A. D. Jørgensen, *Den nordiske Kirkes Grundlæggelse*, Copenhagen, 1874-6.

Poul Johs. Jørgensen, *Dansk Retshistorie*, Copenhagen, 2nd ed., 1947, 1965.

H. Koht, *Innhogg og utsyn i norsk historie*, Christiania (Oslo), 1921.

H. Koht, *Harald Harfagre og rikssamlinga*, Oslo, 1955.

Kulturhistorisk Leksikon for nordisk Middelalder, Copenhagen, etc., 1956– (to be completed). (Contains brief, authoritative articles in alphabetical order over a wide range of Scandinavian medieval culture and civilization. Useful bibliographies, illustrations. Indispensable.)

H. Ljungberg, *Den nordiska religionen och kristendom. Studier över det nordiska religionsskiftet under Vikingatiden*, Stockholm, 1938.

Brita Malmer, *Nordiska mynt före år 1000*, Acta Arch. Lundensia, Lund, 1966.

L. Musset, *Les Peuples Scandinaves au Moyen Age*, Paris, 1951. (A compact, masterly summary.)

Nordisk Kultur, 30 volumes, Copenhagen, etc., 1930–56. (Articles and monographs in the three Scandinavian languages include: *Befolkning i*

Oldtiden, I 1936; *Befolkning*, II, 1938; *Stednavne*, V, 1939; *Runorna*, VI, 1933; *Litteraturhistorie*, VIII A and B, 1942–3; *Våben*, XII B, 1943; *Dragt*, XV B, 1941; *Handel og Samfærdsel*, XVI, 1934; *Bygningskultur*, XVII, 1953; *Religionshistorie*, XXVI, 1942; *Kunst*, XXVII, 1937; *Mønt*, XXIX, 1956. Indispensable for almost every aspect of ancient and medieval Scandinavia.)

F. Paasche, *Møtet mellom hedendom og kristendom i Norden*, Stockholm, 1958.

Th. Ramskou, *Danmarks Historie*, II : *Normannertiden*, 600–1060, Copenhagen, 1963.

Thorkild Ramskou, *Vikingetiden, Skibet, Sværdet og Vægten*, Copenhagen, 1962.

Schultz' *Danmarks Historie*, I–II, Copenhagen, 1941.

H. Schück, *Svenska folkets historia*, Lund, 1914.

H. Shetelig and E. Bull, *Det norske folks liv og historie*, I–II, Oslo, 1929–31.

R. Skovmand, *De danske skattefund fra vikingetid og den ældste middelalder indtil omkring 1150*, Copenhagen, 1942. (Has a résumé in French.)

J. Steenstrup, *Normannerne*, I–IV, Copenhagen, 1876–82. (A classic work, still of great value.)

M. Stenberger, *Die Schatzfunde Gotlands der Wikingerzeit*, I, Stockholm 1958, II, Lund, 1947.

F. Ström, *Nordisk Hedendom*, Göteborg, 1961.

Sønderjyllands Historie fremstillet for det danske Folk, I–II, Copenhagen, 1931–9.

Sv. Tunberg, G. Carlsson, S. Kraft, *Sveriges historia till våra dagar*, II–III, Stockholm, 1926.

Curt Weibull, *Källkritik och historia*, Stockholm, 1964. (Includes 'Om det svenska och det danska rikets uppkomst', *Hist. tidskr. för Skåneland*, VIII, Lund, 1917–21; and 'Sverige och dess nordiska grannmakter under den tidligare medeltiden', Lund, 1921.)

Lauritz Weibull, see p. 444.

III.   *Pre-Viking Scandinavia:*

See Chambers, Shetelig and Falk, Davidson, under I.

Anders Hagen, *Norway*, 1967.

Ella Kivikoski, *Finland*, 1967.

Ole Klindt-Jensen, *Denmark*, 1957.

E. Oxenstierna, *The World of the Norsemen*, 1967. (A translation of *Die Nordgermanen*, Stuttgart, 1957.)

Mårten Stenberger, *Sweden*, 1962.

R. L. S. Bruce-Mitford, *The Sutton Hoo Ship Burial*, British Museum, 1966.

J. G. D. Clarke, *Prehistoric Europe. The Economic Basis*, 1952.

C. A. Nordman, *The Megalithic Culture of Northern Europe*, Finska Fornminnesföreningens Tidskrift, 39, 1939.

Johannes Brøndsted, *Danmarks Oldtid*, I–III, Copenhagen, revised edition, 1957–60.

Johannes Brøndsted, *Danmarks Historie, I: De ældste tider indtil år 600*, Copenhagen, 1962.

G. Ekholm, *Forntid och fornforskning i Skandinavien*, Stockholm, 1935.

P. Herrmann, *Die Heldensagen des Saxo Grammaticus*, Leipzig, 1922.

L. Musset, *Les invasions : les vagues germaniques*, Paris, 1965.

Axel Olrik, *Kilderne til Sakses Oldhistorie*, I–II, Copenhagen, 1892–4.

Axel Olrik, *Danmarks Heltedigtning. I, Rolf Krake og den ældre Skjoldungrække; II, Starkad den gamle og den yngre Skjoldungrække*, Copenhagen, 1903–10. (English translation and revision, L. M. Hollander, *The Heroic Legends of Denmark*, New York, 1919.)

IV. *The Vikings Overseas:*

(*a*) The Movement South and South-West:

See Arbman, Kendrick, Sawyer, Shetelig, under I.

W. E. D. Allen, *The Poet and the Spae-Wife. An attempt to Reconstruct Al-Ghazal's Embassy to the Vikings*, 1960.

Peter Hunter Blair, *An Introduction to Anglo-Saxon England*, 1956.

A. W. Brøgger, *Ancient Emigrants, A History of the Norse Settlements of Scotland*, 1929.

B. G. Charles, *Old Norse Relations with Wales*, Cardiff, 1934.

Michael Dolley, *Viking Coins of the Danelaw and of Dublin*, British Museum, 1965.

R. H. Hodgkin, *A History of the Anglo-Saxons*, I–II, 1952.

E. Joranson, *The Danegeld in France*, Rock Island, 1923.

C. F. Keary, *The Vikings in Western Christendom*, 1891.

S. Körner, *The Battle of Hastings, England, and Europe*, Lund, 1966.

F. M. Stenton, *Anglo-Saxon England*, 1943.

A. Walsh, *Scandinavian Relations with Ireland during the Viking Period*, Dublin, 1922.

R. E. M. Wheeler, *London and the Vikings*, 1927.

D. M. Wilson, *The Anglo-Saxons*, 1960.

H. Arbman and M. Stenberger, *Vikingar i västerled*, Stockholm, 1935.

Fritz Askeberg, *Norden och kontinenten i gammal tid*, Uppsala, 1944.

J. Adigard des Gautries, *Les noms de personnes scandinaves en Normandie de 911 à 1066*, Lund, 1954.

Louis Halphen, *Les Barbares*, Paris, 1940.

E. Lévi-Provencal, *Histoire de l'Espagne musulmane*, Paris, 1950.

F. Lot and L. Halphen, *Le Règne de Charles le Chauve*, I, Paris, 1909.

F. Lot, *Les Invasions barbares et le peuplement de l'Europe*, I–II, Paris, 1937.

Niels Lund, *De Danske Vikinger i England*, Copenhagen, 1967.

A. Melvinger, *Les premières incursions des Vikings en Occident d'après des sources arabes*, Uppsala, 1955.

L. Musset, *Relations et échanges d'influence dans l'Europe du Nord-Ouest (Xe–XIe siècles)*, Paris, 1958.

L. Musset, *Les invasions: le second assaut contre l'Europe chrétienne*, Paris, 1965. (Deals with the Slavs and Steppe peoples as well as the Vikings under the three heads : Instruments de Recherche et Documentation; Nos Connaissances; Problèmes en suspens et Directions de Recherche.)

J. C. H. R. Steenstrup, *Normandiets Historie under de syv første Hertuger*, Copenhagen, 1925.

W. Vogel, *Die Normannen und das Frankische Reich bis zur Gründung der Normandie* (799–911), Heidelberg, 1906.

(*b*) The Movement East:

N. K. Chadwick, *The Beginnings of Russian History*, 1946.

D. M. Dunlop, *The History of the Jewish Khazars*, Princeton, 1954.

B. D. Grekov, *Kiev Rus* (English version), Moscow, 1959.

C. A. Macartney, *The Magyars in the Ninth Century*, 1940.

H. Paszkiewicz, *The Origin of Russia*, 1954.

N. V. Riasanovsky, *A History of Russia*, New York, 1963.

Vilh. Thomsen, *The Relations between Ancient Russia and Scandinavia and the Origin of the Russian State*, 1887. Reissued Burt Franklin, New York, ?1964. Revised in Thomsen's *Samlede Skrifter*, I, Copenhagen, 1919.

G. Vernadsky, *Ancient Russia*, New Haven, 1943.

G. Vernadsky, *Kievan Russia*, New Haven, 1948.

G. Vernadsky, *The Origins of Russia*, 1959.

H. Arbman, *Svear i österviking*, Stockholm, 1955.

T. J. Arne, *La Suède et l'Orient*, Uppsala, 1914.

F. Balodis, *Handelswege nach dem Osten und die Wikinger in Russland*, Stockholm, 1948.

W. J. Raudonikas, *Die Normannen der Wikingerzeit und das Ladogagebiet*, Stockholm, 1930.

A. Stender-Petersen, *Varangica*, Århus, 1953.

(*c*) The Movement West:

G. M. Gathorne-Hardy, *The Norse Discoverers of America*, 1921; 1970.

K. Gjerset, *History of Iceland*, 1925. (Needs revision.)

Halldór Hermannsson, *The Problem of Wineland*, Ithaca, 1936.

Helge Ingstad, *Land under the Pole Star*, 1966.

Helge Ingstad, *Western Way to Vinland*, 1969.

Gwyn Jones, *The Norse Atlantic Saga*, 1964.

Knud J. Krogh, *Viking Greenland*. With a Supplement of Saga Texts by Gwyn Jones, Copenhagen, 1967. (A translation by Helen Fogh of *Erik den Rødes Grønland*: Sagatekster ved H. Bekker Nielsen, Copenhagen, 1967.)

Magnus Magnusson and Hermann Pálsson, *The Vinland Sagas*, 1965.

Fridtjof Nansen, *In Northern Mists. Arctic Exploration in Early Times*, 1911.

Poul Nørlund, *Viking Settlers in Greenland and their Descendants during five hundred years*, 1936.

R. A. Skelton, Thomas E. Marston, and George D. Painter, *The Vinland Map and the Tartar Relation*, 1965.

Kristján Eldjárn, *Kuml og Haugfé úr Heiðnum Sið í Íslandi*, Akureyri, 1956.

S. B. F. Jansson, *Sagorna om Vinland*, I, Lund, 1944.

Jón Jóhannesson, *Íslendinga Saga*, I–II, Reykjavík, 1956–8. (The best history of early Iceland.)

Sigurður Nordal, *Íslenzk Menning*, I, Reykjavík, 1942.

V. *The Scandinavian Community:*

(*a*) Art:

See Arbman, Brøndsted, Wilson and Klindt-Jensen, Shetelig, and Shetelig and Falk, under I.

H. R. Ellis Davidson, *The Sword in Anglo-Saxon England*, 1962.

A. Hagen and A. Liestøl, *Ancient Norwegian Design*, Oslo, 1961.

W. Holmqvist, *Germanic Art during the First Millennium A.D.*, Stockholm, 1955.

T. D. Kendrick, *Late Saxon and Viking Art*, 1949.

P. M. C. Kermode, *Manx Crosses*, 1907.

B. Almgren, *Bronsnycklar och djurornamentik vid övergången från vendeltid til vikingatid*, Uppsala, 1955.

H. Arbman, *Schweden und das karolingische Reich*, Stockholm, 1937.

R. Broby-Johansen, *Oldnordiske Stenbilleder*, Copenhagen, 1967.

A. W. Brøgger, H. Falk, and H. Shetelig, *Oseberg funnet*, I–IV, Oslo, 1917–28. (Also Bjørn Hougen, 'Osebergfunnets billedvev', in *Viking*, IV, Oslo, 1940.)

S. Lindqvist, *Gotlands Bildsteine*, I–II, Uppsala, 1941.

J. Petersen, *De Norske vikingesverd*, Christiania, 1919.

J. Petersen, *Vikingetidens redskaper* (with an English summary), Oslo, 1951.

B. Salin, *Die Altgermanische Thierornamentik*, Stockholm, 1904 and 1935.

(*b*) Camps and fortifications:

See p. 101 n, and p. 360, n. 1.

(*c*) Religion:

W. A. Craigie, *The Religion of Ancient Scandinavia*, 1914. (Needs revision, but still a useful introduction.)

H. Ellis Davidson, *Gods and Myths of Northern Europe*, 1964.

H. Ellis Davidson, *Pagan Scandinavia*, 1967.

E. O. G. Turville-Petre, *Myth and Religion of the North*, 1964.

G. Dumézil, *Les Dieux des Germains*, Paris, 1959.

Olaf Olsen, *Hørg, Hov og Kirke. Historiske og Arkæologiske Vikingetidsstudier*, Copenhagen, 1966 (*Aarbøger for nordisk Oldkyndighed og Historie*, 1965).

J. de Vries, *Altgermanische Religionsgeschichte*, I–II, Berlin, 1956–7.

(*d*) Runes:

See p. 420. Add S. B. F. Jansson, *The Runes of Sweden* (Trans. P. G. Foote), 1962; L. Musset and F. Mossé, *Introduction à la runologie*, I–II,

Paris, 1965; Arndt Ruprecht, *Die ausgehende Wikingerzeit im Lichte der Runeinschriften*, Göttingen, 1958.

(*e*) Ships:

See p. 183, n. 2.

(*f*) Towns and Trade:

See p. 181, n. 1. Add H. Jankuhn, 'Sechs Karten zum Handel des 10 Jhs. im westlichen Ostsee-becken', *Archaeologia Geographica*, Hamburg, I, 1950, pp. 8–16; P. Kletler, *Handel und Gewerbe im frühen Mittelalter*, Vienna, 1924; H. Preidel, *Handel und Handwerk im frühgeschichtlichen Mitteleuropa. Eine kritische Betrachtung*, Lund, 1965; J. R. C. Hamilton, *Excavations at Jarlshof, Shetland*, 1956.

VI *Sources:*

Adam of Bremen: *Gesta Hammaburgensis Ecclesiae Pontificum*, ed. B. Schmeidler, Scriptores rerum Germanicarum, Hanover, 1917. Trans. F. J. Tschan, *History of the Archbishops of Hamburg-Bremen*, New York, 1959.

Ágrip (af Noregskonunga sögum), ed. F. Jónsson, Copenhagen, 1929.

Alfred's *Orosius*, ed. H. Sweet, EETS, 1883. Text and trans. of the passage relating to Ohthere's northern voyage in Alan S. C. Ross, *The Terfinnas and Beormas of Ohthere*, Leeds, 1940; and see B. Schier, 'Wege und Formen des ältesten Pelzhandels in Europa', in *Archiv f. Pelzkunde*, I, 1951.

Anglo-Saxon Chronicle : Two of the Saxon Chronicles Parallel, ed. C. Plummer and J. Earle, 1892, re-ed. D. Whitelock, 1952. Trans. D. Whitelock. D. C. Douglas, and S. I. Tucker, *The Anglo-Saxon Chronicle*, 1961; G. N. Garmonsway, *The Anglo-Saxon Chronicle*, 1960.

Anskar : *Vita Anskarii auctore Rimberto*, ed. G. Waitz, SSRG, Hanover, 1884. Trans. C. H. Robinson, *Anskar, The Apostle of the North*, 1921.

Annales Bertiniani, ed. G. Waitz, SSRG, Hanover, 1883; F. Grat, J. Vielliard, S. Clémencet, Paris, 1964.

Annales regni Francorum, ed. G. H. Pertz and Fr. Kurze, SSRG, Hanover, 1895.

Annales Fuldenses, ed. F. Kurze, SSRG, Hanover, 1891.

Arab Sources: *Rerum normannicarum fontes arabici*, ed. A. Seippel, I–II, Oslo, 1896–1928. Translations of various documents will be found in Harris Birkeland, *Nordens historie i middelalderen etter arabiske kilder*, Det Norske Videnskabs-Akademi i Oslo, Skrifter, II, Hist.-Filos.

Klasse, 2, 1954; Georg Jacob, *Arabische Berichte von Gesandten an germanische Fürstenhöfe aus d. 9 und 10 Jahrhundert*, Berlin-Leipzig, 1927; C. A. Macartney, *The Magyars in the Ninth Century*, 1930; V. F. Minorsky, *Hudud-al-' Alam*, 1937; A. Zeki Validi Togan, *Ibn Fadlan's Reiseberichte*, Leipzig, 1939; M. Canard, 'La Relation du Voyage d'Ibn Fadlan chez les Bulgares de la Volga', Algiers, 1958; H. M. Smyser, 'Ibn Fadlan's Account of the Rus, etc.' (For the last three see p. 164–5 above, n. 1); W. E. D. Allen, *The Poet and the Spae-Wife*, 1960; and others.

Beowulf, ed. Fr. Klaeber, 1936; ed. C. L. Wrenn, 1953. For the references to Hygelac see Gregory of Tours, *Historia Francorum*, and *Liber Historiae Francorum (Gesta Francorum)*, in B. Krusch, Mon. Germ. Hist., Scriptores rerum Merovingicarum, I–II, Hanover, 1885; *Liber Monstrorum (De Monstris et de Belluis)*, in M. Haupt, *Opuscula* II, Leipzig, 1876, and M. A. Thomas, 'Un manuscrit inutilisé du Liber Monstrorum', in *Archivum Latinitatis medii aevi*, Bulletin du Cange, Paris, 1925.

Chronicon Æthelweardi, ed. A. Campbell, 1962.

Constantine Porphyrogenitus: *De Administrando Imperio*, Greek text edited by G. Moravcsik, English translation by R. J. H. Jenkins, I–II, Budapest, 1949–62.

Dudo : *Dudonis sancti Quintini de moribus et actis primorum Normanniae ducum*, ed. M. J. Lair, Caen, 1865.

Edda : *Die Lieder des Codex Regius nebst Verwandten Denkmälern*, ed. G. Neckel, I–II, Heidelberg, 1936. Trans. H. A. Bellows, *The Poetic Edda*, New York, 1923; and others. For an account of the Eddic poems see the relevant chapters of G. Turville-Petre, *Origins of Icelandic Literature*, 1953; Stefán Einarsson, *A History of Icelandic Literature*, New York, 1957; and especially Einar Ól. Sveinsson, *Íslenzkar Bókmentir í Fornöld*, I, Reykjavík, 1962. A new ed. by U. Dronke, Vol.I, 1969.

Edda Snorra Sturlusonar, ed. F. Jónsson, Copenhagen, 1926. Many translations into English.

Egils Saga Skallagrímssonar, ed. Sigurður Nordal, Reykjavík, 1933. Trans. Gwyn Jones, *Egil's Saga*, New York, 1960.

Einhard: *De vita Karoli Magni*, ed. G. H. Pertz, SSRG, Hanover, 1845; *Annales*, ibid.

Encomium Emmae, ed. and trans. A. Campbell, Camden Third Series, 1949.

Ermentarius: *Vie et miracles de Saint Philibert*, in A. Giry, *Monuments de l'histoire des abbayes de Saint-Philibert*, 1905.

Fagrskinna, ed. F. Jónsson, Copenhagen, 1902–3.

Flateyjarbók, ed. G. Vígfússon and C. R. Unger, I–III, Christiania, 1860–8.

Flodoardi Annales: Ph. Lauer, *Les Annales de Flodoard*, Paris, 1905.

Fontes Historiae Religionis Germanicae, coll. C. Clemen, Berlin, 1928.

Gertz, M. Cl., *Scriptores minores historiae danicae medii ævi*, I–II, Copenhagen, 1917–22; reissued 1970.

Grágás, ed. V. Finsen, I–III, Copenhagen, 1852–83.

Grønlands Historiske Mindesmærker, ed. C. C. Hrafn, I–III, Copenhagen, 1835–45, repr. 1976. New ed. of Vinland and related texts with discussion in Ól. Halldórsson, *Grœnland í Miðaldaritum*, Reykjavik, 1978.

Guta Lag och Guta Saga, ed. H. Pipping, Copenhagen, 1905–7.

Hamburgisches Urkundenbuch, ed. J. M. Lappenberg, A. Hagedorn, H. Nirrnheim, I–III, Hamburg, 1842–1953.

Heimskringla, ed. Bjarni Aðalbjarnarson, I–III, Reykjavík, 1946–51. The best edition. For the northern historians see also Bjarni Aðalbjarnarson, *Om de Norske Kongers Sagaer*, Oslo, 1937; G. Turville-Petre, *Origins of Icelandic Literature*, 1953; Hans Bekker-Nielsen, Ole Widding, Th. D. Olsen, *Norrøn Fortællekunst, Kapitler af den norsk-islandske middelalder-litteraturs historie*, Copenhagen, 1965; Svend Ellehøj, *Studier over den ældste norrøne historieskrivning*, Copenhagen, 1965. Trans. (*Heimskringla*) S. Laing, 1844 and 1961–4; W. Morris and E. Magnusson, 1893; Erling Monsen, 1932; L. M. Hollander, Austin, 1964.

Historia Norwegiæ, ed. G. Storm, *Monumenta historica Norvegiae*, Christiania, 1880.

Historia de antiquitate regum Norwagiensium, ed. G. Storm, ibid.

Hrólfs Saga Kraka, ed. D. Slay, Copenhagen, 1960. Trans. Gwyn Jones, in *Eirik the Red and Other Icelandic Sagas*, 1961.

Icelandic Sagas: In *Íslenzk Fornrit*, Reykjavík, 1933– (in progress); *Altnordische Saga-Bibliothek*, Halle, 1891–1929; *Íslendingasagnaútgáfan*, Reykjavík, 1946–50. Numerous separate editions and translations. [The following offer a fair conspectus of the debate concerning the sagas' historicity. Paul Henri Mallet, *Introduction à l'histoire de Dannemarc*, Copenhagen, 1755; A. L. Schlözer, *Allgemeine Nordische Geschichte*, Halle, 1771; Friedrich Rüys, *Die Edda*, Berlin, 1812; P. E. Müller, *Ueber den Ursprung und Verfall der Isländischen Historiographie*, Copenhagen, 1813; *Sagabibliothek*, Copenhagen, 1817; N. M. Petersen, *Historiske Fortællinger om Islændernes Færd*, Copenhagen, 1839; *Den Oldnordiske Literaturs Historie*, Copenhagen, 1866; C. C. Rafn (ed.), *Antiquités russes*, Copenhagen, 1850; R. Keyser, *Efterladte Skrifter, I : Nordmændenes Videnskabelighed og Literatur i Middelalderen*, Christiania,

1866; Konrad Maurer, 'Die Norwegische Auffassung der Nordischen Literatur-Geschichte' in *ZfdPh*, I, 1869; 'Ueber die Hœnsna- þóris Saga', in *K. Bayer. Akad. d. Wiss., München, Philos-Philol. Classe, Abhandl.*, 1871; and various other works; E. Jessen, 'Glaubwürdigkeit der Egils-Saga und Anderer Isländer-Saga's', in *Historische Zeitschrift*, 1872; P. A. Munch, material collected in *Samlede Afhandlinger*, Christiania, 1874; K. Lehmann and Hans Schnorr von Carolsfeld, *Die Njáls-sage Insbesondere in Ihren Juristischen Bestandtheilen*, Berlin, 1883; Finnur Jónsson, many works including *Den Oldnorske og Oldislandske Litteraturs Historie*, Copenhagen, 1894–1902, 2nd ed. 1920–4; *Udsigt over den Norsk-Islandske Filologis Historie*, Copenhagen, 1918; 'Norsk-Islandske Kultur- og Sprogforhold i 9. og 10. Århundrede' in *D. Kgl. Danske Vidensk. Selsk. Hist. of Fil. Meddelelser, 1921*; A. Heusler, particularly *Das Strafrecht der Isländersagas*, Leipzig, 1911; 'Zum Isländischen Fehdewesen in der Sturlungazeit' *Abhandl. d. K. Preuss. Akad d. Wiss., Phil-Hist. Classe, 1912;* L. Weibull, critical works collected in *Nordisk Historia. Forskningar och undersökningar*, I, *Forntid och Vikingatid*, Stockholm, 1948; Knut Liestøl, *Upphavet til den Islendske Ættesaga*, Oslo, 1929 (Trans. *The Origin of the Icelandic Family Sagas*, Oslo, 1930), and other works; Björn M. Olsen, 'Um Íslendingasögur', in *Safn til Sögu Íslands*, 6, 1937–9; Sigurður Nordal, 'Hrafnkatla', *Studia Islandica*, 7, 1940 (Trans. R. G. Thomas, *Hrafnkels Saga Freysgoða*, Cardiff, 1958); *The Historical Element in the Icelandic Family Sagas*, Glasgow, 1957; Einar Ólafur Sveinsson, *Um Njálu*, Reykjavík, 1933; W. Baetke, 'Über die Entstehung der Isländersagas', in *Berichte über die Verhandl. d. Sächs. Akad d. Wiss. zu Leipzig. Philol-Hist. Klasse*, 1956; the *Íslenzk Fornrit* introductions generally. See, too, the references under *Heimskringla* above, and the references to C. and L. Weibull and H. Koht in Section II, and add Theodore M. Andersson, *The Problem of Icelandic Saga Origins. A Historical Survey*, 1964, and *The Icelandic Family Saga. An Analytic Reading*, 1967, debate continues: see the references in R. McTurk's review of W. Baetke (ed.), *Die Isländersagas* (1974) in *Saga-Book*, 1975–6, pp. 320–4]

Ireland-Scotland: *Annala Rioghachta Eireann. Annals of the Kingdom of Ireland by the Four Masters*, I–VII, ed. J. O'Donovan, Dublin, 1851, 1856; *Annala Uladh. Annals of Ulster*, I–II, ed. W. H. Hennessy, Dublin, 1887–93; *Annals of Inisfallen*, ed. S. Mac Airt, Dublin, 1951; *Cogadh Gaedhel re Gallaibh. The War of the Gaedhil with the Gaill*, ed. J. H. Todd, Rolls Series, London, 1867; *Three Fragments of Irish Annals*, ed. J. O'Donovan, Dublin, 1860. All with English translations. See P. Walsh, 'The Dating of the Irish Annals', in *Irish Historical Studies*, II, 1941, pp. 355–75, and *The Four Masters and their Work*, Dublin, 1944;

W. F. Skene (ed.), *Chronicles of the Picts, Chronicles of the Scots, and other Early Memorials of Scottish History*, Edinburgh, 1867; A. O. Anderson, *Early Sources of Scottish History*, I–II, Edinburgh, 1922.

Íslendingabók, ed. and trans. H. Hermannsson, *The Book of the Icelanders (Íslendingabók)*, New York, 1930.

Jordanes: *Getica*, ed. Th. Mommsen, Berlin, 1882. Trans. C. C. Mierow, Princeton, 1915.

Konungs Skuggsjá, ed. F. Jónsson, Copenhagen, 1920; L. Holm-Olsen, Oslo, 1945. Trans. L. M. Larson, *The King's Mirror*, New York, 1917.

Landnámabók, ed. Finnur Jónsson, I–III, Copenhagen, 1900, 1921, 1925. Also *Skarðsárbók*, ed. Jakob Benediktsson, Reykjavík, 1958. Trans. G. Vigfusson and F. York Powell, *Origines Islandicae*, I, 1905; Gwyn Jones, *The Norse Atlantic Saga*, 1964 (in selection).

Langebek, J., *Scriptores rerum Danicarum medii ævi*, I–IX, Copenhagen, 1772–1878.

Langfeðgatal, in Langebek, *Scriptores*, I.

Liebermann, F. *Die Gesetze der Angelsachsen*, I–II, Halle, 1903–16.

Morkinskinna, ed. F. Jónsson, Copenhagen, 1928–32.

Norges gamle Love indtil 1387, I–V, ed. R. Keyser and others, Christiania, 1846–95.

Recueil des Actes de Charles II le Chauve, ed. M. Prou, F. Lot, and G. Tessier, Paris, 1943–55.

Recueil des Actes de Charles III le Simple, ed. Ph. Lauer, Paris, 1940.

Recueil des Actes des ducs de Normandie, 911–1066, ed. Marie Fauroux, Caen, 1961.

Rimbert: *Vita Rimberti*, ed. G. Waitz, SSRG, Hanover, 1884.

Runes: See 'Runes' under V(*d*).

Russian Primary Chronicle: Povest' Vremennykh Let, ed. E. F. Karsky, Leningrad, 1926; V. P. Adrianova-Peretts (text prepared for publication by D. S. Likhachev), Leningrad, 1950. Trans. S. H. Cross and O. P. Sherbowitz-Wetzor, Cambridge ,Mass., 1953.

Samling af Sveriges Gamla Lagar, ed. Schlyter, I–XIII, Lund, 1827–77.

Saxo Grammaticus: *Gesta Danorum*, ed. A. Holder, Strasbourg, 1886; J. Olrik and H. Raeder, Copenhagen, 1931, with Index Verborum ed. Franz Blatt, 1936 and 1938. Trans. O. Elton, *The First Nine Books of the Danish History of Saxo Grammaticus*, 1894.

Simeon of Durham, *Historia Dunelmensis Ecclesiæ*, ed. T. Arnold, I–II, RS, 1882.

Skaldic Verse: Finnur Jónsson, *Den norsk-islandske Skjaldedigtning*, I–II,

Copenhagen, 1912–15; E. H. Kock, *Den norsk-isländiska skaldediktningen*, I–II, Lund, 1946–9. Trans. L. M. Hollander, *The Skalds*, New York, 1945 (a selection); G. Vígfússon and F. York Powell, *Corpus Poeticum Boreale*, I–II, Oxford, 1883.

Skjöldunga Saga, ed. A. Olrik, Copenhagen, 1894; Jakob Benediktsson, *Arngrimi Jonae opera latine conscripta*, in Bibliotheca Arnamagnaeana, IX–XII (text in IX), Copenhagen, 1950–7. See Jakob Benediktsson, 'Icelandic Traditions of the Scyldings', *Saga-Book*, XV, 1957–9, pp. 48–66.

Svenonis Aggones Historia Regum Daniae, in Langebek, Scriptores, I; *Opuscula Historica*, in Gertz, Scriptores, I.

Theodoricus: See *Historia de antiquitate regum Norwagiensium*.

Thietmar of Merseburg: *Merseburgensis Episcopi Chronicon*, ed. R. Holtzmann, SSRG, Berlin, 1935.

Welsh Sources: *Annales Cambriae*, ed. John Williams ab Ithel, 1860; the different texts are more reliably edited by Egerton Phillimore in *Y Cymmrodor*, IX, 1888, and J. E. Lloyd in *Transactions . . . Cymmrodorion*, VIII; *Brut y Tywysogion*, or, *The Chronicle of the Princes*, ed. and trans. Thomas Jones, Cardiff, 1952 (Peniarth MS. 20), 1955 (Red Book of Hergest); *Brenhinedd y Saesson*, or, *The Kings of the Saxons*, ed. and trans. Thomas Jones, Cardiff, 1971; *The History of Gruffydd ap Cynan*, ed. and trans. Arthur Jones, Manchester, 1910; ed. D. Simon Evans, Cardiff (to appear).

Widukind: *Chronica Saxonum*, ed. H. E. Lohmann and P. Hirsch, *Die Sachsengeschichte des Widukind von Korvei*, SSRG, Berlin, 1935.

William of Jumièges: *Gesta Normannorum Ducum*, ed. J. Marx, Rouen and Paris, 1914.

*

L. Weibull, *Nordisk Historia. Forskningar och undersökningar*, I, *Forntid och Vikingatid*, Stockholm, 1948. (Contains a reprint of *Kritiska undersökningar i Nordens historia omkring år 1000*, Lund, 1911, and *Historisk-kritisk metod och nordisk medeltidsforskning*, Lund, 1913, along with other writings.) For a critique of Weibull's methods and significance, see the symposium, 'Source-Criticism and Literary History: Lauritz Weibull, Henrik Schück and Joseph Bédier. A Discussion', in *Mediaeval Scandinavia*, 5, 1972, pp. 96–138.

Index

Abalus (Heligoland?), an island
rich in amber reported on by
Pytheas of Massalia, 21

Abd-al-Rahman II, Moorish ruler
in Spain, 214

Abodrits, a Wendish people, encouraged by Charlemagne to move
into East Holstein at the expense of
the Saxons, 98; invaded by
Godfred the Dane, 98; their king
Drosuk captured and their mart
at Reric destroyed, 98–9; Drosuk
put to death, 100; 101, 103, 244

Adaldag, archbishop of Hamburg-
Bremen, confirmed as head of the
Church in Denmark, 948, 125

Adam of Bremen, his *Gesta*
or *History* of primary importance for northern history and
the conversion of the north,
mentioned or his authority
invoked, 63 *n*, 65 *n*, 109, 111, 113,
126, 127, 129–30, 134, 136, 137,
166, 197, 242, 285, 304, 322, 327,
400, 402, 403 *n*

Adogit, dwellers in Scandza's farthest
north, 25

Ælfeah, archbishop of Canterbury,
as bishop of Winchester assists
at the conversion of Olaf Tryggvason, 132; murdered at Greenwich
1012, 367; Knut honours him as
saint, 374

Ælgifu (Álfífa), Knut's consort and
mother of his son Svein, 372; her
children excluded from the English

succession, 372; arrives in Norway
with Svein 1030, 383; put in charge
there with her son after
Stiklarstadir, 385; later historians
and hagiographers unjust to her,
385; Magnus Olafsson secures a
hold on Norway, 386; her ambitions
for her son Harald, 398

Æsir, the heathen deities of the north
discussed, 316–24; mentioned,
123, 124, 125, 126

Æthelweard, an ealdorman, 132

Agdir, a province in south-western
Norway, 26, 84

Aggersborg, west on the Limfjord,
site of a Danish stronghold, 19,
51, 101 *n*, 360

Ágrip, a source for northern history,
119, 122, 124, 131, 400, 403 *n*

Aïfor, a cataract on the Dnieper,
257, 258

Aisne, a river in France, 224

Aix-la-Chapelle, a seat of Charlemagne, 101, 224

Alamanni, Alamanns, 28, 73

Alanda, a river in Kurland, 243

Åland Islands, Ålanders, 165, 183,
251–2, 388

Ålborg, in Jutland, an early mint, 6;
and mart, 167

Alcuin, describes king Ongendus,
106; laments the viking incursion
and quotes Jeremiah, 194–5, 196

Aldeigjuborg, see Staraja Ladoga

Alexander VI, Pope, his letter *c.*
1490 concerning Greenland, 307, 310

undreamt-of splendour and profitability, 259; Varangian Guard there, 266; Harald Hardradi there, 404–5 and *n*; mentioned, 32, 73, 100; and see Byzantium, Greece

Cordoba, Al-Tartushi a native of, 164, 174

Cork, southern Ireland, 205

Cornwall, viking raids there, 203, 210

Cotentin, Normandy, 230 *n*, 231 *n*

Crete, Varangians see service there, 266

Crimea, 248

Cuckhamsley Knob, 359

Cumberland, 203

Cwenas, see Kainulaiset

Dag, unlikely death of an unlikely king, 37

Dagö (Dagaiþi), an island off Estland, temporary abode of exiled Gotlanders, 252 *n* 2

Dalarna, a province of Sweden north of Värmland, 383

Dalmatia, Varangians campaign there, 266

Dalriada, 203

Dan, son of Ypper, eponymous hero of Danish legends, 44

Danegeld, general name for enforced payment of money, treasure, goods, food to the Danes, 9, 132, 154; first recorded French payment, 212–13; details of seven French payments, 213 *n*; first recorded English payment, 213 *n*; details of English payments, 132, 356, 358, 364–5, 366, 367, 399; annual tax in England 1012–51, 366; Edward the Confessor pays off his northern mercenaries, 366; runic stones referring to, 9, 265

Danelaw, *Denelagu*, a late title for the Scandinavian-held part of eastern England, 12, 355; possible influence on religion in Denmark, 126, and Iceland, 285; its making, 219–23;

activities hostile to the English, 226; its decline, 223–4, 233 ff.; characteristics (boundaries, language, society, law), see Appendix II, 421–4; and see 219–24, 394

Danevirke, the defence works across the neck of the Jutland peninsula, 99; inception and Godfred's share in, 99; described, 99–102, 104–5; Thyri, Gorm's wife, erroneously credited with, 144; Otto II attacks and surmounts, 128; Jarl Hakon Sigurdarson said to have defended, 128

Danevirkesten, runic inscription relating to king Svein's housecarle Skardi, 174 *n*

Dani, the name first used by Jordanes in the sixth century, 26, 45

Danmark, a geographical designation, first recorded usage, 114 and *n*; and see Denemearc

Danube, the river, 20, 22, 23, 103, 261

Denemearc, Denimarca, a geographical designation, first recorded usage, 109, 114 and *n*; and see Danmark

Derby, England, 221, 239

Description of Greenland, see Ivar Bardarson

Diarmaid, king of Leinster, 388

Dicuil, a source of information for Atlantic islands, including the Faroes and Iceland, see his *Liber de Mensura Orbis Terrae*, 269–70

Dir (Dýri), see Askold

Disco, island and mountain, western Greenland, 65, 191, 294

Dnieper, the Russian river, 9, 163, 244; Rus arrival on, 79, 246 *n*; wild tribes of its lower reaches, 249–50; route to from Staraja Ladoga, 252; trade and overlordship of Rus, 254; trade artery from Further Russia to Black Sea and Constantinople, 256–8; *poliudie*, 256; perils of the